War Against the Wolf
America's Campaign to Exterminate the Wolf

Over 100 historical documents and modern articles
documenting the evolving attitudes toward wolves
in America from 1630 to 1995

Rick McIntyre, Editor
Foreword by Bruce Babbitt

Voyageur Press

Edited by Jane McHughen
Designed by Kathryn Mallien
Cover designed by McLean & Tuminelly
Cover illustration by David Danz, based on a photo by William Rideg
Printed in the United States of America
95 96 97 98 99 5 4 3 2 1

Library of Congress Cataloging-in-Publication Data:
  War Against the Wolf : America's campaign to exterminate the wolf / Rick
  McIntyre, editor.
      p.   cm.
  Includes bibliographical references and index.
  ISBN 0-89658-264-7
      1. Wolves—Control—United States—History. 2. Wolves—Control—United
  States—History—Sources. 3. Wolves—Control—Law and legislation—
  United States—History—Sources. 4. Wildlife reintroduction—United
  States—History. I. McIntyre, Rick.
  SF810.7.W65W37   1994
  333.95'—dc20   94-28038
                                            CIP

Distributed in Canada by Raincoast Books
8680 Cambie Street, Vancouver, B.C. V6P 6M9

Published by Voyageur Press, Inc.
P.O. Box 338, 123 North Second Street, Stillwater, MN 55082 U.S.A.
612-430-2210, fax 612-430-2211

For Lobo and Blanca,
TOGETHER IN LIFE,
TOGETHER IN DEATH.

(Drawing by Ernest Thompson Seton, Ernest Thompson Seton Memorial Library and Museum)

"FROM THE BEASTS' POINT OF VIEW WE HUMANS
MUST SEEM THE MOST VICIOUS RACE ON EARTH."
Sir Charles G. D. Roberts,
Canadian naturalist and writer

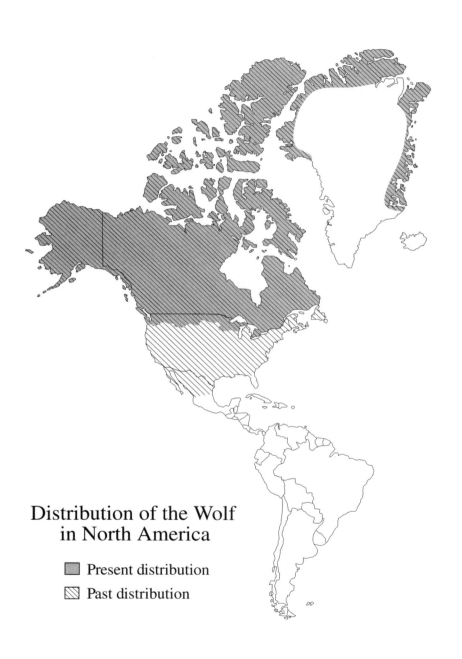

Distribution of the Wolf
in North America

- ▨ Present distribution
- ▨ Past distribution

Contents

Chapter 3: Range War   75

Photo Section I   133

Chapter 4: The Federal Government versus the Wolves   149

Chapter 5: Predators in the National Parks 201

Chapter 6: The Outlaw Wolves 217

Chapter 7: Native Americans and the Wolf 253

Foreword
by Bruce Babbitt

Something happened to Aldo Leopold when he met a wolf in the wild.

Early in this century, in the White Mountains of Arizona, he and a colleague happened upon a small pack. Having "never heard of passing up a chance to kill a wolf," they fired their shotguns at the pack. As they approached the littered carcasses, Leopold and his colleague were stopped in their tracks. "We reached the old wolf in time to watch a fierce green fire dying in her eyes," he later wrote. "I realized then, and have known ever since, that there was something new to me in those eyes—something known only to her and to the mountain."

Changed utterly by the sight of the dying green fire, Leopold has taken many of us on a journey to better understand our place on the land. His encounter with wolves touched me, in part, because it happened in mountains I had explored countless times and thought I knew quite well. I knew wolves once roamed the canyons, and knew my family had played a role in ridding the land of predators. But at the time, I didn't quite grasp the importance of their presence—or the shame of their absence.

Today, the green fire in a wolf's eye stands to change us once more.

In implementing a recovery strategy for the gray wolf in the Northern Rockies, we fulfill one of the Endangered Species Act's most far-sighted requirements. The Act requires us not just to stem the loss of individual species, but to work toward recovering viable populations in their natural surroundings. In this case, the Act encourages consideration of how the Continent's top predator—humans—can coexist with another animal—the wolf—whose intelligence, strength and adaptability place it at the top of the wildlife food chain.

Wolves were eradicated in the Yellowstone region sixty years ago as part of larger efforts to tame a wild land and make a wilderness productive. Now the region, along with the nation, is finding again that wilderness is part of our cultural heritage, and that it must be protected and nurtured.

In crafting a reintroduction strategy for the wolf, wildlife professionals have worked hard to accommodate the concerns of ranchers and local communities. They have taken steps to ensure that Yellowstone's wolves will thrive on a wildlife prey—and not on livestock. They must succeed because the long-term survival of wolves in the Rockies clearly depends on the goodwill of the region's people.

The reintroduction of the wolf is an extraordinary statement for the American people. It enables us to come close to restoring, in one specific area, conditions resembling what Lewis and Clark would have seen as they made their way across the West in 1803-07. It reconnects our historical linkage with the wilderness that is so central to our national character. It admits to past errors and asserts our willingness to correct them. It offers a new vision of a developed society living in harmony with its magnificent wilderness endowment.

Perhaps most important, wolves in Yellowstone will vastly expand our sense of what is possible—that we might restore conditions long thought to be passed. Restoration is not always possible; in many cases, it is either impossible or unreasonable to turn back the clocks and restore natural conditions. But in 1995, we proved that determination, cooperation, and a strong sense of our wilderness heritage can enable us to turn vague memories into magnificent possibilities.

In this anthology, Rick McIntyre presents a vast array of historical documents and modern essays that chronicle how far America has come on the issue of wolves. Just as Aldo Leopold was able to radically change his attitude toward wolves, our country, in the past few decades, has dramatically revised its policy on wolves.

In the Northern Rockies, and throughout America, the green fire that Leopold saw in the eyes of a wild gray wolf will live again. And the fact of its existence, even if we might never see it for ourselves, can challenge and change us all.

—Bruce Babbitt

Bruce Babbit's foreword was adapted and expanded from an essay he wrote for the September 1994 issue of Audubon Magazine.

Witnesses to an Ecological Murder

"Why did they want to kill off all the wolves?"
Inupiaq high school student, Shaktoolik, Alaska

In the spring of 1993, I was invited to northwest Alaska to do a series of slide shows in Native villages along the Bering Strait. The local school districts had been using my book, *Grizzly Cub: Five Years in the Life of a Bear,* in their reading programs and wanted me to talk to village children, first grade through high school, on grizzly bears, wolves, and ravens.

At the mid-point of my trip I flew into Shaktoolik, a coastal Inupiat village with a few hundred residents. Although it was late March, the ten feet of snow on the ground and frigid temperatures made it seem like mid-winter to me. The Shaktoolik children used skis to get to school and to travel around their village. During my three days in town I lived with the principal and his wife, in their apartment on the second floor of the school.

I found the younger kids were extremely interested in anything related to wildlife. At my talks, they enthusiastically answered my questions about their customs and knowledge of animals and pressed me about my experiences with grizzlies and wolves in other parts of the country.

The high school students, like teenagers everywhere, were harder to reach. To avoid appearing uncool to their friends, they were reluctant to interact with me, so I cut the introduction to my wolf slide show short and started the program.

I began to detect some interest when I reached the section dealing with wolf behavior. As I told them about how wolves raise their pups, I could see that some kids were beginning to respond. Then I moved on to the story of our country's attempt to exterminate the wolf in the lower forty-eight states. Within moments I sensed that the mood in the room had shifted dramatically. Every teenager was leaning forward, looking at the historic photos of wolf destruction. When I described the use of strychnine to kill hundreds of thousands of wolves and other predators, the students stared at the pictures of poisoned wolves with shocked, disbelieving expressions.

At first, I was surprised. I had talked with the principal about village customs and he had told me that it was not unusual for local Native people to hunt and trap wolves. One of the villagers owned a large reindeer herd and wolves occasionally killed some of his animals. When that occurred, he or others in the town would track down and kill the offending wolf. The residents of Shaktoolik were certainly not opposed to hunting and killing predators that attacked livestock.

As I dismantled my projector after the program, one of the older teenage boys came up to me. His former attempt to maintain his cool at any cost was now gone. With a troubled look he said, "Those people who poisoned and killed the wolves were really bad people. Why did they want to kill off all the wolves?"

As we talked, I realized that this boy and his fellow villagers had never heard of our country's massive wolf extermination program and couldn't begin to understand the motives behind it. They could agree on the need to kill individual problem wolves, and had done that in the country surrounding their village, but the concept of attempting to destroy all the members of a wildlife species was completely alien to them.

I had just finished the research for my first wolf book, *A Society of Wolves: National Parks and the Battle Over the Wolf,* so I told the young man what I knew from my reading of historical accounts about the motives behind the attempt to exterminate the wolf. Nothing I said seemed to make sense to him. He literally couldn't understand why a country would try to wipe out a fellow species. He walked away shaking his head, dissatisfied with what I had told him. None of it related to the reality of his world, a Native American world of traditions, ethics, and morals that set limits on what humanity can do to fellow forms of life.

I had similar experiences with Native people in other villages on my lecture tour. Few of them knew about our attempt to kill off the wolf, and none could understand why our country would want to do it. On my long flight home, I decided to start a research project, which culminated in this anthology on the war against the wolf.

Taking references from the historic documents I had already gathered on wolf control, I tracked down, in libraries around the country, hundreds of other historic sources, going back as far as our country's first wolf bounty law, passed by the Massachusetts Bay Colony in 1630. I found nineteenth-century articles and books, written by hunters, trappers, and ranchers, that described their attitudes toward wolves. I discovered obscure government reports written by the United States Biological Survey, the federal agency given the mission of wolf extermination.

As I read the historic accounts of the war against the wolf I came to see parallels between what was done to the wolf and my own family history. My Scottish ancestors lived in Glen Noe, a Highland valley, for nearly eight centuries. During the wars between the Scots and the British, title to my family's land continually changed hands. Whoever won the last battle claimed legal ownership.

Around 1800, the English, the winners of the most recent Scottish war, discovered a breed of sheep that could survive the severe Highland winters. With the full support of the law, they threw tenant farmers like my family off their land and forced them to emigrate to Nova Scotia. Like the wolves and many Native American tribes, my family lost their traditional homeland because the ruling class wanted that land for financial gain. Due to that family history, I identify with the plight of the wolf. Everyone who knows of an episode of oppression, victimization, or dispossession in their family history should feel a sense of solidarity with the wolf.

Prior to being thrown out of their Highland glen, my ancestors served as predator control agents for the upper class. In our clan, many men took up the professions of forestry and gamekeeping. Part of their responsibilities would have been to hunt down and kill local wolves. They succeeded at their mission: the last Highland wolf reportedly was destroyed in 1743. With the wolves gone, the Highlands were safe for the defenseless domestic sheep that brought great profit to the ruling class. The thanks my ancestors received for their diligent wolf control work was the loss of their land to sheep. Too late, they realized they had been used as an unsuspecting tool to end their clan's eight century way of life in Glen Noe. Because of that family history, I'm not so quick to assign blame to others for their involvement in predator control work. My ancestors are just as guilty as anyone else who went along with the program.

The pessimism that affected me when I read historic accounts of the persecution of the wolf in North America gradually gave way to a more positive perspective as I found other material proving that a few early voices were raised against the country's prevailing anti-wolf sentiments. Those voices—newspaper editors, biologists, nature writers, and former wolf hunters—spoke out for the wolf and its right to existence.

It took many decades, but these pro-wolf biologists and writers eventually turned the tide. By the late 1960s and the early 1970s, our country's attitude toward the wolf had drastically changed. With the passage of the Endangered Species Act in 1973, our official wolf policy experienced a full reversal. Once we vowed to kill them all off—now our country is doing everything possible to save wolves and to get them reestablished in former ranges, areas where our ancestors, many of them federal employees, had exterminated them.

This anthology sets out to show the evolution of attitudes toward the wolf in our country, from hatred and fear to respect and admiration. My emphasis is not on how bad things were but on how far we've come. Ultimately, this is an optimistic story. It's been a long journey, but we're finally winning the war to save the wolf.

Hunting Their Lost Tribe

"He's part of my heritage."
Young Hispanic girl, Carlsbad, New Mexico

In his 1919 annual report for the New Mexico District of the U.S. Biological Survey (USBS), J. Stokley Ligon spoke of his goal of "absolute extermination" of the wolf. Later in his report he commented: "There are a few stragglers [wolves] in the state drifting and being drifted, hunting their lost tribe, or endeavoring to avoid the hunters' tricking devices, most of them having lost feet in traps." Ligon estimated there were thirty wolves left in his district. He wrote of his hope that they would soon be destroyed "in order to make the finish." By finish he meant total elimination of the wolf in New Mexico.

Ligon's description of those last stragglers, wolves that were "hunting their lost tribe" on crippled legs, is a haunting, unforgettable image of the last survivors of the war against the wolf in the Southwest. Their survivor status was just temporary—every one was hunted down and killed. Ligon achieved his goal.

In assembling this anthology, I've tried to select a broad sample of government reports, legislation, personal letters, journal entries, newspaper and magazine articles, history books, autobiographies, research papers, and traditional Native American stories that document the evolution of American attitudes toward the wolf. To provide additional coverage on current wolf issues, I commissioned nine authors to write new articles specifically for this collection. This introductory essay will attempt to make sense of the historic record and show how far our country has come on the issue of the wolf.

The Roots of the Conflict
Prior to the arrival of the colonists on the eastern shore of our continent,

Native Americans had successfully coexisted with wolves for thousands of years. Paula Underwood's Oneida story, "Who Speaks for Wolf," captures the essence of the Native attitude toward the wolf. The human characters in the story were willing to move to solve a conflict between their village and a community of wolves. They saw this as the preferred alternative to killing the wolves, for they thought:

> A People who took life only to sustain their own
> would become a People who took life
> rather than move a little
> IT DID NOT SEEM TO THEM
> THAT THEY WANTED TO BECOME SUCH A PEOPLE.

That heritage of coexistence with the natural world was alien and unthinkable to the colonists. Europeans brought with them Old World attitudes and ethics toward wildlife and wilderness. Wild areas and wild animals had to be controlled and dominated before the New World would be safe for settlement. Fear played a large role in their response to nature. To them, the sound of "wolves at midnight howling" was a terrifying reminder of just how unsafe and dangerous this new land was.

The animal husbandry practices of the colonists contributed to the conflict between themselves and predators. Few animals were fenced in or closely supervised. As they wandered about looking for grass they were watched by wolves, bears, and mountain lions. These free-roaming, unprotected cattle, pigs, and sheep were easy kills for predators accustomed to hunting wary and swift prey such as deer. Centuries of selective breeding had severely diluted and weakened the alertness, speed, agility, and defensive ability of domestic animals. To a wolf, all livestock are unfit compared to deer and other wild game. Some wolves—not all—took advantage of the situation and preyed on the unsupervised stock animals.

In response, the governing bodies of the colonies established bounties on predators, particularly wolves. The Massachusetts Bay Colony instituted a wolf bounty in 1630 and Virginia followed in 1632. Virginia also required local Native tribes to kill an annual quota of wolves and turn in the hides as a form of tribute. The colonies of Pennsylvania and Rhode Island contracted men to work at wolf extermination full time. Wolves that lived in wilderness areas and preyed on deer were killed along with wolves that had attacked livestock.

Thus, within a few years of colonial settlement, the pattern was set. The war against the wolf was initially carried out on a small scale in a handful of villages clustered on the eastern seaboard, but in the coming centuries, the pattern would be repeated and greatly enlarged to include all of the lower forty-eight states. What the colonists tried to do in their local area—the extermination of all wolves—became the policy of our emerging nation. Destruction of predators became a heritage passed on for generation after generation. That heritage of conflict and destruction became part of the American way of life.

Where We Went Wrong

The final phase of the war against the wolf started in the 1880s, just after the destruction of the vast western herds of bison. The loss of the wolves' natural, traditional prey set off a chain of events that culminated in the extermination of the wolf in the western states and territories. Many wolf packs were forced to turn to the only alternative source of food: the cattle and sheep that ranchers had brought in to replace the bison herds. That conflict between ranchers and wolves escalated to the "final solution" of the "wolf problem," an extermination program carried out by a federal agency, the USBS.

The pattern and heritage set by the earliest colonists was carried out to its logical conclusion. By the 1950s, the wolf population of the lower forty-eight states had dropped from two million to just a few hundred. Wolves had been exterminated in 99 percent of their original range in that vast region.

Most of us would probably agree that settlers had a right to deal with wolves that truly were killing their livestock. Farmers and ranchers have an obligation to guard and properly care for the animals in their care, but if a wolf or other predator targets their herds and flocks, it has to be dealt with. Where we went wrong was to go beyond killing just problem wolves. Just as the colonists had done on a small scale, we targeted all wolves for elimination—guilty and innocent.

The historic record shows that livestock producers and government officials knew that only a small percentage of wolves were preying on domestic animals and that wolf livestock depredation in many areas was very minor.Wallis Huidekoper, a livestock industry spokesman, in a 1916 speech to the annual convention of the Montana Stock Growers Association said, "It is a well-known fact that stock-killing individuals among wolves are only a small proportion of their kind inhabiting a given area." Despite that, he rallied his audience to "wage continuous war" against all wolves.

Ligon, in his 1919 USBS report for New Mexico, admitted that "the damage now being committed in the state [by wolves] is so small . . . that little complaint is heard." Elsewhere in his report, Ligon reaffirms that, despite the declining problems with wolves, the government's goal was still "absolute extermination." To carry out that extermination goal, the U. S. Forest Service, the USBS, and even the National Park Service (NPS) sought out and killed all the wolves on public lands in the West.

The native wolf population of Yellowstone National Park preyed on their natural, wild prey: deer, elk, and bison. But even those Yellowstone wolves were killed by the federal government. It didn't matter that they weren't causing any problems. The policy was to get every single wolf, even the ones in national parks. The national agenda was clear: There was no place for the wolf in our country, not even in remote wilderness areas like Yellowstone.

Blaming the Victims

Even the most anti-wolf writers in this collection understood the fundamental reason for the conflict between the nation and the wolves. Everyone knew that loss of their natural prey forced the wolves to turn to livestock for survival. But understanding of the cause created little sympathy for the wolf. Like our country's treatment of Native American tribes in the nineteenth century, the solution to conflict, even when the opposition was understandably reacting to unfair treatment, was massive retaliation. It was an era of "Might Makes Right" and "Survival of the Fittest."

In an interview published in the December 31, 1922, issue of *The Rocky Mountain News*, Stanley Piper, head of the USBS Control Methods Laboratory in Denver, spoke of the victimization of the wolf:

> The pioneer stockman, entering first upon the great plains about the middle of the last century, suffered some losses from gray wolves, but his real battle with them did not begin until after the buffalo had long been gone. But as man became king, took to himself the land and its products, killed off creatures suitable for his food, stocked the ranges with his herds, extended his fields to the outermost edges of the frontiers and forced his way wherever his life could be sustained, his conflict with animals strong enough to contend has steadily increased.

Despite his understanding of the plight of the wolf, Piper willingly helped his agency exterminate the wolf, an animal that had the effrontery "to contend" with the massive tide of Manifest Destiny—the unchallenged assumption that the Euro-American culture had a right to appropriate and control the lands that became the western states. Piper's lab manufactured the predator poisons relentlessly spread by USBS agents across public and private lands.

Bison hunter John R. Cook, in his 1907 book, *The Border and the Buffalo,*questioned himself on the morality of his involvement with the slaughter of the bison, the primary prey of Indians and wolves:

> What would you do, John R. Cook, if you had been a child of this wonderfully prolific game region, your ancestors, back through countless ages, according to traditional history, having roamed these vast solitudes as free as the air they breathed? What would you do if some outside interloper should come in and start a ruthless slaughter upon the very soil you have grown from childhood upon, and that you believed you alone had all the rights of occupancy that could possibly be given one? Yes, what would you do?
>
> But there are two sides to the question. It is simply a case of the survival of the fittest. Too late to stop and moralize now, and sentiment must have no part in our thoughts from this time on.

Ben Corbin's 1900 book *Corbin's Advice or the Wolf Hunter's Guide* adds a religious mandate and rationalization to the issue of the treatment of Natives and the wolf:

> I can not believe that Providence intended that these rich lands, broad, well watered, fertile and waving with abundant pasturage, close by mountains and valleys, filled with gold, and every metal and mineral, should forever be monopolized by wild beasts and savage men. I believe in the survival of the fittest, and hence I have "fit" for it all my life. . . . The wolf is the enemy of civilization, and I want to exterminate him.

The wolves' response to the extermination campaigns often only made the country hate them more. For example, since wolf-killed animals were often baited with strychnine after the wolves first fed on them, many packs learned that they could not safely return to their own kills. This was an intelligent response to the wide-spread poisoning campaigns of the late 1800s. But that adaptation made it appear that wolves were wasteful of meat. The sight of partially eaten carcasses infuriated hunters and ranchers and gave them further justification to kill every wolf, by whatever means necessary, in their region. An ironic aspect of this issue is obvious today. Is there any species on the planet more wasteful than the human race? What right do we have to demand that another species abide by an ethic that we ourselves nearly always fail to achieve?

The issue of the supposed "wastefulness" of wolves is constantly mentioned in historic writings of the times. The "waste not-want not" ethic of the country was unquestioned during this period and the seeming inability of the wolf to live up to that standard cemented its doom.

Yet in Alaska, I saw that wolves, when not persecuted, finished off each kill they made. When a caribou or Dall sheep was captured, the pack would feed for a few hours then go off to rest and digest their meal. Over the next several days the wolves would return to the carcass and consume the rest of the meat and frequently the marrow in the bones. Some wolves would bury portions of the kill for later use. Any bits of meat left at the site would be eagerly taken by grizzlies, foxes, eagles, ravens, and other animals. Nothing went to waste.

Another frequently expressed complaint against the wolf was its supposed cruelty in killing its prey. Examples of wild animals or livestock that wolves failed to kill in humane ways were used in near-religious terms to justify extermination. This perceived cruelty was also used to rationalize deliberately sadistic methods of killing wolves. John James Audubon described a farmer who captured wolves in a pit trap, severed the tendons in their hind legs, then tossed the defenseless, crippled animals into a pack of dogs. Ben Corbin threw baited fish hooks into wolf dens, waited until the hooks had been swallowed and imbedded in the pups' stomach then yanked them out and killed them. Stanley Young, in his book *The Wolves of North America*, stated that cowboys often roped wolves and dragged them to death across rough ground. USBS trappers wrapped wire tightly around the penises of captive male wolves, making it impossible for them to urinate. Later they killed the animals, carefully cut out the full bladders, and used the urine as scent to attract other wolves to traps.

Nearly all of the older papers in this collection assume that humankind has a clear moral superiority over the wolf and justify extermination on that premise. In today's world, the traditional accusations of the wolf's supposed wastefulness and inhumanity in its killing methods pale beside our knowledge of humanity's record of moral crimes. The unending murders, rapes, and ethnic-cleansing campaigns reported on nearly every news broadcast demonstrate that our race fails to live up to any claim of moral superiority. Our treatment of wolves and other wildlife is often just as cruel as our treatment of our fellow humans. In the conflict between humanity and the wolf, only one species is capable of truly inhumane behavior. With our track record, calling another species inhumane is the height of hypocrisy.

A wolf earns its living by killing large prey with its sole weapon, its teeth. That may not be a pretty process. A wolf's priority is to reach its prey and make the kill without injuring itself. To do that, it bites into whatever part of its prey it can reach. There are no moral components to the process, there is no ethically right or wrong way for the wolf to make its kills. Those people who condemn the wolf's alleged "immoral" behavior might pause to reflect on the implications of their view. To ascribe morals and ethical codes to animals implies that they have the same moral capacity as humans, the same option to choose good or evil, the same type of conscience as people. Do they truly believe that wolves are positioned at an equal level with humanity? If so, how can they justify the mass extermination of a fellow species who possess the same moral sense as the human race? If the wolf is "just an animal," then it merits no moral condemnation for actions that we might not like. It acts out on its instincts just as cats and dogs do. A misbehaving cat who eats a goldfish is not being "sinful," it's just being a cat.

The wolves reacted and adapted to what we were doing to them—killing off their traditional game, taking their home ranges, poisoning, trapping, and destruction of their families—as best as they could. We blamed them for trying to survive and gave them no quarter.

The extraordinary stories of the last outlaw wolves are unforgettable, epic tales of loners who waged guerrilla warfare against the species that sought to destroy their race. Lobo, the Custer Wolf, and Rags became superwolves that, by default, served as champions of their kind, the last defenders of the Wolf Nation. Like any classic heroes, they set themselves against an enemy with vastly superior forces. Rags, like many heroic characters in epic literature, appeared to be motivated by revenge. The destruction of two mates and a litter of pups set him off on murderous rampage that lasted for years. In the end, the only thing that could stop him was a bullet through his heart.

If these outlaws were the champions of their race, the USBS trappers sent out to kill them could also be considered champions of their species. These men were told to kill the renegades by whatever means necessary—bullets, traps, poison—no matter how long it took. The duels between the champions of the two warring races—duels between H. P. Williams and the Custer Wolf, and Bill Caywood and Rags—took place in arenas far removed from civilization. For the wolves, it was a fight they never could win. Surviving the best efforts of one USBS trapper only meant that another, more experienced agent would be sent out to replace the first man. The U.S. government had plenty of men and financial resources, and the

USBS never gave up—agency pride demanded that they "get their wolf."

The predator control agents always killed the outlaw wolves. The doomed champions of the Wolf Nation lost their lives in these duels but their valiant struggles for survival created a respect and admiration among the trappers assigned to kill them. Williams, the killer of the Custer Wolf; Caywood, the killer of Rags; and Ernest Thompson Seton, the killer of Lobo and Blanca, all were forced to change their attitudes toward wolves as a result of their encounters with these courageous champions. The USBS trappers continued to do their duty, but as expressed by a contemporary newspaper reporter, they became "regretful executioner[s]."

Seton was profoundly affected by his involvement in the deaths of Lobo and his mate Blanca. He spent much of the rest of his life giving lectures on their poignant lives, telling the story of the war against the wolf from the wolf's point of view to hundreds of thousands of people. He created a sympathy for the wolf that eventually radically changed the country's policy toward the animal.

The Forest Service, Park Service, and Wolf Control

Two federal agencies I've worked for, the U.S. Forest Service and the National Park Service, once were heavily involved in wolf control. Both agencies carried out wolf extermination programs in wilderness areas where wolf populations were far removed from any livestock. The Forest Service and Park Service enthusiastically implemented the anti-wolf policies of the nation. The employees of those agencies, along with the men of the USBS, thought they were doing the right thing in killing wolves and other predators. Like us, these people were products of their time, applying what they had been taught by their parents and elders as best they could to their lives and jobs. They reflected the biases and misconceptions of their times. It is likely that nearly all of us would have agreed with wolf extermination policies if we had been born into that era.

However, at least one early Yellowstone ranger, Milton Skinner, began to speak and write with enlightenment on the need to change wolf policies in the park (see the next section and Chapter 8). Today, it is easy to argue that the other Yellowstone rangers should have listened to Skinner and changed their ways, but the reality was that the vast majority of early NPS employees continued to think of wolves as pests that needed to be eliminated. The prevailing national attitudes toward predators dominated wildlife management policies during the initial years of Park Service management of Yellowstone and other national parks.

Changing Views of the Wolf

Documenting the gradual change in attitudes toward the wolf was the most fascinating aspect of editing this collection. The earliest pro-wolf statement I found was Henry David Thoreau's journal entry for March 23, 1856. He calls the wolf "one of the nobler animals" and laments that the extermination of the wolf, cougar, wolverine, and bear, and other animals from the Massachusetts woods forced him to live in an "emasculated country."

Writing more than a century before the great environmental movement of the late 1960s, Thoreau demonstrated a sound grasp of the fundamental principles of ecology and biodiversity. Referring to his studies of the vast, complex array of spring phenomena, he sadly comes to a realization: ". . . thinking that I have here the entire poem, and then, to my chagrin, I hear that it is but an imperfect copy that I possess and have read, that my ancestors have torn out many of the first leaves and grandest passages, and mutilated it in many places."

Voicing a sentiment that would later motivate millions of supportors of wolf recovery, Thoreau sums up his feeling about an emasculated environment, "I wish to know an entire heaven and entire earth."

In 1894, thirty-eight years after Thoreau's journal entry, Ernest Thompson Seton published "Lobo: King of the Currumpaw" in *Scribner's* magazine. The story of Lobo and Blanca, as told by Seton in the article, in a popular book, and in hundreds of lectures, had a profound impact on the American conscience. Lobo was seen as a tragic hero of Shakespearean dimensions, an animal that died of sorrow over the sadistic death of his mate.

The first known proposal to reintroduce wolves into a former range came in 1914 in Henry Shoemaker's *Wolf Days in Pennsylvania*. Shoemaker wrote of the wolf's "inherent right to life" and intelligently discussed the positive role wolves played in the balance of nature. He predicted that "a strong demand will be made to stock the Pennsylvania wilds not with more rabbits, quails, ground-hogs and squirrels, but with savage beasts, such as panthers, brown bears and wolves." Shoemaker's motives for the reintroduction are somewhat murky—he hoped that wolf hunting will become "the royal sport of Pennsylvania"—but he also argued that wolves are necessary to the long-term health of wildlife communities.

By 1924, the issue of predator control was being heatedly discussed at professional conferences of biologists. In April of that year, Milton Skinner, the former Yellowstone ranger, read a paper, "The Predatory and Fur-Bearing Animals of the Yellowstone National Park," at the Sixth

Annual Meeting of the American Society of Mammalogists (ASM). Skinner argued for selective control of wolves that were proven livestock killers rather that the current USBS policy of "absolute extermination" of the species.

The ASM annual meetings became battlegrounds between biologists and the USBS. A. Brazier Howell's paper, "At the Cross-Roads," presented at the 1930 ASM meeting, effectively backed the predator control extremists into a corner. Transcripts of that meeting show that the biologists frequently laughed out loud at the rationalizations voiced by USBS bureaucrats. Those justifications of absolute predator extermination could no longer be taken seriously.

Aldo Leopold, a former wolf hunter and USBS cheerleader, eventually became the most effective spokesman for the biological value of the wolf. His essay "Thinking Like a Mountain" has never been equaled for its eloquent explanation of the essential role of the wolf in wild, naturally functioning communities. The power in Leopold's essay comes from his experience of witnessing the death of a wolf he had shot, a mother wolf with "a fierce green fire dying in her eyes."

The process of reevaluating our view of the wolf climaxed during the environmental movement of the late 1960s and the 1970s. The philosophical writing of people like Thoreau, Leopold, and Barry Lopez (*Of Wolves and Men*), along with the scientific studies of the wolf by men such as Sigurd Olson, Adolph Murie, and L. David Mech (*The Wolf*), gave the nation sound, logical reasons for preserving surviving wolf populations and for seeking out ways to restore the wolf to parts of its former habitat.

The Future of Wolf-Human Relations

My research into Native American wolf stories impressed me with the sophisticated attitudes Native people have toward wildlife and humanity's relationship with the natural world. Paula Underwood's Oneida story "Who Speaks for Wolf" provides a model of how to resolve conflicts between wolves and humans. Realizing that they, not the wolves, had created the conflict, the villagers voluntarily gave the land back to the wolves.

The Blackfeet story "When Men and Animals Were Friendly," the Piegan story "The Legend of the Friendly Medicine Wolf," and the inland Dena'ina tale "Tigin Sutdu'a: Wolf Story" all speak of a close connection between wolves and people and the ability of the two species to coexist. Those stories, along with the new essays by Native writers commissioned for this book, set out an ancient ethic and philosophy that could serve as a role model for our modern American culture.

As we will see in Chapter 9, with the passage of the Endangered Species Act (ESA) in 1973 and the implementation of its provisions, our country has begun a process of giving land back to the wolves that is similar to the way the Oneida villagers gave their land back to their brother species. The ESA set forth a new national policy for endangered species such as the wolf. The act defined its purpose in these terms: "To provide a means whereby the ecosystems upon which endangered species and threatened species depend may be conserved, to provide a program for the conservation of such endangered species and threatened species." The ESA further declares it to be "the policy of Congress that all Federal Departments and agencies shall seek to conserve endangered species and threatened species and shall use their authorities in furtherance of the Act."

The act also directed the Secretary of Interior to "develop and implement plans for the conservation and survival of endangered species." In 1987, the U.S. Fish and Wildlife Service (USFWS) announced their plans for implementing this legally mandated aspect of the ESA in their report, *The Northern Rocky Mountain Wolf Recovery Plan*. The goal for wolf recovery was defined as the successful establishment of at least ten breeding pairs of wolves for a minimum of three years in three separate historic wolf ranges: northwest Montana, central Idaho, and Yellowstone National Park.

In 1985 Canadian wolves began recolonizing northwest Montana. The three major federal land management agencies—the NPS, the U.S. Forest Service, the USFWS—are legally required to do everything possible to insure that that recolonization is successful.

Congress, in 1991, directed the USFWS to prepare an Environmental Impact Statement (EIS) on the possibility of reintroducing wolves in Yellowstone and central Idaho. The EIS project, headed up by Ed Bangs, held approximately 120 public meetings and hearings in ten states to solicit opinions on wolf recovery, and analyzed over 160,000 comments on reintroduction. Ed describes the mechanics and emotional issues involved in the process in his paper "Wolf Hysteria" in Chapter 9. The end result of the massive project was the May 1994 release of the final EIS report, *The Reintroduction of Gray Wolves to Yellowstone National Park and Central Idaho*. On June 15, 1994, Bruce Babbitt, the Secretary of the Interior, approved the EIS's proposed wolf reintroduction projects for both Yellowstone and Idaho.

Implementation of the Yellowstone project began in early 1995 with the release of three packs of wolves into the northern range of the park, the prime range of the Yellowstone's original wolf population. Additional packs will be released during the following two to four years. Once the three states achieve the goal of ten breeding pairs for a minimum of three years, wolves will be considered recovered in the northern Rockies and they will be taken off the region's endangered species list. This long political and biological process will essentially accomplish what the Native council did in "Who Speaks for Wolf"—give the wolf back some of its traditional land.

Ligon's 1919 image of wolves "hunting their lost tribe" has a modern counterpart. In Ligon's day, any wolf sighted was hunted down and killed. Today, it is federal policy to assist the wolf in reestablishing itself in the former territories of its "lost tribe." Canadian wolves have already recolonized Montana. Diane Boyd's paper in Chapter 9 describes her personal involvement with this recolonization process. Wolves have entered Washington state, North Dakota, South Dakota, and Maine. Members of the northern Minnesota wolf population have dispersed into Michigan and Wisconsin. Reports from Texas, New Mexico, and Arizona raise the possibility that small remnant populations of Mexican wolves have survived in northern Mexico and that a few individual animals may have crossed the international border, heading north. These wolves may not have found any surviving members of their lost tribe but, unlike their ancestors, they did find a new willingness from humanity to try to coexist. Charles Bowden's and Rick Lobello's papers in the final chapter focus on the Mexican wolf and its chances for survival.

The red wolf has already been reintroduced into North Carolina and Tennessee and gray wolves have just been released into Yellowstone and Idaho. Later reintroductions may take place in Texas, Arizona, New Mexico, Colorado, New York, New Hampshire, and Maine. Tribal officials on the Wind River and Nez Perce Indian reservations are discussing bringing the wolf back to their lands. With natural recolonization and reintroduction projects, the wolf may be back in eighteen states by the turn of the century.

The modern contributions to this book, many of them specially commissioned to bring current wolf issues up-to-date, give an overview of where we stand now. The current attitude toward wolves starkly contrasts with the historical views present in earlier sections of the book. I've become very optimistic on the issue of wolf recovery. The 1973 ESA set a national policy of supporting the reestablishment of the wolf in its former range. That policy is being successfully implemented: Wolves are on their way back. But beyond that, as I travel around the country, speaking on wolves, I consistently find intense public support for wolves and their recovery. At my programs, people constantly ask me what they can do to help wolves get reestablished. A list of wolf organizations working toward that goal can be found at the back of this book.

In the winter and spring of 1994, I traveled to many schools in small ranching communities in West Texas to speak on wolves. Before I said anything to the kids, I would ask them what their favorite animal was. They always picked the wolf. Their response made me realize that children have a natural affinity for the wolf, even in places where adults hate wolves. Kids instinctively like the wolf. That affinity will stay with a child for his or her whole life unless an elder teaches them to fear the animal. Our job is to help maintain that natural love and respect.

Recently I was at the Living Desert State Park, a small zoo in Carlsbad, New Mexico, watching a pair of Mexican wolves that live in a large enclosure. As I studied the wolves, a Hispanic family approached the display. A young girl, perhaps ten years old, ran ahead and immediately spotted one of the wolves. With great excitement, she turned to her family and said, "It's a Mexican wolf! He's part of my heritage!"

This book is about a heritage. Wolves were residents of North America long before any human being set foot on the continent. Wolves witnessed the first migration of people from Siberia, across the Bering Land Bridge, into Alaska. They witnessed the further migration of Native people throughout all of North America. Wolves observed the landings of European colonists in Massachusetts and Virginia. The wolf is a Native, an ancient citizen of America.

Part of our heritage is our nation's war against the wolf. Our ancestors hated the wolf and vowed to exterminate it in the lower forty-eight states. From the 1630s through the 1950s, all means—guns, traps, poison—were used to destroy the wolf. Except for a remnant population of a few hundred wolves in the Upper Midwest, our nation succeeded at its mission. Never before has one species declared such total war on a fellow species.

Now we've reevaluated that heritage and our view of the wolf. We've decided to give it back some land, to invite it back home to its former ranges, to reestablish the wolf as part of the heritage and history of North America. We've finally learned a lesson about our place in the natural world and our responsibility to consider how our actions effect fellow life forms. The traditional Native American attitude of coexistence with the wolf is slowly becoming dominant in the American culture.

It's appropriate to let a wolf have the final say on this issue. In the traditional Blackfeet story, "When Men and Animals Were Friendly," as retold by Jack Gladstone, a wolf character explains why he has saved the lives of a Blackfeet family and why he has invited them into his camp:

> "It is because I feel it is about time that they [human persons] get to know us better and we animal persons come to know them. We are brothers, after all."

Chapter 1

The Colonial and Early American Period

". . . the wolves at midnight howling."
Anonymous woman colonist, circa 1640

It's hard to imagine now, but the entire Eastern seaboard of our country once teamed with wolves, including the area we now call New York City. In the following examples of colonial wolf bounty laws, ranging from Massachusetts to Virginia, we see a consistent picture: the colonists wanted to rid the New World of the wolf.

Beginning in 1630, just ten years after landing in the New World, the settlers in the Massachusetts Bay Colony passed a series of laws offering a cash reward to any resident who killed a wolf. The money to pay for those bounties initially came from assessments placed on livestock owners: one penny for every "beast [cow] and horse" and a half cent for each "swine and goat." In later laws, the colony paid bounties, as high as 40 shillings per wolf, directly out of the public treasury. A 1638 law fixed the minimum wage for a laborer at 18 cents per day, so 40 shillings (one shilling equaled twelve cents) was equivalent to twenty-seven days of a laborer's wages. Such high prices tempted many to seek out and kill wolves. In 1644 and 1645, any Massachusetts Indian who turned in a wolf could choose either three quarts of wine or a bushel of corn as a reward. Other early Massachusetts laws encouraged residents to keep dogs, such as mastiffs and greyhounds, to use in hunting wolves and authorized town governments to use public funds to purchase and keep wolf-hunting dogs. Towns were also required to set out and bait specific numbers of wolf traps. Any town that neglected its obligation to trap wolves was assessed a fine.

The Virginia Colony, like Massachusetts, used varying systems of rewards and legal obligations to kill off wolves. Rewards included the privilege of hunting wild hogs on public land and up to three hundred pounds of tobacco. The Native tribes of Virginia were mandated to turn into the colonial government an annual tribute of 145 wolf pelts. Rhode Island and Pennsylvania sought out professional trappers to rid their colonies of wolves.

Many of the historic accounts in this and later chapters blame wolves for the deaths of great numbers of livestock. As Phil Gipson discusses in his essay in Chapter 9, modern biologists question the reliability of many of these accounts and assume that the livestock depredation figures were greatly exaggerated.

To make the colonial laws of the 1600s more understandable to readers, I have modernized the spelling of words and converted obscure abbreviations to full words.

1630–53: Wolf Legislation in the Colony of Massachusetts Bay

My source for the Massachusetts Bay wolf bounties was Nathaniel Shurtleff, Records of the Governor and Company of the Massachusetts Bay in New England.

November 9, 1630
It is ordered, that every English man that killeth a wolf in any part within the limits of this patent shall have allowed him 1d [one penny] for every beast & horse, & ob. [1/2 penny] for every weaned swine & goat in every plantation, to be levied by the constables of the said plantations.

1637
It is ordered, that there should be 10 shillings a piece allowed for such wolves as are killed.

1640
Ordered, that every man that kills a wolf with hounds shall have 40 shillings allowed him, & whosoever kills a wolf with trap, piece, or other engine, shall have 10 shillings allowed him, to be paid by that town where the wolf is killed, & if he be killed out of any town bounds it shall be paid by the Treasurer.

And it is further ordered, that such as shall keep any hound, mastiff, or greyhound, which shall be aiding to the death of any such wolf, shall not be contributory to the recompense to be given for such wolf.

1641
The order for giving 40 shillings a piece for wolves killed with dogs, &

10 shillings a piece for wolves killed otherwise, is repealed.

1644

It is ordered, that there shall be a bushel of Indian corn or three quarts of wine paid to any Indian by the constable of every town for every wolf killed within the bounds of the town where such constable dwells, upon the town's account, provided that the Indian bring the head to the constable, & make good proof where such wolf was killed, for the better satisfaction that it was killed within the same town bounds.

May 1645

Mr. Bartholmew, John Johnson, Mr. Sprauge, Mr. Winsley, & Mr. Hubbard are chosen a committee to consider of the best ways and means to destroy the wolves which are such ravenous cruel creatures, & daily vexations to all the inhabitants of the colony, & to present their thoughts & conclusions thereabouts to this house.

June 1645

Whereas great loss and damage doth befall this commonwealth by reason of wolves, which do destroy so great numbers of our cattle, notwithstanding provision hath formerly been made by this Court for suppressing of them, and we find little hath been done that way for the better encouraging of any to set about a work of so great concernment, it is therefore ordered, that any person, either English or Indian, that shall kill any wolf or wolves within ten miles of any plantation in this jurisdiction, shall have for every wolf by him or them so killed, ten shillings, to be paid out of the treasury of the country, provided that due proof be made thereof unto the plantation next adjoining, where such wolf or wolves were killed, & also that they bring a certificate under some magistrate's hand, or the constable of the place unto the Treasurer; provided also that this order doth only intend such plantations as do contribute to public charge; & for such plantations upon the river of Piscataq that do not join with us to carry on public charge, they are to make payment upon their own charge.

And the law for allowance of one bushel of Indian corn or 3 quarts of wine to any Indian for killing of any wolf, is hereby repealed.

1648

It is ordered by this court, & by the authority thereof enacted, that any inhabitant, English or Indian, within this jurisdiction, that shall kill any wolf or wolves, making good proof to the constable of the town where such wolf is killed, bringing of their heads, which the constable is to bury, if any English shall kill any, he shall be allowed thirty shillings, at the least, by the constable of the town for the time being, ten shillings whereof the Treasurer, in the next levy that issues out of that town to the country, he shall allow to the constable; & for every Indian that shall kill any wolf, he shall be allowed twenty shillings, ten whereof shall be allowed by the Treasurer, as before, back again to the constable, as aforesaid. This law to be of force for the space of four years.

It is ordered, that the select men of every town shall, & hereby have power given them, to purchase or procure, with the town's stock, so many hounds as they think meete [proper], & to impose the keeping of them on such as they judge fittest, that so all means may be improved for the destruction of wolves, and that no other dog shall be kept in any town but such as the select men shall see meete; provided that no magistrate shall have any hound imposed upon him, nor dog taken from him, without his consent.

1653

Whereas, by a late law, made October, 1648, there was some encouragement both to English & Indians for the destruction of wolves, which hath been found profitable unto the country, but is now expired, it is therefore ordered by this Court, that the said law be again renewed, & stand in force as before.

1636–61: Wolf Legislation in the Colony of New Plymouth

For most of the 1600s, New Plymouth was an independent colony; it was absorbed by the Massachusetts Bay Colony in 1691. Nathaniel Shurtleff's Records of the Colony of New Plymouth *was the source for the New Plymouth bounties.*

1636

That whoever shall kill a Wolf and make it sufficiently known to the Governor or some assistant shall have four bushels of corn to be raised of the Constablerick or liberties.

1642

It is enacted by the Court that all the Towns within the Government shall make wolf traps and bait them and look unto them daily upon the penalty of 10 shillings a trap that shall be neglected. The number that each Town is to make is as followeth.

Plymouth five, Duxbury five, Scituate four, Sandwich three, Taunton two, Barnstable three, Yarmouth three, Marshfield two.

1651
Ordered

That all such wolves as are killed by the Indians at Namassaket or elsewhere from the 15th of March annually to the last of April; the charge of the killing of them shall be borne by the whole colony; and that they shall have for every wolf so killed a coat of trading cloth; and at all other times of the year any either English or Indians that shall kill any wolves each Town shall bear the charge of the killing of them where they are killed.

1658
It is enacted by the Court that if any Indian shall kill a wolf in any township of this Jurisdiction he shall be paid a Coat of Trading Cloth and if any English shall kill a wolf he shall be paid fifteen shillings to be paid by the Country and defrayed by the Treasurer.

1661
Whereas very great spoil hath lately been made by wolves upon all sorts of cattle in sundry townships within this government, to the great detriment thereof, this Court, therefore, presuming on the General Court of Deputies favorable sense hereof in this exigent, do order and declare, that it shall and may be lawful, until the next Court of Election, for the several townships to pay unto any Indian or Indians that shall bring into the constable of any such township any head or heads of wolves half a pound of powder and two pound of shot or lead for every head brought in as aforesaid, besides the coat by Court order in such case provided.

1632–91: Wolf Legislation in the Colony of Virginia
The Virginia wolf legislation comes from William Hening's The Statutes at Large: Being a Collection of All the Laws of Virginia.

September 8, 1632
And for encouragement to destroy the wolves, *it is thought* that whosoever shall kill a wolf, and bring in his head to the commander, it shall be lawful for such person or persons for every wolf so killed, to kill also

one wild hog and take the same for his own use.

1646

Whereas many losses are lately received by the inhabitants by reason of wolves which do haunt and frequent their plantations; for the better prevention and for the destroying of them, *It is enacted* that what person soever shall after publication hereof kill a wolf and bring in the head to any commissioner upon certificate of the said commissioner to the county court he or they shall receive one hundred pounds of tobacco for so doing to be raised out of the county where the wolf is killed.

1668

An Act for Destroying Wolves

Since it is most evident that the inhabitants of this country do receive daily damage by wolves, and no fit way or temper yet found for the destruction or diminishing of them, *It is enacted* that the Indian tributaries be enjoyed and assessed to bring in a certain number annually, that is to say:

		Bowmen or hunters	wolves heads
Into Nanzemond county, the Nanzemonds being about		45	9
Surrey.	Powchay-icks	30	6
	Weyenoakes	15	3
Charles City County.	Men-Heyricks	50	10
	Nottoways, 2 towns	90	18
	Appomattux	50	10
Henrico County.	Manachees	30	6
	Powhites	10	2
New Kent.	Pamunckies	50	10
	Chickahomonies	60	12
	Mattapanics	20	4
	Rapahanocks	30	6
	Totas Chees	40	8
Gloster.	Chiskoyackes	15	3
Rapahanock.	Portobaccoes	60	12
	Nanzcattico & Mattehatique	50	10
Northumberland.	Wickacomico	70	14
Westmoreland.	Appomatux	10	2
		725	145

And for the putting this act into effectual execution, *It is enacted by this grand assembly* that the county courts do appoint a certain person or persons in their counties to receive from the respective Indians, assigned them as aforesaid, the heads which are to be brought in by these Indians, and to keep a just account of the number, and to present to the said court such as are deficient to do, and neglect to bring in their due number, against such, viz. against the great man of the town, the said court to issue out summons for his appearance to show cause for his or their default, and to warn them to fulfill their number, but if after such warning given as aforesaid, the said Indians shall neglect and be wanting in their number, the court shall transmit the contempt to the next assembly for a further remedy. . . .

It is further enacted by the assembly that upon the return of the accounts of wolves heads at the next assembly, It be then considered what satisfaction shall be made the right the honorable governor in lieu of the wolves heads brought in on the account of his tribute; & because some laws prohibit the Indians from coming among the English, the governor is requested by his commission to license them in any county desiring to employ them.

1691
An Act Giving Reward for Killing of Wolves

Whereas it is found by frequent experience since the several former acts of this country giving a reward for killing of wolves have been repealed, and the encouragement which incited many people to use their best endeavors and industry to destroy them wholly taken away, that wolves have and do greatly increase in number, and that frequent spoil and destruction, in every part of this country, is by them made upon hogs, sheep and cattle, to the great injury, damage and loss of the inhabitants. *Be it therefore enacted by their majesties lieutenant governor, council and the burgesses of this General Assembly and the authority thereof, and it is hereby enacted,* That whosoever hereafter shall kill and destroy wolves, either by gun, pit, trap, or other means or ways whatsoever, shall, for every wolf so killed and destroyed, be paid in the county where the same is done, by pit or trap, three hundred pounds of tobacco and casque, and for a wolf killed by gun or otherwise, two hundred pounds of tobacco and casque for his encouragement and reward.

🐺 1673: Wolf Bounties in New Netherland

New Netherland was the area we now know as Manhattan Island, a borough of New York City. The florins (fl.) mentioned in the following law were gold coins used by the Dutch colonists. The New York City wolf bounty comes from E. B. O'Callaghan's Laws and Ordinance of New Netherland, 1638–1674.

November 14, 1673

Whereas We are informed of the great ravages the Wolf commits on the small cattle; therefore to animate and encourage the proprietors who will go out and shoot the same, We have resolved to authorize the Deputy Sheriff and Schepens to give public notice that whoever shall exhibit a Wolf to them which hath been shot on this island on this side *Haarlem* shall be promptly paid therefore by them; For a Wolf, fl. 20, and for a She wolf fl. 30 Wampum, or the value thereof, which said Deputy Sheriff and Schepens shall, by their messenger, levy from those who keep any cattle, large or small, within their district on said Island, each of whom shall, according to the number of cattle, be bound to contribute and pay thereto whatever he shall be taxed thereupon by the Deputy Sheriff and Schepens.

🐺 1640s: *History of the State of Rhode Island and Providence Plantations,* Samuel Greene Arnold

In the 1640s, Rhode Island escalated the war against the wolf by hiring professional hunters to kill wolves. Any employee who killed a wolf received a five pound cash bonus as well as his daily wages. Pennsylvania offered special premium bounties to men who signed on to a predator control program that required them to hunt wolves at least three days each week. This idea, originating in the mid-seventeenth century, of contracting professional hunters to kill wolves was resurrected in 1915 by the federal government in an attempt to devise a final solution to the wolf problem.

Wolves were numerous, and so destructive to the cattle that men were hired by the day to hunt them, and were paid besides, thirty shillings a head for every one killed, which bounty was soon increased to five pounds, and a special tax levied for the purpose, to be paid by the farmers in proportion to their number of cattle. Roger Williams was commissioned to arrange with Miantinomi for a grand hunt to extirpate them, which, however, was not so thoroughly done but that, for several years, they continued to be a source of annoyance.

1705: Wolf Legislation in the Colony of Pennsylvania

January 12, 1705
An Act for the Killing of Wolves
For preventing the destruction of sheep and cattle by wolves:
[Section I.] Be it enacted by John Evans, Esquire, by the Queen's royal approbation Lieutenant-Governor under William Penn, Esquire, absolute Proprietary and Governor-in-Chief of the Province of Pennsylvania and Territories, by and with the advice and consent of the freemen of the said Province in General Assembly met, and by the authority of the same, That if any person within this province shall kill a dog-wolf, he shall have ten shillings, and if a bitch-wolf, fifteen shillings; to be paid out of the county stock; provided such person brings the wolf's head to one of the justices of the peace of that county, who is to cause the ears and tongue of the said wolf to be cut off. And that the Indians, as well as others, shall be paid for killing of wolves accordingly.

[Section II.] And be it further enacted by the authority aforesaid, That all and every person or persons who are willing to make it their business to kill wolves, and shall enter into recognizance before two or more justices of the peace of the respective counties where he or they dwell, with sufficient security in the sum of five pounds, that he or they shall and will make it his or their sole business, at least three days in every week, to catch wolves, shall have twenty-five shillings for every wolf, dog or bitch, that he or they shall so catch and kill within the time mentioned in the said recognizance; to be paid out of the county levies where the wolves are taken as aforesaid.

1633: *New England's Prospect*, William Wood

A great hunger for news from the colonies existed in England, especially for those who contemplated resettling in the New World. William Wood took advantage of that demand by writing a report on his 1633 journey to America. His book, first published in 1634, became wildly popular. Wood wrote several passages on the wolf problem:

The wolves be in some respect different from them in other countries. It was never known yet that a wolf ever set upon a man or woman. Neither do they trouble horses or cows; but swine, goats, and red calves, which they take for deer, be often destroyed by them, so that a red calf is cheaper than a black one in that regard in some places. In the time of autumn and in the beginning of spring, these ravenous rangers do most frequent our English habitations, following the deer which come down at that time to those parts. They be made much like a mongrel, being big boned, lank paunched, deep breasted, having a thick neck and head, prick ears, and long snout, with dangerous teeth, long-staring hair, and a great bush tail. It is thought of many that our English mastiffs might be too hard for them; but it is no such matter, for they care no more for an ordinary mastiff than an ordinary mastiff cares for a cur. Many good dogs have been spoiled by them. Once a fair greyhound, hearing them at their howlings, run out to chide them, who was torn in pieces before he could be rescued. One of them makes no more bones to run away with a pig than a dog to run away with a marrow bone. . . .

These be killed daily in some place or other, either by the English or Indian, who have a certain rate for every head. Yet is there little hope of their utter destruction, the country being so spacious and they so numerous, traveling in the swamps by kennels. Sometimes ten or twelve are of a company. Late at night and early in the morning they set up their howlings and call their companies together—at night to hunt, at morning to sleep. In a word they be the greatest inconveniency the country hath, both for the matter of damage to private men in particular, and the whole country in general.

1638: Letter from Edmund Browne to Sir Simonds D'Ewes

The British Museum has a letter in its collection written on September 7, 1638, by Edmund Browne, a recent immigrant to the New World, to an English friend, Sir Simonds D'Ewes. Browne had graduated from Cambridge University in 1624 and sailed to Massachusetts in 1637. The following year, he helped found the town of Sudbury and served as a minister there until his death in 1678. Browne's letter to D'Ewes includes observations on wolves' fear of humans. This modernized version of Browne's letter comes from Everett Emerson's 1976 book Letters From New England.

Here be yearly many new plantations set upon in both the patents to the great comforts of our spirits. Our greatest enemies are our wolves, but yet [they] flee man, and the musceta, being our English gnat, is exiled out of places inhabited. The Indians are wholly subjected, and we more secure from land enemies and annoyances by thieves than in O[ld] England. I tell you no untruth: our outward door hath stood by a quarter of a year unlocked, and men ride and travel abroad ten or twenty miles without sword or offensive staff, for both wolves and Indians are afraid of us. (The Lord be praised.)

1640: *The History of the Colony of Massachusetts-Bay,* Thomas Hutchinson

In 1764 Thomas Hutchinson, a historian and statesman who later served as Lieutenant Governor of Massachusetts, published a three-volume work covering Massachusetts colonial history from 1628 to 1691. Included in his history is the transcript of a letter written around 1640 by a colonist described as a "gentlewoman." Her letter, sent to a friend considering a move to the colony, comments on the difficulties and fearful things she encountered in the new land.

When I remember the high commendations some have given of the place, and find it inferior to the reports, I have thought the season thereof to be this, that they wrote surely in strawberry time. When I have thought again of the mean reports, and find it far better than those reports, I have fancied the eyes of the writers were so fixed on their old English chimney tops, that the smoke put them out. The air of the country is sharp, the rocks many, the trees innumerable, the grass little, the winter cold, the summer hot, the gnats in summer biting, the wolves at midnight howling, &c. Look upon it, as it hath the means of grace, and, if you please, you may call it Canaan. I perceive some among you have imagined they might enlarge their estates by coming here, but I am taught that great men must look to be losers, unless they reckon that gain which, by the glorious means of life, comes down from heaven. Men (by what I hear) of your rank and worth, will be welcome on New England's coasts; he can advise you best, who can lead you to his place.

1672: *New-England's Rarities Discovered,* John Josselyn

Several authors in this collection divide wolves into species or groups that are not recognized by biologists as valid. There are only two wolves native to North America. The gray wolf (Canis lupus) is found throughout the entire continent except for the southeastern region. The native wolf to that part of the continent is known as the red wolf (Canis rufus). John Josselyn in a 1672 book on the marvels of New England described a newly invented method of killing wolves.

The *Wolf*, of which there are two kinds; one with a round balled Foot, and are in shape like mongrel Mastiffs, the other with a flat Foot, they are like Greyhounds, and are called *Deer Wolfs*, because they are accustomed to prey upon Deer. A *Wolf* will eat a *Wolf*, new dead, and so do Bears as I suppose, for their dead carcasses are never found, neither by the *Indian* nor *English*. They go a clicketing twelve days, and have as many Whelps at a Litter as a Bitch. The *Indian Dog* is a Creature begotten 'twixt a *Wolf* and a *Fox*, which the *Indians* lighting upon, bring up to hunt the *Deer* with. The *Wolf* is very numerous, and go in companies, sometimes ten, twenty, more or fewer, and so cunning, that seldom any are killed with Guns or Traps; but of late they have invented a way to destroy them, by binding four Mackerel Hooks across with a brown thread, and then wrapping some Wool about them, they did them in melted Tallow till it be as round and as big as an Egg; then (when any Beast hath been killed by the Wolves) they scatter by the dead Carcass, after they have beaten off the *Wolves*; about Midnight the *Wolves* are sure to return again to the place where they left the slaughtered Beast, and the first thing they venture upon will be balls of fat.

🐺 1717: *The History of Cape Cod: The Annals of Barnstable County*, Frederick Freeman

In an 1860 book, Frederick Freeman describes a failed 1717 attempt to keep wolves out of Cape Cod through the construction of a six-foot-high wolf-proof fence, intended to run the five miles from Buzzard's Bay to Cape Cod Bay.

This year also the singular project of building "a high fence of palisades or of boards, from Picket Cliff," the north-east boundary between Sandwich and Plymouth, "to Wayquauset Bay in Wareham, to keep wolves from coming into the county," was the theme of general discussion. The town of Sandwich took action on the subject, regarding the enterprise as not only feasible but highly important, but Falmouth alone acceded to the proposition. The other towns, with all which conferences were had, were backward in agreeing to furnish an equitable proportion of the means to meet the expense, and thus the project failed of accomplishment. Some beyond the county limits were opposed to permission being granted by the General Court, as they did "not wish all the wolves to be shut out of the county upon their own limits."

As shown in Chapter 4, this eighteenth-century idea of a wolf-proof fence was revived in the mid-twentieth century by the U.S. Biological Survey (USBS), who proposed that a similar fence be constructed along the United States–Mexico border.

🐺 1739: *An Essay on the Life of the Honorable Major General Israel Putnam*, Colonel David Humphreys

Israel Putnam, later a valiant major general in the Revolutionary War, had a famous encounter with a wolf in 1739 on his farm in Pomfret, Connecticut. The following account of that incident comes from Colonel David Humphreys' 1818 biography of Putnam.

In the year 1739 [Israel Putnam] removed from Salem to Pomfret, an inland fertile town in Connecticut, forty miles east of Hartford: having here purchased a considerable tract of land he applied himself successfully to agriculture.

The first years, on a new farm, are not however exempt from disasters and disappointments, which can only be remedied by stubborn and patient industry. Our farmer, sufficiently occupied in building an house and barn, felling woods, making fences, sowing grain, planting orchards and taking care of his stock, had to encounter, in turn, the calamities occasioned by drought in summer, blast in harvest, loss of cattle in winter, and the desolation of his sheepfold by wolves. In one night he had seventy fine sheep and goats killed, besides many lambs and kids wounded. This havoc was committed by a she wolf, which, with her annual whelps, had for several years infested the vicinity. The young were commonly destroyed by the vigilance of the hunters, but the old one was too sagacious to come within reach of gunshot: upon being closely pursued she would generally fly to the western woods, and return the next winter with another litter of whelps.

This wolf, at length became such an intolerable nuisance, that Mr. Putnam entered into a combination with five of his neighbors to hunt alternately until they could destroy her. Two by rotation, were to be constantly in pursuit. It was known, that, having lost the toes from one foot, by a steel trap, she made one track shorter than the other. By this vestige, the pursuers recognized, in a light snow, the route of this pernicious animal. Having followed her to Connecticut river and found she had turned back in a direct course towards Pomfret, they immediately returned, and by ten o'clock the next morning the blood-hounds had driven her into a den, about three miles distant from the house of Mr.

Putnam: The people soon collected with dogs, guns, straw, fire and sulphur to attack the common enemy. With this apparatus several unsuccessful efforts were made to force her from the den. The hounds came back badly wounded and refused to return. The smoke of blazing straw had no effect. Nor did the fumes of burnt brimstone, with which the cavern was filled, compel her to quit the retirement. Wearied with such fruitless attempts (which had brought the time to ten o'clock at night) Mr. Putnam tried once more to make his dog enter, but in vain; he proposed to his negro man to go down into the cavern and shoot the wolf: the negro declined the hazardous service. Then it was the master, angry at the disappointment, and declaring that he was ashamed to have a coward in his family, resolved himself to destroy the ferocious beast, lest he should escape through some unknown fissure of the rock. His neighbors strongly remonstrated against the perilous enterprize: but he, knowing that wild animals were intimidated by fire, and having provided several strips of birch-bark, the only combustible material which he could obtain, that would afford light in this deep and darksome cave, prepared for his descent. Having, accordingly, divested himself of his coat and waistcoat, and having a long rope fastened round his legs, by which he might be pulled back, at a concerted signal, he entered head foremost, with the blazing torch in his hand.

The aperture of the den, on the east side of a very high ledge of rocks, is about two feet square; from thence it descends obliquely fifteen feet, then running horizontally about ten more, it ascends gradually sixteen feet towards its termination. The sides of this subterraneous cavity are composed of smooth and solid rocks, which seem to have been divided from each other by some former earthquake. The top and bottom are also of stone, and the entrance, in winter, being covered with ice, is exceedingly slippery. It is in no place high enough for a man to raise himself upright, nor in any part more than three feet in width.

Having groped his passage to the horizontal part of the den, the most terrifying darkness appeared in front of the dim circle of light afforded by his torch. It was silent as the house of death. None but monsters of the desert had ever before explored this solitary mansion of horror. He, cautiously proceeding onward, came to the ascent; which he slowly mounted on his hands and knees until he discovered the glaring eye-balls of the wolf, who was sitting at the extremity of the cavern. Started at the sight of fire, she gnashed her teeth, and gave a sullen growl. As soon as he had made the necessary discovery, he kicked the rope as a signal for pulling him out. The people, at the mouth of the den, who had listened with painful anxiety, hearing the growling of the wolf, and supposing their friend to be in the most imminent danger, drew him forth with such celerity that his shirt was stripped over his head and his skin severely lacerated. After he had adjusted his clothes, and loaded his gun with nine buck-shot, holding a torch in one hand and the musket in the other, he descended the second time. When he drew nearer than before, the wolf, assuming a still more fierce and terrible appearance, howling, rolling her eyes, snapping her teeth, and dropping her head between her legs, was evidently in the attitude, and on the point of springing at him. At the critical instant he levelled and fired at her head. Stunned with the shock, and suffocated with the smoke, he immediately found himself drawn out of the cave. But having refreshed himself, and permitted the smoke to dissipate, he went down the third time. Once more he came within sight of the wolf, who appearing very passive, he applied the torch to her nose, and perceiving her dead, he took hold of her ears, and then kicking the rope (still tied round his legs) the people above with no small exultation dragged them both out together.

1818: "The Great Hinckley Hunt," Milton P. Peirce

On Christmas Eve of 1818, pioneers who had recently settled in the "Western Reserve" of northeast Ohio organized an all-out "war of extermination upon the bears and wolves" living in the virgin forests of their district. After the killing had been completed, the wolves were scalped and turned in for bounty payments. The $255 in cash was used to purchase whiskey and other supplies for an all-night party hosted by Judge Hinckley, the organizer of the hunt.

Hinckley township, the epicenter of the six-hundred man campaign, is located just fifteen miles south of downtown Cleveland. Milton Peirce's account, published in the January 4, 1890, issue of American Field, *is based on interviews with participants in the hunt.*

It is proper to state here, that these New England settlers were thoroughly accustomed to raising sheep while in their native states, and they very naturally desired to engage in the industry at their new homes, but were seriously embarrassed by reason of the superabundance of wolves. Their pigpens were also frequently raided by bears. . . . In the early days of sheep-raising upon the "Reserve," quite a number of hunts were organized, in which quite large tracts of forest were surrounded by the settlers and many bears, wolves and deer were killed. Quite a number of persons were also wounded by careless firing of guns, and one or more killed.

Judge Hinckley made no effort to dispose of the lands in the township bearing his name, for some years, and each of the adjoining townships had, by 1818, gained a good many settlers who cleared numerous tracts of land. Hinckley was still an unbroken, virgin forest of the heaviest of timber, and became a harbor for large game which devastated the surrounding settlements. It was not unusual for a settler to lose his entire little flock of sheep in a single night, even though penned within the shadow of his buildings. Finally, late in the Fall of 1818, quite a number of meetings were held in the townships surrounding Hinckley, to make arrangements for a war of extermination upon the bears and wolves. Committees were appointed, and the various committees met for consultation, and made arrangements for a grand hunt which should embrace the entire township of Hinckley and forest lands adjacent thereto. Four captains were appointed, one of whom had supreme command of the entire battalion. Surveyors blazed a line of trees upon a circle half a mile around the center of the township. The programme, which was advertised in various ways so that it was fully known for twenty miles in every direction around Hinckley was as follows: The drive was to take place on December 24. Able-bodied men and large boys joining in the hunt were to assemble as follows: Those from Cleveland, Newburg and Royalton, and adjacent neighborhoods, on the north line of the township of Hinckley. Those from Brecksville, Richfield and adjacent neighborhoods, on the east line. Those from Bath, Granger and adjacent neighborhoods on the south line. Those from Medina, Brunswick, Liverpool and adjacent neighborhoods, on the west line. All were instructed to be on the ground at sunrise.

As the last war with Great Britain had closed only three years before, there were plenty of officers who understood the handling of such bodies of men. Most families also had serviceable muskets, such as the laws of their respective states had required each able-bodied man between the ages of 18 and 45 to own. But still, there were not sufficient firearms to go around. Bayonets were mounted upon poles, butcher knives and improvised lances were similarly mounted, and some carried axes, while many carried hatchets and butcher knives in waist belts. It should be understood that the virgin forests of that region were of large timber, few with limbs nearer than thirty feet from the ground, and as there was but little underbrush in the forest, it was practicable to drive a team with sled, wherever there were no streams to interfere. Many of those from a distance came on sleds, and some reached the ground on the evening of December 23. Nearly six hundred men and large boys were on the lines at sunrise, eager for a start, for a few deer and turkeys had been killed before reaching the lines, and many had been driven in.

Soon after sunrise, the commanding officer gave the words: "All ready!" The words were loudly repeated around the lines to the right, and came around to the starting point in just forty seconds, showing a good organization. Many of the boys and some of the men were provided with horns and conch-shells, and most of them with sonorous voices. The signal to start was by the horns, shouts, etc. The captains and their assistants along each line kept their lines properly spaced (like skirmishers) and each line made its share of noise. In a few moments deer began to show themselves along all the lines, but were quickly fired upon. Many escaped, but about one hundred had been killed before the half-mile limit had been reached; also a few turkeys.

By previous arrangement, a general halt was made at the line of blazed trees, half a mile from the center of the township. There was occasionally a large fallen tree, the top of which afforded hiding-places for the bears and deer. All such within the circle were subsequently found to be occupied by these animals, too much frightened to show fight. Quite a number of dogs had been led by boys and men who did not have firearms. Deer were to be seen running in every direction within the circle, and occasionally a bear or wolf. The dogs, at a given signal, were released and soon created great commotion within the circle. The frightened deer made constant attempts to break though the cordon of men and boys, but most of them were shot upon nearing the circle. The officers constantly cautioned the men not to fire, except toward the center. Finally after the fire had slackened materially and upon a given signal, the most experienced hunters, previously selected, advanced toward the center with orders to kill all the bears and wolves, if they could without endangering each other or those in the lines. They soon succeeded in killing most of those animals within the circle. Then, upon signal, the hunters climbed trees in order to make plunging shots and not endanger those in the circular line who were ordered to advance upon the center without firing, except after an animal had succeeded in passing through the line. A stream, now frozen over and with high banks, was soon reached by a portion of the line. An excellent hiding-place was afforded by this stream, and bears, wolves, deer and turkeys were found under the edge of its banks. As plunging shots could be safely fired here, a lively rattle of musketry took place, and most of the game there hidden was killed. The hunters in the central trees were now kept busy, and many with muskets and ammunition joined them as the line doubled and trebled in ranks by concentration. Finally, late in the afternoon the slaughter ceased, as the game was all killed. Most of the turkeys saved themselves by dint of their wings, but several were killed; one was killed by a farmer with a long-handled hayfork, as it flew low over his head. Several deer were killed with bayonets, pikes, hayforks, etc., while jumping over the heads of those forming the circle.

Orders were then given to each line to return and bring in all the game into the center. The boys and old men had kept the teams well up to the lines, and these were brought into requisition where necessary. The first work in order was the gathering and scalping of the wolves, for their scalps had a fixed cash value (a $15 bounty, according to legend), and a trustworthy man was started with these (with horse and sled), to purchase sundry supplies. He returned before dark and found over four hundred men awaiting his coming. Over fifty of the men and most of the boys had returned home to do the chores. The game had all been collected at the center and counted. A large bear had been dressed and prepared for a barbecue, and was being roasted when the man returned with the supplies. . . . Those who came prepared to stay all night had ample supplies of cakes, bread, salt, etc., and with an ample supple of bear and venison meat, enjoyed a rare game feast as well as a night of hilarity seldom experienced, even during the lifetime of the average frontiersman. All accounts agree that among that entire party, not one became intoxicated, but the old survivors (and there are several still living) say it was because of the honest whiskey made in those days.

A beautiful Christmas morning dawned upon the jolly campers, who were soon visited by numerous parties from surrounding settlements, and some even from twenty or more miles away, who had come to see the game and to spend a jolly Christmas, make acquaintances among neighboring settlers and have a rare time generally. And they scored a decided success.

A committee was appointed to make an equitable division of the game, which they did among the four parties forming the four lines that surrounded the township the previous morning. The few deer which were killed outside the township lines, while the parties were coming to their respective lines in the early morning, were not brought in, but were taken on the return home by those who killed them. An accurate enumeration of the game collected at the center resulted as follows: 17 wolves, 21 bears, 300 deer. The few turkeys killed were not taken into account, they being taken home by parties returning the first night. A few foxes and 'coons were killed, but were not taken into account. . . .

During the past fifty years the writer had read sufficient hunting literature to form several large volumes (if the *American Field* articles are included), and doubts whether there has ever been recorded so successful a hunt in America, or one so well planned and managed.

1835: *Ornithological Biography*, John James Audubon

John James Audubon traveled extensively throughout the United States in the early 1800s, seeking out specimens of native birds and working on paintings that later would appear in his book Birds of America *(1827–38). In the following excerpt from his* Ornithological Biography *(1835), Audubon writes about his experiences with wolves in rural America:*

There seems to be a universal feeling of hostility among men against the Wolf, whose strength, agility, and cunning, which latter is scarcely inferior to that of his relative master Reynard, tend to render him an object of hatred, especially to the husbandman, on whose flocks he is ever apt to commit depredations. In America, where this animal was formerly abundant, and in many parts of which it still occurs in considerable numbers, it is not more mercifully dealt with than in other parts of the world. Traps and snares of all sorts are set for catching it, while dogs and horses are trained for hunting the Fox. The Wolf, however, unless in some way injured, being more powerful and perhaps better winded than the Fox, is rarely pursued with hounds or any other dogs in the open chase; but as his depredations are at items extensive and highly injurious to the farmer, the greatest exertions have been used to exterminate his race. Few instances have occurred among us of any attack made by Wolves on man, and only one has come under my own notice.

Two young Negroes who resided near the banks of the Ohio, in the lower part of the State of Kentucky, about twenty-three years ago, had sweethearts living on a plantation ten miles distant. After the labours of the day were over, they frequently visited the fair ladies of their choice, the nearest way to whose dwelling lay directly across a great cane brake. As to the lover every moment is precious, they usually took this route, to save time. Winter had commenced, cold, dark, and forbidding, and after sunset scarcely a glimpse of light or glow of warmth, one might imagine, could be found in that dreary swamp, excepting in the eyes and bosoms of the ardent youths, or the hungry Wolves that prowled about. The snow covered the earth, and rendered them more easy to be scented from a distance by the famished beasts. Prudent in a certain degree, the young lovers carried their axes on their shoulders, and walked as briskly as the narrow path would allow. Some transient glimpses of light now and then met their eyes, but so faint were they that they believed them to be caused by their faces coming in contact with the slender reeds covered with snow. Suddenly, however, a long and frightful howl burst upon them, and they instantly knew that it proceeded from a troop of hungry, perhaps desperate Wolves. They stopped, and putting themselves in an attitude of defense, awaited the result. All around was dark, save a few feet of snow, and the silence of night was dismal. Nothing could be done to better their situation, and after standing a few minutes in expectation of an attack, they judged it best to resume their march; but no sooner had they replaced their axes on their shoulders, and begun to move, than the foremost found himself assailed by several foes. His legs were held fast as if pressed by a powerful screw, and the torture inflicted by the fangs of the ravenous animal was for a moment excruciating. Several Wolves in the mean time sprung upon the breast of the other Negro, and dragged him to the ground. Both struggled manfully against their foes. But in a short time one of them ceased to move, and the other, reduced in strength, and perhaps despairing of maintaining his ground, still more of aiding his unfortunate companion, sprang to the branch of a tree, and speedily gained a place of safety near the top. The next morning, the mangled remains of his comrade lay scattered around on the snow, which was stained with blood. Three dead Wolves lay around, but the rest of the pack had disappeared, and Scipio, sliding to the ground, took up the axes, and made the best of his way home, to relate the sad adventure.

About two years after this occurrence, as I was travelling between Henderson [Kentucky] and Vincennes [Indiana], I chanced to stop for the night at a farmer's house by the side of a road. After putting up my horse and refreshing myself, I entered into conversation with mine host, who asked if I should like to pay a visit to the wolf-pits, which were about a half a mile distant. Glad of the opportunity, I accompanied him across the fields to the neighbourhood of a deep wood, and soon saw the engines of destruction. He had three pits, within a few hundred yards of each other. They were about eight feet deep, and broader at bottom, so as to render it impossible for the most active animal to escape from them. The aperture was covered with a revolving platform of twigs, attached to a central axis. On the surface of the platform was fastened a large piece of putrid venison, with other matters by no means pleasant to my olfactory nerves, although no doubt attractive to the Wolves. My companion wished to visit them that evening, merely as he was in the habit of doing so daily, for the purpose of seeing that all was right. He said that Wolves were very abundant that autumn, and had killed nearly the whole of his sheep and one of his colts, but that he was now "paying them off in full," and added that if I would tarry a few hours with him next morning, he would beyond a doubt shew me some sport rarely seen in those parts. We retired to rest in due time, and were up with the dawn.

"I think," said my host, "that all's right, for I see the dogs are anxious to get away to the pits, and although they are nothing but curs, their noses are none the worse for that." As he took up his gun, an axe and a large knife, the dogs began to howl and bark, and whisked around us, as if full of joy. When we reached the first pit, we found the bait all gone, and the platform much injured; but the animal that had been entrapped had scraped a subterranean passage for himself and so escaped. On peeping into the next, he assured me that "three famous fellows were safe enough" in it. I also peeped in and saw the Wolves, two black, and the other bridled, all of goodly size, sure enough. They lay flat on the earth, their ears laid close over the head, their eyes indicating fear more than anger. "But how are we to get them out?"— "How, sir," said the farmer, "why by going down to be sure, and hamstringing them." Being a novice in these matters, I begged to be merely a looker-on. "With all my heart," quoth the farmer, "stand here, and look at me through the brush." Whereupon he glided down, taking with him his axe and knife, and leaving his rifle to my care, I was not a little surprised to see the cowardice of the Wolves. He pulled out successively their hind legs, and with a side stroke of the knife cut the principle tendon above the joint, exhibiting as little fear as if he had been marking lambs.

"Lo!" exclaimed the farmer, when he had got out, "we have forgot the rope; I'll go after it." Off he went accordingly, with as much alacrity as any youngster could shew. In a short time he returned out of breath, and wiping his forehead with the back of his hand. "Now for it." I was desired to raise and hold the platform on its central balance, whilst he, with all the dexterity of an Indian, threw a noose over the neck of one of the Wolves. We hauled it up motionless with fright, as if dead, its disabled legs swinging to and fro, its jaws wide open, and the gurgle in its throat alone indicating that it was still alive. Letting him drop on the ground, the farmer loosened the rope by means of a stick, and left him to the dogs, all of which set upon him with great fury and soon worried him to death. The second was dealt with in the same manner; but the third, which was probably the oldest, as it was the blackest, shewed some spirit, the moment it was left loose to the mercy of the curs. This Wolf, which we afterwards found to be a female, scuffled along on its forelegs at a surprising rate, giving a snap every now and them to the nearest dog, which went off howling dismally with a mouthful of skin torn from it side. And so well did the furious beast defend itself that, apprehensive of its escape, the farmer levelled his rifle at it, and shot it through the heart, on which the curs rushed upon it, and satiated their vengeance on the destroyer of their master's flock.

Audubon's story of a fatal wolf attack that occurred "about twenty-three years ago" may or may not be an accurate account. Nancy Jo Tubbs's essay in Chapter 9 reports on the results of a modern investigation into an alleged attack by a wolf on a human. Despite years of diligent searching, no documented record of a healthy wild wolf attacking and killing a person has been found in North American history. Audubon's story is representative of the type of tales people told about wolves on the American frontier.

1856: Proposed Amendment to Iowa's Wolf Bounty Law, Jarius Neal

In December of 1856, shortly after Iowa became a state, the state Senate considered passage of an act to "protect the wool growers from the destruction of wolves." The following text for Jarius Neal's proposed amendment to the bill comes from the state of Iowa's Journal of the Senate *for 1857.*

That any wolf or other voracious beast which shall feloniously, maliciously and unlawfully, attack with intent to kill, or do great bodily injury to any sheep, ass, or other domestic animal shall on being duly convicted thereof, be declared an enemy to our Republican institutions, and an outlaw, and it shall be lawful for the person aggrieved by such an attack, to pursue and kill such beast wherever it shall be found, and if such beast unlawfully resist, the injured party may notify the Governor, who shall thereupon call out the militia of the State to resist said voracious beast, and if the militia of the State should be overcome in such battle, then the Governor is authorized to make a requisition upon the President of the United States, for troops.

I cannot say for sure, but I think Neal intended his amendment to be taken as a satire on the proposed wolf bounty. Neal's suggestion was voted down but the Senate later approved the original bill. The Iowa House of Representatives failed to pass the act but a similar bill, offering a $3 bounty on wolves, was finally enacted in 1858.

1856: Journal Entry, Henry David Thoreau

By the mid 1800s, most of the wolves had been exterminated in the eastern states. Bounties for wolves, beginning with Massachusetts in 1630, had done their job. The first known person to challenge the contemporary attitudes toward wolves was Massachusetts resident, Henry David Thoreau. As in many other areas of thought and politics, Thoreau was far ahead of his time. On March 23, 1856, he wrote the following entry in his journal:

I spend a considerable portion of my time observing the habits of the wild animal, my brute neighbors. By their various movements and migrations they fetch the year about to me. Very significant are the flight of geese and the migration of suckers, etc., etc. But when I consider that the nobler animals have been exterminated here,—the cougar, panther, lynx, wolverine, wolf, bear, moose, deer, the beaver, the turkey, etc., etc.,—I cannot but feel as if I lived in a tamed, and, as it were, emasculated country. Would not the motions of those larger and wilder animals have been more significant still? Is it not a maimed and imperfect nature that I am conversant with? As if I were to study a tribe of Indians that had lost all it warriors. Do not the forest and the meadow now lack expression, now that I never see nor think of the moose with a lesser forest on his head in the one, nor of the beaver in the other? When I think what were the various sounds and notes, the migrations and works, and changes of fur and plumage which ushered in the spring and marked the other seasons of the year, I am reminded that this my life in nature, this particular round of natural phenomena which I call a year, is lamentably incomplete. I listen to [a] concert in which so many parts are wanting. The whole civilized country is to some extent turned into a city, and I am that citizen whom I pity. Many of those animal migrations and other phenomena by which the Indians marked the season are no longer to be observed. I seek acquaintance with Nature,—to know her moods and manner. Primitive Nature is the most interesting to me. I take infinite pains to know all the phenomena of the spring, for instance, thinking that I have here the entire poem, and then, to my chagrin, I hear that it is but an imperfect copy that I possess and have read, that my ancestors have torn out many of the first leaves and grandest passages, and mutilated it in many places. I should not like to think that some demigod had come before me and picked out some of the best of the stars. I wish to know an entire heaven and entire earth. All the great trees and beasts, fishes and fowl are gone. The streams, perchance, are somewhat shrunk.

Chapter 2

The Wolfers

". . . their business was to kill wolves."
James Josiah Webb

During colonial days, wolf pelts had little economic value. The most sought-after fur was beaver. When the Old World immigrants and their descendants first explored the western regions of the North American continent, they were searching for new beaver trapping opportunities. In the early 1800s, at the peak of the beaver pelt trade, a trapper of average abilities could make $16 per day, far more lucrative than the average farm worker's wages of 50 cents. One trapper claimed he took in $50,000 in a single year. Beaver pelts were so valuable on the frontier that they were commonly used as money. Some experts estimate that 500,000 beaver were trapped annually throughout North America during peak years. By 1850, however, near extermination of the beaver and a change in men's fashion (the style now favored silk hats) combined to cause the beaver trapping industry to crash.

During the next few decades, demand for wolf pelts gradually increased. Trappers could earn a good living by killing wolves and to multiply their take, most men killed wolves with poison rather than traps. Calling themselves wolfers, they shot bison, elk, and other animals for bait, then laced the carcasses with liberal amounts of strychnine. The era of the wolfers, from the 1850s to the 1880s, saw the greatest mass slaughter of wolves in world history. Historian Edward Curnow, in his study of wolf eradication in Montana, estimated that wolfers killed 100,000 wolves annually in the territory during the 1870 to 1877 period.

Wolfers and ranchers often used the terms "wolf" and "coyote" interchangeably. In places where authors use the word coyote but obviously meant wolf, I put the word wolf in brackets.

🐺 1854–55: *Adventures in the Santa Fé Trade: 1844–1847,* James Josiah Webb

In 1888, James Josiah Webb began to write a memoir of his days "in the Santa Fé trade." From 1844 to 1861, Webb made a total of eighteen business trips between St. Louis and Santa Fe. The following passage from the 1931 edition of his autobiography gives an account of what may have been one of the earliest wolfing operations:

To give some idea of the numbers of wolves on the prairie in the buffalo range, I will give an account of two men formerly conductors of the mail from Independence to Santa Fé. I think it was in 1854 or 1855 [that] they went to Walnut creek [near Great Bend, Kansas] and built a small mud fort, and in summer they would sell what few knickknacks they could to traders and other passing travelers, and in winter their business was to kill wolves for the skins. They would kill a buffalo and cut the meat in small pieces and scatter it about in all directions a half a mile or so from camp, and so bait the wolves for about two days. Meantime, all hands were preparing meat in pieces about two inches square, cutting a slit in the middle and opening it and putting a quantity of strychnine in the center and closing the parts upon it. When a sufficient amount was prepared, and the wolves were well baited, they would put out the poisoned meat. One morning after putting our the poison, they picked up sixty-four wolves, and none of them over a mile and a half from camp. The proceeds from that winter's hunt were over four thousand dollars.

🐺 1872: *Buffalo Land: A Manual for Sportsmen and Hand-book for Emigrants Seeking Homes,* W. E. Webb

Another account of the early days of wolfers comes from W. E. Webb's book. During an excursion from his base in Hays City, Kansas, Webb observed the techniques of wolfers:

As night approached, our Mexicans prepared for wolf-baiting. During the day they had shot two or three old bulls, which wandered within half a mile of camp, and now the swarthy fellows intended to turn an honest penny. For these purposes professional hunters, and occasionally teamsters on the plains, provide themselves with bottles of strychnine, and a quantity of this was accordingly produced. We went with the men to see the operation, as it clearly came within the province of our studies. With their knives the Mexicans cut from the carcass lumps of flesh about the size of one's fist, into which gashes were made, doses of strychnine inserted, and the flesh then pressed together again. The balls, thus charged, were scattered close around the carcass, and a few laid upon it. Cuts were also made, and the poison introduced in various parts of the hams. As many as fifty doses were thus prepared, and we then returned to camp.

No coyote [*sic*] serenade occurred that night, the musicians evidently being busy drawing sweetness from the cords of the slain. A solemn hush lay over the land, for the bisons are a quiet race, and, except in novels, never take to roaring any more than they do to ten-mile charges.

The next day's life began, as did the previous one, before sunrise, and while breakfast was cooking, we followed the Mexicans down to examine their baits. The ground around the carcasses was flecked with forms which, in the early light, looked like sleeping sheep. A half-dozen or more wolves which were still feeding, scampered away at our approach. From the number of animals lying around, we at first supposed most of them simply gorged, but the rapid, satisfied jabbering of the Mexicans quickly convinced us that the strychnine had been doing its work more effectively than we had given it credit for. Twenty-three dead wolves were found, and the even two dozen was made up by a large specimen of the gray variety—or timber-wolf, as it is called in contradistinction from the coyote—who was exceedingly sick, and went rolling about in vain efforts to get out of the way.

Before proceeding to skin the dead wolves, the Mexicans captured this old fellow and haltered him, by carbine straps, to the horns of one of the buffalo carcasses, near which he sat on his haunches, with eyes yellow from rage and fright. Just to stir him up, we tossed him a piece of bone; he caught it between his long fangs with a click that made our nerves twitch. Man never appreciates the wonderful command that God gave him over the other animals until away from his fellows, and surrounded by the wild beasts of the solitudes, in all their native fierceness. Here were a few mortals of us encompassed by wolves, in sufficient numbers and power to annihilate our party, and yet one solitary man walking toward them would have put the whole brute multitude to flight.

Although we wondered, at the time, that so many wolves were gathered from a single baiting, we soon learned that this success was by no means unusual. At Grinnel Station [70 miles west of Hays City], where a corporal's guard was stationed, we afterward saw over forty dead wolves, and most of them of the gray variety, stacked up, like cord-wood, as the result of one night's poisoning by the soldiers.

1865: *Twenty Years on the Trap Line*, Joseph Henry Taylor
*Joseph Henry Taylor, a professional trapper, wrote about the wolfers'
life in his 1891 autobiography. This excerpt includes Taylor's observations
on the hatred Indians felt toward the wolfers, the sad fate of a dog who
survived Custer's last stand, and the wolf phantoms that gave his fellow
wolfers nightmares:*

Wolf skin overcoats becoming a part of the uniform of soldiers of portions of the Russian army, and the popularity of the wolf robe in all fur
wearing countries, made the demand steady and profitable to the fur
dealer and the wolf trapper, so that new and more systematic ways were
devised to destroy wolves for their fur value.

About the year 1865, those trappers who made killing a specialty,
became generally termed wolfers. In those days large herds of the buffalo still roamed over many parts of the Great Plains, though even at
that date their range limits became so circumscribed that they were
divided into two great divisions, the northern and southern.

The southern range constituted that portion of the plains south of
Platte River, reaching down to the northern borders of the State of
Texas, while the northern range, stretched from the Platte northward to
the Saskatchewan Valley, in Her Majesty's domain.

Following every buffalo herd, were packs of ravenous wolves that
watched warily for wounded or decrepit buffalo that would fall an easy
prey to their savage onslaught. Old bulls, no longer able to stand the
bluffs and butts of their younger fellows, were forced to the outskirts
there in turn to meet the dreaded wolf. While buffalo were ever careful to give protection to their young, their aged especially the males,
were literally "turned out to die," when no longer able to hold their
own in a single butting combat.

Every band of buffalo great or small, was therefore encircled by gangs
or packs of wolves, coyotes, foxes and swifts [foxes]. The three latter
were ranged on the outer circle, and forced to wait, as it were, for second table.

With a full knowledge of the movements of his game, the wolfer
riggs [sic] up an outfit similar to that of the hunter or the trapper with
the exception of traps and baits. In the place of these, he supplies himself liberally with strychnine poison.

If it was in the autumn, he moved slowly in the wake of a buffalo
herd, making open camp, and shooting down a few of the beasts, and
after ripping them open, saturating their warm blood and intestines
with from one to three bottles of strychnine to each carcass.

After his line of poisoned buffalo had been put out to his notion, the wolfer makes a camp in a ravine or coulee and prepares for the morrow.

With the first glimmer of light in the eastern sky, he rises, makes his fire, and cooks his coffee, then hitches up, if he has a team, or saddles up if with packs, and follows his line to the finish. Around each buffalo carcass will probably be from three to a dozen dead wolves, which he packs off some distance from his baits, and skins them.

The most frequented winter grounds of the professional wolfers on the southern plains were along the Republican and Smoky Hill Rivers of Western Kansas, and the country about the neighborhood of the Staked Plains in northern Texas. The northern wolfer found their best grounds along the Milk, Musselshell and Judith Rivers, and around the Bear Paw Mountains of Montana, and the Peace River country in Manitoba.

The northern wolfers had the business well systemized, and while many lost their lives by Indian hostility, and the exposure incident to that kind of life, yet many of them made small fortunes at times, but an infatuation born of the calling held them as in a serpent's charm until some reverse in his affairs, left him where he began — in vigorous poverty.

The wolfer's winter life was much the same in his general rounds as his autumn experience. If on the plains near camps of hostile Indians, a small party gets together, from a common camp, and erect a "dug out," a kind of half underground house. These dug outs can be made warm and comfortable. Being thus partly below the prairie level, they are enabled to resist the bitter cold, blowing blizzards that sweep over the Great Plains with terrible fury at intervals during the winter months.

These underground habitations are also used by the wolfers to thaw out the frozen carcasses of the wolves and foxes so that they could be skinned.

A few days warm sun often neutralizes the poison put in the buffalo carcass, so that the effect is only to sicken the wolf that eats the poisoned meat. It then wanders off alone to die by inches in some secluded place out of the lines, and being undiscovered, a loss to the wolfer. Other times these victims of the poison recovers from its fits with the loss of their coat, and no phantom of horror presented itself in such ghastly way, as the reappearance of a sick and famished wolf, with a hide denude of fur or hair, staggering around in a dazed sort of way in search of food to prolong life. Such a sight will sometimes haunt a wolfer from his calling—callious [sic] though his nature to suffering may be.

The Indians have an especial antipathy to the wolfer. Poisoned wolves and foxes in their dying fits often slobber upon the grass, which becoming sun dried hold its poisonous properties a long time, often causing the death months or even years after, of the pony, antelope, buffalo or other animals feeding upon it. The Indians losing their stock in this way feel like making reprisals, and often did.

The writer well remembers a case of strychnine's far reaching effects. On one of the closing days of my trapping experience, a companion and myself were wolfing and trapping around Lake Mandan. We were also accompanied by a large greyhound, formerly the property of General Custer. While out attending some otter traps, we came to a staked beaver skeleton, which I remembered of poisoning and putting out as a wolf bait five winters before. The dog commenced to play with it, then to licking it, when we were pained to see him fall over in a fit and die. The hound had been a notable one. He had followed his former master on his last charge at the Little Big Horn, and made his way alone to Fort Abraham Lincoln, where he arrives on the second night after that battle.

Wolves and buffalo passed off the face of the plains about the same time, though a few coyotes still remain, and an occasional buffalo wolf. These hang around the great cattle herds, and the professional wolfer has merged his occupation with that of the cowboy and the shepherd.

1866–67: *Forty Years on the Frontier*, Granville Stuart

One of the earliest Montana ranchers, Granville Stuart, witnessed the days of the wolfer and the reaction of local Native American tribes to their work. The following excerpt from Stuart's book relates his observations on wolfers and Natives.

The wolfer was the successor of the trapper. About the time that the beaver began to be scarce in the streams, men who had followed the avocation of trapping turned their attention to wolfing. Not until about 1866–67 were the skins of the wolf valuable but from that time on there was a good market for the pelts and wolfing became quite an important industry in Montana.

It was a hard and perilous life led by these brave intrepid men but all the more attractive to them because of the dangers encountered. Every tribe of Indians whether hostile or not to other white men was the avowed enemy of the wolfer as they lost many of their dogs from eating of the poison bait. The friendly tribes would on every occasion cut up and destroy his skins or steal his horses "setting him afoot" when the poor wolfer would be obliged to make his way to the nearest trading post without food or blankets. The hostile Indians lurked about waiting for a chance to get his scalp but were very careful not to attack unless the wolfer could be taken unawares or at a very great disadvantage. The Indian learned early in the game to keep well out of range of his deadly rifle. They usually traveled two together for company and for greater safety.

A wolfer's outfit was a pack horse, a saddle horse each, flour, beans, sugar, coffee, and salt; a pair of blankets, a buffalo robe, the best rifle he could procure, a good revolver, plenty of ammunition, a hunting knife and a supply of strychnine. These supplies were purchased in the fall at one of the trading posts and at the first freeze the wolfers took to the plains and did not return until spring.

The most valuable pelts were those of the gray or timber wolf. These wolves spend the summer in pairs on the timbered mountain sides, having their whelps in caves under the large rocks. They subsist on the fawns of the elk and deer with an occasional grouse or rabbit for a change of diet. As soon as it turns cold they collect in large packs, as many as fifty or sixty together, go to the plains and follow the buffalo.

Just after the first freeze the wolfer begins to set his baits: a buffalo would be killed and the meat poisoned. He would then follow on a short distance and repeat the operation. The baits were usually set in a circle but extended over a wide section of open valley and blizzard swept plains and the poor wolfer suffered severely from the cold while attending the baits. As soon as the wolves ate the poisoned meat they would die and the bodies freeze solid. One poisoned carcass would often kill a hundred or more wolves. When a chinook came or a thaw it was necessary to prevent the hides from spoiling. These visits to the baits were always attended by much danger from hostile Indians and at times the danger would be so great that the most fearless wolfer dare not venture out and many valuable skins would be lost. Occasionally a chinook or a prolonged warm spell would come at an inopportune time and hundreds of the skins would spoil, causing the loss of almost an entire season's work to the unfortunate wolfer. A good season was very remunerative, often netting from two to three thousand dollars.

The money rarely did him much good as the wolfer usually came to a trading post, disposed of his skins, and then joined in a wild carousal, drinking and gambling until the money was all gone. Then he would chop wood for the steamboats, hire out to freighters or engage in some work about the fort until winter, when he would again return to the old life of peril and privation.

The wolfer's lines of baits extended from far up into Canada to Colorado and Nebraska. Their principal trading posts were Fort Peck, Fort Benton, Fort Hawley, Fort Brown, the Crow Agency, Fort Pease, and Bozeman.

1884: *How to Hunt and Trap*, Joseph H. Batty

Joseph Batty, who described himself as "official taxidermist and hunter for government surveys and taxidermists for numerous universities and colleges," wrote an 1884 how-to manual for hunters and trappers that included a chapter entitled "Poisoning Carnivorous Animals":

Though many hunters poison animals for their hides, the practice is indulged in as a profession, on the Northern plains, by a class of men know as "Wolfers." They are Yankees and half-breeds, and are brave and courageous beyond expression. The buffalo wolf is chiefly sought after, though the coyotes, and red, gray and kit foxes are often taken. The wolfers are exposed to greater hardship than any other class of hunters; they have to live in the most barren country, exposed to the severe weather and winds of the plains, which, in their fierce and cutting sweep, seem to imitate tornadoes. Remote from civilization, deeply drifted in with snow, they can scarcely travel, and often wonder how life will be sustained for the Winter; but their pluck seems to keep them alive until Spring dawns on them and their half-starved ponies. They often make a good winter's work on the upper Missouri and Milk rivers; but their hard-earned money too frequently goes for Indian whiskey, for which they pay a fabulous price.

In the process of poisoning, one or more buffalo are killed for baits; their skins are partially removed, bodies laid open and contents of thorax taken out. The viscera and blood which settles is poisoned, the upper quarters are gashed with a knife, and strychnine is put in the incisions. The crystals soon dissolve and penetrate the flesh. The carcasses often freeze before the wolves find them, and they first eat the frozen blood from the thorax, and die in from twenty minutes to an hour afterwards. In warm weather the action of the poison is much quicker. It takes two bottles of strychnine to a buffalo, costing the hunter a dollar and a half. Occasionally the poison is unsuccessfully used, but the hunter is almost sure of a few pelts, and is often richly rewarded. Seventy-eight wolves have been taken in Montana in a single night with one buffalo.

When poisoned, the animals often freeze, and are piled up like cord-wood, until the weather is sufficiently warm to skin them. Occasionally a few are thawed out by the camp fire and the pelts removed; but if one "strikes the buffalo right," he will have plenty to do to kill for bait the stragglers that come near camp, and to pack the wolves.

The carcass of one buffalo will do long service, but fresh ones are best, and should be obtained if possible. When buffalo are scarce, it is often necessary to lay baits five, ten or fifteen miles from camp. Three wolves are enough to carry behind a saddle at once, and when the baits are so far away from camp, the great difficulty of securing poisoned animals in a northern Winter may be imagined. Wolfing is carried on in Minnesota, Dakota, Montana, and in the British Provinces. Strychnine has made great havoc among the immense bands of gray wolves that frequented the Northern buffalo prairie. In Spring, the wolfers used to come down the Missouri river in mackinaw boats loaded with packs of pelts, the skin of the buffalo wolf predominating. When we were once camped with wolfers, traders were giving one dollar per pelt; in St. Paul they were bringing one dollar and a half, and in New York City two dollars.

1870s: "The Eagle Creek Wolfers," James Willard Schultz

The following article appeared in the January 5, 12, and 19 issues of Forest and Stream *magazine in 1901. The author is listed as the "Scribbler," but it is generally acknowledged that James Willard Schultz wrote the story. Schultz lived in the western territories and states as a hunter, trapper, and guide during the second half of the 1800s. He knew from first-hand experience what the life of a wolfer was like. His colorful account incorporates the frontier dialect that wolfers used when conversing with each other:*

Years ago, in the buffalo days, three wolfers looking about for a likely place to pass the coming winter and ply their vocation, decided to locate near the mouth of Eagle Creek. This streamlet, as old-timers know, enters the Missouri River from the north about fifty miles below Fort Benton, Mont. It was then, and for that matter is to-day [sic], one of the wildest and most picturesque places in the Northwest. Loading a Mackinaw boat with sufficient supplies for the winter, the three left Fort Benton one day early in September, and in due time, without much effort on their part, the swift current carried them to their destination. Just below the mouth of Eagle Creek, and on the south side of the river, was a narrow stretch of bottom land, and there they built a cabin of green cottonwood logs, roofing it with poles and a layer of dirt several feet thick. In one corner they constructed a broad fireplace of stones and clay, the chimney being built of the same material, and extending far enough above the roof to insure a good draft. All in all, it was a very comfortable shack.

Directly in front of the cabin was a narrow but dense growth of cottonwood and willow, which sheltered it from the north wind, and incidently [sic] hid it from the sharp eyes of any prowling war party of Indians who might be passing up or down the valley. At least that was what the wolfers hoped. Immediately behind it, the sage brush hills slanted upward at an acute angle to the foot of the frowning sandstone cliffs where ends the great plain lying between the Yellowstone and the Missouri. . . .

After building the cabin, there was absolutely nothing for the wolfers to do but loaf around and wait for cold weather, when they could begin operations against the wolves. Of the three men, crusty Ben Underwood, and careless, happy Jack Fenn, were old-timers who had passed their lives on the plains. The third was the writer, then very much of a youth and tenderfoot, whom the others called the "Scribbler," because "he was always wastin' his time writing things that no Eastern newspaper fish would ever believe or print." They were good, faithful friends, Jack and Ben, and very kind to the Scribbler, albeit they loved to joke him. Peace to their shades; they have long since returned to Mother Earth. . . .

For a long distance above and below the mouth of Eagle Creek there were but few places where the game could get down from the plains to the river, both rims of the valley being walled by cliffs. Here and there these had broken down, or terminated in a steep bare hill, and at intervals they were pierced by long deep cañons. At such places the buffalo, the antelope and deer had for centuries traveled up and down on their way to and from the river, and had worn trails many feet in depth, even in the comparatively hard sandstone. Of course, where the game traveled the wolves were also continually passing, and that was why the wolfers had located there. They felt that one or two poisoned baits on each thorofare would be worth many times that number promiscuously scattered about on the plains.

The Scribbler never tired of gazing at the immense herds of buffalo and other game which were continually passing in and out of the valley. Of course, there were many bands in sight at all times, but every morning a solid stream of buffalo could be seen pouring down over the rim of the valley by some narrow trail, and then spreading out like a fan as they hurried to the shore of the river. With them came band after band of antelope from the plains, and mule deer from the pine-clad slopes and buttes, where they made their homes; and often a bunch of bighorn, led by some wary old ram, plunged down the steep hills into the bottom. But the latter never tarried long; their thirst assuaged, they lost no time in returning to the cliffs and buttes near by. Then there were bears, numbers of them, especially the light colored grizzly, which Lewis and Clarke called the "white bear," and which they dreaded to encounter. Elk and whitetail deer were also abundant, especially further down the river, where they frequented the large timbered bottoms. And then the wolves! There seemed to be thousands and thousands of the great shaggy fellows. By day and night their long-drawn, melancholy howls echoed and re-echoed through the valley and along the beetling cliffs. There was something indescribably sad in the cry of the wolf, something that made even the most lighthearted and careless of men pause and listen. Many persons could not bear the sound; yet to the true lover of nature it had a peculiar—if perhaps undefinable—charm. How the deep, clear, plaintive, minor strains of their voices used to grow and swell down in that lonely valley, as the shades of night drew on. Often a single old male, sitting on a commanding ridge or barren butte, would start it. Throwing back his head until the long, keen, muzzle pointed straight up to the zenith, he shuts his eyes, and from his powerful throat, through parted black lips, offset by gleaming fangs, came the wail o-o-o-o-o-o-o-o-o-o; faint at first, then rising to a resonant crescendo, and finally dying away. And presently, perhaps from the far shore of the river, came the long drawn answer; and before it was finished others took up the refrain; here two or three, there an old female and her nearly grown family of young; and then far up and far down the valley, and out along the frowning cliffs, others and still others joined in, until the still air trembled with the burden of their voices. Oh, never, never again shall we hear the like! The days of the buffalo and wolf have forever vanished; days when it was possible for the adventurous spirit to view nature as yet unsoiled by the ruthless cupidity of civilized man; days when her children, the wild creatures of forest and plains, and the still wilder redmen, were almost the sole inhabitants of a boundless domain. . . .

A tall mountain man named Longhair walks into the wolfers' camp and

*tells how he had just lost all his belongings in a skirmish with Indians.
Despite his destitute condition, the wolfers offer to make him a partner in
their enterprise. When they describe Longhair as a rustler in the passage
below, they mean that he hustles hard to earn a living in the wilderness.*

"Never mind about bein' broke." Ben continued. "Here's lots o' grub
'n' ca'tridges 'n' strychnine, 'n' they's lots o' wolves prowlin' round jest
achin' to be poisoned. Yer a rustler all right, 'n' so fur as I'm consarned
yer can go in whacks on the hull business."

"Sure," Jack exclaimed, thumping the table.

"Certainly you are welcome," echoed the Scribbler.

"Fellers," said Longhair, rising and shaking hands solemnly all
around, and there was a tremor in his voice, "Fellers, all I kin say is, yer
white. Old Longhair will do his best. The preacher said they was a
silver linin' to every cloud, 'n' by gosh he didn't tell no lie." . . .

Winter set in in a few days. . . . One morning when they awoke they
found a little pile of snow in the fireplace which had sifted down the
chimney during the night, and when the door was opened they saw
that a real blizzard was on. The bitterly cold wind was from the east,
and the snow was falling so fast that the opposite shore of the river was
invisible. They were delighted at the change; their days of enforced
idleness were over; from that time until spring they would be busy poisoning and skinning wolves.

Very early the day after the storm they started out to kill and poison
some baits, Jack and Ben going to the west, Longhair and the Scribbler
quartering up the hills to the east of the cabin. It was very cold; a thin,
sparkling feather of frost hung in the air, and great clouds of fog arose
from the narrow black line of open water in the channel of the river.
The storm and intense cold had driven unusual numbers of game in
from the plains. The bottoms and slopes of the valley were fairly black
with buffalo, checkered with the light forms of the antelope, which
were also there in thousands. A band of mule deer, alarmed by the
approach of the two men, suddenly rushed out of a low coulée and
then stopped to gaze foolishly about. But they were safe; even the big
buck with the massive set of antlers was too small for a good bait, and in
those days his kind were seldom killed for food. . . . So little did the
wolfers think of them that they never shot one; buffalo meat was their
preference, varied occasionally by a feast of fat bighorn or antelope or
white-tail deer.

About half a mile from the cabin a well traveled game trail entered the valley from the plains through a break in the prevailing cliffs. As Longhair and the Scribbler approached the place, a small herd of buffalo was just coming through on their way into the valley. They kept on until they were directly opposite the two hunters, a coulée about 200 yards wide intervening between them. "Paste that big cow in the lead, Scrib," said Longhair, "an' be sure to hit her so she'll drop right there on the trail; we don't want no baits down in the coulées."

The Scribbler refused the shot. "You are a better marksman than I am," he replied; "shoot her yourself."

Longhair brought his gun to his shoulder and fired with the ease and celerity of the professional hunter. The crack of the rifle sounded very faint in the cold, thin air. Thud! went the bullet against its mark, and down dropped the cow in her tracks, shot through the shoulder and heart, as was afterwards ascertained. . . .

When Longhair fired the herd lost no time in scampering back up the trail. The hunters made their way over to the fallen cow, turned her on her back, propping up the body by turning the head sharply around against a foreshoulder, and then removed the entrails. A large amount of blood remained in the cavity, and they quickly poured two bottles of strychnine into it, thoroughly mixing it with the rapidly congealing fluid and smearing the whole inside. The contents of another bottle was sprinkled into the deep gashes cut in the body and upon the heart and organs lying beside it. Before they had half finished several interested spectators arrived. A couple of magpies were the first to come, and they were so bold that they fluttered about the men, chattering and scolding almost within arm's reach. Next came a kit fox sniffing the air and picking up his ears and alternately advancing and retreating in the trail just above. Poor creatures! they fell victims to the deadly poison before the wolfers passed out of sight of the bait.

The next trail entering the valley was three miles further on. There also a buffalo was killed and poisoned, and the two swung down the ridge to the river. Here were more buffalo, and the Scribbler shot one, which tumbled over the steep bank onto a sand bar at the water's edge. In winter the wolves traveled up and down stream a great deal on the ice, and although the snow had fallen but a couple of nights before, they already had a well-beaten trail near each shore. It was a sort of boulevard, a strolling place, where they met of nights to practice their weird and melancholy chorus. It was an ideal place for a bait, that sandbar beside their well-beaten road, and Longhair surveyed the carcass of the buffalo with great satisfaction. "Them two up on the hills is all right," he said, "but here's where we make the biggest killin'. There, we've poisoned it to rights. Come on; le's go home."

Tired of tramping through the deep snow, they chose the easier route homeward over the ice, following the wolf road. On their way they saw where a buffalo had walked out on the ice to get a drink from the open water in the channel, but there was no returning track, and the broken ice at the edge of the narrow opening explained the reason—it had crashed through the thin sheet and drowned. A great many of them lost their lives in that way every winter.

Arrived at camp, Longhair and the Scribbler found that their partners had preceded them and had supper ready. How warm and cozy the cabin was after the long tramp in the cold and snow! How cheerful the ruddy glow from the fireplace illuminating every detail of the rude interior. And how they did relish that meal of boiled ribs, beans, and bread!

Jack and Ben had put out four baits, and on their way home had found three wolves lying dead around the carcass of the first buffalo they had killed. As they were not frozen, they skinned them and brought in the pelts. It was a good beginning, and proved one most important point—that their strychnine was good.

The next morning the river was found to have frozen solid, so all hands crossed over and put out some baits on that side and up Eagle Creek. The succeeding day the baits first put out were examined, and sixty-three wolves were found, to say nothing of coyotes and kit foxes, which were of no value in those days. Around every bait the snow was strewn with the long-haired animals. Some had died with their heads on the carcass; a few had got away several hundred yards before falling; the majority lay within a circle of 50 yards. Some were very dark colored; some a light gray; a few as white as the snow they lay upon. "We're sure in luck," Ben said that evening. "Le's see: five times sixty-three— three hundred an' fifteen dollars' worth o' pelts in two days, baits acrost the river not counted. If we could keep that lick up all winter we'd come out millionaires next spring."

"The Lord tempers the wind to a sheared sheep, as the preacher says," Longhair remarked. "Looks as if I was goin' to make enough ter buy some more pack mules 'n' a saddle hoss 'n' a new outfit o' stuff."

And now the days passed quickly, one much like another. When it was pleasant the wolfers wandered around among their baits, noting with great satisfaction the increasing number of wolves lying about them. When it was very cold or stormy they remained in their comfortable cabin, happy and contented. Nothing worried them. As the season advanced, a less and less number of wolves fell victims to the deadly baits, perhaps because the greater part of those in the vicinity had already partaken of the poisoned meat, or because the survivors had become educated and were wary of the food so temptingly offered them. One would naturally think that at sight of a number of his kindred lying stiff and stark about a bait, any sensible wolf would become panic stricken and immediately strike out for other regions. Unfortunately for the wolfers, there were but two or three chinooks during the winter and they were of such short duration that the frozen animals never thawed out so they could be skinned. After January no more baits were poisoned, for it was evident that when warm weather did set in many of the pelts would decay before they could be removed. In fact, there were already more dead wolves than could be cared for. . . .

. . . [Later] a chinook set in, and they were soon busy removing the hides from the poisoned wolves, and pegging them out on the ground to dry. It was hard work, and a greasy, disagreeable job, but they kept steadily at it, begrudging even the time required to eat their midday lunch. It was their harvest time; every well-haired and well-cured hide, they knew, was worth a five-dollar bill. No wonder they worked with tireless energy. . . .

One day in April the long expected and long looked for smoke of a steamer was discovered far down the river, and the wolfers hurried to get their belongings out on the bank, ready to put aboard. The result of their season's work made a goodly showing; there were 900 prime wolf skins, twenty in a bunch, pressed, baled and bound with rawhide thongs. There were also some bear hides . . . and a few beaver pelts which Jack had caught at odd times in the river near by. It seemed to the impatient men as if the steamer would never arrive, but finally she came puffing slowly along against the swift current, and in answer to a rifle shot swung in to the bank. The gang plank was lowered, the hawser made fast to a tree, and as the deck hands ran out to carry on their pelts and things, the wolfers stepped aboard, the cynosure of all eyes. There were many passengers, including a number of women, come to try their fortunes in the boundless West, and they crowded around the new arrivals and began to ask all sorts of questions. Ben and Jack and the Scribbler fled from them, but Longhair was in his element, and the lies he told those pilgrims were monumental. "Are the buffalo very fierce animals?" one thin, consumptive looking man was heard to ask.

"You bet they be," Longhair replied: "They rush at a feller on sight an' eat him up if they catch him. They don't like white men much, though. They live mostly on Injuns."

"What do you hunters eat mostly?" a woman asked.

"Meat."

"What? No vegetables? No green things of any kind?"

"Well, we eat grass in the spring when it's young an' tender like; we bile it an' put on vinegar, an' it goes fust rate.

The tenderfeet believed everything he said.

Fort Benton was sighted the evening of the second day after the wolfers went aboard. The steamer whistles blew, a cannon at the old adobe fort boomed a salute to the first boat of the season, and all the people of the town thronged to the levee to see her come in. There were merchants and soldiers, gamblers, saloon keepers and hurdy gurdy girls, traders and trappers, miners from the Rocky Mountains, bull whackers, mule skinners and Indians; a motley crowd. The wolfers were vociferously greeted by their friends, their hands nearly shaken off. "Come on," they cried, "and bring your friend. What's his name? Longhair? Come on, Longhair, the town's yours."

1861–62: *The Wolf Hunters*, George Bird Grinnell

The editor of Forest and Stream *magazine and author of many books, George Bird Grinnell had a deep interest in documenting life on the American frontier. A number of his books were based on his experiences of living with various tribes of plains Indians and hunting with James Willard Schultz.*

Grinnell discovered an unpublished manuscript written by Robert Morris Peck, a professional wolfer who detailed his adventures in western Kansas in the winter of 1861–62. Using the manuscript as his main source, Grinnell described the lives of Peck and his fellow wolfers in the 1911 book, The Wolf Hunters. *The first excerpt, from Grinnell's "Introductory Note" to the book, notes the Indians' hatred of the wolfers' poisoning activities.*

In the days of the buffalo, wolfing was a recognized industry. Small parties—two or more men—with team, saddle-horses, and camp outfit, used to go out into the buffalo range, establish a camp, and spend the winter there, killing buffalo and poisoning the carcasses with strychnine. The wolves that fed on these carcasses died about them, and their pelts were taken to camp, to be stretched and dried.

The work was hard and not without its dangers. Storms were frequent, and often very severe, and the Indians were bitterly opposed to the operations of these wolf hunters, who killed great numbers of buffalo for wolf baits, as well as elk, antelope, deer, and other smaller animals. . . .

The following pages describe the adventures of Mr. Peck and two companions—all recently discharged soldiers—during the winter of 1861–1862. . . .

In this passage, Peck is asked to scout for signs of hostile Indians as he hunts for fresh meat for the wolfers' camp:

"Now, Peck, while Jack goes to set his traps for beaver, suppose you saddle up Black Prince and go out and kill a buffalo calf or yearling and bring in a quarter or so of fresh meat. And, as there's plenty of time yet before night, while you're at it you may as well make a complete circuit of the camp, say about a mile or two out, and see if there's anybody or any sign of anybody in this neighborhood besides ourselves."

"Tom," I said, "I believe it would be better for me to go out and kill a yearling first and bring in some meat and then take a ride around the country afterward; for if I kill the yearling first and leave the carcass till I make the circuit of the camp the wolves will get away with the meat before I get back to it; and if I make the round first before killing our meat I'll be scaring all the near buffalo away."

"You're right," replied the old man; "do as you say. I'm glad to see that you do a little thinking of your own once in a while."

"And I believe I can kill two birds with one stone," I continued, "by taking some strychnine along and baiting the remains of the yearling after I cut off the hind quarters, and in the morning I'll have a few coyotes [wolves] to skin to give us a start in business."

"That's a good idea, too; but don't fool away too much time, for I want you to make that round of the neighborhood before night."

As I got our package of strychnine out of the wagon, opened it, and took out one of the phials to put in my pocket, Tom suggested:

"You'd better open that bottle here an' put in a little water to dissolve the crystals; you'll find it's easier to handle in liquid than in crystals, and also more savin'."

Tom's suggestion was a good one and I did as he advised. Then hanging the hatchet and fieldglass to my saddle, I mounted and rode away.

Crossing the creek just below the beaver dam, where Jack was already looking out locations for his traps, I rode through the timber to look for the most convenient band of buffalo, and espied one that suited my purpose about a mile down the prairie bottom, strung out in single file on the trail, coming in to the creek for water.

Recrossing the creek so as to keep out of their sight behind the timber, I rode down to a point that would intercept them and prepared to await my game. The place I had chosen to wait for them was an old buffalo crossing, the converging trails, deeply worn in the banks on either side, showing that it was much used. They would have to pass me here, and, again recrossing the creek to the north side, I rode down into the timber, tied my horse behind some bushes, and returned afoot to the crossing, being careful not to give the buffalo my wind.

Soon they passed me, went on down, drank, and climbed the hills on the other side of the stream. As the young cattle filed past me I selected a yearling and, as he came opposite, shot him, and he dropped dead in the trail. The rest gave a jump or two and went on. I cut off the hind quarters and with some trouble put them on Prince.

Then stripping back the skin from the fore quarters, I applied my solution of strychnine, a few drops here and there over the meat and entrails, and left them for wolf bait.

Having left my meat at camp, I rode away on my scout, reaching camp again about sunset.

Just after we finished supper the howling of a pack of coyotes—which we seldom noticed—prompted me to exclaim:

"Make the most of your time, my lads, for if you happen to scent that bait I put out for you I'll be skinning some of you in the morning."

The howling and barking of wolves was such familiar music to us that it seldom provoked remark, for we had scarcely passed a night since entering the buffalo range that we had not been serenaded by the shrill, discordant notes of the coyote, varied occasionally by the deeper bass of the big, gray buffalo wolves, or "lobos," as the Mexicans call them.

Next morning Jack and I hurried through the work of watering and changing the animals to fresh grass, while Tom prepared breakfast. We were impatient to be off, and after the meal, taking our rifles in addition to revolvers, we started out to our respective tasks, Jack afoot and I on Black Prince.

As I approached my wolf baits I disturbed a couple of coyotes—probably late comers that had but recently found the carcass, for they certainly gave no evidence of the effects of strychnine as they loped off on the prairie a little way and there sat on their haunches licking their chops and watching me as though reluctant to leave their feast.

I tied Prince a few rods away from the bait, of which but little remained, while I walked about through the tall grass, looking up the dead wolves, three of which I noticed lying by the bait before dismounting. On looking about I found five more, at varying distances from the carcass, none of them more than a few hundred yards away. Some of them were still warm.

I put down the rifle, drew my knife, and went to work. Having had considerable experience in skinning wolves, I was quite expert at it and soon had the eight pelts stripped off the dead coyotes and rolled up together ready for tying on behind my saddle.

The process of skinning was simple. I turned the wolf on his back and with the point of my knife split the skin from the point of the chin down the throat and belly to the root of the tail; then split the inside of each leg from the foot to an intersection of the first, or belly cut; then stripped back the skin from belly, legs, and sides. The tail was then slipped off the bone whole, without splitting, in this way: strip the skin of the tail away from the bone for about an inch at the root; then slip a split stick over the bone, take an end of the stick in each hand, clamping the bone tightly, and give a jerk toward the end of the tail. The bone slips out of its skin as if it were greased.

Peck and Tom later kill a bison and poison it with strychnine. The following passage shows how wolfers would return to their bait station to freshen up their poison:

"First come, first served, will be the rule here to-night," I remarked as we started to camp. "The first wolves to reach the bait will probably get laid out before they have time to get half a feed, while those that come later may not get strychnine enough to give them a bellyache."

"How many do you expect to find in the morning?" asked Jack.

"Oh, about eight or ten for the first night will be a pretty fair haul; but by to-morrow night I'll poison the bait again, and by that time it ought to catch more—maybe as many as twelve or fifteen—for the scent of the dead buffalo will then attract them from a greater distance."

I did even better than I anticipated, for next morning I found thirteen dead wolves lying around the bait awaiting my skinning knife. Jack remained in camp until I had skinned the wolves, brought in the pelts and pegged them down to dry, after which he took the team and went out to the hay-field where Tom was mowing.

The dead buffalo only lasted for three nights' baiting, by which time I had taken nearly fifty pelts, some big gray wolves but mostly coyotes and little yellow foxes. . . .

. . . Our winter's catch of wolfskins numbered something over three thousand. These were all dried and baled in one of Weisselbaum's warerooms. About one fourth of these pelts were of the large gray wolves, or "lobos," as the Mexicans call them, which, at that time, were rated on the plains at one dollar and twenty-five cents each. The other three fourths were coyotes, worth seventy-five cents each. Besides these, there were several bales of the skins of the little yellow fox, worth twenty-five cents each. At these figures, the entire lot should bring us something over twenty-six hundred dollars.

1871: "Buffalo Days," L. C. Fouquet

In a 1922 letter addressed to the Kansas State Historical Society, L. C. Fouquet described his experiences with bison and Indians in Kansas during the 1870s. Fouquet visited a village of bison hunters and wolfers near Hutchinson, Kansas, in the fall of 1871 and found that the men had used a unique material to pave a nearby road:

My next experience with buffalos and hunters, etc., was in the late fall of 1871. Many more people took to the killing of buffalos for the meat, which they dried, but mostly for the skins.

There was a little village started on Turkey creek about 16 miles North and some west of the new Medicine Lodge town.

Some of the hunters had made a number of rooms (homes) side by side by cutting spaces in the creek bank (east side). They placed logs overhead, then brush and dirt; also sods on top to a level with the rest of the land. No buffalo could ever guess that there was any human around, and they would come sometimes right over to their habitations, and about.

Those people would kill them, take the skins and the very finest part of the meat to dry for the Hutchinson market. They placed poison on the rest for the gray wolves and cayotes [sic] who had become very plentifull [sic] in that land of their plentifull food. And the first thing after breakfast the hunters did was to go to their job of skinning wolves. Any newcomers would have been astonished at the amount of buffalo and wolf carcasses laying around in that neighborhood.

Not far above this cave village was a road going thro the swampy creek valley, about 75 yards wide, and this had been artistically and scientifically paved with gray wolf carcasses and I drove over this bone road several times.

1850s–80s: *The Wolves of North America,* Stanley P. Young

Nearly every possible living creature was killed and poisoned by the wolfers. The following passage, from Stanley Young's 1944 book shows that wolfers even used songbirds as bait:

Sometimes small birds, such as the junco or horned larks, were killed and used for bait. The bird was slit down its breast-bone, and into the slit was placed a pinch of strychnine. The cut was squeezed together again, and the bird placed on the ground along a wolf runway, or along trails that led to water.

1893: *Trail of an Artist-Naturalist,* Ernest Thompson Seton

While working on this section of the book I often wondered what sufferings an animal went through after ingesting strychnine. Ernest Thompson Seton, in his 1940 autobiography, described two cases of strychnine poisoning in vivid detail. Both of these incidents occurred in late 1893 when Seton was working as a wolf hunter on ranches in northeast New Mexico. The first story took place just after Seton had begun a poisoning campaign against the wolves and coyotes of the Currumpaw region of the territory.

Then two incidents happened which gave me plenty of food for thought. Early one morning I was riding the drag of the day before, when I saw, nearly a quarter-mile ahead, a coyote also on my drag. He stopped at something, evidently a poison bait, and devoured it. He went on 200 yards, then fell in the first horrible convulsion of strychnine poisoning. I galloped up, and drew my gun to end his suffering. The ball went over his head. However, now he knew his enemy. He staggered to his feet, vomited all he had in his stomach, then sought to escape. He dragged his paralyzed hind legs on the ground, but worked desperately with fore-feet, snapping at his own flank and legs with frenzied jaws.

I rode and fired again—and again missed. He made another desperate effort.

I followed fast and far, and soon realized that I was making him take the remedy that was the only successful solution: "puke up the poison, get up and fight for your life."

I fired again and again, but gradually his desperate efforts found response in his hind legs. He drove his willpower into them—they worked—he went faster and faster; and, at length, although I followed for half a mile on a good horse, he gradually faded away and was finally lost in a great stretch of scrubby gullies.

These things I now realized: Had I let him alone, he would have died where first he took the bait; but I made him take the one possible remedy—get up and fight for his life. Next he would ever after know and fear the smell of strychnine, and would teach other coyotes to do the same.

I had often found my poison victims with gashes on loins and on limbs; I knew now that these were self-inflicted in their agony.

The other incident, a never-to-be-forgotten tragedy, took place at a neighboring ranch. It was a cold wet night in late November, frost in the air, wet snow everywhere, when Natty Lincoln rode in about ten o'clock. He was nearly frozen. The resident boys were in bed.

Nat turned his horse loose, and walked in.

"Say, Jack," he called, "have you any quinine? I'm all in."

"Sure," said Jack. "On the shelf back of the stove."

Yes, there it was in the dim light—a fat little bottle, the familiar ounce container of the quinine.

Nat took a dipper of water, and swallowed a spoonful of the quinine.

"Gosh," he exclaimed, "that's the bitterest quinine I ever tasted." Then he fell on the ground, writhing and screaming in agony.

The other boys jumped out of their beds in sudden terror.

"What is it? What's up?"

"Jack, Jack, if ever in my life I done you a kindness, for God's sake, take your gun and kill me! I got the wrong bottle; I got the wolf poison."

Shrieking in agony, poor Nat went down again; and in three more minutes was dead.

I was not in that ranch house at the time, but I was in the neighborhood, and got the story first-hand from those who were there. It affected me deeply. What right, I asked, has man to inflict such horrible agony on fellow beings, merely because they do a little damage to his material interests? It is not right; it is horrible—horrible—hellish!

And I put out no more poison baits.

Chapter 3

Range War

". . . a war to the bitter end."
Stanley Young

As the American frontier steadily moved west, settlers encountered wolves in nearly every region. At first, these encounters were not necessarily troublesome. Early Texas and Colorado ranchers apparently had few problems with wolves. Their belligerent longhorn cattle were more than a match for the local packs.

The pioneers who settled Oregon brought breeds of cattle other than longhorns with them, breeds less able to defend themselves against wolves, bears, and mountain lions. In 1843, losses to these predators prompted the newly arrived immigrants to hold a series of public assemblies known as "wolf meetings." The first wolf bounties in the West were passed at those meetings. In the following decades, nearly all of the other western territories and states passed their own wolf bounties.

Western expansion caused the destruction of vast numbers of bison and other game animals, the traditional prey of both wolves and Native Americans. General Phil Sheridan and other military men encouraged the wildlife slaughter as a means to better control the Native tribes of the Great Plains. Loss of the game and subsequent starvation drove many Native people onto reservations. For the wolves, the same loss forced many packs to turn to livestock for survival.

All hands seemed to be against the wolf, from professional bounty hunters, such as Ben Corbin, to ranchers, such as Theodore Roosevelt (who defined wolf killing as a manly sport). But despite the best efforts of westerners to exterminate the wolf, remnant populations of wolves persisted well past the turn of the century. As shown in S. W. McClure's 1914 speech, the ranching industry eventually demanded that the federal government take over the campaign and kill off the last of the wolves.

1831: *Visit to Texas: Being the Journal of a Traveller*

In 1831, five years before Texas won independence from Mexico, an American investor bought twenty thousand acres of Texas land from a New York real estate company. On arriving in Texas, he discovered that his deed was worthless — the land company had swindled him. Returning to the States, in 1834 he published an account of his trip. The anonymous author of the book included an observation on the ability of longhorn cattle on an east Texas ranch to protect their calves from wolves.

But a sudden accident changed the whole aspect of this tranquil scene. A bellowing was heard on the verge of a wood, which caused the cattle to raise their heads and listen, and soon began to attract them towards the spot. Those at a distance soon left feeding and proceeded thither also — not at a slow and leisurely gait — but with a rapid motion, a wild and angry look, and occasionally with a loud bellowing in return. To me the scene was entirely new, and I was quite at a loss to account for it. All hurried with one consent towards one point, evidently influenced by similar and violent feelings, nor did they give over their race nor slacken their speed until they reached the place. Some of them we could see starting from a distance of two, and I presume even three miles, and steering in a direct line across the Prairie. Others were arriving every moment from different quarters, until the number assembled was so great, that it was much easier than before to realize the size of this noble herd. The cause of this muster was explained, when we were informed that a wolf had seized a calf on the borders of the wood, whose cries had called all the cattle to its succor. This is an affair of frequent occurrence, as I was assured. The herd are always ready to repel such an assailant; and I am sure would have been sufficient to overwhelm a far more powerful enemy, excited as they were, and ready to rush in a mass, as they seemed to be, on any opponent.

The people represent it as dangerous to venture among cattle while thus enraged; and we did not approach the spot until the following day, when however, we were unable to discover any traces of the wolf or his prey, and therefore presumed that the former had fled and the latter had escaped without fatal injury.

1860s: *A Tenderfoot in Colorado*, R. B. Townshend

Another account of the fierce protectiveness of the Texas longhorn breed comes from R. B. Townshend. Townshend had immigrated from England to Colorado in the 1860s and established a ranch in the mountains west of Colorado Springs. Beginning in the 1890s, he published maga-

zine articles on his early ranching experiences. These stories, along with additional material, were published in book form in 1923. His observations on the longhorns' "system of mutual protection" contrasts with his later experiences with shorthorn cattle who act "helpless" on the open range.

I turned back to the rolling prairie, where I was still hoping to find my stray horse, and as I went I noticed half a dozen dun and brindle Texas cows, who had already slaked their thirst, travelling steadily away from the water in the same direction as myself. A few young heifers and steers accompanied them, though the mass of the cattle, as I well knew, would stay by the water till the heat of the day was over; but this party of long-horned, long-legged Texas ladies clearly had business elsewhere. They struck into one of the innumerable cattle trails leading from the high pastures to the water and pressed up it, travelling one close behind the other at a steady walk that occasionally became a trot. I rode parallel to them, curious to see the goal they were making for so eagerly.

Up we went into the high rolling sand-hills, and there, in the middle of them, in a little cup-like hollow, I saw a regular Texas nursery. Eight little dun-coloured Texas calves lay there, squatted close to the sandy ground with which their coats matched so well, their heads lying out flat, with the chins pressed down on the sand, just as little antelope fawns would have crouched. In this pose they were all but invisible. Beside them lay two elderly Texas cows, whose office had been to guard the crèche.

The mothers, who had travelled till now in perfect silence, began to low loudly and lovingly when they caught sight of their offspring, and in a moment each young hopeful had jumped up and rushed to his own dam, where his wriggling tail and nuzzling head, the busy lips frothing with milk, soon showed he was getting the dinner he had waited for so patiently. Meantime the two guardian cows had risen to their feet, and lost no time in starting off in their turn to make their trip to the water, leaving their own two calves safe in the care of the rest of the band.

The system of mutual protection was perfect. Brer' Wolf might prowl around and watch with hungry eyes till his lips watered — there was no chance for him to get veal for his dinner while the sharp horns of those fierce Texas mothers guarded their children. Broadly speaking, one might say the Texas cow, the cow of the wilderness, had evolved an institution that has enabled her and her offspring to survive the dangers of savage life.

This institution had been long superseded by the civilized life of the farm for the well-bred shorthorn cow; but take her away from her sheltered surroundings and turn her loose on the range, and she is as helpless as most duchesses would be if left on a desert island. The pedigree daughter of fifty prize-winners must inevitably succumb to the dangers of her new life unless she has initiative enough to revert to the social system of her own primitive ancestors who fought with the wolf and bear in the woodlands of early Britain.

As seen in the two previous selections, the Texas longhorns were readily able to protect their calves from wolves. Ranchers later switched from the longhorns to the "well-bred shorthorn cow." These cows, bred for higher milk and beef production, had little ability to defend themselves or their calves from wolves and other predators. Compared with bison and the longhorns, these animals were easy targets for the wolf.

1845: *The Emigrants' Guide to Oregon and California,* Lansford W. Hastings

The first mass migration to the far West occurred in the early 1840s, on the Oregon Trail. Starting in Independence, Missouri, the trail moved west through what are now the states of Kansas, Nebraska, Wyoming, Idaho, and Oregon. Most wagon trains needed four to five months to complete the journey. Lansford Hastings, an early Oregon settler, wrote a 1845 book that served as both a trail guide and history of the first settlements. In the following passage, Hastings writes about the abundance of wolves seen on the trail west.

Wolves are very numerous in all portions of this section, among which, are the black, gray, and the prairie wolves; the latter of which, are very small, but they are much the most numerous and troublesome. Of the former, the gray wolf is much the most numerous, but the black wolf is much the largest, being generally about the size of our common large mastiffs. All the different kinds of wolves, are very troublesome in all the various settlements, into which they make frequent inroads, not only destroying the hogs and sheep, but also, frequently attacking and destroying even the grown cattle. The cause of there being such an abundance of all the different kinds of wolves, is, perhaps, that they are never killed, either by the Mexicans or foreigners. They do not kill them, because they are entirely worthless, and because the people in that country, have not a superabundance of ammunition. In traveling through the valleys of this section, you will pass many hundreds of them, during the day, which appear to evince no timidity, but with heads and tails down, in their natural crouching manner, they pass within a very few rods of you. As shooting them would be a waste of so much ammunition, you allow them to pass unmolested, and thus, their timidity is diminished, and their familiarity and numbers are increased.

1843: *The River of the West,* Frances Fuller Victor

In early 1843, the settlers of Oregon's Willamette Valley, the destination of travelers on the Oregon Trail, began to talk about organizing some form of government. At the time, the United States and Britain jointly claimed and occupied the region. Differences between local Catholic French Canadians voyageurs, and the more numerous, newly arrived Americans, many of whom were associated with the Methodist Mission, presented a seemingly insurmountable obstacle to forming a provisional government.

Several politicians developed a scheme that would be certain to attract all local citizens: advertise a meeting to deal with the "wolf problem." After the wolf issue had been discussed, the organizers would then move on to the true mission of the meeting: political organization of Oregon. This process, which began as a local meeting on wolves, culminated in the creation of the Oregon Territory by the U.S. Congress in 1848. Statehood followed in 1859. The following description of the Oregon Wolf Meeting comes from Mrs. Frances Fuller Victor's 1870 book, The River of the West:

Some truly long-headed politicians had hit upon an expedient to unite the population, Canadian and American, upon one common ground of interest.

The forests which clad the mountains and foot-hills in perpetual verdure, and the thickets which skirted the numerous streams flowing into the Wallamet [*sic*], all abounded in wild animals, whose depredations upon the domestic cattle, lately introduced into the country, were a serious drawback to their natural increase. Not a settler, owning cattle or hogs, but had been robbed more or less frequently by the wolves, bears, and panthers, which prowled unhindered in the vicinity of their herds.

This was a ground of common interest to all settlers of whatever allegiance. Accordingly, a notice was issued that a meeting would be held at a certain time and place, to consider the best means of preventing the destruction of stock in the country, and all persons interested were invited to attend. This meeting was held on the 2d of February, 1843, and was well attended by both classes of colonists. It served, however, only as a preliminary step to the regular "Wolf Association" meeting which took place a month later. At the meeting, on the 4th of March, there was a full attendance, and the utmost harmony prevailed, notwithstanding there was a well defined suspicion in the minds of the Canadians, that they were going to be called upon to furnish protection to something more than the cattle and hogs of the settlers.

After the proper parliamentary forms, and the choosing of the necessary officers of the Association, the meeting proceeded to fix the rate of bounty for each animal killed by anyone out of the Association, viz: $3.00 for a large wolf; $1.50 for a lynx; $2.00 for a bear; and $5.00 for a panther. The money to pay these bounties was to be raised by subscription, and handed over to the treasurer for disbursement; the currency being drafts on Fort Vancouver, the Mission, and the Milling Company; besides wheat and other commodities.

This business being arranged, the real object of the meeting was announced in this wise:

"*Resolved,*—That a committee be appointed to take into consideration the propriety of taking measures for the civil and military protection of this colony."

A committee of twelve were then selected, and the meeting adjourned. But in that committee there was a most subtle mingling of all the elements—missionaries, mountain-men, and Canadians—an attempt by an offer of the honors, to fuse into one all the several divisions of political sentiment in Oregon.

1875: *The Border and the Buffalo,* John R. Cook

The slaughter of the great herds of bison that took place in the American West during the 1870s and 1880s had a deep, long-lasting impact on Native Americans, wolf populations, and the coming tide of white settlers. The tribes who lived on the plains based their economy on bison hunting. As is shown by John R. Cook's story of a 1875 speech given to a joint assembly of the Texas Senate and House of Representatives, General Philip Sheridan encouraged the professional buffalo hunters in their annihilation of the herds. The following episode from Cook's book took place in January of 1875 as his party of buffalo hunters were camped near the Pease River, northeast of the current location of Lubbock, Texas.

The Texas Legislature, while we were here among the herds, to destroy them, was in session at Austin, with a bill drawn up for their protection. General Phil. Sheridan was then in command of the military department of the Southwest, with headquarters at San Antonio. When he heard of the nature of the Texas bill for the protection of the buffaloes, he went to Austin, and, appearing before the joint assembly of the House and Senate, so the story goes, told them that they were making a sentimental mistake by legislating in the interest of the buffalo. He told them that instead of stopping the hunters they ought to give them a hearty, unanimous vote of thanks, and appropriate a sufficient sum of money to strike and present to each one a medal of bronze, with a dead buffalo on one side and a discouraged Indian on the other.

He said: "Those men have done more in the last two years and will do more in the next year, to settle the vexed Indian question, than the entire regular army has done in the last 30 years. They are destroying the Indians' commissary; and it is a well-known fact than an army losing its base of supplies is placed at a great disadvantage. Send them powder and lead, if you will; but, for the sake of lasting peace, let them kill, skin, and sell until the buffaloes are exterminated. Then your prairies can be covered with speckled cattle, and the festive cowboy, who follows the hunter as the second forerunner of advanced civilization."

His words had the desired effect, and for the next three years the American bison traveled through a hail of lead.

Cook's party of buffalo hunters continued on to the Salt Fork of the Brazos River, where they found themselves in a "vast sea of animals." They established a camp and for the next three years worked at their mission "to destroy them." By 1878, with the Texas bison herds wiped out, the professional hunters were leaving the state, heading north to the killing fields in the Black Hills of South Dakota. In the next passage, Cook reflects on the morality of what they were doing:

And at times I asked myself: "What would you do, John R. Cook, if you had been a child of this wonderfully prolific game region, your ancestors, back through countless ages, according to traditional history, having roamed these vast solitudes as free as the air they breathed? What would you do if some outside interloper should come in and start a ruthless slaughter upon the very soil you had grown from childhood upon, and that you believed you alone had all the rights by occupancy that could possibly be given one? Yes, what would you do?"

But there are two sides to the question. It is simply a case of the survival of the fittest. Too late to stop and moralize now. And sentiment must have no part in our thoughts from this time on. We must have these 3361 hides that this region is to and did furnish us inside of three months, within a radius of eight miles from this main camp. So at it we went.

John Cook questioned the right of white society to take over the homeland of Native Americans, and to kill off their traditional prey. He then quickly rationalized his involvement in this illegal and unfair process by arguing that it was "simply a case of the survival of the fittest."

As Sheridan had hoped, the buffalo hunters did destroy the Indians' commissaries. Once the herds were gone, it became far easier for the U.S. Army to pacify and force onto reservations the Native tribes who had formerly subsisted on the seemingly limitless numbers of bison.

It might be said that the bison were also the commissary of the wolves of the plains. Once their main prey disappeared, the wolf packs were forced to turn to the "speckled cattle" that General Sheridan had confidently predicated would replace the wild bison. That dilemma—loss of natural wild prey and subsequent switching to livestock—created the conflict that eventually exterminated the wolf from the western states. Sheridan's medal could have added the image of a dead wolf next to the picture of the dejected Native American.

🐺 1870s: *Twenty-Seven Years on the Texas Frontier,* Captain William Banta

As they plied their trade, bison hunters frequently encountered wolves. William Banta, a man who later served twenty-seven years as a Texas ranger, tells an astonishing story of a fellow bison hunter who found himself at the mercy of a pack of hungry wolves:

It was agreed that each [of his party of eight] should select his buffalo, and a charge was ordered. It was not long before the herd was on the move, and a wild scene presented itself. The herd scattered in every direction. Bang, bang, in every direction could be heard. It was not long before everything was still but the whistling north wind, and it getting colder every minute.

By 4 o'clock all were back in camp except John Rotman; he was missing. By dark it was sleeting and freezing; well, it was cold. Three buffalo were killed and brought into camp, but no tidings from Rotman. Guns were fired off, hoping to attract the attention of the missing man, but in vain; and the later the hour the colder it got. About 12 o'clock it cleared off, and the cold increased. The firing of guns was kept up all night, but no tidings of the lost man was received. Early the next morning preparations were made for a search, but no one had any hopes of finding him alive. Four of us mounted our horses and started, firing off guns at intervals, hoping if he was alive, he would hear us and come to us. About 1 o'clock we fired again, and to our joy heard him answer us. We went at full speed in the direction of the report of his gun, and soon found him on foot. We were then about fifteen miles from camp. He was taken up behind one of us and we went into camp, where we arrived about dark. It was still very cold, and of course he was hungry, having been out two days and one night without anything to eat.

After supper he gave us a history of his experience during his absence, which was as follows: "I followed the buffalo eight or ten miles, shooting at him as fast as I could load, and finally he fell. It was cloudy, and I could not tell what time it was. I thought after I had killed the buffalo I would return to camp, but I was completely turned around. I rode until dark, almost frozen to death; I was so numb I had but little feeling in my hands, so I walked and led my horse. Finally, just after dark, I came to the dead buffalo. I decided to try to skin him and wrap up in the hide to keep from freezing. Finally I got the hide off, and tying my horse to a bush, spread the hide out, with the wool side up, and laid my gun by my side and rolled up in the green hide. I got warm and went to sleep. About daybreak, I was disturbed by wolves, which had gathered about the carcass of the buffalo. There were so many of them of all sizes that the largest ones fought off the small ones and caused them to work on the hide in which I was rolled up. It had frozen as stiff as a board, and I could not move hand or foot; I could see out at a small place. When it came day, and when they began to grit their teeth near my head, I fairly trembled with fear, and could not help saying "suy". The wolves would look all around, and not seeing anything, they would begin to eat on the frozen hide so close to my head I could almost feel their teeth clipping my ears. In this condition I lay until about ten o'clock before the sun thawed the hide so I could crawl out. On my release from the hide I found my horse frozen to death, and I was left to wander on foot, hungry, stiff, and alone."

Another bison hunter, Jim Ennis, had a similar encounter with wolves. Like Rotman, Ennis rolled himself in a fresh bison hide on a cold night. After it froze solid, a pack of wolves appeared and chewed off bits of meat. They then ripped through a section of the hide and chewed off parts of Ennis's clothes. The warmth of the morning sun later freed the trapped man. When he staggered into camp, his partners did not recognize him—his black hair had turned gray during his ordeal. This story was told by J. Wright Mooar in a 1927 letter to J. Evetts Haley. The letter is in the collection of the Panhandle-Plains Historical Museum in Canyon, Texas.

1886: "Montana Wolves and Panthers"

The July 22, 1886, issue of Forest and Stream *magazine contained a letter entitled "Montana Wolves and Panthers" written the previous February by a correspondent identified only as Carl. His report, sent from Fort Keogh, is an eyewitness account of how the Montana cattlemen waged an "industrious war" against the wolf in the 1880s:*

Montana is simply overrun with destructive wild animals at present. During the year 1884, soon after the last buffalo disappeared across the Canadian border, and when the great herds of domestic cattle succeeded to the stamping grounds of the native bison, there was a remarkable increase in the number of gray wolves on the Montana ranges. To be accurate, this species of wolf, together with his cousin, the prairie coyote, always did hang around the buffalo herds, ever watchful to pounce upon some superannuated bull driven from the band by the younger ones, or to snap up some weak calf or unwise animal that chanced to stray too far from the main body. With the disappearance of the buffaloes from Montana, these scavengers of the prairie also disappeared, because, being left without sufficient food supply, they of course followed the wild herds as they retired to more remote pastures. In 1884 the great buffalo herds in the Canadian northwest became pretty well decimated, and so the wolves returned to their old haunts. Not being so particular as to object to beefsteak when buffalo hump was not to be had, they played sad havoc with the cattle herds that year. Cattlemen did not begin to pay much attention to the matter until last year, when it was found that it knocked considerably from their profits to support such immense swarms of these pests. Cattle and especially young and weak calves, dropped during the winter time, have been the food upon which they subsisted.

In 1884 the Territory offered a bounty for the scalps of destructive wild animals brought in to be punched. The bounty is fifty cents on a coyote, one dollar on a wolf, eight dollars on mountains lions or panthers, and the same on bears. This law cost the Territorial Treasurer $12,740.50 that year, besides which nearly every county offered as much, if not more for the scalps of wild animals than did the Territory. Many cowboys entered into the scheme of poisoning wolves, which besides affording them plenty of sport and winter amusement, also yielded a handsome largess for the ear punching, after which the skins were sold. In this way a number of the cowboys more than doubled their summer's pay which they received for rounding up and herding cattle. Some of the counties also offered strychnine to all who would use it, and even some of the cattlemen volunteered to subscribe a beef or two. This latter alternative, however, was not necessary, as there are always sufficient dead animals lying around to be used for bait and even the wolves and coyotes themselves manufactured plenty of material for their own destructions in the animals they killed for food. Such an industrious warfare has been carried on for two years against the coyotes and wolves, that one would suppose the rascally thieves would begin to show a diminution in numbers, but such is not the case.

In 1885 they were on the ranges in greater swarms than ever and the damage they did counted heavily against the profits for the year. On the chestnut range in Northwestern Montana the stockmen came to the front with a handsome offer to wolf killers, which will make it a paying business for anybody to engage in that occupation alone. It will give the wolfer plenty of poison and not less that $5 for each skin, after which he is at liberty to sell the hides for what he can get.

Mr. Wallace Taylor, of Choteau County, in a recent letter, reported a bad state of affairs in his section of the country, occasioned by the wolves devouring cattle and sheep. He says, "The animals are rapidly increasing and getting bolder every day. They even attack bulls and large cows, and in many instances get away with them. The stockmen are doing everything in their power to exterminate them by the liberal use of poison and the increase of bounty; but thus far the animals have not diminished, and the stockmen fear they will actually be obliged to leave that part of the Territory and secure other quarters." Mr. Taylor is a reliable gentleman, who is not given to exaggeration, so we may receive with the utmost confidence what he says. Mr. Chas. Smith, inspector of the cattle district in and around Helena, in his last report speaks particularly of the great loss of lambs by depredating wolves. "The animals are rapidly increasing," he says, "and getting bolder and more ferocious each day. The sheepmen are becoming frightened over the rapid disappearance of their flocks and are using every means to exterminate the pests." At the last convention of cattlemen, held at Miles City, the question of destroying wolves was one of the principal topics discussed. The discussion developed the fact that the number of calves destroyed by the wolves is simply astounding, and a campaign in earnest was organized against these nuisances. One stockman stated he could show carcasses of fifteen or twenty calves which had been killed by wolves near his ranch. Another stockman had found four in one day near his ranch that the wolves had slain and all agreed that there had been a large increase of wolves in the country this year. One hundred and fifty dollars was in a few minutes paid into the hands of the chairman of the committee to purchase poison to be given to those who wished to kill wolves. In addition to the above, the chairman of the wolf committee informed all that it was expected of each stockman to keep on hand a large supply of poison, and have his employees put it out judiciously and persistently. Mr. Van Buren, a member present, announced his intention of putting out a supply of poison 150 miles in length, and many of the stockmen present offered to furnish him meat to use for bait. This species of wolf, the animal referred to, is not the ordinary black wolf of the States, but is a great big animal nearly the size of a young calf, gaunt and hungry looking even when well fed, and has plenty of pluck and grit. This gray wolf is a good traveler, and may be found today in one country and tomorrow many miles from there. . . . The States wolf above mentioned has never been found in Montana to my knowledge, but several parties on the Shonkin range in Choteau county assert that they saw a genuine black wolf a few days ago, although no one succeeded in getting a shot at him. He is certainly not a native of Montana, and where he came from it is hard to say. Perhaps he is a straggler who drifted down from some one of the Canadian Provinces. As before remarked, some of the cowboys have gone regularly into the business of wolf killing. J. W. Proctor, of Billings, arrived a day or two ago from the Musselshell, where he spread a string of poisoned meat thirty miles long, for the delectation of the gray wolves and coyotes out there. Unfortunately a heavy snow storm covered up the bait, but nevertheless a great many "varmints" were bagged; certainly sufficient to pay all expenses and leave a handsome margin besides.

In Yellowstone County the boys have struck quite a bonanza. In addition to the territorial bounty the county offers one dollar on a coyote, and two dollars on a wolf. This just doubles the territorial bounty on each animal killed or brought in.

A young fellow named Martin, with not much on his hands except idle time, practiced a week at the business in Yellowstone county, and the result was nine wolf skins and twenty-six coyote skins. To sum up he got $13 and $26 for coyote ears, and $9 and $18 for those of the wolves; after which he sold the hides for and average of about $1.50 each to a fur dealer in Billings. Total profit, $118.50 and lots of fun; cost about $5.00 for strychnine and time. Bait was had in one dead animal picked up on the range.

1897: "Wolves and Wolf Nature," George Bird Grinnell

In 1897, Theodore Roosevelt and George Bird Grinnell, the editor of Forest and Stream *magazine, teamed up to write and edit a volume entitled* Trail and Campfire. *Both men had extensive personal experience in living in wolf and bison country in the West. Grinnell's section of the book, "Wolves and Wolf Nature," comments on the effect of the extermination of the buffalo on the wolf and on the relationship of wolves and ranchers:*

Notwithstanding the fact that ever since the settlement of America the wolf has been pursued with guns, traps and poison, it is certain that no blow ever befell the race so severe as the extermination of the buffalo. Their natural prey gone, the wolves also in great measure disappeared. Probably they scattered out in search of food, and starved in great numbers. Those that survived were then forced to turn their attention to the herds of the stockmen, which furnished them an easy prey. They began to increase, and for years their depredations have resulted in very heavy loss to raisers of horses and cattle on the Northern plains. . . .

Conditions have changed for the wolf. In early days he was disregarded, but now a very large class of people in the West take an active interest in wolves. As these animals began to be troublesome, and to prey on the stock of the cattlemen, people who had heard of the old-time industry of wolfing took to poisoning them, since, as a rule, the work of trapping them called for more patience and skill than the average ranchman possessed, and they were too wary to be shot. At last, however, the wolves refused to take the poison, refused to eat any meat, in fact, except a carcass freshly killed by themselves. This, of course, put an end to the poisoning, and recourse was had again to steel traps. With these, trappers have had some success. I know of a case last winter where six wolves were trapped in a very limited area, and, curiously enough, all of these were she wolves. After people had become discouraged with their lack of success in poisoning, a great many greyhounds and staghounds were taken into the West, and efforts were made to use these to kill off the wolves on the ranges. No doubt many wolves have been killed in this way, as it is certain that many coyotes have, but this method of hunting, while an exhilarating sport, is inefficient as a means of exterminating the wolves.

1880s: *The Wolf in North American History,* Stanley P. Young

In looking back at this period in his 1946 book, The Wolf in North American History, *Stanley Young, a man who had helped to exterminate the wolf in the West, wrote*:

> Consequently, as far as the prairie West was concerned, the wolf became a predominant factor to cope with in livestock production. Its common prey, the buffalo, was entirely eliminated, and livestock took the place of them. . . . The wolf depredations were becoming very apparent, owing to the fact that wolves obtained their food more and more from the cattle herds which were now occupying the former buffalo, antelope, elk, and deer ranges. This brought the wolf into direct competition with the producer of prairie cattle, and it became a war to the bitter end. Every known means at the livestock's producer's disposal—guards, guns, traps, poisons, bounties, wolf-proof enclosures—were employed to secure protection from wolf depredation. The cowman of the Old West wrought his vengeance on the wolf because of a typical psychological twist, so noticeable among many of the early western cattlemen, with regard to wolf depredations. For instance, disease might decimate his flocks and herds, or drought or severe winters might result in extreme loss by death; but none of these factors seemed to arouse such outstanding resentment and determination to adopt every means of elimination as when the wolf entered corrals, killed on the open prairie or mountain range, or maimed and mutilated his range cattle or other domestic stock. The wolf brought all its killing traits into play as it sought a substitute for its former food of buffalo meat. It was an obvious conclusion that beef cattle and other stock would rapidly become the logical and favorite substitute.

1880s: *Life-Histories of Northern Animals,* Ernest Thompson Seton

Writing about the same period, in his 1909 publication Life Histories of Northern Animals, *naturalist Ernest Thompson Seton described how the few surviving wolves learned to counteradapt to the trapping and poisoning methods used by ranchers to destroy them.*

> The range of the Gray-wolf had a known history. When the Buffalo swarmed over Western America from the Alleghanies [*sic*] to the Rockies, and from Great Slave Lake to Central Mexico, their herds were followed by troops of Buffalo-wolves that preyed on the weak and helpless. As the Buffalo disappeared the Wolves were harder put for a living. When the last great Buffalo herds were destroyed and the Wolves were left without their usual support, they naturally turned their attention to

the cattle on the ranges.

The ranchmen declared vigorous war against them: traps and poison were imported in vast quantities, a bounty was offered for each Wolf scalp, and every inducement held out to wolf-hunters.

In those days the Wolves were comparatively unsuspicious and it was easy to trap or poison them. The result was that enormous numbers were killed in the early days of 1880 to 1888 or 1889; so many, indeed, that the species seemed on the verge of extinction. The remnant of the race continued on the foothills of the Rockies or the Badlands, but they were so rare as to be no longer a factor in the cattle question. Then new knowledge, a better comprehension of the modern dangers seemed to spread among the Wolves. They learned how to detect and defy the traps and poison, and in some way the knowledge was passed from one to another, till all Wolves were fully possessed of the information. How this is done is not easy to say. It is easier to prove that it *is* done. Few Wolves ever get into a trap, fewer still get into a trap and out again, and thus learn that a steel-trap is a thing to be feared. And yet all Wolves have that knowledge, as every trapper knows, and since they could not get it first-hand, they must have got it second-hand; that is the information was communicated to them by others of their kind.

It is well known among hunters that a piece of iron is enough to protect any carcass from the Wolves. If a Deer or Antelope has been shot and is to be left out over night, all that is needed for its protection is an old horseshoe, a spur, or even any part of the hunter's dress. No wolf will go near such suspicious looking or human-tainted things; he will starve rather than approach the carcass so guarded.

With poison, a similar change has come about. Strychnine was considered infallible, when first it was introduced. It did vast destruction for a time, then the Wolves seemed to discover the danger associated with that particular smell, and will no longer take the poisoned bait, as I know from numberless experiences.

It is thoroughly well known among the cattle men now that the only chance of poisoning Wolves is in the late summer and early autumn, when the young are beginning to run with the mother. She cannot watch over all of them, the whole time, and there is a chance of some of them finding the bait and taking it before they have been taught to let that sort of smell-thing alone.

The result is that the Wolves are on the increase, have been, indeed, since the late 80's. They have returned to many of their old hunting-grounds in the cattle countries, and each year they seem to be more numerous and more widely spread, thanks to their mastery of the new problems forced upon them by civilization.

1880s–90s: *Cattle Brands: A Collection of Western Camp-Fire Stories*, Andy Adams

Andy Adams worked as a cowboy in Texas and Oklahoma in the late 1800s. In this passage from his 1906 book, Adams tells the story of a six-hundred man wolf round-up on the Salt Fork of the Cimarron River in Oklahoma. Like the Great Hinckley Hunt of 1818, this round-up was intended to be operated with military precision but it turned out to be an embarrassing comedy of errors, especially to cowboys who prided themselves on their marksmanship. This fight, cowboys versus the wolves, is one of the most bizarre episodes in the war against the wolf.

An hour before daybreak one Christmas morning in the Cherokee Strip, six hundred horses were under saddle awaiting the dawn. It was a clear, frosty morning that bespoke an equally clear day for the wolf *rodeo*. Every cow-camp within striking distance of the Walnut Grove, on the Salt Fork of the Cimarron, was a scene of activity, taxing to the utmost its hospitality to man and horse. There had been a hearty response to the invitation to attend the circle drive-hunt of this well-known shelter of several bands of gray wolves. The cowmen had suffered so severely in time past from this enemy of cattle that the Cherokee Strip Cattle Association had that year offered a bounty of twenty dollars for wolf scalps.

The lay of the land was extremely favorable. The Walnut Grove was a thickety covert on the north first bottom of the Cimarron, and possibly two miles wide by three long. Across the river, and extending several miles above and below this grove, was the salt plain—an alkali desert which no wild animal, ruminant or carnivorous, would attempt to cross, instinct having warned it of its danger. At the termination of the grove proper, down the river or to the eastward, was a sand dune bottom of several miles, covered by wild plum brush, terminating in a perfect horseshoe a thousand acres in extent, the entrance of which was about a mile wide. After passing the grove, this plum-brush country could be covered by men on horseback, though the chaparral undergrowth of the grove made the use of horses impracticable. The Cimarron River, which surrounds this horseshoe on all sides but the entrance, was probably two hundred yards wide at an average winter stage, deep enough to swim a horse, and cold and rolling.

Across the river, opposite this horseshoe, was a cut-bank twenty feet high in places, with only an occasional cattle trail leading down to the water. This cut-bank formed the second bottom on that side, and the alkaline plain—the first bottom—ended a mile or more up the river. It was an ideal situation for a drive-hunt, and legend, corroborated by evidences, said that the Cherokees, when they used this outlet as a hunting-ground after their enforced emigration from Georgia, had held numerous circle hunts over the same ground after buffalo, deer and elk.

The rendezvous was to be at ten o'clock on Encampment Butte, a plateau overlooking the entire hunting-field and visible for miles. An hour before the appointed time the clans began to gather. All the camps within twenty-five miles, and which were entertaining participants of the hunt, put in a prompt appearance. Word was received early that morning that a contingent from the Eagle Chief [Ranch] would be there, and begged that the start be delayed till their arrival. A number of old cowmen were present, and to them was delegated the duty of appointing the officers of the day. Bill Miller, a foreman on the Coldwater Pool, an adjoining range, was appointed as first captain. There were also several captains over divisions. . . .

The question of forbidding the promiscuous carrying of firearms met with decided opposition. There was an element of danger, it was true, but to deprive any of the boys of arms on what promised an exciting day's sport was contrary to their creed and occupation; besides, their judicious use would be an essential and valuable assistance. To deny one the right and permit another, would have been to divide their forces against a common enemy; so in the interests of harmony it was finally concluded to assign an acting captain over every ten men. "I'll be perfectly responsible for any of my men," said Reese, a red-headed Welsh cowman from over on Black Bear. "Let's just turn our wild selves loose, and those wolves won't stand any more show than a coon in a bear dance."

"It would be fine satisfaction to be shot by a responsible man like you or any of your outfit," replied Helicoid, superintendent of the "L X." "I hope another Christmas Day to help eat a plum pudding on the banks of the Dee, and I don't want to be carrying any of your stray lead in my carcass either. Did you hear me?"

"Yes; we're going to have egg-nog at our camp to-night. Come Down."

The boys were being told off in squads of ten, when a suppressed shout of welcome arose, as a cavalcade of horsemen was sighted coming over the divide several miles distant. Before the men were allotted and their captains appointed, the last expected squad had arrived, their horses frosty and sweaty. They were all well known west end Strippers, numbering fifty-four men and having ridden from the Eagle Chief, thirty-five miles, starting two hours before daybreak.

With the arrival of this detachment, Miller gave his orders for the day. Tom Cave was given two hundred men and sent to the upper end of the grove, where they were to dismount, form in a half circle skirmish-line covering the width of the thicket, and commence the drive down the river. Their saddle horses were to be cut into two bunches and driven down on either side of the grove, and to be in readiness for the men when they emerged from the chaparral, four of the oldest men being detailed as horse wranglers. Reese was sent with a hundred and fifty men to left flank the grove, deploying his men as far back as the second bottom, and close his line as the drive moved forward. Billy Edwards was sent with twenty picked men down the river five miles to the old beef ford at the ripples. His instructions were to cross and scatter his men from the ending of the salt plain to the horseshoe, and to concentrate them around it at the termination of the drive. He was allowed the best ropers and a number of shotguns, to be stationed at the cattle trails leading down to the water at the river's bend. The remainder, about two hundred and fifty men under Lynch, formed a long scattering line from the left entrance of the horseshoe, extending back until it met the advancing line of Reese's pickets.

With the river on one side and this cordon of foot and horsemen on the other, it seemed that nothing could possibly escape. The location of the quarry was almost assured. This chaparral had been the breeding refuge of wolves ever since the Cimarron was a cattle country. Every rider on that range for the past ten years knew it to be the rendezvous of El Lobo, while the ravages of his nightly raids were in evidence for forty miles in every direction. It was a common sight, early in the morning during the winter months, to see twenty and upward in a band, leisurely returning to their retreat, logy and insolent after a night's raid. To make doubly sure that they would be at home to callers, the promoters of this drive gathered a number of worthless lump-jawed cattle two days in advance, and driving them to the edge of the grove, shot one occasionally along its borders, thus, to be hoped, spreading the last feast for the wolves.

By half past ten, Encampment Butte was deserted with the exception of a few old cowmen, two ladies, wife and sister of a popular cowman, and the captain, who from this point of vantage surveyed the field with a glass. Usually a languid and indifferent man, Miller had so set his heart on making this drive a success that this morning he appeared alert and aggressive as he rode forward and back across the plateau of the Butte. The dull, heavy reports of several shotguns caused him to wheel his horse and cover the beef ford with his glass, and a moment later Edwards and his squad were seen with the naked eye to scale the bank and strike up the river at a gallop. It was known that the ford was saddle-skirt deep, and some few of the men were strangers to it; but with that passed safely he felt easier, though his blood coursed quicker. It lacked but a few minutes to eleven, and Cave and his detachment of beaters were due to move on the stroke of the hour. They had been given one hundred rounds of six-shooter ammunition to the man and were expected to use it. Edwards and his cavalcade were approaching the horseshoe, the cordon seemed perfect, though scattering, when the first faint sound of the beaters was heard, and the next moment the barking of two hundred six-shooters was reechoing up and down the valley of the Salt Fork.

The drive-hunt was on; the long yell passed from the upper end of the grove to the mouth of the horseshoe and back, punctuated with an occasional shot by irrepressibles. The mounts of the day were the pick of over five thousand cow-horses, and corn-fed for winter use, in the pink of condition and as impatient for the coming fray as their riders.

Everything was moving like clockwork. Miller forsook the Butte and rode to the upper end of the grove; the beaters were making slow but steady progress, while the saddled loose horses would be at hand for their riders without any loss of time. Before the beaters were one third over the ground, a buck and doe came out about halfway down the grove, sighted the horsemen, and turned back for shelter. Once more the long yell went down the line. Game had been sighted. When about one half the grove had been beat, a flock of wild turkeys came out at the lower end, and taking flight, sailed over the line. Pandemonium broke out. Good resolutions of an hour's existence were converted into paving material in the excitement of the moment, as every carbine or six-shooter in or out of range rained its leaden hail at the flying covey. One fine bird was accidentally winged, and a half a dozen men broke from the line to run it down, one of whom was Reese himself. The line was not dangerously broken nor did harm result, and on their return Miller was present and addressed this query to Reese: "Who is the captain of this flank line?"

"He'll weigh twenty pounds," said Reese, ignoring the question and holding the gobbler up for inspection.

"If you were a vealy tow-headed kid, I'd have something to say to you, but you're old enough to be my father, and that silences me. But try and remember that this is a wolf hunt, and that there are enough wolves in that brush this minute to kill ten thousand dollars' worth of cattle this winter and spring, and some of them will be your own. That turkey might eat a few grasshoppers, but you're cowman enough to know that a wolf just loves to kill a cow while she's calving."

This lecture was interrupted by a long cheer coming up the line from below, and Miller galloped away to ascertain its cause. He met Lynch coming up, who reported that several wolves had been sighted, while at the lower end of the line some of the boys had been trying their guns up and down the river to see how far they carried. What caused the recent shouting was only a few fool cowboys spurting their horses in short races.

As the beaters and shooters continued their work, the buck and doe reappeared, swimming the river. A volley of bullets failed to hit either animal. Then a band of antelope was sighted and fifty men shot at them until their guns were empty. As with the deer, none of the antelope were hit. In frustration, a dozen men raced after the animals, twirling their lassoes. Only two riders managed to rope an antelope. Finally done with these distractions, the men went back to their assigned place in the wolf rodeo.

The line had been closing gradually until at this juncture it had been condensed to about five miles, or a horseman to every fifty feet. Wolves had been sighted numerous times running from covert to covert, but few had shown themselves to the flank line, being contented with such shelter as the scraggy plum brush afforded. Whenever the beaters would rout or sight a wolf, the yelling would continue up and down the line for several minutes. Cave and his well-formed circle of beaters were making good time; Reese on the left flank was closing and moving forward, while the line under Lynch was as impatient as it was hilarious. Miller made the circle every half hour or so; and had only to mention it to pick any horse he wanted from the entire line for a change.

By one o'clock the drive had closed to the entrance of the pocket, and within a mile and a half of the termination. There was yet enough cover to hide the quarry, though the extreme point of this horseshoe was a sand bar with no shelter except driftwood trees. Edwards and his squad were at their post across the river, in plain view of the advancing line. Suddenly they were seen to dismount and lie down on the brink of the cut-bank. A few minutes later chaos broke out along the line, when a band of possibly twenty wolves left their cover and appeared on the sand bar. A few rifle shots rang out from the opposite bank, when they skurried back to cover.

Shooting was now becoming dangerous. In the line was a horseman every ten or twelve feet. All the captains rode up and down begging the men to cease shooting entirely. This only had a temporary effect, for shortly the last bit of cover was passed, and there within four hundred yards on the bar was a snarling, snapping band of gray wolves.

The line was halted. The unlooked-for question now arose how to make the kill safe and effective. It would be impossible to shoot from the opposite bank without endangering the line of men and horses. Finally a small number of rifles were advanced on the extreme left flank to within two hundred yards of the quarry, where they opened fire at an angle from the watchers on the opposite bank. They proved poor marksmen, overshooting, and only succeeded in wounding a few and forcing several to take to the water, so that it became necessary to recall the men to the line.

These men were now ordered to dismount and lie down, as the opposite side would take a hand when the swimming wolves came within range of shotguns and carbines, to say nothing of six-shooters. The current carried the swimming ones down the river, but every man was in readiness to give them a welcome. The fusillade which greeted them was like a skirmish-line in action, but the most effective execution was with buckshot as they came staggering and water-soaked out of the water. Before the shooting across the river had ceased, a yell of alarm surged through the line, and the next moment every man was climbing into his saddle and bringing his arms into position for action. No earthly power could have controlled the men, for coming at the line less than two hundred yards distant was the corralled band of wolves under the leadership of a monster dog wolf, evidently a leader of some band, and every gun within range opened on them. By the time they had lessened the intervening distance by one half, the entire band deserted their leader and retreated, but unmindful of consequences he rushed forward at the line. Every gun was belching fire and lead at him, while tufts of fur floating in the air told that several shots were effective. Wounded he met the horsemen, striking right and left in splendid savage ferocity. The horses snorted and shrank from him, and several suffered from his ugly thrusts. An occasional effective shot was placed, but every time he forced his way through the cordon he was confronted by a second line. A successful cast of a rope finally checked his course; and as the roper wheeled his mount to drag him to death, he made his last final rush at the horse, and, springing at the flank, fastened his fangs into a stirrup fender, when a well-directed shot by the roper silenced him safely at last.

During the excitement, there were enough cool heads to maintain the line, so that none escaped. The supreme question now was to make the kill with safety, and the line was ransacked for volunteers who could shoot a rifle with some little accuracy. About a dozen were secured, who again advanced on the extreme right flank to within a hundred and fifty yards, and dismounting, flattened themselves out and opened on the skurrying wolves. It was afterward attributed to the glaring of the sun on the white sand, which made their marksmanship so shamefully poor, but results were very unsatisfactory. They were recalled, and it was decided to send in four shotguns and try the effect of buckshot from horseback. This move was disastrous, though final.

They were ordinary double-barreled shotguns, and reloading was slow in an emergency. Many of the wolves were wounded and had sought such cover as the driftwood afforded. The experiment had barely begun, when a wounded wolf sprang out from behind an old root, and fastened upon the neck of one of the horses before the rider could defend himself, and the next moment horse and rider were floundering on the ground. To a man, the line broke to the rescue, while the horses of the two lady spectators were carried into the mêlée in the excitement. The dogs of war were loosed. Hell popped. The smoke of six hundred guns arose in clouds. There were wolves swimming the river and wolves trotting around amongst the horses, wounded and bewildered. Ropes swished through the smoke, tying wounded wolves to be dragged to death or trampled under hoof. Men dismounted and clubbed them with shotguns and carbines,—anything to administer death. Horses were powder-burnt and cried with fear, or neighed exultingly. There was an old man or two who had sense enough to secure the horses of the ladies and lead them out of immediate danger. Several wolves made their escape, and squads of horsemen were burying cruel rowels in heaving flanks in an endeavor to overtake and either rope or shoot the fleeing animals.

Disordered things as well as ordered ones have an end, and when sanity returned to the mob an inventory was taken of the drive-hunt. By actual count, the lifeless carcasses of twenty-six wolves graced the sand bar, with several precincts to hear from. The promoters of the hunt thanked the men for their assistance, assuring them that the bounty money would be used to perfect arrangements, so that in other years a banquet would crown future hunts. Before the hunt dispersed, Edwards and his squad returned to the brink of the cut-bank, and when hailed as to results, he replied, "Why, we only got seven, but they are all *muy docil* [very docile]. We're going to peel them and will meet you at the ford."

"Who gets the turkey?" some one asked.

"The question is out of order," replied Reese. "The property is not present, because I sent him home by my cook an hour ago. If any of you have any interest in that gobbler, I'll invite you to go home with me and help to eat him, for my camp is the only one in the Strip that will have turkey and egg-nog to-night."

1880s–90s: *The XIT Ranch of Texas and the Early Days of the Llano Estacado*, J. Evetts Haley

Historian and rancher J. Evetts Haley has compiled an extensive account of the XIT Ranch of northern Texas. This operation, over three million acres in size, was the largest ranch in the western states. Established in the mid-1880s, the ranch employed from 100 to 150 cowboys who ran herd on 150,000 cattle. Haley's book, published in 1929, describes how some of the ranch's cowboys were given wolf hunting assignments during the slack winter months:

Two cowboys were given a wagon, camp equipment, and saddle horses about the first of January and put to "wolfing" upon those divisions where lobos, the great predatory wolves of the plains, were most numerous. They were paid no salary from then until the cow work started in April or May, but they capitalized on a bounty of five to ten dollars paid by the company upon every lobo caught. Some counties paid an additional ten. With good fortune the "wolfers" made more money during these few months than they did during all the rest of the year as cowpunchers.

These lobos, or "loafers," were about the size of a Newfoundland dog, very cunning, and difficult to trap. The principal ways of killing them were by running them down horseback and by finding their dens. Cowmen estimated the annual depredations of a lobo at seventy-five head of cattle. The wily fellows preferred fresh meat, rarely returning to a carcass, which made poisoning practically impossible. Several, banding together, rounded up a small bunch of cattle, and choosing a weak cow or steer, ran at its hind legs every time it came to the outer edge of the bunch, slashing at the great tendons in its hind legs. When they had cut its hamstrings and disabled it, the killing was easy. Big calves and yearlings were common prey, and losses amounted to thousands of dollars annually.

The lobo took shelter along the caprock and in the breaks, and at night ventured out upon the plains for several miles in search of meat, and after gorging on his fresh kill, returned to shelter in the roughs. Early of a morning the two "wolfers" saddled their horses and rode along the edge of the plains just above the caprock to cut off any late-returning lobo as he lazily trotted back to the shelter of the broken country. Upon intercepting a wolf, they turned him back across the level plain and gave chase. The wolf was usually so full of beef that he could run but poorly, and after a chase of from two to four miles the "wolfers" were usually able to ride upon and shoot or rope him.

In March the lobo pups began to arrive. Then a she wolf, jumped by hunters or dogs, headed for her den in all haste. During this season the wolfer used a pack of hounds in trailing and locating dens. When he arrived at the cave or den, the hunter took a short candle in one hand, his six-shooter in the other, wiggled into the den, and shot the wolf by the reflections of the light in her eyes. Rarely did he have to crawl inside more than ten or twelve feet, though sometimes the holes were deeper. The dens were often so narrow that he could worm his way in only by keeping both arms extended ahead of him. The explosion from his gun always put out his candle. He backed out of the hole to re-light it and went in again before he could be sure of the effect of his shot.

Charlie Orr and Frank Fuller were "wolfing" one spring on the Escarbada. Obviously, it was an eerie sort of business, and a question of propriety as to who should go first led to a delay at the entrance to a lobo's den. Being men of sporting blood, they settled the argument by drawing straws. Orr drew the long straw and had to go first. With six-shooter in hand he crawled until he could see the wolf's eyes gleaming at him. Up came the six-shooter and the reverberation shook dust from the walls and dinned the cowboy's ears. Unfortunately he missed his aim, and the lobo, seeing a gleam of light over Orr's back, made a break for the outside. The space was not enough for her to pass through and she wedged over Orr's back. Frantic with fear she began scratching furiously in an attempt to dig out, and every scratch carried away some of the cowboy's clothes. Finally she dug through and Fuller shot her as she came out. Nine pups were found in the den, but Orr's back was bare and showed marks of the powerful claws. This mattered little, for it was a profitable day's work since a cowboy's back is tough and work shirts were cheap.

A lobo disturbed at her den leaves at the first opportunity and does not come back. Thus to leave a den meant to lose the wolf. Dumas Hall, an eighteen-year-old boy keeping camp at Toro in 1906, crawled into a lobo's den, and while feeling around in the dark, was bitten through the hand by the old bitch. After backing out to survey the damage, he armed himself with his lariat and skinning knife and went into the den again. When he came to a narrow place through which he could barely squeeze, he thought he heard his horse running away. For a cowboy far from camp this was genuinely disconcerting, but when he stopped to listen to the rhythmic beat of his horses's hoofs, he heard instead the pounding of his own heart. Squeezing through the narrow place, he crawled on. By striking ahead of him with his knife, he crowded the wolf into a small hole, tied his lariat around her hind legs, pulled her out, and killed her with rocks. He went back and got ten pups from the hole, one of the largest litters found upon the ranch.

Allen Stagg, another XIT cowboy well versed in lobo lore, hunted along the Canadian for several seasons. He killed eighty-four lobos in 1896 alone, and upon one or two occasions was wedged into their dens in narrow places. After crawling into the den and killing the mother lobo, he fished the pups out by means of a long pole to which was attached a metal hook.

Lobos, when not gorged, were fleet and hard to run down. Few horses could equal their speed for the first four or five miles. Therefore the cowboy who undertook to catch one held his horse down to a "long lope." When the wolf began to tire, he let out his horse a little, and after a long chase, often of ten to fifteen miles, he was able to ride upon and rope the animal. J. Walling, one of the camp men on the Yellow Houses, once ran a lobo twenty-five miles. He got the wolf, but "just the same as killed the horse," breaking his wind and leaving him unfit for further use. Yet experienced hunters claim that Walling could have saved his horse if he had known how to run a lobo. There was more than one way to handle a wolf.

During the late nineties, the company paid annual bounties upon approximately 200 lobos, and its cowboys did much to clear the plains of this predatory animal, the last of which was killed in this section in 1916.

1880–1920: *Wolves: Being Reminiscent of My Life on an Eastern Montana Ranch*, Elbert F. Bowman

Elbert Bowman grew up on a ranch in Custer County, Montana, during the height of the cattleman's war against the wolf. In 1938, after retiring, Bowman wrote a memoir that conveys a valuable account of contemporary wolf-human relations. Note his observations on the reaction of wolves to sick and healthy cattle.

Wolves—black wolves, white wolves, yellow wolves and grey; timber wolves, mountain wolves, swamp wolves, desert wolves, werewolves,— blood brothers all, associates with stock men from ancient days when both hung on the edges of the vast herds of wooly elephant and auroch, of wild horses and musk ox, of reindeer and caribou, of bison and antelope, and stole each other's meat. Dim, ghostly shapes in faint, grey dawn and starlight night, that lope tirelessly on the long ridges and across the wide flats.

Man has exterminated the wolf almost completely, but in the war he has lost all but the puny sheep, the thin-skinned cow, and the pampered horse; and the horse has almost gone with the others now.

The wolf of our Northwest was a great, sleek, well-fed brute, who grew sometimes to a length of seven and a half feet, tip to tip, and who stood nearly three feet high, possibly weighing 150 pounds. He was never hungry for long—meat was too plentiful and easy for one of his ability to get.

After the buffalo was gone, the buffalo hunter turned wolfer from necessity, and by the skillful use of poison thinned the wolves to a mere remnant, and also sharpened their cunning to an acuteness that made them an enemy to be respected to the last; but government and private trappers, aided by bounties raised by the states and by individuals, finished them in the Northwest.

Many were the schemes and plans used, but until we learned the art of den hunting, there was little success in any of them. Dogs aided in smooth country, but let a wolf get far enough away from the horsemen to have what he considered a fighting chance, he would make a stand at some gulch crossing or narrow trail, leave a jumble of dead and crippled dogs, and go on his way, while the survivors raced yipping back with the bad news.

Seldom was a grown wolf hurt much in a battle of this kind, for a thick, wooly coat, a tough skin, and a savage ability to kill and maim took care of that. An animal that could pull out the big muscle at the back of a yearling steer's hind leg, or break a shoulder joint with one chop and yank of his jaws, is easily capable of killing and crippling a pack of any dogs able to run as fast as he, if only the man he really fears is out of sight. . . .

. . . I never knew the wolves to eat much mutton. Being a cow man, I don't blame them for that, either. . . . Calves and yearlings were the wolves' main dish, but there were times when nearly all the cattle in quite a large region were grown animals. Then the wolves would buckle down and kill even three and four year old steers and cows. But the lame, the halt, and the blind were safe from these killers; for never did they attack anything that would not run, and sick stock are surly and refuse to be scared into any footracing. . . .

As far as men were concerned, wolves were never a danger in our country. The Indians called them "Brother," very seldom killed them, and otherwise paid little attention to them. They also called the coyote "Little Brother." But they paid the wolf due respect for his cunning, for the sign for wolf was used in the sign language to mean such things as "I will find out," "we saw so-and-so," and "our scout (making the sign for wolf) says," and in other phrases as to the giving or finding out of information. . . .

It would seem that dogs that could trail by scent would be the answer to a lot of the trouble in cases of this kind [a wolf killed calf], and many were the men who tried using them. But there is something about the smell of a fresh wolf track that so fills a trail hound or any kind of smelling dog with a great fear and nervousness, so that he will not follow. Some dogs actually get sick and vomit on getting a few good whiffs of wolf scent. Others will look for rabbits or anything of that kind. Often they will branch off on a fresh coyote track if they can find one, but they will not take to the fresh trail of the wolf. . . .

After supper he [a neighboring rancher] and I were sitting on some logs that were piled up about a hundred feet from the house. It was pleasant sitting there in the warm dusk, smoking and talking. Presently we heard some wolves howling way off in the red scoria hills to the south. Then another pack answered far off to the northwest. The rancher's dog, a big, fat old collie who posed as an all-round tough dog, ran off a little way into the deepening dark, barking and growling defiance to the whole wolf race. However, he went out to the west, toward the barn and hay corral, although the sounds came from the south and east.

Suddenly there came the deep savage howl of a big wolf who must have been out that way not more than a couple of hundred yards. A dark streak rushed past us, followed by a crash against the screen porch. We ran down to see what had happened and found that the dog had missed the screen door, which opened in, and had run right though the screening alongside it.

We found him lying under the table in the kitchen, and while he would thump his tail on the floor when we spoke to him, he refused to budge. He was so scared that his master let him stay in the house all night. He must have nearly broken his neck when he hit the screen, for he could not turn his head for a couple of days.

The next morning we found the half-eaten remains of a yearling steer about a half-mile to the west, and the usual couple of coyotes hanging around it.

Poison, properly put out, seemed to be about the best way of getting the grown wolves. Nearly always they would come back to their kill after some days, perhaps a week later, and lunch a little if there was anything left. By that time, they seemed to like to chew on the spongy ends of the rib bones, and sometimes would drag the head and hide and other remains around in the grass without eating much.

On different occasions I have poisoned several wolves from one family. Of course, the chance of finding them before the hides were spoiled was very slim, but who cared, for they would kill no more calves and colts, and the survivors would move elsewhere.

Traps were all right if you could put them where the wolf was going to step, but there was a horde of smaller harmless wild folk to spring them before the wolf came. Coyotes, bobcats, badgers, eagles, magpies, rabbits, skunks, ferrets, were likely to be the victims, or the lumbering, clumsy porcupine and even the great horned owl, to say nothing of the cattle. . . .

A big old wolf in a trap is as dangerous looking a customer as you can imagine. While you are quite a way off, he will make a desperate effort to escape, and many a wolf has broken a trap and escaped in this way. When you come close to a trapped wolf, he will just stand there with a sort of sneering grin on his face, the big teeth bared, seeming to calculate the length of his chain to an inch. His snarls are full of hatred instead of fear, and he will wait for you to make the first move.

A coyote will cow down on the ground with a pleading look in his yellow eyes, and if you want you can walk up and push him over, tie his mouth shut with a stout string, fasten him behind your saddle, and take him away like a bag of meal. You could not do that to a wolf, and you would not want to, either.

However, with all these troubles, a lot of wolves were trapped and killed by the stockmen and by the professional trappers. Wolves were merely a sideline, a sort of piece of velvet with these last gentry. It was the coyote, bob cat [sic], badger and skunk that furnished him a living, to say nothing of the beaver and muskrat, his mainstay for a couple of centuries.

Usually the wolfer and trapper were fairly well liked by the stock man, and generally was of quite a bit of benefit. He killed off the chicken-eating coyotes and bobcats around the ranch, and thinned the wolves a good deal. All he asked was the local bounty that was usually given on wolves, in addition to the state bounty, and perhaps a hopelessly lame or wire-cut horse or a big-jawed steer for bait.

Sometimes, however, he was a bird of another feather altogether, and killed a calf or a yearling to eat as slyly as any of the wolves he hunted, besides shooting the gentle black-tail doe that stayed in the meadow pasture or some nice antelope out of the bunch that had always lived around the beef pasture.

There have been instances where trappers of this kind have even shot good horses and cattle to provide bait, and in latter years, when game was better protected, some of this type were always getting into trouble because of killing antelope or deer for bait. I knew of one who even went to the extreme of killing deer to feed a pack of mongrel hounds which he had to run coyotes with.

Later a few of the best trappers were hired by the government, the Bureau of Predatory Animal Control, as they called the department that looked after that sort of thing. Wolfers were paid so much as a salary and given a bonus, determined when the trapper turned the hides or some part of everything they trapped, shot, or poisoned into the main office. Those who became government trappers were hard-working, reliable men who knew their business, and they produced results.

The old-time trapper would not trap when the fur was not prime; neither did he like to hunt dens, as the young pups were not worth anything for fur and not much for bounty. Besides, if the wolves got unusually thick on a certain range the stock men might get desperate and put on a private bounty of ten or fifteen dollars in addition to the bounty offered by the state, which was usually ten dollars. After the head was cut off and sent in to check with the bounty claim stubs, the trapper still had most of the hide left to sell, and this brought him five to seven dollars.

I dare say nearly every county in the western states has had a bounty fraud scandal at one time or another, and some went on between the states. At one time Montana required the skin of the lower jaw to be cut off and sent in to check up by, while Wyoming cut off the whole head and ears. A business of smuggling hides minus the skin of the lower jaw, but with the rest of the head still on the pelt at once sprang up between Montana and Wyoming, and went on until the method of checking up was changed, and some of the fraudulent ones punished. At this time there was a three-dollar bounty on coyotes, and of course the main traffic was in coyotes.

Den hunting was the method that in time did more to exterminate the wolf in our country than any other two methods combined. It was a kind of wholesale slaughter, sometimes netting one or, more rarely, both old wolves and all the pups at one stroke.

As I look back, it seems strange that it was not done in the earlier times, but in our country it was not really gone into by every stock man until 1908 and 1910.

The pups are born somewhere about April first, sometimes as early as March fifteenth, or as late as April tenth, but usually nearer the first of April. The greatest number of pups I ever knew to be taken from one den was fourteen, but eight to twelve was usually the number. I have heard of sixteen being taken, but I believe that was a case of two wolves denning in the same group of bad lands [sic] holes, as often was the case, a mother and her grown daughter, most likely.

The pups are born blind, and do not open their eyes till they are about nine days old. They are almost black, a sort of dark brindle with irregular black markings on their sides and black tips on tail and ears, and black feet. They are fat, chubby little rascals, and until they are about three weeks old will snuggle up to you as friendly as any puppy you ever saw.

No matter where the den is it will be hard to find. It may be hid away in a badland cave way back in the cedar brakes, or it may be under the rim rock on some high knife-blade ridge between two buttes, or in a fissure in some castle-like group of gigantic sandstone rocks. It may be in one of these honeycomb formations that have boiled up out of the earth and turned to stone, up in the pine hills, or it may be found in a bunch of little washouts in a pasture, or even a dug-out den among the roots of a big cottonwood down by the river bank; but whatever it is it will take keen eyes and patience and hard work to find it.

There will be no trail at this early stage, no padded-down path showing the marks of paws bigger than the palm of your hand. Only a track here and there, and prints going in all directions give you a clue. If you get too close and still do not find the den the mother will move the pups a mile or two overnight, and you may go to all the trouble of digging to the nest and find it empty. . . .

We always liked to have the weather turn bad along about the first week in April and give us a few days of snow; it made tracking better and more sure, but it also made it very disagreeable riding around in the mud and slush, perhaps chilled to the bone.

An old she-wolf seems to have inherited some of the wisdom that used to be associated with witches and devils. She will pick out several dens and fix them up for the blessed event and then maybe not use any of them. I have known a wolf to pick one out and then for some reason go over two creeks away, about eight miles, to den.

The wolf hunter's ambition was always to catch the two old wolves in the den, or almost as good, the mother, but this was rare. Seemingly the mother wolf did not stay in the den any longer than it took to feed and lick the babies. But she and her mate were where they could keep an eye on the place without being seen, you may be sure.

I have always heard that if you went in the den when the old she-wolf was there you were in danger of the mate going in after you with real murder in his heart. I don't know. I've never been able to find the mother at home, but let me say that going into a den alone is not very safe anyway; too much chance for a chunk of dirt to fall behind a man's knees and wedge him in. Then if the old wolf were in, he would need help most likely. . . .

The wolf will show fight if the den is in a room or large place, and here a small calibre pistol like a .22 comes in handy, since the stockman's usual .38 .40 or .45 will all but knock a man unconscious from concussion in such a small place, or make him deaf for a week or two, and a rifle is equally bad. Then there is the danger of the jar making a piece of the roof fall in.

Some men carried a weapon like a fish spear with the barbs filed off, mounted on a handle about two feet long to keep the wolf off with while trying to shoot a small pistol with one hand. Most of us, however, just trusted to luck and expected to use a hatchet and sharpened forked stick. . . .

For some time after birth the wolf pups are satisfied with milk and during this time the mother needs huge, frequent meals to make up for the strain of feeding them. Later they will begin on partly-digested meat which their parents will bring in and disgorge for them. Often one will see where the old wolves have had to unload some of their burden on the way home, particularly if they have been disturbed or frightened. A scout around where this had been done will often tell the hunter the direction in which the den is.

There is no great difficulty in telling, within a mile or two, where there is a den. There will be tracks and trails radiating from some patch of roughs or hills like the spokes of a great wheel, but closer together. A jumble of tracks will be found going all ways and into and out of many holes, but little signs like the vomited meat or fresh bones are hints to wolf hunters that are gladly taken.

As the pups grow, so do their appetites, and both old ones now bring home pieces of flesh and bones as heavy as they can carry; about ten or fifteen pounds seems to be the average size of these morsels, but these are often carried five or six miles, sometimes more. . . .

Charley [one of Bowman's cowboys] was coming down the high divide between Sheep Creek and Devil's Hole when his keen eyes happened to see two wolves lying on a little red shale-covered hill with a few cedars and sage brush for cover. They were quite well hidden but he made them out plainly enough to be sure. He didn't stop to prowl around as he had no rifle or any equipment for digging, just rode on as if he had never seen them. It was about two P.M. and a nice day in early April.

The next morning he and I left the ranch about half past three and were up over the place by the time it was light enough to see, but there was nothing in sight. We waited until sun-up and then really began to look for the den.

About eight we found it, no mistaking it, the entrance was worn smooth and hairs rubbed off and all that sort of thing. After looking around pretty carefully for back doors we went to work. We had one of those little auto spades and a hatchet, a couple of traps, a lot of candles and—don't overlook this if you do the same—a jug of water.

From then on it was dig out and enlarge the underground water passage that was the den, turn about, sometimes having to carry some of the dirt and rocks quite a way to make room.

It was all of seventy-five or eighty feet into the nest. Charley was digging ahead at the time, and as he rounded a bend, there was the nest. I heard him gasp as he saw the litter, then he said, "There are at least fifty of these little devils here. How can we carry them all out?" The way we did was this. I backed out, taking two with me which I knocked on the head. I had on two pairs of pants and I tied pieces of saddle strings around the bottoms of the legs of one pair and took them back into the den.

It seemed a long way to crawl into a small, rough passage as deep and crooked as this one was, all littered with cactus that the pack rats had brought in. There were fourteen of them in all, nice, fat, cuddly, little rascals. One we saved to try to use as a decoy for the old wolf; the rest we killed.

I have done it many times before and since, but I have never had to do anything that goes against the grain much more than to kill the pups at this stage. Potential murderers they may be, and as cruel as man himself after they are grown, but at this time they are just plump, friendly, little things that nuzzle you and whine little, pleased whines.

We both felt somewhat ashamed and guilty, but it was duty; so we tied the live pup back in the den about ten feet where the old wolf could see and hear him and then carefully concealed two big wolf traps nearer to the mouth of the den and went home. It was about three in the afternoon and we were hungry.

After dinner we skinned out the pups and threw the bodies over a high cut bank behind the blacksmith shop, cleaned up and called it a day.

Early the next morning we scouted around and we found that the old she-wolf had followed the trail of her dead children clear to the ranch. She had even been down under the cut bank and smelled the bodies we had thrown there.

Whether in revenge or just because she felt mean, she and her mate had also killed a couple of fall calves in the horse pasture not over a half mile from the ranch.

We waited another night, then went out on a point where we could see into the mouth of the den with field glasses but no wolf [was] in the traps. Later that day I missed a fair shot at her in a little pass four or five miles away. . . .

The trap and pup did not do any good. She waited until a little rain sent a rill of water down the den floor and washed the dirt down over the traps so they would not work, then went in and looked her dead pup over.

We had failed to get her or her mate, but she was so disgusted with the country that she moved over on the North Alkali about forty miles south and was caught in a den by a man over on the head of Fallon Creek the next year. . . .

About 1918 or 1920 saw the last of the wolves in our country. A few perhaps stayed on a little longer in some places, as around the Devil's Tower in Wyoming and in the big red hills on the upper part of the Little Powder River. Once in a while a lone adventurer of the clan would cross the country.

One of these travelers I traced by inquiry and found he came from the Box Elder Creek brakes in the southeastern corner of Montana. He followed the old trails of drifting people of his kind, down the divide between Sheep and Trail Creeks, then across Sheep at a long diagonal, crossing a little way below our ranch, and so on in a northwest course that took him across the Yellowstone at the place that is called Wolf Rapids, and then on the Sheep Mountains, about fifty miles in almost a straight line.

Yes, the wolves are gone. Never again in my time and country will dim ghostly shapes lope tirelessly on the long ridge and across the sage flats. Never again will I hear the strange savage music of their howling. I miss them, yet I would not wish them back. But if in the hereafter comes a time when we can meet as wolf to wolf and man to man I shall be glad.

1890s: "Wolves and Wolf-Hounds," Theodore Roosevelt

Before becoming president, Theodore Roosevelt wrote a number of books about his ranching experiences in western North Dakota. Hunting the Grisly [sic] and Other Sketches, *published in 1902, one year after he assumed the presidency, contains a chapter entitled "Wolves and Wolf-Hounds." This example of Roosevelt's writing sets forth many of the contemporary feelings toward the wolf and describes the "sport," as practiced by ranchers, of hunting wolves with packs of dogs:*

The wolf is the arch type of ravin, the beast of waste and desolation. It is still found scattered thinly throughout all the wilder portions of the United States, but has everywhere retreated from the advance of civilization. . . .

Formerly wolves were incredibly abundant in certain parts of the country, notably on the great plains, where they were known as buffalo wolves, and were regular attendants on the great herds of the bison. Every traveller and hunter of the old days knew them as among the most common sights of the plais, and they followed the hunting parties and emigrant trains for the sake of the scraps left in camp. Now, however, there is no district in which they are really abundant. The wolfers, or professional wolf-hunters, who killed them by poisoning for the sake of their fur, and the cattlemen, who likewise killed them by poisoning because of their raids on the herds, have doubtless been the chief instruments in working their decimation on the plains. In the '70's and even in the early '80's, many tens of thousands of wolves were killed by the wolfers in Montana and northern Wyoming and western Dakota. Nowadays the surviving wolves of the plains have learned caution; they no longer move abroad at midday, and still less do they dream of hanging on the footsteps of hunter and traveller. Instead of being one of the most common they have become one of the rarest sights of the plains. A hunter may wander far and wide through the plains for months nowadays and never see a wolf, though he will probably see many coyotes. However, the diminution goes on, not steadily but by fits and starts, and, moreover, the beasts now and then change their abodes, and appear in numbers in places where they have been scarce for a long period. In the present winter of 1892–'93 big wolves are more plentiful in the neighborhood of my ranch than they have been for ten years, and have worked some havoc among the cattle and young horses. The cowboys have been carrying on the usual vindictive campaign against them; a number have been poisoned, and a number of others have fallen victims to their greediness, the cowboys surprising them when gorged to repletion on the carcass of a colt or calf, and, in consequence, unable to run, so that they are easily ridden down, roped, and then dragged to death.

Yet even the slaughter wrought by man in certain localities does not seem adequate to explain the scarcity or extinction of wolves, throughout the country at large. In most places they are not followed any more eagerly than are the other large beasts of prey, and they are usually followed with less success. Of all animals the wolf is the shyest and hardest to slay. It is almost or quite as difficult to still-hunt as the cougar, and is far more difficult to kill with hounds, traps, or poison; yet it scarcely holds its own as well as the great cat, and it does not begin to hold its own as well as the bear, a beast certainly more readily killed, and one which produces fewer young at birth. . . .

. . . Near my own ranch the wolves have sometimes committed great depredations on cattle, but they seem to have queer freaks of slaughter. Usually they prey only upon calves and sickly animals; but in midwinter I have known one single-handed to attack and kill a well-grown steer or cow, disabling its quarry by rapid snaps at the hams or flanks. Only rarely have I known it to seize by the throat. Colts are likewise a favorite prey, but with us wolves rarely attack full-grown horses. They are sometimes very bold in their assaults. . . . In the spring of '92 we put on some eastern two-year old steers; they arrived, and were turned loose from the stock-yards, in a snowstorm, though it was in early May. Next morning we found that one had been seized, slain, and partially devoured by a big wolf at the very gate of the stockyard; probably the beast had seen it standing near the yard after nightfall, feeling miserable after its journey, in the storm and its unaccustomed surroundings, and had been emboldened to make the assault so near town by the evident helplessness of the prey.

The big timber wolves of the northern Rocky Mountains attack every four-footed beast to be found where they live. They are far from contenting themselves with hunting deer and snapping up the pigs and sheep of the farm. When the weather gets cold and food scarce they band together in small parties, perhaps of four or five individuals, and then assail anything, even a bear or a panther. A bull elk or bull moose, when on its guard, makes a most dangerous fight; but a single wolf will frequently master the cow of either animal, as well as domestic cattle and horses. In attacking such large game, however, the wolves like to act in concert, one springing at the animal's head, and attracting its attention, while the other hamstrings it. . . .

Where there are no domestic animals, wolves feed on almost anything from a mouse to an elk. They are redoubted enemies of foxes. They are easily able to overtake them in fair chase, and kill numbers. If the fox can get into the underbrush, however, he can dodge around much faster than the wolf, and so escape pursuit. Sometimes one wolf will try to put a fox out of a cover while another waits outside to snap him up. Moreover, the wolf kills even closer kinfolk than the fox. When pressed by hunger it will undoubtedly sometimes seize a coyote, tear it in pieces and devour it, although during most of the year the two animals live in perfect harmony. I once myself, while out in the deep snow, came across the remains of a coyote that had been killed in this manner. Wolves are also very fond of the flesh of dogs, and if they get a chance promptly kill and eat any dog they can master — and there are but few that they cannot. Nevertheless, I have been told of one instance in which a wolf struck up an extraordinary friendship with a strayed dog, and the two lived and hunted together for many months, being frequently seen by the settlers of the locality. This occurred near Thompson's Falls, Montana. . . .

. . . I have never known wolves to attack a man, yet in the wilder portions of the far Northwest I have heard them come around camp very close, growling so savagely as to make one almost reluctant to leave the camp fire and go out into the darkness unarmed. Once I was camped in the fall near a lonely little lake in the mountains, by the edge of quite a broad stream. Soon after nightfall three or four wolves came around camp and kept me awake by their sinister and dismal howling. Two or three times they came so close to the fire that I could hear them snap their jaws and growl, and at one time I positively thought that they intended to try to get into camp, so excited were they by the smell of the fresh meat. After a while they stopped howling; and then all was silent for an hour or so. I let the fire go out and was turning into bed when I suddenly heard some animal of considerable size come down to the stream nearly opposite me and begin to splash across, first wading, then swimming. It was pitch dark and I could not possibly see, but I felt sure it was a wolf. However after coming half-way over it changed its mind and swam back to the opposite bank; nor did I see or hear anything more of the night marauders.

Five or six times on the plains or on my ranch I have had shots at wolves, always obtained by accident and always, I regret to say, missed. Often the wolf when seen was running at full speed for cover, or else was so far off that though motionless my shots went wide of it. But once have I with my own rifle killed a wolf and this was while travelling with a pack train in the mountains. We had been making considerable noise, and I never understood how an animal so wary permitted our near approach. He did, nevertheless, and just as we came to a little stream which we were to ford I saw him get on a dead log some thirty yards distant and walk slowly off with his eyes turned toward us. The first shot smashed his shoulders and brought him down.

The wolf is one of the animals which can only be hunted successfully with dogs. Most dogs however do not take at all kindly to the pursuit. A wolf is a terrible fighter. He will decimate a pack of hounds by rabid snaps with his giant jaws while suffering little damage himself; nor are the ordinary big dogs, supposed to be fighting dogs, able to tackle him without special training. I have known one wolf to kill a bulldog which had rushed at it with a single snap, while another which had entered the yard of a Montana ranch house slew in quick succession both of the large mastiffs by which it was assailed. The immense agility and ferocity of the wild beast, the terrible snap of his long-toothed jaws, and the admirable training in which he always is, give him a great advantage over fat, small-toothed, smooth-skinned dogs, even though they are normally supposed to belong to the fighting classes. In the way that bench competitions are arranged nowadays this is but natural, as there is no temptation to produce a worthy class of fighting dog when the rewards are given upon technical points wholly unconnected with the dog's usefulness. A prize-winning mastiff or bulldog may be almost useless for the only purposes for which his kind is ever useful at all. A mastiff, if properly trained and of sufficient size, might possibly be able to meet a young or undersized Texan wolf; but I have never seen a dog of this variety which I would esteem a match single-handed for one of the huge timber wolves of western Montana. Even if the dog was the heavier of the two, his teeth and claws would be very much smaller and weaker and his hide less tough. Indeed I have known of but one dog which single-handed encountered and slew a wolf; this was the large vicious mongrel whose feats are recorded in my *Hunting Trips of a Ranchman.*

General Marcy of the United States Army informed me that he once chased a huge wolf which had gotten away with a small trap on its foot. It was, I believe, in Wisconsin, and he had twenty or thirty hounds with him, but they were entirely untrained to wolf-hunting, and proved unable to stop the crippled beast. Few of them would attack it at all, and those that did went at it singly and with a certain hesitation, and so each in turn was disabled by a single terrible snap, and left bleeding on the snow. General Wade Hampton tells me that in the course of his fifty years' hunting with horse and hound in Mississippi, he has on several occasions tried his pack of fox-hounds (southern deer-hounds) after a wolf. He found that it was with the greatest difficulty, however, that he could persuade them to so much as follow the trail. Usually, as soon as they come across it, they would growl, bristle up, and then retreat with their tails between their legs. But one of his dogs ever really tried to master a wolf by itself, and this one paid for its temerity with its life; for while running a wolf in a canebrake the beast turned and tore it to pieces. Finally General Hampton succeeded in getting a number of his hounds so they would at any rate follow the trail in full cry, and thus drive the wolf out of the thicket, and give a chance to the hunter to get a shot. In this way he killed two or three.

The true way to kill wolves, however, is to hunt them with grey-hounds on the great plains. Nothing more exciting than this sport can possibly be imagined. It is not always necessary that the greyhounds should be of absolutely pure blood. Prize-winning dogs of high pedigree often prove useless for the purposes. If by careful choice, however, a ranchman can get together a pack composed both of the smooth-haired greyhound and the rough-haired Scotch deer-hound, he can have excellent sport. The greyhounds sometimes do best if they have a slight cross of bulldog in their veins; but this is not necessary. If once a greyhound can be fairly entered to the sport and acquires confidence, then its wonderful agility, its sinewy strength and speed, and the terrible snap with which its jaws come together, render it a most formidable assailant. Nothing can possibly exceed the gallantry with which good greyhounds, when their blood is up, fling themselves on a wolf or any other foe. There does not exist, and there never has existed on the wide earth, a more perfect type of dauntless courage than such a hound. Not Cushing when he steered his little launch through the black night against the great ram Albemarle, not Custer dashing into the valley of the Rosebud to die with all his men, not Farragut himself lashed in the rigging of the Hartford as she forged past the forts to encounter her iron-clad foe, can stand as a more perfect type of dauntless valor.

Once I had the good fortune to witness a very exciting hunt of this character among the foot-hills of the northern Rockies. I was staying at the house of a friendly cowman, whom I will call Judge Yancy Stump.

Judge Yancy Stump was a Democrat who, as he phrased it, had fought for his Democracy; that is, he had been in the Confederate Army. He was at daggers drawn with his nearest neighbor, a cross-grained mountain farmer, who may be known as old man Prindle. Old man Prindle had been in the Union Army, and his Republicanism was of the blackest and most uncompromising type. There was one point, however, on which the two came together. They were exceedingly fond of hunting with hounds. The judge had three or four track-hounds, and four of what he called swift-hounds, the latter including one pure-bred greyhound bitch of wonderful speed and temper, a dun-colored yelping animal which was a cross between a greyhound and a fox-hound, and two others that were crosses between a greyhound and a wire-haired Scotch deer-hound. Old man Prindle's contribution to the pack consisted of two immense brindled mongrels of great strength and ferocious temper. They were unlike any dogs I have ever seen in this country. Their mother herself was a cross between a bull mastiff and a Newfoundland, while the father was described as being a big dog that belonged to a "Dutch Count." The "Dutch Count" was an outcast German noble, who had drifted to the West, and, after failing in the mines and foiling in the cattle country, had died in a squalid log shanty while striving to eke out an existence as a hunter among the foot-hills. His dog, I presume, from the description given me, must have been a boarhound or Ulm dog.

As I was very anxious to see a wolf-hunt the Judge volunteered to get one up, and asked old man Prindle to assist, for the sake of his two big fighting dogs; though the very names of the latter, General Grant and Old Abe, were gall and wormwood to the unreconstructed soul of the Judge. Still they were the only dogs anywhere around capable of tackling a savage timber wolf, and without their aid the Judge's own high-spirited animals ran a serious risk of injury, for they were altogether too game to let any beast escape without a struggle.

Luck favored us. Two wolves had killed a calf and dragged it into a long patch of dense brush where there was a little spring, the whole furnishing admirable cover for any wild beast. Early in the morning we started on horseback for this bit of cover, which was some three miles off. The party consisted of the Judge, old man Prindle, a cowboy, myself, and the dogs. The judge and I carried our rifles and the cowboy his revolver, but old man Prindle had nothing but a heavy whip, for he swore, with many oaths, that no one should interfere with his big dogs, for by themselves they would surely "make the wolf feel sicker than a stuck hog." Our shaggy ponies racked along at a five-mile gait over the dewy prairie grass. The two big dogs trotted behind their master grim and ferocious. The track-hounds were tied in couples, and the beautiful greyhounds loped lightly and gracefully alongside the horses. The country was fine. A mile to our right a small plains river wound in long curves between banks fringed with cottonwoods. Two or three miles to our left the foot-hills rose sheer and bare, with clumps of black pine and cedar in their gorges. We rode over gently rolling prairie, with here and there patches of brush at the bottoms of the slopes around the dry watercourse.

At last we reached a somewhat deeper valley, in which the wolves were harbored. Wolves lie close in the daytime and will not leave cover if they can help it; and as they had both food and water within we knew it was most unlikely that this couple would be gone. The valley was a couple of hundred yards broad and three or four times as long, filled with a growth of ash and dwarf elm and cedar, thorny underbrush choking the spaces between. Posting the cowboy, to whom he gave his rifle, with two greyhounds on one side of the upper end, and old man Prindle with two others on the opposite side, while I was left at the lower end to guard against the possibility of the wolves breaking back, the Judge himself rode into the thicket near me and loosened the track-hounds to let them find the wolves' trail. The big dogs also were uncoupled and allowed to go in with the hounds. Their power of scent was very poor, but they were sure to be guided aright by the baying of the hounds, and their presence would give confidence to the latter and make them ready to rout the wolves out of the thicket, which they would probably have shrunk from doing alone. There was a moment's pause of expectation after the Judge entered the thicket with his hounds. We sat motionless on our horses, eagerly looking through the keen fresh morning air. Then a clamorous baying from the thicket in which both the horseman and dogs had disappeared showed that the hounds had struck the trail of their quarry and were running on a hot scent. For a couple of minutes we could not be quite certain which way the game was going to break. The hounds ran zigzag through the brush, as we could tell by their baying, and once some yelping and a great row showed that they had come rather closer than they had expected upon at least one of the wolves.

In another minute, however, the latter found it too hot for them and bolted from the thicket. My first notice of this was seeing the cowboy, who was standing by the side of his horse, suddenly throw up his rifle and fire, while the greyhounds who had been springing high in the air, half maddened by the clamor in the thicket below, for a moment dashed off the wrong way, confused by the report of the gun. I rode for all I was worth to where the cowboy stood, and instantly caught a glimpse of two wolves, grizzled-gray and brown, which having been turned by his shot had started straight over the hill across the plain toward the mountains three miles away. As soon as I saw them I saw also that the rearmost of the couple had been hit somewhere in the body and was lagging behind, the blood running from its flanks, while the two greyhounds were racing after it; and at the same moment the track-hounds and the big dogs burst out of the thicket, yelling savagely as they struck the bloody trail. The wolf was hard hit, and staggered as he ran. He did not have a hundred yards' start of the dogs, and in less than a minute one of the greyhounds ranged up and passed him with a savage snap that brought him too; and before he could recover the whole pack rushed at him. Weakened as he was he could make no effective fight against so many foes, and indeed had a chance for but one or two rapid snaps before he was thrown down and completely covered by the bodies of his enemies. Yet with one of these snaps he did damage, as a shrill yell told, and in a second an over-rash track-hound came out of the struggle with a deep gash across his shoulders. The worrying, growling, and snarling were terrific, but in a minute the heaving mass grew motionless and the dogs drew off, save one or two that still continued to worry the dead wolf as it lay stark and stiff with glazed eyes and rumpled fur.

No sooner were we satisfied that it was dead than the Judge, with cheers and oaths and crackings of his whip, urged the dogs after the other wolf. The two greyhounds that had been with old man Prindle had fortunately not been able to see the wolves when they first broke from the cover, and never saw the wounded wolf at all, starting off at full speed after the unwounded one the instant he topped the crest of the hill. He had taken advantage of a slight hollow and turned, and now the chase was crossing us half a mile away. With whip and spur we flew toward them, our two greyhounds stretching out in front and leaving us as if we were standing still, the track-hounds and big dogs running after them just ahead of the horses. Fortunately the wolf plunged for a moment into a little brushy hollow and again doubled back, and this gave us a chance to see the end of the chase from nearby. The two greyhounds which had first taken up the pursuit were then but a short distance behind. Nearer they crept until they were within ten yards, and then with a tremendous race the little bitch ran past him and inflicted a vicious bite in the big beast's ham. He whirled around like a top and his jaws clasped like those of a sprung bear-trap, but quick though he was she was quicker and just cleared his savage rush. In another moment he resumed his flight at full speed, a speed which only that of the greyhounds exceeded; but almost immediately the second greyhound ranged alongside, and though he was not able to bite, because the wolf kept running with its head turned around threatening him, yet by his feints he delayed the beast's flight so that in a moment or two the remaining couple of swift hounds arrived on the scene. For a moment the wolf and all four dogs galloped along in a bunch; then one of the greyhounds, watching his chance, pinned the beast cleverly by the hock and threw him completely over. The others jumped on it in an instant; but rising by main strength the wolf shook himself free, catching one dog by the ear and tearing it half off. Then he sat down on his haunches and the greyhounds ranged themselves around him some twenty yards off, forming a ring which forbade his retreat, though they themselves did not dare touch him. However the end was at hand. In another moment Old Abe and General Grant come running up at headlong speed and smashed into the wolf like a couple of battering-rams. He rose on his hind-legs like a wrestler as they came at him, the greyhounds also rising and bouncing up and down like rubber balls. I could just see the wolf and the first big dog locked together, as the second one made good his throat-hold. In another moment over all three tumbled, while the greyhounds and one or two of the track-hounds jumped in to take part in the killing. The big dogs more than occupied the wolf's attention and took all the punishing, while in a trice one of the greyhounds, having seized him by the hind-leg, stretched him out, and the others were biting his undefended belly. The snarling and yelling of the worry made a noise so fiendish that it was fairly bloodcurdling; then it gradually died down, and the second wolf lay limp on the plain, killed by the dogs unassisted. This wolf was rather heavier and decidedly taller than either of the big dogs, with more sinewy feet and longer fangs. . . .

During the last decade many ranchmen in Colorado, Wyoming, and Montana, have developed packs of greyhounds able to kill a wolf unassisted. Greyhounds trained for this purpose always seize by the throat; and the light dogs used for coursing jack-rabbits are not of much service, smooth or rough-haired greyhounds and deer-hounds standing over thirty inches at the shoulder and weighing over ninety pounds being the only ones that, together with speed, courage, and endurance, possess the requisite power.

One of the most famous packs in the West was that of the Sun River Hound Club, in Montana, started by the stockmen of Sun River to get rid of the curse of the wolves which infested the neighborhood and worked very serious damage to the herds and flocks. The pack was composed of both greyhounds and deer-hounds, the best being from the kennels of Colonel Williams and of Mr. Van Hummel, of Denver; they were handled by an old plainsman and veteran wolf-hunter named Porter. In the season of '86 the astonishing number of 146 wolves were killed with these dogs. Ordinarily, as soon as the dogs seized a wolf, and threw or held it, Porter rushed in and stabbed it with his hunting knife; one day, when out with six hounds, he thus killed no less than twelve out of the fifteen wolves started, though one of the greyhounds was killed, and all the others were cut and exhausted. But often the wolves were killed without his aid. The first time the two biggest hounds— deer-hounds or wire-haired greyhounds—were tried, when they had been at the ranch only three days, they performed such a feat. A large wolf had killed and partially eaten a sheep in a corral close to the ranch house, and Porter started on the trail, and followed him at a jog-trot nearly ten miles before the hounds sighted him. Running but a few rods, he turned viciously to bay, and the two great greyhounds struck him like stones hurled from a catapult, throwing him as they fastened on his throat; they held him down and strangled him before he could rise, two other hounds getting up just in time to help at the end of the worry.

Ordinarily, however, no two greyhounds or deer-hounds are a match for a gray wolf, but I have known of several instances in Colorado, Wyoming, and Montana, in which three strong veterans have killed one. The feat can only be performed by big dogs of the highest courage, who all act together, rush in at top speed, and seize by the throat; for the strength of the quarry is such that otherwise he will shake off the dogs, and then speedily kill them by rabid snaps with his terribly armed jaws. Where possible, half a dozen dogs should be slipped at once, to minimize the risk of injury to the pack; unless this is done, and unless the hunter helps the dogs in the worry, accidents will be frequent, and an occasional wolf will be found able to beat off, maiming or killing, a lesser number of assailants. Some hunters prefer the smooth greyhound, because of its great speed, and others the wire-coated animal, the rough deer-hound, because of its superior strength; both, if of the right kind, are dauntless fighters.

Colonel Williams' greyhounds have performed many noble feats in wolf-hunting. He spent the winter of 1875 in the Black Hills, which at that time did not contain a single settler, and fairly swarmed with game. Wolves were especially numerous and very bold and fierce, so that the dogs of the party were continually in jeopardy of their lives. On the other hand they took an ample vengeance, for many wolves were caught by the pack. Whenever possible, the horsemen kept close enough to take an immediate hand in the fight, if the quarry was a full-grown wolf, and thus save the dogs from the terrible punishment they were otherwise certain to receive. The dogs invariably throttled, rushing straight at the throat, but the wounds they themselves received were generally in the flank or belly; in several instances these wounds resulted fatally. Once or twice a wolf was caught, and held by two greyhounds until the horsemen came up; but it took at least five dogs to overcome and slay unaided a big timber wolf. Several times the feat was performed by a party of five, consisting of two greyhounds, one rough-coated deer-hound, and two cross-bloods; and once by a litter of seven young greyhounds, not yet come to their full strength.

Once or twice the so-called Russian wolf-hounds or silky coated greyhounds, the "borzois," have been imported and tried in wolf-hunting on the western plains; but hitherto they have not shown themselves equal, at either running or fighting, to the big American-bred greyhounds of the type produced by Colonel Williams and certain others of our best western breeders. Indeed I have never known any foreign greyhound, whether Scotch, English, or from continental Europe, to perform such feats of courage, endurance, and strength, in chasing and killing dangerous game, as the homebred greyhounds of Colonel Williams.

🐺 1875–1913: Wolf Bounty Laws in Wyoming Territory and State

Colorado, in 1869, became the first territory in the Rocky Mountain region to pass a wolf bounty law. During the next few years, most of the other western territories and states follow suit. Wyoming serves as a typical example of how these bounty laws evolved. Bounties offered for wolves gradually increased, from 50 cents in 1875 to $8.00 in 1893. Note the 1913 law that stipulates a fine of up to $300 as punishment for freeing a wolf from a trap.

1875

An Act to Protect Sheep
Be it enacted by the Council and House of Representatives of the Territory of Wyoming:

Section 1. The county commissioners of the various counties in this Territory are hereby authorized and required to encourage the destruction of wolves by making payment out of the county fund to any person who shall engage in the destruction of wolves, the sum of fifty cents for each wolf killed by such person. The person so engaged who may desire the compensation above named, shall present to the chairman of the board of county commissioners of the county, in which the wolves were killed, the scalp of such wolves, together with an affidavit, that the wolf from which said scalp was taken was killed by the person presenting said scalp which scalp and affidavit shall be evidence that the wolves were killed by the person so producing it. It shall thereupon be the duty of the chairman of the board to so mark or destroy such scalp that it cannot be again used as evidence, and give the person so producing it a certificate stating the number of scalps so presented, and to what sum the person is entitled under this act, which certificate may be filed with the county clerk as a claim against the county, to be by him presented to the board at its next meeting thereafter, at which time the board of county commissioners shall allow the claim and order a warrant drawn upon the treasury of the county, as in other cases; *Provided*, This section shall not be construed to prevent the board from disallowing such claim, should it appear in any way to have been fraudulently made or obtained.

Sec 2. This act shall be in force from and after January 1st, 1876.

1879

An Act to Amend an Act Entitled "An Act for the Protection of Sheep"

Be it enacted by the Council and House of Representatives of the Territory of Wyoming:

Section 1. The county commissioners of the various counties in this Territory are hereby authorized and required to encourage the destruction of wolves, by making payment out of the county fund to any person who shall engage in the destruction of wolves, the sum of one dollar for each wolf killed by such person.

1884

An Act to Encourage and Protect the Interest of Wool-Growers

Section 1. . . . For each wolf or coyote, one dollar and fifty cents.

1890

An Act to Encourage the Destruction of Predatory Wild Animals, for Other Purposes

Section 1. . . . for each gray or black wolf so destroyed, three dollars.

1893
An Act to Amend and Re-enact Section One of an Act Entitled, "An Act to Encourage the Destruction of Predatory Wild Animals, and for Other Purposes."
Section 1. . . . for each gray and black wolf so killed, eight dollars.

Excerpt from Wyoming's 1913 Wolf Bounty Law
Section 16. Any person who shall have captured alive any of the animals named in this act and who shall turn said animals loose shall be guilty of a misdemeanor and upon conviction thereof be fined in a sum not less than $40 and more than $300.

1905: Wolf Mange Law in the State of Montana

In 1905, the State of Montana passed a law that required the State Veterinarian to assist in a program of capturing wolves alive, infecting them with the contagious form of mange, and then releasing them in hopes that they would return home and infect their fellow pack members:

"An Act to provide for the extermination of wolves and coyotes by inoculating the same with mange, and to place such duties under the charge of the State Veterinarian, and to make an appropriation for such experiments."
Be it Enacted by the Legislative Assembly of the State of Montana:

Section 1
The State Veterinarian is hereby instructed and it shall be his duty to at the earliest possible moment secure a sufficient number of wolves, wolf pups, coyotes and coyotes pups to demonstrate fully the feasibility of producing among them the contagious disease known as Mange and that not less than six wolves and six coyotes shall be so obtained in each of the following counties of the State: Dawson, Custer, Valley, Fergus, Chouteau, Teton, Meagher and Rosebud.

Section 2
A suitable person shall be selected in each county who shall be a person that is an owner of and interested in live stock growing, such designated person shall have charge of and keep in captivity such wolves and coyotes, and shall when the same are fully infected with said disease or diseases, convey the same in six different directions from the place said animals are kept, not less than eight miles away in each direction.

Section 3
For capturing, detaining in captivity and distributing such wolves and coyotes, said person shall receive not more than Fifteen ($15.00) Dollars per head to be paid out of the fund herein provided for.

Section 4
It shall be the State Veterinarian's duty to inoculate such wolves and coyotes with said disease and to assure himself that all such wolves or coyotes are fully infected before being released; and it shall be his further duty to obtain reports from stockmen in the various counties in which said disease is produced and make a detailed report of results to the next Legislature.

Section 5
There is hereby appropriated for this purpose the sum of Two Thousand, Five Hundred ($2,500.00) Dollars, which sum shall be used in payment for and the keeping and distribution of such wolves and coyotes and to defray any necessary expense of the State Veterinarian in carrying out the provisions of this Act.

Section 6
This Act shall take effect and be in full force from and after its passage and approval by the Governor.
Approved March 10, 1905.

1984: Current Wolf Bounty Law in the State of Colorado
It is generally thought that the last wolf in Colorado was killed in 1945. That apparently was not good enough for the Colorado Legislature. The 1984 edition of the Colorado Revised Statues *shows that the state still offers a bounty on wolves. This despite the fact that, according to the federal Endangered Species Act, the intentional killing of a wolf is a felony punishable by up to $100,000 in fines and up to one year in jail.*

35–40–107. Bounty on coyote, wolf. Any person who kills any wolf, coyote, or any number of such animals within this state, shall receive a premium of one dollar for each coyote killed, and for each wolf killed two dollars, to be paid as provided in sections 35–40–107 to 35–40–112.

1890: Wolf Fund Letter, Wyoming
Ranching associations commonly raised funds for their own private wolf bounties. The following 1890 letter from the Laramie County Protec-

tive Association assesses the Teschemacher and de Billier Cattle Company $65.37 as their share of the Association's Wolf Fund:

The Laramie County Protective Association, Cheyenne, Wyoming, September 20, 1890

DEAR SIR: A meeting of representative stockmen of Laramie County, Wyoming, was held in Cheyenne on Friday, September 19th, for the purpose of devising ways and means to prevent the continual and alarmingly increasing ravages of wolves upon the live stock grazing in this county. After an extended discussion the meeting appointed a committee of three consisting of Dr. John F. Carey, Mr. John H. Gordon and Mr. Hugh J. Gaisford to confer with "The Laramie County Protective Association" with the object in view of obtaining the co-operation of that association in this matter.

At the conference meeting held this morning at the office of The Laramie County Protective Association it was decided to offer a reward of five dollars per head (in addition to the bounty of three dollars per head now paid by this county) for every grey or black wolf killed in Laramie County, Wyoming, after the first day of October, A.D. 1890. It was also decided to raise at once the sum of five hundred ($500.00) dollars for the payment of the rewards so offered.

. . . In order to obtain the funds necessary to carry out this plan it is proposed to levy an assessment of one cent per head upon cattle and horses and one-half cent per head upon sheep, and to take the county assessment for the purposes of taxation, during the present year, as the basis for the proposed assessment.

At the unanimous solicitation of the committee representing the stockmen of this county, "The Laramie County Protective Association" has consented to take charge of the collection of this "Wolf Fund" and pay the rewards offered upon the presentation of the pelts and such other evidence or affidavit as may be required in order to establish the good faith of the party seeking the reward.

Taking the assessment roll of Laramie county for 1890 as the basis of the levy, your assessment for the benefit of the "Wolf Fund" is as follows, viz.:

6537 head of horses and cattle, 1 c. per head   65.37
—— head of sheep, 1-2 c. per head

                                        Total $65.37

Kindly favor us with an early reply enclosing a check for the amount of your assessment. All checks and drafts should be drawn payable to the order of "The Laramie County Protective Association."

Yours Very Truly,
M. M. Mason, Secretary

🐺 1900: *Corbin's Advice or the Wolf Hunter's Guide,* Ben Corbin

In 1900, North Dakota hunter Ben Corbin, a man who called himself "the Boss Wolf Killer," published an extraordinary book, Corbin's Advice or the Wolf Hunter's Guide. *Born in Virginia in 1835, Corbin had learned the secrets of the wolf trapping trade from his father, a man who had "hunted redskins with Daniel Boone." After serving with the Union Army in the Civil War, Corbin moved to Iowa and earned his living by hunting and trapping. High bounties encouraged him to specialize in wolf trapping. In 1883, he relocated to North Dakota, where he perfected his own special methods of catching wolves and earned good money by teaching those techniques to novice trappers.*

In the first excerpt, taken from the book's preface, Corbin uses the lives of Abraham and Jesus to argue that God wants us to end the monopolization of the continent by "wild beasts and savage men."

In Genesis we read that he [Abraham] was rich in cattle, in silver and in gold—something like the ranchmen and stockmen of North Dakota. Indeed the pastoral life preceded every other profession. The Patriarchs were all shepherds. . . . Those shepherds wandered from place to place wherever there was the best pasture, just as we do in Dakota. . . .

In the New Testament, the parable of the Good Shepherd shines like a star. If Jesus did not disdain to call himself the Good Shepherd, why should any man in Dakota not be proud to be called by that name, or to be associated as I am, with the men who are feeding their flocks on the rich and abundant pastures of this great commonwealth? Largely my life has been spent in protecting these flocks against the incursions of ravenous beasts of prey. I know it is but a step and the first step, which counts in the march of civilization. God made the country, but man made the town—and some of these towns are pretty tough, like most of men's work. I can not believe that Providence intended that these rich lands, broad, well watered, fertile and waving with abundant pasturage, close by mountains and valleys, filled with gold, and every metal and mineral, should be forever monopolized by wild beasts and savage men. I believe something in the survival of the fittest, and hence I have "fit" for it all my life. Civilization is a fine thing, and it may spread itself like a green bay tree in the cities, and lordly mansions of the millionaires, with all their silks and broadcloths, but it has to have plenty of beef and pork and mutton—yes, yes, and wool too, and plenty of it. But my lord and lady would go bare-footed, and that would be bad form, and naked, and that would be worse, and empty, and that would be awful, if somebody, somewhere and somehow, would not send them leather, and wool and beef and mutton. But the herds and flocks must be raised and protected here for my lord and lady, if it takes the last man and the last dollar. The wolf don't [sic] like them, and I trust the wolf will never come near their doors, or that any of them will turn out "wolves in sheep clothing," but if he comes near mine I will take him in, and it will be the saddest day of his life. That's why I am here. The wolf is the enemy of civilization, and I want to exterminate him. If he eats up the flocks, where are your wool and mutton to come from, and what's the use of a tariff on wool, and free trade in wolves? I would place the duty higher on both.

In later sections, Corbin describes several of the special methods he uses to kill wolves but adds that use of poison bait, the technique used by the wolfers, would violate his "wolf code of honor."

The time to kill the old wolf is when you locate the den [for] sure, for they will come closer to you now then [sic] ever again. There are several ways to get and shoot the old ones.

Tie a small dog close to the den, and then hide. About sunset the wolf will attack the dog—then shoot quick. Another way is, tie a cub close to the den and let the old wolf see it. Then tie your dog close by, and conceal yourself—not long—soon the dog will begin to howl and the old wolf will go for him in defense of the cub—then shoot.

Never kill the young one till you play this game to a finish. You may carry the young ones five miles at night, and the old ones will be with you next morning—such is their affection for their young. The old ones will outwit you unless you consult me first by letter or otherwise. I could catch more old ones, but I won't as long as the bounty is so slow. I can make more catching cubs. . . .

In warm or soft weather I trap them this way. I take some old horse or cow with the big jaw or some disease that renders them worthless and plant it in a shallow pond or lake, and kill it, and cut it open, set my trap, and there you are, Mr. Wolf, early next morning. I catch scores that way. . . .

One of my best tricks is to locate the den at breeding time and pull the cubs out with my peculiar hooks and long ash or fishpole—I haul them all out—sometimes get ten and leave the den for the next year's crop O.K. I have wire and hooks for the purpose, and have applied for a patent. . . .

I always darken the den—always bait the first hook on the end of my pole with fresh meat, and wait till morning with best results. Another plan I have is to tie my dog to a ten foot pole behind the buggy and drive by the den. The old wolves think, of course, the dog is after their young, and they rush at the dog, then I shoot. . . .

My wolf code of honor bars poison. It is unsafe, unfair, uncivilized. I draw the line at honest fresh bait, fish pole, and hooks for the purpose, and my trusty dog and gun, and I put up my hunter wisdom, experience and cunning against that of the wolf, and I find him sometimes more than a match at my best, for a fact, for anyone who takes the wolf for a fool gets left every time.

Corbin mentioned using fish hooks to catch pups but failed to fully explain the technique. Included in his book is what appears to be a newspaper article entitled "Corbin's Wolf Farm" from the Emmons County Record, *his local North Dakota newspaper. Corbin described this fishhook method in detail to the reporter who, in turn passed it on to the paper's readers:*

Corbin's methods of catching young wolves is one which he devised himself, and which, so far as known, is employed by no other wolf hunter in the state. . . . He catches the young wolves with fishhooks and a steel line, and has been known to land eight young wolves on the same line in one night.

The wolves live in dens in the earth, after the manner of badgers, except that the dens are larger. When Corbin locates the den, he waits until night and then brings his fishing line and hooks into play. The steel line is fastened to a stout stake driven into the ground and is then carried beneath the soil through the region immediately about the den. From the main wire are numerous smaller wires projecting in all directions, to the end of each of which is a spring fishhook. These hooks are baited with good-sized pieces of chicken breast or other tempting morsels.

When the young wolves leave the den at night to prowl about in search of food the first thing they encounter is these scattered bits of meat. The wolf is a ravenous animal, and bolts small bits of meat whole. The young ones attack these bits of meat and swallow them, snap goes the bolted spring hook, and the wolf is fast. Every effort made by the wolf to get away adds to the pain inflicted by the hook, which had found lodgement in his stomach or throat, and he soon learns that absolute quiet is the best method under the circumstances. Not infrequently Corbin returns to the den in the morning to find every one of the young wolves caught on the spring hooks. The steel wire prevents their biting it in two and escaping in this fashion, and as the animals are all securely fastened, it is no difficult task to knock them in the head with a club, take their scalps and leave the bodies for the buzzards.

This process is repeated at every den which may be discovered by the hunter, and seldom without success. Hundreds of young wolves are caught every season, and their scalps brought in for the bounty. The same ground is gone over every season, with the same results, and Corbin pockets annually hundreds of dollars as the result of his ingenuity. He has endeavored to have the fishhook and line patented as a means of catching wolves but the patent office does not consider an old device patentable as applied to a new end, and he has been unable to secure a patent.

Throughout his book, Corbin repeatedly complains about the low bounties offered for adult wolves. At the time of publication, 1900, the county paid only $2.00 for adult wolves and $1.00 for pups. Corbin argues that the counties and state must raise the wolf bounties. After detailing the great financial loss they cause ranchers, he adds this unsubstantiated statement: "There are instances where they have attacked children going to and from school." The following passages show how Corbin lobbied for his cause:

In a careful search of the statutes enacted by several states for the past half century or more I have found that less than $5 has seldom been offered for each wolf or coyote killed. It would seem, from the testimony of the laws on the subject and from the experience of old hunters, that $5 is about the least that the service can be done for. If there is a market price at which any labor can be performed, why should not this business have its market price, also? The measure is this: what is the least that good service can be obtained for in any industry? Ascertain this and it becomes the wage rate for that kind of labor — its fixed average value—by every canon in industrial economy. . . .

But the fact is patent that the restoration of the state bounty would encourage the hunting and trapping of these destructive brutes, and go a long way toward securing at least a partial protection to all domestic animals. With the fecundity of the wolf as great as it is, there is no other way to stop their increase. It will not do to say that the stockmen should be left to do the necessary work themselves, and that if they do not protect their own sheep they should lose them. This is a narrow and selfish view of the matter. A question of public policy, of justice and of fairness come in and requires the state to protect the general interests of the people and defend them from every public enemy; and what greater enemy can the state have than one that is able to wage war on the state's chief industry both day and night. . . .

They [politicians who didn't vote for increased bounties] have no state pride—care nothing for our live stock or for my hunting business. Why, sir, some of these blasted fools would rather see all the stock and half the children eaten up by the wolves than to see me make $5—yes, or even $3—by my business. Jealousy is a mean thing. So is envy. . . .

The small bounty is all right for the young wolves, for an experienced wolf hunter will catch a whole litter of them at once and make something out of it, but if you want the old wolves killed off, something that takes hard work and does more good than killing off 100 young ones, put a higher bounty on them. Put a bounty of $5 or even $10 on old wolves, and shut off the wolf supply factory. No hunter will work to kill an old wolf for $2 when he can in the same time kill half a dozen young ones and get $1 apiece for them. But if you make it an object for him to kill the old ones, he will clean them out, and then there will be no young ones, at $1 apiece. . . . I make a bare living at the business, and yet I keep the wolves cleaned out so that you can make a fortune in the stock business in a few years. It is to get scientific wolf hunters to make a business of destroying them. It should be the aim of the stockmen to pay enough bounty to make the object of experienced hunters to devote their time to killing off wolves. Other states pa big bounties. In many places the stockmen pay a side bounty for all wolves killed on their range.

Despite Corbin's complaints about the low wolf bounties and his statement that he makes "a bare living at the business," he continually brags about how much money he made from those bounties. He offers to sell, for $25.00 (more than a month's wages for most men), his expertise in "wolfology" to *anyone wanting to get into the lucrative wolf bounty business. In the previous passage, Corbin speaks of the need to shut off "the wolf supply factory," but he himself left twenty breeding pairs "alive and well" to insure a continuous crop of pups for harvest on his "wolf farm."*

I fool away no time on the old ones however, for I get $1 for each cub, and only $2 for the adults, and so I take the old ones if I can easily, otherwise I gather in the cubs and pass on.

Out of 1,500 wolves I have killed the past nine years, not more than sixty-one were grown up.

I have twenty old females on my farm of twenty-five miles square that have cost the people from $150 to $200 each in the last nine years, when they could have got rid of the whole tenty for $100 or even less money, by offering an inducement for their capture. In 1897, I caught twenty-one litters of wolves, averaging seven to the litter. I kill about one old wolf for every twenty young ones. I spot the same old pair every year, get the increase and let the old ones o free. I particularize five old wolves whose offspring I have caught every year. These five wolves have cost on bounty $945 and are still alive and well. . . .

Any one interested can easily prepare himself for the business of wolf hunting for $25 under my personal instruction in a thousand matters I can put in no books, and that no book can teach. A ride with Uncle Ben, a few weeks at my fireside will cost you nothing, and before you leave my college you will drop me a $25 and get your diploma as W.H.L.L., which means doctor of wolf hunters. No other college can confer the degree—no other university than my open prairies, grand woods, and crystal streams, where the air is pure, the sunlight clear, and nature's open book before us teaches all you need to know for wolf hunters.

At the end of his book, Corbin relates a sickening story about bringing a litter of wolf pups on a lobbying trip to Bismarck. A year prior to the following incident, Corbin had discovered a wolf den and killed all the pups. He returned the next denning season, hoping to kill the breeding female for a special $5.00 bounty offered by a local rancher. This story begins with Corbin's arrival at the den:

A a glance I saw the dog wolf sneaking off, and I knew the mate was not far away. So I grasped my Winchester, and at the same moment the female ran out of the den and I shot her. Performing the Caesarian operation, I soon had the cubs, as yet unborn. There were four of them alive and kicking, and using the appliance used for delicate babies, I soon had four likely little pets and I then went to the den, dug it out and found two more pups, six in all. I laid them down beside their dead mother for their first meals and this is according to Scripture, "although you may be dead you yet shall live." I then loaded them in the wagon, as the county commissioners had just taken the county bounty off. I saw my chance to place it back on again. I drove to the capital city, Bismarck of course, bought a rubber tit, and a pint of sweet milk and kept them on the bottle for three days, drove around the town with the outfit in the wagon, showed it up in good shape, got about thirty men to sign my petition to place the bounty back on. . . . Still they didn't restore the bounty.

Corbin didn't disclose the fate of those six pups but, after using them as a living exhibit on wolf bounties, he presumably killed them and collected the bounties on them as well as the $5.00 the rancher had offered for the carcass of the mother wolf.

1914: "The Wolf at the Stockman's Door—Sheep and Cattle Killers Breed in the National Reserves," S. W. McClure

The wolf bounties offered by the counties, territories, states, and ranching associations of the American West caused the death of untold numbers of wolves but failed to accomplish their ultimate purpose: total eradication of the wolf. Just after the turn of the century, western stockmen and their associations mounted a campaign demanding that the federal government organize and fund a final solution to the wolf problem. The following article by S. W. McClure, which appeared in the November 14, 1914, edition of The Country Gentleman, *is a typical example of the lobbying effort of the times:*

Depredations of carnivorous wild animals annually ause a loss of not less than $15,000,000 to stockmen in the territory west of the Missouri River. This was the conclusion reached at the National Wool Grower's Convention in Omaha some years ago, and after 14 years' residence in the section I am satisfied that it is a conservative estimate. It is important to every consumer as well as to every producer of meat that this menace be removed. For 20 years this territory lying west of the Missouri River has been the chief source of the country's supply of sheep and cattle, and if I am right nature has intended this section to be for all time the breeding ground for the Nation's meat.

The states most affected by the wild-animal menace are public-land States in which the Federal Government still retains enormous areas of lad—Washington, Oregon, California Arizona, New Mexico, Colorado, Utah, Nevada, Idaho, Wyoming, Montana, and South Dakota. These States were originally the home of the buffalo, elk, deer, goat, and mountain sheep. Also they were and still are the home of the bear, wolf, coyote, cougar, and wildcat. As they have been settld, the herbivorous wild animals have been greaty reduced in numbers—in some cases exterminated. The carnivorous animals, however, still remain, and some species exist in greater numbers than ever before. Originally the food supply of these carnivorous animals was limited. Now, with the land filled with poultry and domestic animals, the marauders find an abundant food supply, easily obtainable.

In the order of losses they occasion the importance of these carnivorous animals is about as follows: Coyotes, wildcats, bears, cougars, and wolves. Probably the coyote causes the loss of more stock and poultry than all the others combined, not because he is more vicious and daring, but because he exists in greater numbers and finds the new conditions of living in a semisettled country distinctly to his liking. For downright viciousness the wolf exceeds all our native wild animals, but the lands that he most loves to frequent have been largely settled; hence the number of wolves is not so great as formerly. . . .

Next in destructiveness to the coyote come[s] the wild cat. . . .

. . . then there are the bears, and probably as many of these animals as in the old days. . . .

. . . The cougar, or mountain lion, is a vicious carnivorous animal, found only in the mountains or in the broken lands along rivers. Mostly he preys upon elk and deer, but in the summer and fall it is no unusual thing for him to kill sheep, cattle, and colts while they are being pastured on the mountain ranges.

Last in importance is the wolf. Originally the West was filled with wolves, and in some parts of the Southwest, notably in Texas, there are still many of them. But the wolf does not relish settlement, and the war that has been waged against him in many Western States has greatly reduced his numbers. However, the loss occasioned in Wyoming, Montana, South Dakota, and New Mexico is considerable and falls heavily upon our beef supply, as the wolf prefers beef to any other food. A single wolf can kill outright a cow of almost any age, although attacks are generally confined to cattle under 2 years of age. Frequently wolves travel in bunches of two or three, and kill out of sheer devilishness. The loss to cattlemen from wolves is great—in some sections so great that a bounty as high as $100 may be paid for the destruction of a single wolf that has made a reputation as a killer. . . .

The actual destruction of livestock is not the only loss caused by these pests. In a country abounding with wild animals the expenses of handling stock are materially increased. Sheep must constantly be protected, and western flockmasters annually pay for labor about $1 a head for each sheep they own. This labor charge, the highest in the world, could be reduced 50 per cent if the wild-animal menace was removed. Sheep do not do well when they are constantly herded: if they could be turned loose in a pasture they would produce an average of 1 pound more wool apiece and more and better lambs would be obtained.

Is there a single reason for allowing these predatory wild animals to live? Certainly not. They do not perform a solitary service of value to mankind. Even their hides, in most cases are inferior to the pelts produced by the domestic animals they destroy. . . .

A continuous war has been waged against these wild animals in all the western stock States, most of which pay bounties for the destruction of the marauders. Counties have also paid bounties, and the stockmen offer liberal rewards. In the aggregate these bounties have amounted to millions of dollars.

MONEY IS NECESSARY.

Why have these animals not been eradicated? Simply because the Federal Government has withdrawn from settlement or development millions of acres of land on which carnivorous wild animals breed by the hundreds of thousands and will continue to breed as long as the land is held as present. Just look at some of the withdrawals in these 12 States: For national forests, 135,602,892 acres; for national parks, 4,435,143 acres; for game preserves, 1,492,928 acres; for national monuments, 1,962,012 acres,; for power sites, 1,991,285 acres; for reservoir sites and water reserves, 221,097 acres; unallotted Indian lands, 32,909,108 acres; oil-land withdrawals, 4,228,513 acres; phosphate-land withdrawals 2,750,294 acres; potash-land withdrawals, 225,989 acres. In addition, the Government has withdrawn 41,041,660 acres of land containing coal. These lands are opn to agricultural entry, but the entryman can secure title only to the surface of the land and up to the present time there have been very few settlers to take advantage of the openings. Here is a total area withdrawn from settlement in 12 States amounting to 226,860,921 acres, upon which carnivorous wild animals are permitted to breed without molestation. Under such conditions is it any wonder that the States and the stockmen have failed in their efforts to exterminate wild animals?

I have not the slightest complaint about these lands being withdrawn; in fact, I am in full accord with a conservation policy that preserves for the present and for the future. However, with the exception of the lands withdrawn for power sites and water reserves, these withdrawn lands are held for the benefit of the entire Nation as much as for the benefit of the States in which they are located. The Nation, therefore, should assume the obligations which the withdrawals impose, at least to the extent of keeping the lands from becoming a menace to the surrounding country. To do this I believe that Congress should at the earliest moment appropriate $100,000 for the use of the Forest Service in destroying carnivorous wild animals within the national forests and $250,000 for the destruction of these animals outside of the forests. The consumers of the country should understand that there can be no appreciable increase in livestock production in the West until the question of the destruction of these predatory wild animals has been definitely settled.

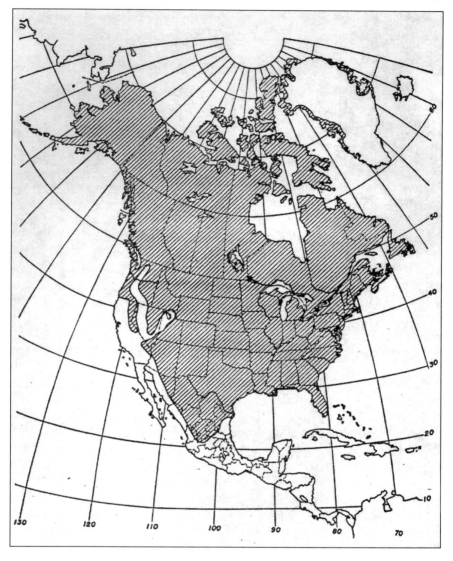

The former range of gray and red wolves in North America. Nature writer and naturalist Ernest Thompson Seton estimated that the original wolf population of the lower forty-eight states was two million. By the 1950s, the number of wolves in the same area had dropped to just a few hundred. (Map from The Wolves of North America, 1944, by Stanley Young and Edward Goldman. Used by permission of Dover Publications)

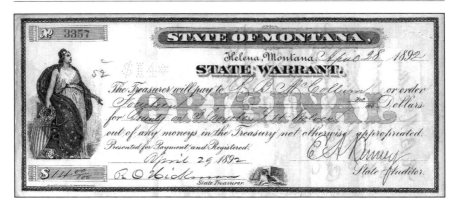

An 1892 Montana state warrant for $14—bounty payment for three coyotes and four wolves. Beginning in 1630, various forms of government in North America offered bounties as a means of encouraging destruction of wolves. (Warrant from the Montana Historical Society)

The Great Hinckley Hunt of December 24, 1818, was a "war of extermination upon the bears and wolves," carried out by an army of six hundred volunteers. It netted a profit of $255 in wolf bounties. The cash was used to buy whiskey and other supplies for an all-night Christmas Eve party. (Photo from the Ohio Historical Society)

"Long Dog." The poison baits wolfers put out to kill wolves also destroyed countless numbers of bears, coyotes, foxes, badgers, wolverines, mountain lions, bald eagles, and other species. Native Americans hated the wolfers and often killed them. The original caption to this sketch reads: "Long Dog the Trapper Killer and Slayer of the Wolfers. The Red Robin Hood of the Upper Missouri country, who ranged that section at the head of a band of Sioux outlaws between the years 1858 and 1883." (From Twenty Years on the Trap Line, *1891, by Joseph Henry Taylor. Photo from the DeGolyer Library, Southern Methodist University)*

"Slaughter of Buffaloes on the Plains." Buffalo were the main prey of the wolves of the Great Plains. Initially, the wolves profited from the mass slaughter committed by the buffalo hunters, but by the early 1880s, the buffalo were nearly extinct and many wolves starved. (From Harper's Weekly, February 24, 1872. *Photo from the Kansas State Historical Society, Topeka)*

"*Poisoning Carnivorous Animals.*" *Historian Edward Curnow estimated that wolfers poisoned* 100,000 *wolves in Montana annually during the years* 1870–77. *The practice was widespread across the plains, and as many as* 120 *wolves could be killed at one poisoned carcass.* (From How to Hunt and Trap, 1894, *by Joseph Batty*)

With their traditional wild prey gone, some wolves began targeting livestock. From the wolves' point of view this made sense—it was either that or starvation for their families. (Sketch entitled Lobo Showing the Pack How to Kill Beef *by Ernest Thompson Seton. Ernest Thompson Seton Memorial Library and Museum*)

Charles M. Russell's 1904 painting Roping a Wolf. *Cowboys hunted down wolves to earn large bonuses from ranchers. Once caught, the animals were often dragged to death over rough ground. (Museum archive #1961.183, Amon Carter Museum, Fort Worth, Texas)*

R. McBride, a cattle rancher in Jackson, Wyoming, with a pack of six wolves he killed in 1902. (Photo from the Jackson Hole Museum and Teton County Historical Society, Jackson, Wyoming)

Billy Weldon and George Theis Jr., with their dog pack, getting ready for a wolf hunt. Theodore Roosevelt was an enthusiastic proponent of "the excellent sport" of hunting wolves with dog packs: "The true way to kill wolves, however, is to hunt them with greyhounds on the great plains. Nothing more exciting than this sport can be imagined." (Photo from the Kansas State Historical Society, Topeka)

In the early 1900s, the ranching industry demanded that the federal government kill wolves on the public lands. The U.S. Forest Service, the U.S. Biological Survey, and the National Park Service all responded with wolf-extermination campaigns. This photograph shows Forest Ranger Aldo Leopold in Arizona in 1910, working in the Apache National Forest: "In those days we had never heard of passing up a chance to kill a wolf." (Negative #X25 900, University of Wisconsin–Madison Archives)

Stanley Young, who started out as a U. S. Biological Survey trapper, eventually directed the agency's national predator control program. Here Young is carrying a live Mexican wolf back to his camp in Arizona's Huachuca Mountains. According to Philip Gipson, a former Animal Damage Control biologist, after chaining and muzzling a male wolf, USBS trappers would wrap a thin wire around the wolf's penis, making it impossible for the animal to urinate. The government man then would kill the wolf, collect the urine, and use it as a scent to attract other wolves to traps. (Photo from the Smithsonian Institution Archives)

G. W. Brown, a government trapper who worked in a national forest in Montana, displaying wolf and coyote pelts. (Museum archive #5935, Arizona Historical Society Library, Tucson)

Crouching on a piece of canvas to place a barrier between his human scent and the site, a U.S. Biological Survey agent carefully digs out a shallow hole for his traps. After covering them with a thin layer of dirt, he will bait the plants to the left of the traps—stalks previously used by wolves as a scent post—with a few drops from a mixture that likely includes urine and excretions from the gall and anal glands of previously captured wolves. When the wolf notices the foreign scent on its scent post, it will investigate the site and step into the trap. (Photo from the Stanley Young Collection, Denver Public Library, Western History Department)

Lobo exposing the traps.

Only the most intelligent and cunning wolves survived the massive poisoning and trapping campaigns. Survivors knew all the trappers' tricks and taught their packs how to avoid capture. (Sketch Lobo Exposing the Traps *by Ernest Thompson Seton. Ernest Thompson Seton Memorial Library and Museum)*

This U.S. Biological Survey official is updating the agency's location map of its predator control agents. In military fashion, the USBS deployed its trappers to any part of the country that had remnant wolf populations. Unlike most government agencies, the USBS actually fulfilled its congressional mandate — destruction of all the remaining wolves in the western states. (Photo from the Stanley Young Collection, Denver Public Library, Western History Department)

This mother wolf and her ten newborn pups were killed in March 1916 by a U.S. Biological Survey agent. The practice of wiping out entire families at the den, know as "denning," was common at the time. (Photo by Bennie Baker. Stanley Young Collection, Denver Public Library, Western History Department)

The government predator control agent might temporarily spare the life of one pup after killing its mother and littermates. The trapper would chain the pup to a tree and then lie in wait to shoot any surviving adults who heard the pup's frightened howls and rushed to save it. The adult wolves' instinctive response enabled the USBS men to wipe out entire packs with this method. (Photo from the Stanley Young Collection, Denver Public Library, Western History Department)

Bill Caywood, a professional U.S. Biological Survey wolf killer, met his match in 1921, when he was told to track down the outlaw wolf Rags the Digger, so-called because of his habit of digging up the traps that were laid for him. Caywood's final confrontation with Rags became a Colorado legend. (Photo from the Stanley Young Collection, Denver Public Library, Western History Department)

In 1920, the U.S. Biological Survey sent out master trapper H. P. Williams (left) to get the infamous Custer Wolf. His instructions were simple: "Stay after the wolf until he was taken, no matter how much time was required." Note the trap still on the left front foot of the dead wolf. (Photo from the Stanley Young Collection, Denver Public Library, Western History Department)

Blanca, mate of Lobo, caught in the trap set by Ernest Thompson Seton in 1894. Seton had been brought in by local ranchers to kill Blanca and Lobo because of the raids their pack conducted on local livestock. Modern scientists Dr. Philip Gipson and his colleagues Dr. Warren Ballard and Dr. Ronald Nowak have examined the skulls of Blanca and Lobo and estimate the ages of the wolves when they died at four to five years for Lobo and six to seven years for Blanca. (Photo by Ernest Thompson Seton. Ernest Thompson Seton Memorial Library and Museum)

Lobo, King of the Currumpaw, caught in four traps when he sought out the body of Blanca. Seton said of Lobo's capture: "Poor old hero, he had never ceased to search for his darling, and when he found the trail her body had made he followed it recklessly, and so fell into the snare prepared for him." Seton was profoundly affected by the deaths of Lobo and Blanca, and his later stories and lectures contributed to the country's changing attitude toward the wolf. (Photo by Ernest Thompson Seton. Ernest Thompson Seton Memorial Library and Museum)

Old Three Toes of the Apishapa and her killer, Roy Spangler, near Thatcher, Colorado, in 1923. After her mate, pups, and pack had been killed, Old Three Toes—the last wolf in her range—became an outlaw marked for death by the U.S. Biological Service. Spangler wanted a job as a trapper with the agency and offered to go after the renegade for free. The USBS agreed to hire him if he got the wolf. Setting aside all other responsibilities, including caring for his sick wife, Spangler relentlessly tracked Old Three Toes. When he finally caught the wolf, Spangler rushed home to tell his wife, only to find she had died of smallpox in his absence. Spangler got his USBS job. Old Three Toes is still alive in this photo. (Photo from the Stanley Young Collection, Denver Public Library, Western History Department)

Shishoka in the chains placed on him by Buffalo Bill Cody. The wolf later escaped and sought out his mother, Wosca. Mother and son then terrorized local ranchers until Wosca went blind. According to Ernest Thompson Seton, Shishoka cared for his mother until they both died in an ambush. (Sketch by Ernest Thompson Seton from Great Historic Animals, 1937. *Ernest Thompson Seton Memorial Library and Museum)*

Chapter 4

The Federal Government versus the Wolves

". . . the most systematic and successful war
on these pests ever undertaken."
Vernon Bailey, USBS

The federal government responded favorably to the ranchers' demand for help in exterminating the last of the wolves. In 1907, rangers in national forests were ordered to trap wolves in their districts. The following year, each western forest proudly reported the number of wolves it had eliminated. The U.S. Congress, in 1915, began funding a wolf control program and gave the mission of implementing it to the U.S. Biological Survey (USBS). As is shown in the USBS reports, the agency's goal was "absolute extermination" of the wolf. The ranching industry and sportsmen's organizations made sure, through their lobbying of Congress, that the USBS had sufficient funding to achieve its mission.

🐺 1907: *Wolves in Relation to Stock, Game, and the National Forest Reserves*, **Vernon Bailey**
In January of 1907, Vernon Bailey, a biologist with the U.S. Biological Survey, wrote a report entitled Wolves in Relation to Stock, Game, and the National Forest Reserves. *This document, published and distributed by the Forest Service, served as a how-to guide on wolf control for forest rangers. Those rangers used the wolf-trapping techniques recommended by Bailey to clear out the wolves from their respective national forests.*

The enormous losses suffered by stockmen on the western cattle ranges and the destruction of game on forest reserves, game preserves, and in national parks through the depredations of wolves have led to special investigations by the Biological Survey in cooperation with the Forest Service, to ascertain the best methods for destroying these pests. The results appear in the present report, which includes also field notes on the distribution, abundance, and breeding habits of wolves.

The chief object of the report is to put in the hands of every hunter, trapper, forest ranger, and ranchman directions for trapping, poisoning, and hunting wolves and finding the dens of young. If these directions are followed it is believed that the wolves can be so reduced in number that their depredations will cease to be a serious menace to stock raising. Prime wolf skins are worth from $4 to $6 each, enough to induce trappers and enterprising ranch boys to make an effort to secure them if a reasonable degree of success is assured. Stock owners need little encouragement to catch or kill wolves on their own ranges, and it is believed that the forest rangers will be able to keep them down on the forest reserves. Their complete extermination on the western range is not, however, to be expected in the near future, and it is only by constant and concerted effort that their numbers can be kept down sufficiently to prevent serious depredations.

After describing wolf predation on cattle, Bailey adds the following comments on wolves and domestic sheep:

Herded sheep are rarely troubled by wolves, which are kept at a distance by the presence of herders and dogs. Occasionally, however, an unguarded herd is raided and a large number of sheep are killed, but so rarely that in open country sheep men have little fear of wolves in comparison with coyotes and wild-cats. In timbered regions wolves kill more sheep, and small herds are not safe even in pastures unless inclosed [*sic*] with wolf-proof fences. In extensive sections of eastern Texas, Louisiana, and Arkansas, and in the northern parts of Michigan, Wisconsin, and Minnesota, few sheep are raised on account of the abundance of wolves. . . .

Bounties
Bounties, even when excessively high, have proved ineffective in keeping down the wolves, and the more intelligent ranchmen are questioning whether the bounty system pays. In the past ten years Wyoming has paid out in State bounties over $65,000 on wolves alone, and $160,156 on wolves, coyotes, and mountain lions together, and to this must be added larger sums in local and county bounties on the same animals.

In many cases three bounties are paid on each wolf. In the upper

Green River Valley [Wyoming] the local stockmen's association pays a bounty of $10 on each wolf pup, $20 on each grown dog wolf, and $40 on each bitch with pup. Fremont County adds $3 to each of these, and the State of Wyoming $3 more. Many of the large ranchers pay a private bounty of $10 to $20 in addition to the county and State bounty. Governor Bryant B. Brooks, of Wyoming, paid six years ago, on his ranch in Natrona County, $10 each on 50 wolves in one year, and considered it a good investment, since it practically cleared his range of wolves for the time. It invariably happens, however, that when cleared out of one section the wolves are left undisturbed to breed in neighboring sections, and the depleted country is soon restocked.

A floating class of hunters and trappers receive most of the bounty money and drift to the sections where the bounty is highest. If extermination is left to these men it will be a long process. Even some of the small ranch owners support themselves in part from the wolf harvest, and it is not uncommon to hear men boast that they know the location of dens, but are leaving the young to grow up for higher bounty. The frauds which have frequently wasted the funds appropriated for the destruction of noxious animals almost vitiate the wolf programs of some of the States. If bounties resulted in the extermination of the wolves or in an important reduction in their number, the bounty system should be encouraged, but if it merely begets fraud and yields a perpetual harvest for the support of a floating class of citizens, other means should be adopted. . . .

Destruction of Wolves
The methods usually employed for the destruction of wolves are hunting with rifle or with dogs and horses, capturing the young in the dens, trapping, and poisoning.

Hunting. Hunting wolves with dogs and horses has been so fully described by President Roosevelt from his own and his associates' experience that little can be added. For thrilling sport and for a test of skill and nerve it can hardly be excelled, but as a method of destroying wolves it is costly in horseflesh, dogs, and the time of the best riders. Nevertheless, this is often the only method employed by the ranchmen.

In the upper Green River Valley, in April, 1906, the three Alexander brothers showed me the skins of 8 wolves which had been taken the previous fall and winter, in most cases by running with horses. They had bought considerable grain at a high price to keep their horses up and had devoted a good deal of time to the hunt. Near Big Piney the same winter several wolf hunts were organized, on one of which 2 wolves were killed by a party of riders. Occasionally a rider surprises a wolf at close quarters and, if well mounted, overtakes and ropes or shoots it. There are also authentic records of wolves having been shot after being followed all day on soft snow, but few hunters will adopt so tiresome a method.

Ordinary trail hounds are said to drive the wolves out of a section, but the relief afforded is only temporary. The dogs can not catch the wolves, and the wolves sometimes turn and kill a number of the pack. Several packs of Russian wolfhounds and large greyhounds are kept in the Green River Valley, but I could not learn that a wolf had ever been killed by their aid.

Men who have made a business of hunting wolves for the bounty assert that they are usually able to shoot one or both of the old wolves at the den by watching the trails, or hiding near the den early in the morning before the wolves return from the night's round. These statements are fully corroborated by my own experience. While watching dens in Wyoming I could easily have shot the male who was doing sentinel duty; for although he watched from a high point from which he could see a man long before being himself seen, still in his anxiety to decoy me away he often came within rifle range.

Capture of Wolf Pups. In no other way can the number of wolves be kept down so surely and so economically as by destroying the young in the breeding dens. It is now positively known that wolves always pair, at least for the breeding season, and a knowledge of their habits, time of breeding, and customary breeding ground renders it a simple matter to find the dens and secure the pups. The large size of the litters makes this method peculiarly important. The usual number is 8, 9, 10, or 11, and the outside limits 5 and 13. In six dens found in the Green River Valley in March and April, 1906, the young numbered, respectively, 5, 5, 8, 9, 10, and 11. . . .

Location of Dens. In Wyoming, as already said, the wolves do not breed far up in the mountains, but after the breeding season follow the cattle to their summer range in the mountains. The twenty breeding dens located and mapped in the Green River and Wind River valleys were mainly along the foothills of the Wind River and Salt River ranges, while a few were in bad-land ridges out in the open valley. On the Gila

the trap between two tufts of grass or weeds, so that it can be readily approached from one side only.

Use of Scents. Success in trapping depends mainly on the use of scents that will attract the wolves to the neighborhood of a trap and keep them tramping and pawing until caught. Meat bait alone is of little use, for as a rule the wolves kill an ample supply for themselves. Many tests of scents, both prepared baits and various animals musks, have been made with wolves in the field and in the National Zoological Park. While some have given a fair degree of success, others have proved worthless, and no one odor has proved entirely satisfactory. Experiments are being continued, however, and new odors tried.

Beaver musk (castoreum) and the commercial perfumery sold as musk have proved effective in many cases by causing the wolf to turn aside to follow the scented cross line and so walk into the trap. Siberian musk (from the Siberian musk deer) is very attractive to wolves in the Zoo. Oil of anise and oil of rhodium seem to have no attraction for wild wolves, and are scarcely noticed by those in confinement. Asafetida is mildly attractive to wolves and coyotes at the Zoo, but used alone is very slightly, if at all, attractive to those on the range.

Wolf urine taken from the bladder is used by some trappers, and is said to be very successful. It is bottled and kept until rancid and then sprinkled over the trap. The sexual organs of the female wolf immersed in the urine are said to add efficacy to this bait. The urine of the female in the rutting season is said to be especially attractive to males; it should be used in January or February.

Fetid Bait. The bait that has proved most effective may be called, for lack of a better name, fetid bait, because of its offensive odor. It has been long in use in variously modified forms by the most successful wolf trappers, and its preparation is usually guarded as a profound secret. It can not be credited to any one trapper, since no two prepare it in just the same way, but in most cases its fundamental odors are the same. It may be prepared as follows:

Place half a pound of raw beef or venison in a wide-mouthed bottle and let it stand in a warm place (but never in the sun) from two to six weeks or longer or until it is thoroughly decayed and the odor has become as offensive as possible. If the weather is not very warm this may require several months. When decomposition has reached the proper stage, add a quart of sperm oil or some liquid animal oil. Lard oil may be used, but prairie dog oil is better. Add half an ounce of asafetida dissolved in alcohol and one ounce of tincture of Siberian musk, or, if this can not be procured, one ounce of pulverized beaver castor or one ounce of common musk sold for perfumery. Mix thoroughly and bottle securely until used. Apply the scent to the grass, weeds, or ground back of the trap with a stick or straw dipped in the scent, or by pouring from the bottle. A teaspoon should be enough for baiting one trap, but in some cases more may be used to advantage.

1908: *Destruction of Wolves and Coyotes: Results Obtained During 1907*, Vernon Bailey

The year after publishing the above paper, Vernon Bailey wrote a follow-up report that listed the total number of wolves and coyotes killed by forest rangers and other hunters in national forests and nearby federal lands. Bailey noted that the techniques suggested in his previous report had resulted in "a marked increase in the number of wolves destroyed."

Wolves and coyotes cause a loss to the stockmen and farmers of the United States of several millions of dollars annually, and in some of the Northern States they threaten the extermination of deer on many of the best hunting grounds. These losses can be prevented only by intelligent and concerted action throughout the wolf-infested country, and the Biological Survey aims to furnish information that will aid in securing the best results in the war against these pests. Early in 1907 a bulletin and two circulars on wolves were widely distributed in the region where the animals are most destructive. These publications contain brief records of losses from wolves, and directions for finding the dens and capturing the pups, for trapping and poisoning the old wolves, and for building wolf-proof fences. A year has passed since the publications were distributed, and while complete returns giving total results are not at hand, the records received indicate a marked increase in the number of wolves destroyed.

Bounty Records

Wyoming is the only wolf-infested state from which satisfactory bounty records are obtainable. During the year ending October 1, 1906, or previous to the distribution of the wolf circulars, approximately 1,607 wolves were presented for bounty. During the year beginning March 1, 1907, or after the wolf circulars were distributed, 2,035 wolves were presented, showing an increase over the preceding year of 328. . . .

Dates of Breeding and Number of Pups

Of primary importance in the warfare against wolves is a thorough knowledge of their breeding habits, since the location of the dens and capture of the young constitute the most effective means of reducing their numbers. Every record of dens found, with date, age of pups, and character of den, adds to our knowledge of the breeding habits of the animal, makes it easier to find other dens, and stimulates hunters to search for them. . . .

Wyoming

In the spring of 1906, at the instance of the Forest Service and Biological Survey, I visited the upper part of Green River Valley, west of the Wind River Mountains, Wyoming, to investigate the damage done by wolves and study their breeding habits. Four wolf dens containing a total of 32 pups were found, and much interest in locating the dens was aroused among the ranchmen in the valley, first by personal intercourse and later by the distribution of publications.

The following spring (1907) 47 pups were taken by residents from 6 dens—evidently all there were in the valley. In fact, the competition in hunting wolf dens was so keen that all 6 were located by ranchmen before the 2 forest rangers detailed for the purpose got into the valley. Although excellent hunters, the rangers could find no more occupied dens. . . .

Elk As Enemies of Wolves

A statement of great practical significance bearing on the protection of stock from wolves is contained in a manuscript report on elk farming, by George W. Russ, of Eureka Springs, Ark., dated March 7, 1908. Mr. Russ states: "An elk is the natural enemy of dogs and wolves. We suffered great losses to our flock until we learned this fact; since then we have had no losses from this cause. A few elk in a thousand-acre pasture will absolutely protect the flocks therein. Our own dogs are so well aware of the danger in our elk park that they can not be induced to enter it." These observations in connection with the previously published evidence that wolves do not molest elk on their native range suggest an important use for this noblest of our game animals, especially as the domestication and breeding of elk has become an assured success and promises profitable returns.

Wolves and Coyotes Killed In and Near National Forests In 1907
The Forest Service has made vigorous efforts to destroy wolves and other predatory animals on and near the national forests, and through its force of forest rangers has carried on the most systematic and successful war on these pests ever undertaken. Besides the regular force of rangers a number of expert hunters and trappers have been employed in the worst infested regions and gratifying results have been obtained. It must be borne in mind, however, that the areas thus protected are but widely separated spots in a vast extent of wolf country, and unless ranchmen and settlers are stimulated to similar efforts permanent results are not to be expected.

Following is a record of wolves and coyotes killed in 1907, furnished by the Forest Service. [Editor's note: table with list of predators killed in each national forest deleted from this excerpt.] In many cases the records are incomplete or approximate, but they come from widely scattered localities and serve to give an idea of the success of the war against these animals. Numerous bears, mountain lions, bobcats, and other animals also were killed. In making up these reports the supervisors of the various national forests have added to the number of animals killed by forest rangers and hunters employed by the Forest Service those killed in the vicinity of the forests by ranchmen, cowboys, and professional hunters, and in many cases it has been impossible to separate the records. Also in a few cases bounty records for the county have been included. Hence the Forest Service should not be credited with the total number of animals killed.

The capture of 1,723 wolves is reported from 39 national forests, which comprise an area of 72,760 square miles. The surrounding country included may amount to as much more, making an area of about 145,520 square miles to which the reports relate, or about one-tenth of the total area inhabited by wolves in the United States.

The capture of 23,208 coyotes is reported from 77 national forests, which comprise and area of 106,746 square miles. This if doubled to include the surrounding country to which the reports also refer makes an area of approximately 213,492 square miles, or about one-ninth of that inhabited by coyotes in the United States.

1915: United States Senate Debate on Funding Wolf Control Projects

As shown in the previous papers by Bailey, by 1907 the USBS had taken an active role in advising the U.S. Forest Service on the best methods of eradi-

cating wolves and other predators on federal land. The Survey's involvement in predator control escalated in 1914 when Congress appropriated $115,000 to the agency for wildlife research. Part of that appropriation funded "experiments and demonstrations in destroying wolves."

The following year, Congress authorized a much larger budget for the USBS and ordered the agency to start its own program of wolf control on public lands. Now, instead of just advising others, the Bureau would direct the final solution to the wolf problem. On February 25, 1915, the U.S. Senate debated the issue of funding a Biological Survey wolf-control program. The following excerpts from that budgetary debate reveal the thinking behind Congress' decision to commit the federal government to the mission of wolf extermination.

Originally, the Senate's proposed 1916 fiscal year (July 1, 1915–June 30, 1916) budget allocated $100,000 to the Biological Survey for research into "the food habits of North American birds and mammals," rodent eradication programs, and wolf and coyote control "experiments and demonstrations." The first portion of the Senate debate discussed increasing the budget for predator control operations. The Secretary of Agriculture requested $110,000 for all of the programs listed above. Some Senators wanted to triple that requested amount so that more money would be available for killing wolves and coyotes.

Because the debate swung back and forth between unrelated topics, I have made some minor rearrangements in sequence in order to better show the development of arguments for predator control.

The VICE PRESIDENT. The next amendment [to the 1916 federal budget for the Biological Survey] passed over was, on page 54, line 19, after the word "marten," to strike out the sum "$100,000" and in lieu thereof in insert "$300,000," so as to read:

For investigation the food habits of North American birds and mammals in relation to agriculture, horticulture, and forestry, including experiments and demonstrations in destroying wolves, coyotes, prairie dogs, and other animals injurious to agriculture and animal husbandry, and for investigations and experiments in connection with rearing of fur-bearing animals, including mink and marten, $300,000. . . .

MR. THOMPSON [Kansas]. I hope the committee amendment will not prevail in this instance. It must strike everyone familiar with this item that, to say the least, the amount is extremely extravagant in view of the other appropriations made in the bill. It should be borne in mind that he amount heretofore appropriated for this purpose has never exceeded $115,000 in any bill of this character; $110,000 is all that the department has asked for this year, and it is the amount fixed by the other House, but it has been increased by the committee $190,000. In comparison with the other items in the bill of greater importance, it does seem to me that the amount is extremely extravagant. Conditions in this country at the present time are certainly such as to justify economy in appropriations. If there is any place in the bill where we can resort to a little economy, it is in items of this character. . . .

The largeness of the proposed increase so challenged my attention that I directed a letter to the Secretary of Agriculture to ascertain whether there was any necessity for this great increase, and received the following reply:

I have your letter of February 15 regarding the item in the Agricultural appropriation bill . . . for investigating the food habits of North American birds and mammals in relation to agriculture, etc., including experiments and demonstrations in destroying wolves, coyotes, prairie dogs, etc. . . . The department has already made excellent progress in its investigations of the best methods of destroying predatory animals, especially wolves and coyotes, which are so destructive to livestock. . . . Experiments and demonstrations for controlling wolves and other predacious animals have been inaugurated in Texas, Colorado, Idaho, and Nevada. The amount carried in the House bill of $110,000 covers the estimate submitted for the work, and the department does not desire to change its recommendations in the matter at this time.

Very truly, yours,
D. F. Houston, Secretary.

It does seem to me that when the department which is charged with the expenditure of this money for this purpose is asking only for $110,000, which amount in itself seems sufficient, the Senate ought not to increase the appropriation to such an extravagant figure, and I hope the amendment will not prevail. . . .

MR. GRONNA [North Dakota]. I desire to ask the Senator from Kansas if it was not shown to the committee that upwards of $15,000,000 worth of animals were being destroyed annually by wolves and coyotes and other predatory animals, and if that was not the reason why this appropriation was increased?

MR. THOMPSON. There was some statement or some resolution of that character presented; but the Secretary of Agriculture, who has this matter in charge, says that he can get along, do the necessary work, protect the live stock, and prevent injury with $110,000. It does seem to me that is a sufficient amount.

MR. GRONNA. Is it not a fact that we had before us concurrent resolutions from the Legislature of the State of Oregon, calling attention to the great number of animals that were being killed every year in the Western States by wolves and coyotes and other predatory animals?

MR. THOMPSON. There were some resolutions of that character it is true; but I believe that the cattle in these States will be just as fully protected with the amount asked by the department as with a larger amount which is evidently not needed.

MR. WARREN. Mr. President—

MR. GRONNA. The Senator from Wyoming, of course, knows more about this matter than I do, and I will be glad to yield to him.

MR. WARREN. . . . we are expending from $12,000,000 to $15,000,000 to eradicate the foot-and-mouth disease, to protect those who are growing cattle, and, what is more to the point, to protect the meat supply and consumers who are those most interested.

Now, so far as the foot-and-mouth disease is concerned, the Government is under no specific or special obligation, except that for the best interests of the public and for the protection of a great product it is deemed expedient that the Government should enter this field and do its share of the work. Take the other side of the question: We have now reached the point where it is claimed—and the claim is very well backed up by argument—that we will lose enormously in live stock because of predatory animals, not of course from prairie dogs and animals of that kind, but from wolves and coyotes, and in connection with this loss and in contradistinction to the losses from foot-and-mouth disease, the Government is directly responsible to the greatest degree if it permits such destruction by wolves and other predatory animals to continue. The Government owns and controls over 200,000,000 acres of land carved out and segregated in United States reservations in the various States. Half, or more than half, of the State from which I come [Wyoming], two-thirds of the adjoining States, and from a quarter to three-quarters of some other States are embraced in various national reservations. The Government is maintaining those great areas, which amount to a large section of the United States, and which practically furnish the breeding grounds for wild animals, which come from there out onto the lands of the settlers and destroy their stock. Now, the United States Government pays no taxes to the States or municipalities. The States make liberal appropriations for the extermination of these wild beasts. They make very large appropriations from State funds; the counties make further appropriations, and live-stock associations and individuals contribute large sums for the destruction of these pests; but, meanwhile, they are surrounded by these United States forests, and so we can spend millions of dollars and hardly make a mark in eradicating these animals, since the Government had taken these great areas, has barred all outsiders, and allows such animals to breed.

Everyone who knows anything about forestry and the western country knows that there is the breeding ground for all the predatory animals. Is it fair that the Government should take the larger part of a State and take the money of cattle and sheep men for pasturage there in those reservations and not properly protect that pasturage against a pest which the States and the people around the reserves are engaged in destroying?

The States have made large appropriations for the purpose. For instance, here are the annual appropriations of a few of them: The State of Montana, $178,047 in one year. And, by the way, these figures merely show what the State itself pays; but counties, associations, and individual stock growers also pay large additional amounts. Indeed, associations pay very large amounts for the same purpose. Texas spends $88,930; Oregon, fifty-two thousand and some odd dollars; Utah, over $54,000; and so on down the list of other Western States, some paying much more and some a little less. . . .

It is said that the department has not asked for quite so much money. That is true; and the department, I am glad to say—I support it therein— so far as I have information, confined its estimates to what was allowed in the appropriation bill of the year before. There is always difficulty in getting the first appropriation for even a small amount. There is twice as much said against it; and all that the department says now is that it has made that certain estimate, and it does not add to it.

In the destroying work that has already been carried on for the last five years in those little restricted areas, it is reported that between 35,000 and 36,000 animals have been destroyed. Over 1,000 were the gray and black wolves, and those who know them know how many farm animals they destroy. They do not stop to eat an animal. They simply throw it down, take its blood, and go on and bring down another. I have known one wolf to destroy scores of young stock, cattle or sheep, in a night. . . .

MR. JONES [Washington]. As I understand, heretofore this appropriation bill has carried an appropriation of this kind providing for experiments and demonstrations in destroying wolves. Now, what have they accomplished? What have they shown to be the best methods of destroying wolves, or have they made any demonstrations at all?

MR. WARREN. I have just stated what the result has been as to destroying these animals and as to the experiments. They have performed their own experiments, and are working under them.

MR. JONES. I do not understand that this appropriation is simply for the purpose of killing wolves. It is for experimenting and demonstrating the best methods of doing it.

MR. WARREN. Oh, Mr. President, of course that is a technicality that the Senator, if he reads the appropriation, will understand may not have particular place there. It is, in the first instance, for the establishment of a system, and in the next for destroying the wild animals; because as I say, with a small appropriation and in a restricted area the agents of the department have destroyed up into between thirty and forty thousand. . . .

MR. FALL [New Mexico]. If the Senator will allow me for just one moment to make a statement along the lines of his statement, in New Mexico, for instance, we have 11,000,000 acres in reserves, and we can not go upon them to demonstrate the knowledge which we gain by experience in killing these animals. We must leave it to the Government. The consequence is, as the Senator has said, that the reserves themselves are the breeding grounds for these animals. The matter has reached such proportions, I may say to the Senator from Kansas, that the State Department of the United States Government has taken up the matter with foreign Governments. The State Department of this Government has taken up this very question of the destruction of predatory animals with the Mexican Government and with the different governors of the northern States of Mexico because so much destruction was being continually caused by the depredations of these animals in the Southwestern States and along the border.

The Senator is absolutely correct. The breeding grounds for the animals are the Government reserves. In New Mexico we are spending $100,000 or $200,000 a year in the attempt to destroy those animals that are breeding and the stock of which is being continually renewed upon the forest reserves, upon which we can not go. . . .

MR. WARREN. . . . I do not stand here pleading for any one interest alone. It is, of course, to the interest of the live-stock growers that the Government shall protect those from whom it gets money through leases of forest reserves, and those around them who pay the taxes, while the Government pays none, in the States; but the great final trouble lies in the question of the meat supply of this country, which must be rapidly diminishing, as shown by the increased price. The [livestock] societies have sent in the most urgent appeals on this subject, and the legislatures the same way. I send to the desk and ask to have the Secretary read senate joint memorial No. 1, adopted by the State of Oregon, on this subject.

The Presiding Officer (Mr. Myers in the chair). In the absence of objection, the Secretary will read as requested.

The Secretary read as follows:

Senate joint memorial No. 1
Memorial to the Congress of the United States of America petitioning the United States Government to appropriate $300,000 for suppressing carnivorous wild animals destructive to live stock in the public-land States of the West.

To the honorable Senate and House of Representatives of the Congress of the United States:

Your memorialists, the governor and Legislature of the State of Oregon, respectfully represent that—

Whereas in the Western States, known as the public-land States, the losses of live stock and poultry, due to the attacks of coyotes, wolves, wildcats, cougars, and bears, amount to not less than $15,000,000 annually; and

Whereas in these western public-land States the State, county, and stockmen do now, and have for years, paid large bounties and used other means to bring about the eradication of these carnivorous animals; and Whereas in these western public-land States there is now withdrawn from settlement in some form or other approximately 225,000,000 acres of Federal land, which land constitutes the principal breeding ground and refuge of these carnivorous wild animals, and enables them to increase their numbers in spite of the efforts made by the State, county, and stockmen to exterminate them; Now, therefore, be it

Resolved, That the Legislature of the State of Oregon does hereby most respectfully urge and request that Congress immediately appropriate the sum of $300,000, to be used by the United States Department of Agriculture for the destruction of coyotes, wolves, wildcats, cougars, and bears in these western public-land States in order that the meat supply of the Nation may be increased and the proper development of the West encouraged.

Adopted by the house January 13, 1915.

Ben Selling,
Speaker of the House.

Adopted by the Senate, January 13, 1915.

W. Lair Thompson,
President of the Senate.

MR. SMITH of Arizona. If the Senator will permit me right at that point, I will say that the Legislature of Arizona also passed a memorial at the last session very much like that. . . . I would like to say to the Senate . . . that the people of Arizona living on the edges of these forest reserves are losing enormous amounts of property through the depredations of these animals. They have no right, however, to invade these forest reserves in great numbers and protect themselves. It seems to me that it is absolutely incumbent on the part of the Government, as the Senator is arguing, to give relief to these cases.

MR. WARREN. Mr. President, I ask to have inserted in the Record, without reading, a short article in the Country Gentleman referring to exactly what we have had under consideration.

S. W. McClure's article, "The Wolf at the Stockman's Door—Sheep and Cattle Killers Breed in the National Reserves," is placed in the *Congressional Record.*

MR. THOMAS [Colorado]. Mr President, I sympathize very much with the views of the Senator from Kansas [Mr. Thompson] regarding this amendment. . . . Mr. President, why should the Government of the United States appropriate this enormous sum of money at this time for the purposes of investigating the food habits of North American birds and mammals, of destroying wolves, coyotes, prairie dogs, and other animals injurious to agriculture and animal husbandry. . . . All of these things may be important in themselves and yet all of them directly concern the States where these animals are found and where these investigations are to be made. . . . I look with some apprehension upon the constant tendency of the States in these days not only to shirk their responsibilities, but to do so with alacrity, and insist that the National Government shall exercise functions with which they are properly clothed and which they only should exercise. . . .

I am aware, Mr. President, of the fact that the forest reserves have eliminated a large amount of territory in the Western States from the jurisdiction of the State governments and that they are supervised, superintended, controlled, inspected, examined, dissected, and guarded by a large army of Government employees at the expense of the Public Treasury. We have just appropriated, or will appropriate in this bill, over five and a half million dollars for the care of our forest reserves. If it is true, as here asserted, that they have become safety places for the predatory animals of the region, which can not be attacked or exterminated by the State authorities, it is very easy to provide in the bill that the forest rangers and the inspectors and supervisors and assistant supervisors and deputy assistant supervisors and deputy inspectors and the other members and attachés of that army of employees who bask in the sunshine of the civil service be required to devote a part of their valuable time in exterminating these animals. . . . Why should they not be destroyed without this extra appropriation, all of which means additional agents and representatives of the Government to carry out this work? If this bill passes, we will have a superintendent of coyote destruction and a supervisor of prairie dogs and a bureau of investigation on fur-bearing animals, together with assistants, deputy assistants, and stenographers, with the result that this $300,000 will be expended in the making of investigations accompanied by voluminous reports that will be laid upon our desks at the next session, but which none of us will ever read. . . .

. . . we ought to find something for these forest inspectors and rangers, and so forth, to do. Let us charge them with the duty either of expelling or exterminating these predatory animals that are said now to find a refuge and haven of safety within the borders of the forest reserves. . . . We can get at it through the Forest Service if it is good for anything. We can require them to do it and then we can determine by the result whether they are or are not good for anything.

I think, Mr. President, under the circumstances the addition of $190,000 in this item should not at this time be made. I very much question whether the sum of $110,000 is not, under the circumstances, extravagant. I hope the committee amendment therefore will not be agreed to.

MR. MYERS [Montana]. . . . I do not believe there is an appropriation provided for in this bill which is more worthy and meritorious or more founded on reason than this item and this increase of the amount appropriated over the amount estimated by the Agricultural Department. I believe that this appropriation and the increase recommended has substantial merit back of it, which should appeal to Members of this body and to the people of the whole country—to the entire United States. I am sorry to see Senators on this side from great agricultural and stock-raising States oppose this increase, not that I think it will be especially beneficial in any discriminatory way to their States or to the West or to any particular part of the country, for I believe here is an appropriation that is beneficial not alone to any one section of the country, not to any one class of people, but to the whole country and to all the people. . . .

The Senator from Colorado [Mr. Thomas], for whom I have the very highest esteem for his ability and sincerity, seems to have a nightmare of fear that this Government is going to put on a vast army of officials and employees every time a new appropriation is brought before this body. . . .

There is, seriously speaking, nothing in this item, neither in the original appropriation nor in the proposed increase, that provides for any inspectors or clerks or bureau officers or any increase of officials or employees whatever. I do not believe that is contemplated. I do not believe there is any reason to apprehend that it will require any more than are now required to administer the expenditure of this fund.

I regard this as a most serious and important matter. I believe that one of the greatest benefits which can be conferred upon the people of the United States is to reduce or at least to keep down the ever-increasing price of meat. The price of meat to the consumer in this country has become a serious matter. The time has come when meat is almost beyond the reach of the ordinary laboring man in this country at the price at which it is retailed. . . . Indeed it may be classed with jewelry in price but not in need. . . . I say if the Congress of the United States by any legislation or by making a small appropriation or by increasing an appropriation can do anything to keep down the price of meat, it will confer a boon upon the people of this country that can not and will not be surpassed by anything else that Congress may do. . . .

. . . For many years past the number of cattle in this country has been steadily diminishing and the price of meat has steadily gone onward and upward. I believe one of the most serious duties that confronts this country—not only the Government of the country, but the citizens themselves—is to induce and bring about a larger meat supply in the country.

I am glad to see from statistics recently given out by the Agricultural Department that last year there were a slight number more of cattle in this country than there were the year before; that there was a slight increase. If we can encourage that increase and cause the increase to continue it is bound to result in good to the people of this country, to the consumers of meat; and in what better way can we encourage it, in what better way can we promote it or bring it about, than by stopping the useless destruction of millions of dollars' worth of live stock in the country every year by predatory wild animals, by wild beasts? Every calf, every sheep, every head of live stock that is destroyed by one of these animals of prey is simply that much taken away from the people of the country. It is meat destroyed that might be consumed by some workingman, by some citizen, and would go to supply food to the people of the country, to make brain and brawn for our workers. These animals destroy millions of dollars' worth of live stock every year. Is it not our duty, is it not a plain and manifest duty, to address ourselves to that subject and stop it, if it may be stopped, and thereby keep the wolf away from the door, as might be suggested? . . .

It is not a sectional provision. Its benefits will be felt by all the people of the country. It is not especially for the benefit of stock growers, but is more for the benefit of the great number of people in this country who do not raise live stock but consume meat. . . .

I believe the increase [in the appropriation] ought to be made. I believe there is good ground for it, and I hope it will be made. It will be money well expended. It will furnish meat to hungry mouths. By it we can feed the hungry. Let no child go hungry for meat if we can help it.

Later in the debate, Senator Jones of Washington suggested that the bill specifically mandate that the Biological Survey spend a minimum amount of money on predator-control projects:

MR. JONES. Mr. President, what I really want to emphasize is this: If we are to make an additional appropriation, then we ought to provide specifically for the use of a certain amount of it for the purposes that we want served, because if you do not do that you will have a great part of the money used, just as surely as you appropriate it, for experiments with reference to mink, marten, and other fur-bearing animals and investigating the food habits of North American birds; you will not serve the purpose everyone here has in mind, which is the destruction of wolves, coyotes, and other predatory animals which destroy the valuable animals of the settlers and of those who are trying to furnish a food supply for the people of the country. . . .

I am in favor of appropriating money for the destruction of these animals, but I am not in favor of increasing this appropriation by a large sum of money and leaving it to the discretion of these officials to be used under the general terms of this clause in the bill. Those who want predatory animals destroyed ought to provide for their destruction, and we ought to so frame the law that the money will be used for that very purpose.

Near the end of the debate, Senator Thomas raises a question that challenges a basic assumption made by proponents of the bill. Much of their argument was founded on the concept that predators were breeding prolifically on federal lands and that private citizens were prohibited from going onto those lands for the purpose of killing predators. As Vernon Bailey's previous reports demonstrated, forest rangers were killing large numbers of predators in the national forests. In addition, no federal law prohibited the hunting and trapping of predators on the national forests. To put it mildly, most of these senators didn't know what they were talking about. The following exchange between Senators Thomas and Jones shows this ignorance:

MR. JONES. . . . I do not suppose the citizens outside of the reserves can go on the forest reserves and kill these animals in order to get these bounties. That is the principal evil complained of by the Senator from Wyoming [Mr. Warren] and the senior Senator from Montana [Mr. Myers]—that these forest reserves are a sort of harbor or refuge, and that the ordinary citizen of the State can not get at these animals on the reserves, whether the bounty is large or small.

MR. THOMAS. Mr. President, does the Senator understand that a citizen is prohibited from going upon a forest reserve for the purpose of killing a predatory animal? I do not understand that the regulations go to that extent. I know they are innumerable and are designed to cover almost every element of human activity, but I do not believe there is any such prohibition as that.

MR. JONES. I do not know what all their prohibitions are, but I think they are so many and so uncertain that most citizens would not run the risk of going on there to hunt these coyotes and wolves.

MR. THOMAS. It may be, but I do not believe the regulations have extended to that subject and excluded the inhabitants of the respective States from hunting game during the open season, or at any time killing these animals that are inimical to civilization.

MR. JONES. Of course the Senator understands that on some of these reserves, I think, they have some regulations that, if strictly construed, would not permit us to go on at all without a permit.

MR. THOMAS. It may be. I am prepared for information going to any extent upon that subject, but I do not believe the subject has been covered specifically.

MR. JONES. At any rate, that has been the basis of the argument that has been presented here to-day—the fact that these reserves constitute a harbor of refuge for these animals.

MR. THOMAS. Yes; that is the reason why I asked the question. It has been assumed here that such was the case.

MR. JONES. I know that they have a great many regulations and they are very restrictive, and I would not be surprised to find that by a technical enforcement of their regulations they could pretty nearly prevent a person from going on there with a gun for almost any purpose, except to follow along certain trails or lines to get across.

Senator Thomas's pertinent questions about the validity of a major argument for the bill were ignored and the amended budget resolution passed the Senate by a vote of forty-three yeas to fifteen nays. Senators Thomas (Colorado) and Thompson (Kansas) voted against it. In the bill's final version, a clause was added to insure that at least $125,000 (28 percent of the total budget of the USBS) be specifically devoted to wolf and coyote control:

For investigating the food habits of North American birds and mammals in relation to agriculture, horticulture, and forestry, including experiments and demonstrations in destroying wolves, coyotes, prairie dogs, and other animals injurious to agriculture and animal husbandry, and for investigations and experiments in connection with rearing of fur-bearing animals, including mink and marten, $280,000. *Provided . . .* that of this sum, not less that $125,000 shall be used on the National forests and the public domain in destroying wolves, coyotes, and other animals injurious to agriculture and animal husbandry.

🐺 1916: "The Wolf Question and What the Government Is Doing to Help," Wallis Huidekoper

Senator Myers' assertion that the predator control program conducted in the western states by the Biological Survey would not result in "any increase of officials or employees whatever" soon proved false. The agency hired three hundred professional hunters and trappers and stationed them throughout the western states. By 1928, five hundred men were doing predator control work for the USBS.

On April 18, 1916, Wallis Huidekoper, vice-president of the American

National Live Stock Association, gave a speech at the annual convention of the Montana Stock Growers' Association on "the wolf question." Huidekoper enthusiastically reviewed the progress the Biological Survey had made with its "corps of hunter-trappers" during the first year of its campaign against predators and then added his thoughts on the outcome of that campaign: "I predict a successful war." His speech shows the ranchers' view of the USBS's work and the close cooperation that existed between livestock associations and the Survey.

Members of the Montana Stock Growers' Association, Ladies and Gentlemen: I spoke to you last year about what had been accomplished in the state legislature by the enactment of new bills for the protection and benefit of the live-stock industry in Montana. These laws have now been in force over a year, and the results are most beneficial. At this meeting I want to give you a little talk on the wolf question, and to tell you what is being done by the federal government in an effort to destroy these pests.

An appropriation by Congress, at the session a year ago, allowed an expenditure of $125,000 by the Biological Survey of the Department of Agriculture for the destruction of predatory animals within the national forests and on the public domain. The question had been strongly brought to the attention of the department through the American National Live Stock Association. It was made plain that great efforts were being made to rid the West of wolves, coyotes, and mountain lions, at heavy expense, which was being borne by individuals, associations, and states. The argument was used that the newly created forest reserves were harboring, and being used as breeding-places by predatory wild animals, and that the government should take some part, and assume its share of the expense, in an organized effort to exterminate these animals. A committee of three (of which I am a member) was appointed at the San Francisco meeting of the American National Live Stock Association, in March, 1915. This committee was to confer with the government officials and encourage these appropriations, as well as make practical suggestions as to the best means of working in order to accomplish the greatest results at the least practicable cost. This work is now being carried on over the entire West; but it is the destruction of these animals within our own state that is of most interest to us.

As the time for preparations was short, and as the federal authorities wished to act as quickly as possible, they decided that the best results could be obtained by employing trappers to work through the winter just passed, and to hunt out dens this spring.

As in the case of all new organizations, errors in judgment will occur, the wrong men be employed, and other mistakes happen, so that the results this first year are not what they should be, and are considerably less than what can reasonably be expected in the future, It is, however, a great stride in the right direction, and we are pleased to have accomplished this beginning. I predict a successful war, with the federal government, the state, and individuals working together for the extermination of these animals.

There never has been any organized effort or preconceived methods or system adopted to rid the ranges of these depredations. Large bounties have been offered by cattle and horse companies, and by individuals, for the past thirty years, for wolves killed on their ranges; but what has been the result? The cowboys kill a few, and the renegade wolves are temporarily run out of that particular country to some adjoining range where no bounty is offered.

Mange has been inoculated into coyotes, and results have been claimed; but I can find no very authentic assurances of the success of this method. In my opinion, the only reliable plan is to wage continuous war with traps, guns, and poison, and to supplement these by the destruction of dens in the spring of the year. This may only be accomplished by united effort; and, to get that, we must have a strong and positive organization. The United States Department of Agriculture has Dr. A. K. Fisher in charge of investigations by the Biological Survey, and Mr. S. E. Piper has entire charge of the work in the field. Both of these gentlemen are well fitted for their positions. They have their hearts in the work, and are untiring in their efforts for good results.

In carrying out the campaign against predatory animals injurious to live stock, they have divided the worst-infested area inhabited by wolves and coyotes into nine districts, as follows: Oregon and Washington; Idaho; Utah; Wyoming; Nevada and California; Colorado; Arizona and New Mexico; and Texas. Each of these districts is in charge of a competent inspector, who has under him a corps of hunter-trappers. These men, for the most part, have been recommended by the Forest Service officers and officers of live-stock associations. If, after a reasonable trial, they do not get results, they are replaced by more promising men. They are paid a flat salary of $75 a month, which later may be increased by an allowance for equipment and horses. These men must turn in all skins as government property, and they are not allowed to receive bounties from any source. A good hunter can make more money by the salary system than by collecting bounties and skins. It is conceded that during a few months in the year skins and bounties will bring a little more money, but during the long period from April to November they get practically no returns.

It is a well-known fact that stock-killing individuals among wolves are only a small proportion of their kind inhabiting a given area. Moreover, these stock-killing individuals are the most wary and cunning of their kind in shunning traps and hunters, as nearly all of them are survivors of continued campaigns for their destruction. It, therefore, requires a more persistent and well-studied plan to secure them, thus taking a much longer time for the destruction of each renegade animal. By adopting the plan of operating chiefly against stock-killers, a dozen or more animals may cost more than a hundred captured by the bounty system. A bounty hunter traps in areas where predatory animals are most numerous, regardless of whether they interfere with stock or not; and when he has killed the least wary of the animals, and reduced the numbers to a point where large catches are no longer possible, he moves to another locality, leaving the more destructive and wary animals to continue their depredations.

Montana is one of the nine districts mentioned, and the work in this territory is in charge of Mr. R. E. Bateman. The available appropriation of $125,000 had been divided among the nine districts, Montana receiving $11,000 as her share. With this amount we now have sixteen trappers working, which number will soon be increased to twenty-one, and they will be kept employed until after the wolves remove their pups from the dens. As I have stated, big results should not be expected the first year. During the first part of the winter just passed Montana had only nine trappers as her proportion, and several of these were not provided with sufficient traps. However, the results the first few months were the killing of 6 wolves, 204 coyotes, and 22 bobcats, at a total cost of $4,059, or an average of $17.50 per animal. This is of course, too expensive a business on this basis, but I am confident it will adjust itself; in fact, later advices give much better results, and a good many wolf dens have been found and the pups killed.

The great consideration is that we have the government started in this work. Another strong feature is that all animals killed are appropriated by the United States. Montana, through her stockmen, is not called upon to contribute one cent of bounty on these animals. Thus our bank accounts are considerably protected.

While speaking of protecting our bank accounts, I want to tell you how successfully a law, which our Association helped to pass last winter, has worked out. You will recall that prior to last year a tax of four mills was levied on all live stock, and of this four mills, three and one-mills was for bounties. Under the terms of the bill passed last winter, the levy on live stock is reduced to three mills, and of this only one and a half mills may be used for bounties. We are, therefore, called upon to pay only one and a half mills on Montana's live stock valued at $46,000,000, instead of three and a half mills heretofore assessed for bounties; and this means a savings on bounties of $92,000. You will also be pleased to know that the state has sufficient money to meet all claims.

In the year just passed there have been turned in for bounty 20,997 coyotes and 11,118 coyote pups, 702 gray wolves and 383 wolf pups, and 61 mountain lions. On these scalps must be paid $108,629. To meet this, we have a tax on live stock amounting to $69,354, and we receive an income from the tax on liquor licenses, available for bounty purposes, of $38,448, making a total of $107,802, or just about enough to break even. Just how we will replace this income from liquor when good old Montana goes dry I have not figured out, but I hope that by that time we shall have fewer wolves to pay for.

From the bounty figures of the last few years it is interesting to note that the coyotes are about holding their own; that is, we are paying on about the same number each year. The number of bounties on gray wolves was 192 less for 1915 than for 1914; also the number of wolf pups was 223 less. Mountain lions have, on the other hand, apparently increased. . . .

Appropriate resolutions have been adopted by the American National Live Stock Association and other live-stock organizations, expressing their confidence in the work of the Biological Survey, and asking Congress for a continued appropriation, so that the good work may continue. I would strongly urge that this Association also adopt a resolution along this line. . . .

In closing, I quote from a letter received from Dr. A. K. Fisher, who is in charge of the work of the Biological Survey. He says: "I may be considered too optimistic, but I believe that in three years, if allowed to take our course under an intensive campaign, with the support of Congress, we shall have practically exterminated the big wolf from the Rocky Mountain region, and the coyotes so reduced that the damage to the live stock will be merely nominal." (Applause.)

At the conclusion of his talk, Huidekoper read a resolution passed at the Annual Convention of the American National Live Stock Association, held at El Paso in January 1916. The resolution called for increasing the budget *of the Biological Survey's predator control program from $125,000 to $500,000:*

> Whereas, The work carried on under the direction of the Biological Survey during the past year gives promise of being the most practical and economical method of handling the predatory-wild-animal problem; therefore be it
>
> Resolved, That the American National Live Stock Association urges Congress to appropriate the sum of $500,000 for the continuation and maintenance of this work on the forest reserves and public lands of the United States.

Huidekoper described the results of the Biological Survey's first year of work in its Montana District. The following eight selections from USBS reports document the progress of the wolf control campaign in the states of Arizona and New Mexico.

1916: *Annual Report, Predatory Animal Control, New Mexico–Arizona District, U.S. Bureau of Biological Survey*, J. Stokley Ligon

In 1915 the Biological Survey appointed J. Stokley Ligon as the first "Predatory Animal Inspector," of the New Mexico–Arizona district and gave him a budget of $20,000. In this position, Ligon, the son of a Texas sheep rancher, supervised all of the Bureau's predator work in the Southwest Region. On frequent occasions, he went out into the field and trapped notorious wolves that his men were unable to kill. The annual reports written by Ligon and his successors offer a vivid insider's picture of the early days of the Biological Survey's war against the wolf. In this selection from his first annual report, Ligon describes how he started the predator control program in his district and how he supervised his hunters. Then, like any good bureaucrat, he uses dollar figures to estimate, to the penny, how much money his agency saved the ranchers of his region. Ending with a plea for continued funding, he guarantees success in "our fight against the wolves."

> Since the work for the year has been largely an experiment with hunters, I have as might be expected, had some hunters that have made very poor records; but such hunters have now been culled out until the following year will see little, if any, of this discredit attached to the work, as I now have the responsible and irresponsible men fairly well divided. Much better results may be expected from even the best of the hunters in the future as all are improving their records under this sys-

tem of organization, and organization and personal instruction have been greatly aided in the District by the appointment to it of an Assistant Inspector, giving, either the Inspector or Assistant much more freedom in the field. For the best of results, I find that it is absolutely necessary that an experienced hunter be constantly mixing with the hunters, instructing and encouraging them in their work.

The first Predatory Animal Hunter was employed in the District in September, 1915—September 1, and the number was increased as suitable men could be located. The number that worked during the month of June was 24. During the year a total of 32 hunters have worked.

The work has been confined mostly to the State of New Mexico because there are more destructive animals in this state and also because the most complaint of damage being done is made here, although my plan is to extend the work into Arizona more freely in the future. The work has been directed, largely, against wolves as these do the greatest damage and with the limited funds at command, I felt that the best showing could be made by concentrating efforts against these.

Damage by Wolves

Wolves are well distributed over the state of New Mexico and a portion of Arizona. At present, they seem to be most abundant in that portion of New Mexico that lies West of the Rio Grande in the northwest portion of the state. Although, until recently, little complaint came from the region from the fact that these wolves have confined their depredations mostly to the Mustang horses that have been rather abundant throughout this entire region.

I think it a very conservative estimate when I place the number of adult gray wolves in New Mexico, at the close of the Fiscal Year at 300. If each of these old wolves averaged the killing of three (3) cattle, anywhere from calves to grown stock, or their equivalent in horses or sheep per month, which is also a moderate estimate, [this] means that each of these wolves gets 36 head of stock a year, or a total of 10,800 head per year. Valuing these stock at $30.00 per head we find that it costs the huge sum of $324,000 annually to feed this wolf pack alone. Contrast these figures with the sum [Stokley's own budget] that is appropriated with which to fight them. In support of these figures I desire to state that on the range of the V-T CattleCompany alone the loss in 10,000 head of cattle per year from wolves has been from 600 to 1,000 head per year according to my own estimation and that of the managers and others who know the conditions in this range. The V-T range lies in the Datil and Gila National Forests in western New Mexico, and is under the management of Mr. Cole Railston, Magdalena, New Mexico. I have many other figures that prove the great loss the wolves cause, but owing to the fact that wolves range over such vast areas their killing is not noticed so much as if it were confined to smaller areas; but it is a well known fact that wolves not only eat meat almost constantly—cattle, horses or sheep, but they eat the very best obtainable and generally want it fresh. If it costs $1,080.00 each to keep these wolves for a year's time, our record of 33 wolves for the year means a saving of $35,640.00 to the ranchmen of the state.

Cooperation

Ranchmen can do a great deal in the way of cooperation with very little effort on their part, and give the work immediate aid, and I am getting this fact impressed upon them as rapidly as possible. The greatest draw back [*sic*] is the conflict that arises between bounty hunters and Government wolf hunters, and I am of the opinion that the cattlemen will remove this trouble within the next six months. The hunters also need protection from disinterested persons and especially from sheep herders. There is hardly a hunter but who has lost from one to a half dozen traps as well as quite a lot of animals. In many locations the warning notices are torn down as fast as they can be put up, but I am of the opinion that this is mostly the work of Mexicans. As a general thing when a sheep or sheep dog is caught in a trap the trap is carried away or broken to pieces.

I desire to acknowledge here, with appreciation, the great amount of aid given the work by the Forest Department, without which the work could not have been nearly so successful as it has been.

The ranchmen, and especially the cattlemen, have given the work their approval and support. The various Cattle Raisers Associations of the country have given our methods much attention and publicity.

I have made the statement, and with the greatest of faith, that if we are given proper cooperation by ranchers in our fight against the wolves, with a reasonable amount of funds with which to bear the expense, that the wolf will have ceased to be a menace, in three year's time from the beginning of operations against him.

1917: *Annual Report, Predatory Animal Control, New Mexico–Arizona District, U.S. Bureau of Biological Survey*, J. Stokley Ligon

In Ligon's second annual report, he relates "with a certain amount of pride" and "with pleasure" the success the Biological Survey has had in killing off

wolves in New Mexico and Arizona. Ligon estimates that the two states
now contained only 140 wolves. In a later paragraph, Ligon describes the
characteristics a government wolf hunter should possess in order to success-
fully fulfill his mission:

It is with a certain amount of pride that I submit this, my second annual report, realizing, however, that the most important part of the
work is yet to be accomplished. While we have not carried on the wolf
work so extensively in Arizona as we have in the State of New Mexico,
we have done some good services in Arizona, and it is with pleasure
that I state that it is my belief that at least fifty per cent reduction in the
damage done by wolves has been accomplished in New Mexico, during the last twelve months. I give credit of this good showing on these
animals to a few trained and faithful hunters. The efforts of the Inspector are, practically, powerless without the aid of efficient hunters, especially is this so in the case of wolf, mountain lion and bear work. My
estimate is that there are not more than 70 adult gray wolves in the
State of New Mexico, at the present time, and perhaps the same number in Arizona. In the case of Arizona, we have not made so close a
study and are, therefore, not able to give an accurate census. While the
running down of the renegade wolves will require some time yet we are
gradually strengthening our system of control to the point where the
getting of these animals actually becomes, not a question at all, but a
method with a little time only as a consideration.

Getting the larger predatory wild animals is a line of work that has
many peculiar phases. In no other work can I realize the importance
of efficiency of each individual, so much. In no other work is there so
much peculiar fascination, yet none that calls for so rare a type of
physical and mental manhood, rendering applicants, who can truly
make a success, few. Wild animals have been hard to bring under control in the Rocky Mountain Region and the vast forests of the North,
because, first, no organized system of operations were employed, and
second, because an iron constitution, and great sacrifice of personal
privileges, in many cases, must be the requirements exacted. Not only
is hard labor, and a keen insight into the nature of the wild things,
important, yes absolutely necessary, but one must have a love for the
big outside, stimulated by a desire for a certain amount of seclusion, is
the key to the situation. Success is at the will of the hunter himself,
although without complete organization of the whole system, the eradication of the shy pests for good and all time, would be prolonged in-

definitely. A professional wolf hunter never tells the secrets of his success in luring these wily animals into his traps. It is not to his own interests to do so, and though, at times, high prices may be paid to him for his methods, his real valuable secrets generally remain to him a secret except to some favored companion who remains equally as selfish after his instructor is dead. Baits in themselves are very simple when we once know them, but even baits are not all, in fact not the most important consideration. On the other hand, in the Government work, we have an unlimited field for experimental work, and this, in connection with what experienced hunters bring to us, established the system that will eventually eliminate these pests that are now such expense to the livestock industry of our land. In fighting wolves, we find that we must fight them with scientific methods, and advance our methods, for without a doubt the gray wolf advances in his efforts to retain his existence . . . and the hunter who brings the wily fellows to bag, is a master of his trade. . . .

. . . The number of adult gray wolves taken in 1916 was 33 while in 1917 68 were taken, however 36 pups were taken in 1916, while in 1917 only 6 were killed. This fact has its significance in that there were fewer females to produce the pups in 1917. While no doubt there were a few litters of pups that have gotten by during the last spring, I feel that we will have little trouble getting these before an other [sic] breeding season. . . .

The average cost of the total number [of all predators: wolves, lion, bears, coyotes, bobcats, golden eagles and jaguars], 750 animals taken in 1916, was $11.30. The average cost of the total number, 1,537 animals taken in 1917, was $9.57. The average salary paid hunters in 1916 was $2.64 per day. The average salary paid hunters in 1917 was $2.90. (This increase in wage is caused by raising the salaries of those hunters who stay in the Service and accomplish efficient work.)

1919: *Annual Report, Predatory Animal Control, New Mexico District, U.S. Bureau of Biological Survey,* J. Stokley Ligon

In 1919 the USBS split Arizona and New Mexico into separate districts. Ligon remained in charge of the New Mexico operation. By this point, just four years after the federal predator control program had begun, he could proudly state that "little complaint is heard" in New Mexico about wolves. However, as seen in these excerpts from his annual report for that year, a few animals still survived. Ligon vowed to continue his work until the goal of "absolute extermination" was achieved:

No reasonable argument can be advanced in favor of preservation of any lobo and timber wolves, mountain lions or predatory bears. Their case is simplified by revolving into a common channel—that of absolute extermination on the open range. . . .

There are a few stragglers [wolves] in the state drifting and being drifted, hunting their lost tribe, or endeavoring to avoid the hunters' tricking devices, most of them having lost feet in traps. . . .

Dispensing with the gray wolf in the state has been prolonged beyond time anticipated by the Inspector. Inability to keep the best hunters constantly after the animals, weather conditions, and the permitting of pups to escape from dens, are factors that have aided the animals in their fight. Invasion from other states, and especially from Mexico has also had considerable bearings.

It is a practical impossibility to prevent increase, so long as there is a pair of wolves at large, although they may be old, minus toes or entire feet, or carry wounds made by bullets. Such afflictions have no serious bearing on prolific reproduction—with the single exception of age.

There are probably a dozen adult wolves in the state at the end of the fiscal year, not including those that enter and leave over the border, but this number is probably increased one hundred per cent by pups that have not been taken this season. This means that thirty wolves will have to be taken during the first half of the coming year in order to make the finish.

During the year some notorious animals have been taken. Of the total number of fifty-two adults killed, as far as is known, only one was secured with poison. The balance were trapped. Fewer made their escape with traps than in previous years.

The damage now being committed in the state is so small, compared to previous years, that little complaint is heard. However, adults that remain are costing $2000 each, or at the rate of $24,000 annually.

1920: *Annual Report, Predatory Animal Control, New Mexico District, U.S. Bureau of Biological Survey,* J. Stokley Ligon

The 1920 Congressional budget for the Biological Survey (Act of May 16, 1920) left out wording that had previously limited the agency's predator control work to "public domain" or federally owned lands. Now the federal war against the wolf could be carried out anywhere, without restriction.

In his 1920 annual report, Ligon repeatedly complains about the diffi-culties he has in running the New Mexico predator control program with the "scant appropriation" of $25,000. Although only twelve wolves were left in the entire state, he pleads for an increased budget to provide for an "ex-pansion of the organization." During this year, his costs per kill had signifi-cantly risen and he tries to explain "the factors that should be considered" on that declining return on federal investment in predator control:

For a time the matter of scant appropriations was not felt, on account of lack of supervisory force as well as for lack of suitable, efficient hunters; but this period has past, and both leaders and laboring men are now available. Conditions are sufficiently well in hand to use a big force to advantage. As the work advances, additional men are needed, and it becomes more important that funds should be available to keep a ca-pable force constantly in the service. It is not sufficient to hold the ground that we gain; we must advance and expand. . . .

The average cost of state animals taken during the last six months, deducting returns from specimens and furs that were sold, was $16.63 plus, each. This does not take into account specimen skins retained and more than one hundred furs and hides carried over to be sold next season. Among the animals taken were fifty-seven wolves, lions and bears. It is difficult to figure the net cost of animals taken by Govern-ment hunters, with the over-head expenses involved in administration and lack of statement of fur sales. Other factors should be considered, such as animals killed and not accounted for by poison, educational and organization advancements. . . .

Expenditures of the Bureau are entirely out of proportion to the sav-ing involved and to the state-wide damage committed. An annual two million dollar damage suit against predatory animals cannot be suc-cessfully fought to a finish with an annual expenditure of $25,000. . . .

As has been stated, the most serious problem that confronts the preda-tory animal department at present in this state, is lack of adequate funds with which to meet the demands and expansion of the organization. A force of twenty regular hunters, constantly after wolves, mountain lions and bears, is very necessary. . . .

The objects and problem of the Service are two-fold; to exterminate or control the injurious species and increase the desirable—both do-mestic and wild. . . .

The wolf situation is one that will require intensive organized effort until the last animal is taken, not only in Texas and New Mexico, but in every state where they find suitable harbors and when this is accomplished, we will have to guard the gateways to Mexico so long as there is a supply in that country. The gray wolf tribe will die hard to the last hybrid, and long after we think we have them out of the way, they will make their appearance. . . .

Progress against the remaining gray wolves of the state was up to expectations during the past year, taking into consideration curtailed operations caused by limited funds. While it is now rather early to make predictions regarding the increase, it is not probable that any young will reach the age of maturity. July 1st, there was known to be no more than twelve adult wolves that make their home wholly in the state. In addition to these, one family or more of hybrids is in the Black Range. The survivors are easily giving way under our trapping methods.

🐺 1922: *Annual Report, Predatory Animal Control, New Mexico District, U.S. Bureau of Biological Survey,* Charles Bliss

Ligon, in his 1920 report, had written that "we will have to guard the gateways to Mexico so long as there is a supply [of wolves] in that country." Now that nearly all the native wolves of New Mexico had been killed off, the Survey's main problem was dealing with "illegal alien" wolves who crossed over from Mexico. In duty that become known as "The Border Patrol," government trappers were assigned to the Mexican border and told to track down and kill any wolf entering the state. As is shown in this excerpt from Charles Bliss's 1922 annual report for the New Mexico District, plans were also being developed for the Survey to do something about the wolves living in Mexico:

Old Mexico wolves migrate in from both the state of Sonora and Chihuahua. With the example of interests in Chihuahua and with all the strength of the original entertainment of the proposal to raise a fund to hire a hunter providing the Biological Survey would recommend a reliable hunter and place him under supervision of the Bureau, an additional fund for a year-long hunter in Sonora section is not doubtful. The Old Mexico activities of the hunter they hired would receive the best the government had in methods of trapping and poisoning and would have the subsequent supervision of our government Bureau. The cooperation is permanent as long as results justify expenditures.

Wolves are killing burros and horses penned in corrals for the night. A decrease in lobos will effect an immediate saving of livestock in Old Mexico, and more or less directly save many dollars for stockmen on the San Francisco and Gila Watersheds, as well as all the livestock industries in New Mexico.

🐺 1946: *Annual Report, Predatory Animal Control, New Mexico District, U.S. Fish and Wildlife Service, L. H. Laney*

In a 1940 reorganization of federal agencies, the U.S. Biological Survey was absorbed by the U.S. Fish and Wildlife Service (USFWS). Wolves crossing over from Mexico continued to be a problem during this period. In the following 1946 annual report for the New Mexico District, L. H. Laney, the district supervisor, proposes that the U.S. government build a wolf-resistant fence along the international border to stop the influx:

Reports show greater losses to wolf during this current year than during recent years and a greater number of wolf have been taken. Stockmen of the Western States who have herds in Mexico have in some instances discontinued predatory animal control in Mexico, and if control there is not resumed, no doubt we will be compelled to take more predatory animals on this side of the border. My opinion is that unless an International boundary fence of wolf-repellent type is constructed, this patrol along the border will become more of a problem each year as the predatory animals in Mexico increase in numbers. We are therefore hopeful that an International fence that will turn back many of the predators will be constructed in the near future.

🐺 1950: *March Quarter Narrative, Predatory Animal Control, New Mexico District, U.S. Fish and Wildlife Service, L. H. Laney*

In 1948, the USFWS began using Compound 1080, a deadly canine poison, for its wolf and coyote control work in New Mexico. The poison proved so effective that L. H. Laney sent two of his agents into Mexico in 1950 to teach local residents how to use Compound 1080.

A cooperative wolf control demonstration in northern Mexico was carried on during the quarter. Assistant District Agent Crook and Mammal Control Agent Davis went into Mexico, and in cooperation with the Pan American Sanitary Bureau and the Mexican Government, demonstrated to American ranchers in the Casa Grande area wolf control methods. Three wolves were taken and their report indicated that wolves are abundant a short distance in Mexico, south of the International Boundary.

1958: *Annual Report, Predatory Animal Control, New Mexico District, U.S. Fish and Wildlife Service,* L. H. Laney

By 1958, just eight years after the initial demonstration of Compound 1080 in Mexico, Laney could state that the USFWS had achieved "complete control of the wolf" along the border:

We wish to make the following observations regarding wolf control by Compound "1080" in Mexico. At the 1950 demonstration, wolf populations were extremely heavy throughout the mountain country worked, and reports by stockmen and by Dr. Bernardo Villa who was present at the 1955 demonstrations indicate that a heavy population of wolf [sic] existed in some of the demonstration areas worked. The 1958 demonstration covered a large portion of country treated with "1080" in 1950 and 1955, and observations lead me to believe that complete control of the wolf has been obtained and has existed for a 3 to 8 year period.

Observation is attained from the reports of reliable stockmen and personal inspection of the known wolf habitat in 1950 and again in 1958. Mr. Alberto Verle, Pat Keenan, Ted Farnsworth, Lee Finn, Martin Jeffers, Otis Jeffers, Alberto Whitten, and Alvin Whitten said they had not had any livestock losses from wolf since the first "1080" was put into operation, and that very little wolf sign had been noted in the past several years. Three separate wolf tracks were noted in the Gavilan River area during the 1958 demonstration. The New Mexico Branch of Animal Control has not taken a wolf along the International Border since 1952. Therefore, the Border stockmen in New Mexico have benefitted considerably from the demonstrations given in Mexico.

The preemptive strike by the U.S. government against the native wolf population in northern Mexico proved to be the final solution to the wolf problem in New Mexico and the rest of the Southwest. The deadly Compound 1080 killed off the last of wolves living near the border.

According to records in the Stanley Young Collection at the Denver Public Library, the successful poisoning program in Mexico brought in requests for information, aid, and advice on predator control from thirty-five other nations, including Argentina, Cuba, Egypt, Russia, South Africa, Taiwan, China, Indonesia, the Congo, and Australia. The experience of the USFWS in predatory control and poisoning techniques became a valued export to developing countries.

In February 10, 1972, President Richard Nixon, in a speech that was billed as an "environmental State-of-the-Union," announced that he was banning the use of Compound 1080, strychnine, and cyanide as predator poisons on federal lands and would also make use of such poisons illegal on private lands.

🐺 1915: "The Varmint Question," Aldo Leopold

The Biological Survey not only had the powerful backing of the livestock industry, it also was strongly supported by associations of hunters and sportsmen. These special interest groups proved to be powerful allies of the Survey's predator control work and could be counted on to effectively lobby Congress for increased funding.

The following selections from Aldo Leopold, a U.S. Forest Service employee and early supporter of the Survey's predator control mission, show how he worked with sportsmen's groups to solidify their backing of the federal predator control program in Arizona and New Mexico.

Leopold, after graduating in 1909 from the Yale School of Forestry with a masters degree, headed west for a Forest Service job on the Apache National Forest in Arizona. During a portion of his next two years on the Apache, Leopold headed a timber-cruising crew working in the remote drainages of the Blue River, a section of the White Mountains. Wolves were common in that country and Leopold, like other forest rangers, shot any that came within rifle range. His experiences in the Arizona mountains caused Leopold to become a committed proponent of the federal campaign to exterminate wolves and other predators.

By 1915 Leopold was working at the Forest Service regional office in Albuquerque. During this period he helped hunters organize game protective associations in the Southwest and became editor of the Pine Cone, *the newsletter of the Albuquerque Game Protection Association. In December 1915, Leopold wrote an editorial calling for an alliance between the hunting associations, the livestock groups, and the Biological Survey against wolves and other predators.*

For some unfathomable reason, there appears to have been a kind of feeling of antagonism between men interested in game protection and between some individuals connected with the stock growing industry.

There have been some very notable exceptions to this rule, particularly among the stockmen themselves. It would, for instance, be a fair statement to say that certain individual stockmen have saved the antelope for New Mexico. But speaking generally the statement is true.

It seems never to have occurred to anybody that the very opposite should be the case, and that the stockmen and the game protectionists are mutually and vitally interested in a common problem. This problem is the reduction of predatory animals.

It is well known that predatory animals are continuing to eat the cream off the stock grower's profits, and it hardly needs to be argued that, with our game supply as low as it is, a reduction in the predatory animal population is bound to help the situation. If the wolves, lions, coyotes, bob-cats [sic], foxes, skunks, and other varmints were only decreasing at the same rate as our game is decreasing, it might at least be said that there was no serious occasion for worry, but that they are not so decreasing is an established fact in the mind of every man familiar with conditions. Whatever may have been the value of the work accomplished by bounty systems, poisoning, and trapping, individual or governmental, the fact remains that varmints continue to thrive and their reduction can be accomplished only by means of a practical, vigorous, and comprehensive plan of action.

How, how is this action to be obtained? How, for instance, is the Biological Survey to receive a larger appropriation for the excellent work they have begun? How, for instance, is a more satisfactory bounty law to be enacted? How, for instance, is trapping to be made attractive to real trappers? Obviously by a united and concerted demand for these things. The stockmen alone have been demanding these things for years, and while they have accomplished a great deal, they have not accomplished enough. Why should the organized game protectionists not join with the stockmen in making these demands, and would not their added weight possibly give the necessary added effectiveness? Would not the manifestation of a sincere desire on our part to co-operate to the limit of our ability also remove the last vestige of [bad] feeling between us and the stock associations? Would not everybody, except the varmints, be benefited by such a move?

There is nothing connected with a properly conducted stock-growing operation which is going to operate against our game program. Conversely, there is nothing in our game program which is going to hurt the stock industry, or deprive any stock of their established range. Why, then, should we not get together?

Plans to have our Association actively develop this idea are already well under way. We have had an informal conference with Mr. Ligon, Predatory Animal Inspector of the Biological Survey, and obtained his personal ideas as to what ought to be done. We have had an informal conference with Mr. E. M. Otero, President of the New Mexico Wool Growers, and he was much pleased with the idea of co-operation. Shortly we shall formally tender our co-operation to the Executive Committee of the Wool Growers and, as soon as suitable occasions arise, to every other stock growing body in the Albuquerque region. If our offers are accepted, we will confer with these bodies on the question of ways and means [of predator destruction], and there is every reason to hope that we can arrive at a mutual agreement which will bring the desired results.

It can hardly be gainsaid that we need the aid and co-operation of the powerful stock growing associations. It seems equally obvious that they could make good use of such help as we are able to give them. It is therefore to be hoped that we can get together.

Four years later, in a January 1919 Pine Cone *article, Leopold wrote: "New Mexico is leading the West in the campaign for eradication of predatory animals." With approval, he noted, "The sportsmen and the stockmen . . . demand the eradication of lions, wolves, coyotes, and bobcats."*

James Kennedy, a professor at Trinity College in Dublin, commented in a paper for the Wildlife Society Bulletin *that Leopold's 1919 anti-predator article "reads like a page from* Mein Kampf."

1920: "The Game Situation in the Southwest," Aldo Leopold

In early 1920, Leopold gave a speech entitled, "The Game Situation in the Southwest" at the National Game Conference of the American Game Protective Association in New York City. He now was the assistant district forester for the Forest Service's Southwest Region. Leopold's proposed alliance between southwestern hunters and ranchers was now a reality. The two groups had followed through on Leopold's suggestion that they make "a united and concerted demand" for increased funding of predator control work. Due to their lobbying, New Mexico had created a Council of Defense, which contributed state funds to the Biological Survey's control work throughout the state. Leopold proudly announced that, as a result of this cooperation, the New Mexican wolf population had been reduced from three hundred to thirty in just three years.

Now that the Survey had achieved so much in its first few years of its predator control work, Leopold set out to share with the convention audience his vision that, with one final push, the ultimate goal of the USBS-stockmen-sportsmen alliance—complete extermination of wolves, mountain lions, and other predators—could be accomplished. They must stay united through the final "clean-up" or killing off of the last of the predators.

The Southwest has more possibilities and perhaps more difficulties in the matter of game production than any region I know of in the United States. I hope to give this meeting a few observations as to these possibilities, to the end of awakening a more active interest in our Southwestern problems, and to get from you a great many ideas which will help untangle some of its knots. . . .

I wish deliberately and emphatically to state that the settlement of the West is improving rather than destroying the possibilities for successful game production. Why? Because: (1) The stock industry which covers the entire West is demanding the destruction of predatory animals, and the U.S. Biological Survey is doing the job, rapidly and well. (2) The stock industry is placing water and salt on millions of acres of range that were originally waterless and, therefore, largely gameless. (3) Forestry and agriculture are doing away with the forest fire and the prairie fire. (4) Irrigation is spreading cover, feed and water over great areas and improving them from the game standpoint. (5) Stock watering places and irrigation reservoirs are literally creating fishing and ducking grounds that in the old days did not exist. (6) All industries are evolving toward a fenced range, which means the cessation of overgrazing, which in the past has been very bad for the game.

It stands to reason, of course, that these artificial improvements involve an adjustment in the economy of nature. Some species, like the elk and buffalo, are damaged and must be relegated to areas offering exceptional conditions. Other species are benefited or damaged in varying degrees. And, of course, there are certain things we must do to aid in the adjustment. But the net result can be made a benefit, not a loss. The march of empire, therefore, is no excuse for lying down on this job.

And now there is one more point which I advisedly segregate to emphasize its importance. The time will never come when even an appreciable fraction of the Southwest will be actually usurped by the works of man. Cities and villages, ranches and irrigation, mines and factories will cover millions of acres in each western state, but each state measures its area in scores of millions. There will always remain vast areas suitable only for forests, grazing, game and recreation. To raise game, both large and small, on these areas will always be possible. To fail to do so will always be an economic and social waste. Our problem [raising the maximum numbers of game animals], I admit, is big and new and complicated; but its successful solution is perfectly practicable. . . .

Leopold then argues for strict regulation of hunting to a level consistent with the sustained yield of the game population. After making that point, he recommends two other methods to protect and increase the game species:

There are two outstanding needs that, to my way of thinking, ought to be taken care of at once. It so happens that these needs are not only imperative at present, regardless of what else is done, but will also be necessary to the success of the plan for the regulation of kill whenever that plan, or something like it is adopted. These two needs are:

1) A well planned system of game refuges.
2) The eradication of predatory animals. . . .

. . . I have just stated that a well-planned system of game refuges is not only a present necessity, but also a logical adjunct to any plan for regulation of kill to be adopted in the future. Why? Because such refuges will act as a safety device for keeping up the breeding stock, for protecting the ranges of rare species and for preventing buck shortages. . . .

The eradication of predatory animals is a matter that is already being handled very efficiently by the U.S. Biological Survey with the co-operation of the stockmen and the states. Remarkable progress has been made; in New Mexico, for instance, there were about 300 wolves three years ago and these have now been reduced to 30. But there are two points about this work which I believe the sportsmen as a whole do not yet fully understand: (1) The real destructiveness of predatory animals to game. (2) The fact that it will be more difficult and costly to finish the eradication work than it was to start it.

As to the first point, take the single case of the mountain lion in National Forests in New Mexico. There are roughly 100 adult lions left in New Mexico, mostly within the National Forests. A special study is being made by Mr. J. S. Ligon and Mr. S. E. Piper of the Biological

Survey, as to how many deer per year each lion gets away with. This study is not yet completed, but I have seen enough evidence to justify me in venturing on my personal responsibility the statement that each lion kills at least 30 deer per year, mostly fawns. Any of our experienced lion hunters will, I think, call this figure very conservative. This means a total loss through lions of at least 3,000 deer per year. The hunters kill about 700 deer per year, according to our rangers' reports. This means the lions are at least four or five times as destructive as the hunters. No plans for game refuges or regulation of kill will get us anywhere unless these lions are cleaned out. Conversely, it is readily apparent that when they are cleaned out, the productiveness and resistance of our deer stocks, and the effectiveness of our proposed refuges, and plans for regulation of kill will be very greatly increased.

I have already stated that the Biological Survey is making splendid progress in eradication work. But let us remember this: as the work progress the remaining animals become fewer, more sophisticated and more expensive to catch. It is going to take patience and money to catch the last wolf or lion in New Mexico. But the last one must be caught before the job can be called fully successful. This may sound like a strong statement, but if any of you have lived in the West and seen how quickly a piece of country will restock with wolves or lions, you will know what I mean. Now the point is, will the public back up the Biological Survey with funds until this job is finished? When the wolves are mostly gone, will the necessary appropriations be forthcoming? They will only if the organized sportsmen and the more far-sighted stockmen throw their full weight into the balance at the strategic moment and insist that the Biological Survey be given the money so that a clean-up can be made. Unless this is done, it will only be a few years before the job will have to be done all over again. A clean-up will pay best in the end, but it is going to take vision to see it and work to get it. This meeting, I think, should not adjourn until everything possible has been done to show Congress that the sportsmen of America are behind this predatory animal campaign, and are going to stay behind it until it is finished. . . .

1928: "Wild Life Conservation and Control in Wyoming Under the Leadership of the United States Biological Survey" Albert Day and Almer Nelson

This report, summarizing the accomplishments of the Biological Survey in Wyoming from 1916 to 1928, was written by Albert Day, supervisor of the

Survey's Predatory Animal and Rodent Control Division (PARC) in Wyoming, and by Almer Nelson, the reservation warden at the Winter Elk Refuge in Jackson. It contains several passages that refer to the Survey's poisoning campaign and to the criticism that state residents were raising against it. The controversy over the use of poison baits that killed both predators and non-targeted "useful" species would intensify in coming years.

Introduction
Wyoming—the State where once the broad expanse of rolling plains harbored great colonies of prairie dogs, with the coyote lurking stealthily in the background, where the antelope herds fed timidly, where the mountains were inhabited by the slinking fox, the shadowy deer, the stately elk and moose, where the rugged crags were scarred with the trails of the mountain sheep—now has abundant wild life problems.

Invasion by man has disturbed nature's balance. The prairie dog, whose early fare consisted of native plants, soon found the homesteaders' cultivated crops more palatable. The wolf, which formerly followed the buffalo herds, developed an acute taste for domestic stock. The coyote turned its attention to sheep, poultry, and pigs. The antelope, which formerly was given the freedom of the prairies, found succulent millet and oats a more choice tidbit. The elk herds, which formerly migrated to the foothills to pass the winter away from the snow-clad mountains, now find their former feeding grounds fenced and producing hay. The inevitable result is hunger, starvation, death.

Our modern civilization requires that we harmonize as nearly as possible the lives of our wild native animals with our agricultural activities. This calls for the protection and preservation of elk, deer, antelope, moose, mountain sheep, and other valuable forms of wild life. To do this, we must eliminate certain predatory animals that prey upon those wild mammals that we consider beneficial, and on domestic stock. The control of rodents is necessary to produce forage and crops. Thus, the Bureau of Biological Survey, that branch of the United States Department of Agriculture that is concerned with wild life problems, finds ample opportunity for service in Wyoming.

Approximately half of Wyoming's 62,000,000 acres is still public domain—national forests, national parks, and military and Indian reservations. The Federal Government thus has a great obligation in assisting the people of Wyoming to solve the problems that arise from man's encroachment on the haunts of nature's denizens. . . .

Headquarters of the Biological Survey in Wyoming

In Wyoming the Biological Survey maintains two offices to assist the farmers and ranchers and to conduct activities relating to wild life. These are:

1. Predatory Animal and Rodent Control. This office is a combination of two former offices. The predatory Animal Control work was formerly under the leadership of Charles J. Bayer, but on July 1, 1928, when he resigned, it was combined with the Rodent Control Division under the leadership of Albert M. Day, with headquarters at Cheyenne, Wyoming.

The Predatory Animal Division is conducted in cooperation with the Wyoming State Game and Fish Commission and State Extension Service. It maintains a force of trained hunters who relentlessly hunt down the stock killers, including wolves, coyotes, mountain lions, and bobcats. These men use poisoning, trapping, and den-hunting methods to accomplish the desired results.

The Rodent Control Division is conducted in cooperation with the State Extension Service and the State Department of Agriculture. Farmers and ranchers of Wyoming are assisted in the control of crop and range-destroying pests, such as prairie dogs, ground squirrels, jack rabbits, field mice, and porcupines. Help also is given poultry growers in the control of magpies, which in some localities, do great damage to young turkeys and chickens.

2. Game Refuge. The Winter Elk Refuge is maintained by the Biological Survey in cooperation with the Wyoming State Fish and Game Commission, the Forest Service, the National Park Service, and the Izaak Walton League of America, to assist in preserving the elk herds of Wyoming. A vitally important part of this work, the winter feeding of elk, and raising hay for the purpose, is under the direction of Almer P. Nelson, with headquarters at Jackson. Here, on lands held for this express purpose, these cooperating agencies feed the elk each winter, sometimes as many as 10,000 head, the actual number depending on the severity of the winter and the number that are driven to the feed grounds for sustenance. Jackson, Wyoming, is also the headquarters of O. J. Murie, a biologist, who is carrying on investigations of the life history of the elk.

Predatory Animal Control

Organized predatory animal control operations were first started in Wyoming in 1915, under the direction of the Biological Survey. Federal funds annually allotted have ranged from $15,000 to $20,000, and a force of 10 to 12 hunters were employed up to and including the year 1920. During this period, in view of the fact that gray wolves and mountain lions were the most destructive beasts of prey, the work was directed mainly against these species to bring them under control first, although thousands of coyotes were killed at the same time.

When work was first started, gray wolves were numerous in Wyoming, and with the coyotes did enormous damage to livestock and game. In the early days of Wyoming, they were comparatively easy to take, because of their abundance. As livestock increased, losses from wolves increased correspondingly, and as the animals were hunted more they grew so wary that at last it took an expert to capture them.

While wolves and mountain lions were gradually losing ground, it was not until state cooperation was obtained in 1921 that it became possible practically to clean up these animals in the state. At this time, the state appropriated $15,000 a year, which was largely used in paying salaries of hunters in cooperation with the Federal Government. This made it possible to double the force of hunters, and the gray wolves and mountain lions were brought under control within the course of four years. Since then they have been gradually reduced until at present there probably are no more than five adult wolves left in Wyoming, and mountain lions now are very scarce.

Various livestock associations have contributed financially to cooperative work, and in addition have furnished State and Federal hunters with board and horse feed, and with bait material. When this was started, hunters used traps and guns only. Later, poison work and den-hunting methods were developed and at present, employing these is considered the most effective and most economical method of control. A specially processed poison is manufactured by the Biological Survey. This is furnished to all regular hunters and in cooperation with the State Extension Service is issued free to cooperating farmer-stockmen hunters. Much more success is had with this than with commercial poisons. Each year newer and better methods of poisoning are being developed. The best methods of use are demonstrated to the cooperating farmer-stockmen hunters who work within districts assigned them and keep the skins of all the animals they take. Skins taken by the Federal, State and association employees become the property of the respective agencies.

If western ranges are ever to be entirely cleaned of predatory animals, it will undoubtedly be through systematic and patient work of salaried hunters, men who are kept on the work after private hunters have stopped through lack of sufficient animals to make it profitable enough to hunt them for their furs.

Wolves

Wolves in the early days ranged the length and breath of Wyoming killing the buffalo, elk, deer, and other big game animals at will. With the advent of the early settlers, the passing of the buffalo, and the thinning of the other game herds, the beasts of prey turned to cattle and horses. Fifty years ago the wolf menace was one of the worst problems of the cattle industry. In the year 1896, the State paid bounties of $3 each on 3,458 wolves. From 1895 to 1927, 36,161 wolves have been taken in Wyoming by regular Federal, State, and bounty hunters. In the early stages of wolf control, bounties reduced them greatly, but it was left to the expert State and Federal Government hunters to thin the ranks of the last few, and if possible exterminate them entirely. In 1915, when the Biological Survey first started work in Wyoming, there were over 1,000 adult wolves in the State, doing damage to livestock and game estimated to exceed $1,000,000 annually. At the present time, excepting those in Yellowstone Park, there are probably no more than five adult wolves left ranging in Wyoming. Two of these are known to be in the Jackson Hole region, where they are doing little damage to domestic stock, but live largely on the elk abounding in that section.

A great number of notorious wolves have been taken by Federal and State Hunters in Wyoming. Notable among these are: Scar-Face, Five-Toes, Cusion-Foot [sic], Two-Toes, Three-Toes (the notorious "Split Rock" wolf), Big-Foot, Red Flash, and a pair of Sheridan wolves. Stockmen will well remember them. Some were very remarkable animals. Red Flash, for instance, was an unusually large wolf with a gorgeous coat of glossy red-tipped fur, and was taken in his prime by a Government hunter, Orin Robinson, who, mounted on skiis [sic], gave chase, ran down this wolf, and shot him. Another off-color wolf was a blue one taken by Hunter Ed Stearns. Four of a pack of fifteen wolves eliminated by Biological Survey Hunters H. P. Williams and Del Dearth near Big Piney were black and bob-tailed.

Another wolf, Old Angora, taken in Jackson Hole, had a long record of killing. He was unusually large and was supposed to be the oldest wolf ever taken in Wyoming. The Wyoming wolves are gray, and it is only when they reach extreme age that they get white. This wolf was entirely white and had very long hair, thus earning for himself the title, "Old Angora." His teeth were practically worn to the gums. In connection with this wolf, a Jackson Hole dude man tells the story of having an eastern man out on a big game hunt when a band of elk was sighted and a rush made through the timber to get nearer for a shot. While going through the timber, the guide saw Old Angora standing on a log only a few yards distant, and dropped beside the trail to give his "dude" a chance. The man refused to shoot thinking he had seen a ghost wolf. Old Angora fathered numerous notorious stock and game killers.

The authors next discuss the life and death of the Custer Wolf. Chapter 6 has a detailed account of this wolf's career.

Only slightly less notorious than the famous Custer Wolf was old female "Three-Toes," known also as the "$10,000 Split Rock Wolf."

This killer had exacted a tribute of at least 50 head of cattle annually before being trapped by C. J. Bayer of the Biological Survey. Old "Three-Toes" got her name from her track, which was always recognized wherever she did her killing from the fact that one toe had been taken off nearly a year previously in a trap set by Hunter Evans of the Biological Survey. In the interval between her two trappings she had killed nearly 200 head of cattle and probable had gotten her share also of the antelope and deer in whose country her depredations were conducted. Her last stand was in a trap seven miles northwest of Split Rock, the wolf drag attached to the trap having caught in the rocks. It is such wolves as this that are given up by bounty hunters, and are caught by salaried predatory animal men of the Biological Survey and its cooperators, even though, as in this case, two or more men stick to the trail until the marauder is captured.

Day and Nelson next list the number of other predators taken by state and federal hunters in Wyoming since 1916: mountain lions (18), bobcats (1,524), lynxes (31), and bears (169). The authors then try to refute the criticism leveled at the Survey's poisoning campaign.

Destruction of Fur-Bearing Animals in Control Operations

Many trappers have criticized the Biological Survey from time to time for conducting poisoning operations against predatory animals, because, they assert, the distribution of poison has been seriously destructive to such fur animals as foxes, martens, minks, weasels, and raccoons. It is

not denied that an occasional useful animal falls in the extensive operations against the thousands of stock-killing predators and the crop-
destroying rodents, and the reports of operations made by the hunters
give specific information on this point. These show that during the
eleven years, 1916–1927, in which 63,145 wolves, coyotes, bobcats, bears,
mountain lions, and lynxes were destroyed, relatively few valuable wild
animals were victims. Of greatest numbers were badgers, 1,450 in all,
but in extenuation of their destruction it is to be borne that badgers
have harmful habits that may make them decidedly objectionable locally, and many are purposely killed because the burrows they dig injure horses and trap many young lambs. They are also occasionally
destructive when they come in contact with poultry. On the average,
however, only 112 badgers are known to have been killed for each year
of the operations against predatory animals.

Except for the badgers, the only animals useful at all for fur were 293
from miscellaneous species, including 44 foxes, 186 skunks, 16 raccoons,
and 3 civet cats, many of which were taken at the request of farmers on
whose lands they had become objectionable; 19 beavers, taken under
State permit on lands where they were a nuisance; 1 muskrat, 3 martens, and 1 mink, all of which had gotten into traps; and 10 ferrets and 12
weasels. Thus it is readily seen that relatively few fur animals were accidental victims of poisoning operations, and excepting the badger, less
than one-half of one percent of the total number of animals taken were
fur-bearers. Many of the animals other than true predatory animals were
intentionally taken because of their depredations about poultry yards
and of their destructive habits in other places, and it is significant that
the muskrats, martens, and minks killed were not poisoned but were
trapped accidently. From the Wyoming evidence, therefore, it appears
that fears entertained by trappers and by persons connected with the
fur trade regarding the safety of fur-bearers during the operations against
predatory animals are built largely on a lack of information concerning
the actual facts in the case.

*The Survey men conveniently forgot that they themselves had stated that
poison baits put out for predators killed many coyotes that "were never found."
A table at the end of their report estimates that during the period 1916 to
1928 21,255 coyotes were poisoned but never recovered. Those baits would
have killed far more non-targeted animals than the authors admit to recovering in the previous paragraphs. Since the Survey was already being criticized for its indiscriminate poisoning operations, the personnel in the field*

had little incentive to look for and accurately tabulate the true numbers of "useful" animals killed. For these reasons, the figures used by Day and Nelson are suspect.

Two other USBS reports from this era document the agency's extensive use of poison. The 1924 USBS annual report claimed a kill of 34,092 coyotes throughout the country, but estimated that an additional 100,000 poisoned coyotes were never found. The 1926 annual report states that the USBS distributed 127,000 ounces of strychnine during its control campaigns. Truly an overkill—that amount of poison could have killed 28,000,000 coyotes or 14,000,000 wolves!

Another table in Day and Nelson's report lists the total federal, state, county and livestock association funds spent on predator control in Wyoming during the years 1921–28: $374,749. Of that total, $338,013, or 90 percent, came from federal, state, or county taxpayer funds.

1915–41: *The Wolf in North American History,* Stanley P. Young

Stanley Young worked for the Biological Survey for twenty years, from 1917 to 1939. Starting out as a predator control agent in Arizona, he later directed the USBS's predator campaign in Colorado, New Mexico, and Kansas. In 1929 he was promoted to the Survey's Washington, D.C., office. By the late 1930s, Young was the chief of the Predatory Animal and Rodent Control Division. In this position, he directed the Bureau's national predator control campaign. His 1946 book, The Wolf in North American History, *contains Young's tabulation of the total number of wolves directly killed by his agency through 1941:*

> With the close of the fiscal year 1941, the Service and its cooperators had tallied a grand total of 24,132 wolves of the species *Canis lupus* (large gray wolf) and *Canis niger* (red wolf) taken between July 1, 1915, and June 30, 1941.

An additional 45,654 gray and red wolves were killed by the USBS/USFWS between 1942 and 1970, according to the 1972 Caine Report. Combining that figure with Young's 1915 to 1941 count brings the known number of wolves killed by the USBS/USFWS from 1915 to 1970 to 69,786. That number does not include wolves killed by the U.S. Forest Service or the National Park Service, or wolves poisoned but never found.

Like many USBS men, Young often expressed conflicting attitudes toward the wolf. In 1930 he received a letter from his former writing partner

Arthur Carhart (Last Stand of the Pack) *that criticized the agency's predatory control policies. Young's response to Carhart on November 24, 1930, contains the following contradictory views of the wolf: "The gray wolf has no place in modern civilization. . . . In my opinion this animal is one hundred percent criminal. . . . Nevertheless, in spite of all that is bad about the wolf I personally consider this animal our greatest quadruped and have often wished that it would change its ways just a little so that the hand of man would not be raised so constantly against this predator."*

Young's earlier book, The Wolves of North America, *co-authored in 1944 with Edward Goldman, another longtime Survey employee, contains an irony that typified attitudes toward wolves during this era. Goldman, using wolf pelts and skulls collected by the Survey's predator control agents, divided the gray wolf species into twenty-three subspecies. Three of those subspecies (*Canis lupus baileyi, Canis lupus ligoni, *and* Canis lupus youngi*) were named after Vernon Bailey, J. Stokley Ligon, and Stanley Young, men who helped manage the Biological Survey's wolf control and extermination program.*

Chapter 5

Predators in
the National Parks

". . . every effort is being made to exterminate them."
Superintendent, Crater Lake National Park

Our modern conception of a national park as a sanctuary for all forms of wildlife is the end result of an evolutionary process that began in 1872 with the creation of Yellowstone National Park. The early managers of Yellowstone and other national parks valued game animals such as deer and elk far more than predatory species. To "save" the "good" animals, the "bad" species were exterminated. The selections in this chapter document how our national parks were once a killing ground for wolves, coyotes, mountain lions, and other predatory species.

1880–1916: Yellowstone National Park Monthly and Annual Reports

The predator control campaign conducted on federal lands by the U.S. Forest Service and the U.S. Biological Survey (USBS) was also carried out in many national parks. In 1872, when Yellowstone was established as a national park, the area contained an "exceedingly numerous" population of wolves. Initially, Yellowstone was administered by a civilian staff. The U.S. Army managed the park from 1886 until 1918, when it relinquished control to the National Park Service (NPS). The following excerpts from early Yellowstone annual and monthly reports, written by both civilian and military superintendents, show how the native wolf population fared in the pre-NPS period.

The first selection, from Philetus Norris's 1880 superintendent's annual report, describes the poisoning campaign conducted by wolfers within the park during the 1870s. Excerpts from later annual and monthly reports document the Army's policy toward wolves and other predators. The 1898 report mentions that the Army set out poisoned carcasses to kill predators. As shown in the 1916 report, the Biological Survey advised the Army on how best to "exterminate carnivorous animals in the park."

1880 Annual Report

The large, ferocious gray or buffalo wolf, the sneaking, snarling coyote, and a species apparently between the two, of a dark-brown or black color, were once exceedingly numerous in all portions of the Park, but the value of their hides and their easy slaughter with strychnine-poisoned carcasses of animals have nearly led to their extermination.

1889 Annual Report

The carnivora of the Park have, in common with other animals, increased until, I believe, something should be done for their extermination.

1898 Annual Report

Coyotes—Very numerous in certain sections. They do some damage to the young elk, but the young deer and antelope are their particular prey. Efforts are made in winter to keep their numbers down by poisoning carcasses of dead animals, and to a certain extent it has been successful.

1914 Annual Report

Gray wolves have made their appearances in the Park in considerable numbers, having been seen traveling in packs of ten or less. While efforts have been made to kill them, thus far none have been taken inside of the Park though a few have been killed just outside, along the northern border. They are very destructive of game, and efforts will be made to kill them.

1915 Annual Report

Gray wolves are increasing, and have become a decided menace to the herds of elk, deer, mountain sheep, and antelope. Several were killed in the park last winter, and an effort will be made the coming winter to capture or kill them.

1916 Annual Report

From October 6, 1915, to June 30, 1916, two special rangers were employed by advice of the United States Biological Survey for the purpose of exterminating carnivorous animals in the park. They succeeded in shooting and trapping 83 coyotes, 12 wolves, and 4 mountain lions. The skulls and such of the skins as were desired as specimens were sent to the National Museum, and the other skins were sold and the money deposited to the credit of the park revenues. Other park employees succeeded in killing 97 coyotes, making a total killed of 180. Two young male wolves captured in the spring of 1915 by the employees at the buffalo farm were shipped alive on November 16 to the National Zoological Park [Washington].

1907: U.S. Army Rules, Regulations and Instructions for Yellowstone

The following excerpt from a U.S. Army manual for soldiers stationed in the park shows that scouts and noncommissioned officers were ordered to personally kill wolves and other predators.

Scouts and noncommissioned officers in charge of stations throughout the park are authorized and directed to kill mountain lions, coyotes, and timber wolves. They will do this themselves, and will not delegate the authority to anyone else. They will report at the end of the month, in writing, the number of such animals killed, and will retain all skins or scalps in their personal possession until directed what to do with them.

1918–28: Yellowstone National Park Monthly and Annual Reports

When the NPS took over management of Yellowstone in 1918, it continued the predator control program initiated by the U.S. Army. The 1918 reports mention Biological Survey trappers who were doing predator control work inside Yellowstone, at the request of the Park Service. The monthly report for April 1922 states that "poison was used extensively" in the park. Other reports document that park rangers were "ordered" to find wolf dens and kill the pups and mother wolf, the same denning technique mentioned in the previous chapter.

April, 1918 Monthly Report

Wolves: Nineteen wolves were killed during the month, 16 of them by Mr. Steve Elkins, 2 by Scout Dewing, and 1 by Mr. Donald Stevenson, a predatory animal hunter representing the Biological Survey. There are indications of many more wolves on Specimen Ridge and

Hellroaring [Creek], and Stevenson and Dewing are still hunting them.

1918 Annual Report

Coyotes and wolves: These animals have done much damage to other game, and for that reason much pains have been taken to hunt them down and trap them. Two expert hunters were employed as scouts during the winter, and spent most of their time hunting and trapping. Steve Elkins, the famous guide and mountain lion hunter, was also employed for several weeks with his pack of lion hounds hunting lions, wolves, and coyotes, and the U.S. Biological Survey sent one of its hunters here for a time last spring, but he was not so successful as were some of our own men, and was finally called away by the draft. Another Biological Survey hunter, Mr. Wm. D. Clemons, has been working on the Upper Yellowstone since August 1st, and is trapping and hunting wolves and coyotes along the park line, on both sides of it. In all 190 coyotes and 36 wolves were killed in the park during the year. While there are more of these animals in the park than are desirable, I am of the opinion that there are not so many found among the game animals as there are among domestic animals in farming communities outside, as I have been informed by the State Game Warden of Montana that during 1917 there were killed 848 coyotes in the County of Gallatin, 1533 in Park and Sweetgrass Counties, and 301 in Carbon County.

February 1919 Monthly Report

Wolves and coyotes: Two wolves were killed during the month, one by Ranger Dewing and the other by Hunter Elkins. Signs seen, however, indicate the presence of several ranging from Mammoth to Soda Butte, and in the Soda Butte district they have been responsible for the death of quite a number of elk. Efforts are being made to exterminate them.

  Mountain lions: Steve Elkins was employed with his trained dogs throughout the month hunting lions, but the fact that he secured none indicates that they are becoming scarce. His services were valuable, however, in that he killed 10 coyotes and 1 grey wolf during the month.

1920 Annual Report

Coyotes, wolves and mountain lions. These are by far the most destructive of our carnivorous animals, and efforts are constantly made to keep them down to a reasonable number. It is hardly practicable, even if it were desirable, to entirely exterminate these animals, but a certain amount of hunting and trapping by our rangers each year has a most salutary effect.

They usually kill annually quite a large number of young elk, deer, antelope, and mountain sheep. This year, however, their depredations have not been heavy. Apparently the mountain lions left the Park altogether during the severe weather, and the coyotes and wolves found so many dead and dying animals that they gave over their hunting to a large extent. Two rangers gave all their attention from Jan. 1st to May 31st to hunting and trapping the carnivores, and other rangers aided whenever possible. In all, 107 coyotes and 28 wolves were destroyed.

The 1920 annual report denies that the NPS *was trying to exterminate Yellowstone's predators, but the April 1921 monthly report clearly states that park rangers "continued their efforts of trying to exterminate coyotes, wolves, and mountain lions."*

March 1921 Monthly Report
Carnivorous Animals: Rangers Henry Anderson and Dewing devoted most of their time during the month of March to hunting coyotes, and preparing to hunt wolves in their dens during April when they have their young. Several dens have been located and are being watched.

April 1921 Monthly Report
Carnivorous Animals: Park Rangers Henry Anderson and Court Dewing continued their efforts of trying to exterminate coyotes, wolves, and mountain lions. During the month they succeeded in killing one male wolf, an extremely large one, and located and dug out one den of wolves and killed 11 pups. The mother escaped.

April 1922 Monthly Report
Predatory Animals: About 25 coyotes were accounted for in the park during the past month. It is impossible to get an accurate estimate of the number of these animals killed, as poison was used extensively and there have been many killed that have never been found. H. Anderson, the trapper at Gardiner, was sick during a large part of the month, and was unable to hunt out these dead animals.

Figuring those that were reported as being killed last month, and a few that have not been reported to this office, the total number of predatory animals killed in the park is about 175 coyotes and 1 wolf.

Ranger H. Anderson has been ordered to look for wolf dens in the

Blacktail and Hellroaring country and is now on this work. Since April 1st he has succeeded in locating a den of wolves, killed the mother and captured 10 puppies alive. [The pups were later destroyed.]

May 1922 Monthly Report
Predatory Animals: Only one coyote was reported killed by rangers during the past month. Park Ranger Anderson cleaned up a den of 1 female and 10 wolf pups. He is still operating in the country where wolves are known to den and he will probably get several more dens during the spring. To date there has been a total of about 175 coyotes and 15 wolves accounted for during the winter. It is not possible to get the exact number of coyotes as many were know to have taken poison and their carcasses were never found. Anderson was sick during the time that coyotes were taking the poison readily and was not able to trace them down.

It is likely that wolves also had taken the poison baits but their remains were never found by the rangers.

. . . It is evident that the work of controlling these animals must be vigorously prosecuted by the most effective means available whether or not this meets with the approval of certain game conservationists.

August 1922 Monthly Report
Predatory Animals: Park Ranger Henry Anderson has been hunting out the summer haunts of park wolves and has succeeded in finding out what he believes to be their main summer range. This is in a section of the park that is practically inaccessible due to bog holes, rim rock, down timber and jack pines. The area is the part of the Mirror Plateau lying near the head of Timothy, Raven, Pelican and Broad Creeks. Ranger Anderson found numerous signs in this region and due to its inaccessibility and the fact that there is a large amount of game making its summer range near this point, there is no reason why the wolves should not find this area ideal summer home. Anderson will spend the remainder of the month in this locality in an attempt to exterminate as many of these predatory animals as possible.

April 1923 Monthly Report
Predatory Animals: The feature of the month with reference to predatory animals, was the cleaning out of a wolf den near Tower Falls. The

Predators in the National Parks / 207

old female was killed and the five pups brought to Mammoth where they will be placed in a cage and kept for exhibition purposes during the summer.

September 1924 Monthly Report
Predatory Animals: This animal we have always with us despite our best efforts to destroy him, particularly the coyote. There were no reported instances of wolf or mountain lion activities in the park last winter apart from an occasional lone track. None were actually seen within the park and there was no evidence of any kills by either of these animals during the entire winter season. The situation this fall gives promise of a recurrence of the wolf as we have two reports of recent date indicating their presence in the park. Park Ranger Hall reports having seen three near Heart Lake and a wolf pack numbering 12 are reported to have been seen at Elk Park by two members of a road crew on duty near that point. This last report has not been definitely confirmed and may be exaggerated but in any case we have reason to consider that the wolf will have to be reckoned with this winter. Coyotes do not appear to be any more numerous than usual at this time of the year and rangers have accounted for five this season.

October 1926 Monthly Report
Predatory Animals: 36 coyotes have been killed this season to date as compared with 64 to November 1st last year. Comparatively few have been seen; they are alert and unapproachable and are widely scattered over the entire park area. Weather conditions have not been favorable for hunting or trapping predatory animals. A timber wolf is alleged to have been seen by some road workmen along the old freight road near Fountain Station but this report has not been confirmed. Signs of a mountain lion were seen in the Tower Falls District late in September. There is believed to be a very limited number of wolves and mountain lion in the park.

October 1928 Monthly Report
Predatory Animals: Rangers will carry on as usual with predatory animal control work this year. . . . Eighty-one coyotes have been destroyed this season as compared with 44 to November 1st last year, 36 in 1926 and 64 in 1925. There have been no wolf or lion signs reported this season.

John Weaver, in his 1978 NPS report, The Wolves of Yellowstone, *stated that a minimum of 136 wolves were killed in the park between 1914 and 1926. Eighty of those wolves were pups. Since many wolves killed by poison bait were never found, the true tally of kills is likely much higher. The last two wolves killed in the park's predator control program died in October of 1926. After that date, wolves were occasionally reported in the park but did not appear to represent a viable breeding population. Those reported sightings may have been transient animals born outside the park who failed to establish themselves in Yellowstone.*

1930: *Animal Life of Yellowstone National Park,* Vernon Bailey

During this period, Vernon Bailey, the USBS biologist who wrote the 1907 and 1908 reports on wolf control on national forests, was serving as the chief field naturalist of the Survey. Bailey frequently visited Yellowstone to investigate predatory animal populations and advise the park staff on predator control programs. His 1930 book contains several passages that refer to those early trips to the park.

Bailey was almost certainly the Survey official referred to in Yellowstone's 1916 annual report: "From October 6, 1915, to June 30, 1916, two special rangers were employed by advice of the United States Biological Survey for the purpose of exterminating carnivorous animals in the park." Donald Stevenson, mentioned several times in Bailey's book, was called "a predatory hunter representing the Biological Survey" in the April 1918 monthly report. The presence of Stevenson and other Survey-trained hunters was likely arranged by Bailey. Army officers and early park rangers eagerly adopted Vernon Bailey's philosophy of wildlife management ("wolves and game can not be successfully maintained on the same range") and made it park policy. This was despite Bailey's own observation that game was "abundant" in the park.

Gray Wolf; Buffalo Wolf

The large gray wolves at times have become abundant in the park and wrought great havoc among the game animals, but at present they are being hunted so persistently over much of the outside range as well as in the park that they have become extremely scarce. During the summers of 1914 and 1915, they were especially destructive in the park and were following the elk herds to the high pastures of Mirror Plateau, returning with them in winter to the valleys along the Lamar and Yellowstone rivers. In the summer of 1915, Mr. Frazier, at the Buffalo

Ranch [a buffalo compound within the park], told me that wolves had been very troublesome during the preceding winter and had killed many elk. He said that from the ranch he would often hear an elk bawling in the night and the next morning see ravens circling over a half-eaten carcass. During June of that year, Mr. Frazier killed two half-grown wolf pups and caught two more, which were kept chained up at the ranch. During July and August, 1915, I found where a family of wolves had killed and eaten a young elk in Slough Creek valley and found wolf tracks along Slough Creek and Lamar valleys up to the mouth of Mist Creek, also along Pelican Creek, and later a few tracks on Fox Creek at the southern edge of the park. Tracks were especially numerous along Pelican and Raven creeks, where at least ten or a dozen wolves hunted in one pack.

In November, 1915, Donald Stevenson counted nine separate tracks, where a band of wolves had crossed a sandbar on Pelican Creek, but at that time they were leaving that section of the park and following the elk herds to lower levels. In January, 1916, they were found in the Lamar and Yellowstone valleys, where Stevenson and Black secured four of the old wolves and later a family of seven pups. With persistent hunting and trapping during the spring this band of wolves was broken up, and apparently most of those not procured were driven out of the park. Evidently a few remain, however, and, as they breed rapidly, constant care must be exercised to prevent their becoming reestablished in numbers to do serious damage to the game. . . .

Destruction of Game: — Wolves are powerful animals, and their habit of hunting in pairs, families, or packs enables them to pull down and kill any game animals, even to the size of full grown buffalo or elk. Where game is abundant, as in the park region, they kill mainly those animals easiest to obtain, which are generally the young and cows. They prefer freshly killed meat and can usually kill one or more animals every night for food. On Pelican Creek, in 1915, along the trails which they were constantly using, their droppings were made up entirely of elk hair, and a scarcity of elk calves was very noticeable among the herds in that section. Ravens were especially numerous there at that time, as in sections where game is being regularly killed. One game animal killed every twenty-four hours is probably not too much to allow for each adult wolf where game is abundant. It is therefore evident that wolves and game can not be successfully maintained on the same range.

🐺 1918–23: National Park Service Annual Reports

Stephen Mather served as the first director of the NPS. *The early annual reports that Mather and his staff published show that predator control work occurred in many of the national parks. The following excerpts from Mather's reports, written by the superintendents of the parks where the predator work was being done, reveal that the bias of the times deeply influenced the* NPS's *wildlife management practices. Note the mention of Vernon Bailey's visit to Glacier National Park in the 1918 report.*

1917 Annual Report

Rocky Mountain National Park: A start was made last winter to exterminate predatory animals, but as a great amount of necessary improvement work had to be carried on by the ranger force, little was accomplished, the killing of five foxes and seven martens being the extent of this work. Two mountain lions were reported as having been seen within the park, but we were unsuccessful in our attempt to trap them. Two deer and one sheep have been reported killed by mountain lions. Much better results are expected from this work during the coming winter.

1918 Annual Report

Sequoia and General Grant National Parks: Predatory wild animals as well as food-bearing animals inhabit the parks at all times, but the former being of a more or less migratory nature fluctuate in their numbers throughout the parks during certain periods, and as this consequence more lions and wolves came into the Sequoia Park last winter than at any time previous in recent years. As soon as their increasing presence was discovered a campaign for their destruction was organized during the month of February in which 2 large lions, 5 coyotes, 3 lynx, and 6 foxes were killed. These species of animals being of a very wary nature when finding they were being pursued soon left the park for other regions before damage of consequence was done.

Crater Lake National Park: The park abounds in black and brown bear, black-tailed deer, pine marten, porcupines, grouse, pheasants, and numerous varieties of birds. Deer and bear are more plentiful each year and are growing quite tame. Cougar, lynx, timber wolves, and coyotes are seen occasionally, and every effort is being made by the ranger force to exterminate them.

Mesa Verde National Park: The park, if fenced and the predatory animals hunted out, would be an ideal game preserve, for it contains both summer and winter range.

Glacier National Park: The protection afforded the many species of wild animals found in the park is beginning to show in their increasing numbers and their tameness. This is especially apparent as regards the Rocky Mountain sheep, goats, and deer. In previous years a good view of a band of sheep or of a goat jumping from one crag to another on the mountainside was a rare sight indeed; but now it is a common thing to see tourists viewing these animals through field glasses from hotel or chalet veranda. Deer are also increasing in numbers and the campaign of extermination that is being inaugurated against the predatory animals in the park will help greatly in removing this menace to the deer. . . .

During the early part of the summer the park was visited by Mr. Vernon Bailey, chief field naturalist for the Bureau of Biological Survey. Conditions relative to the destruction of game by predatory animals were investigated and considered sufficiently serious to warrant action being taken toward their extermination. A cooperative agreement was reached between the National Park Service and the Biological Survey under which the Biological Survey would train hunters and oversee the work and the National Park Service pay the salaries.

It was originally planned to send four hunters from the Idaho district, these men to devote about two months of the present fall season in systematically clearing the park of predatory animals and later returning to their regular stations. For several reasons it became necessary to abandon this arrangement, the most important of these being increased pressure of the Army draft and the conviction that more permanent and less expensive results could be obtained through securing local men and training them for the work. Experience has shown that no lasting benefit may be had through a brief period of work, however thorough. As the park is surrounded by hundreds of miles of infested territory, and predatory animals are more or less migratory, a small area is quickly restocked when work is relaxed. . . . Success in this venture will depend on the permanent employment of the required number of hunters and the job will be a question of years, not months.

Mr. L. J. Goodman, of the Biological Survey, arrived at park headquarters on August 22. He spent several days in familiarizing himself with local conditions, perfecting plans, and locating desirable material for hunters. In this work he was assisted by the assistant chief ranger and one ranger, every assistance possible being provided. . . . One hunter was established at Anaconda Creek, as this is a central point for the area where coyotes are most abundant and trapping most feasible. Another hunter was assigned the territory from Logging Creek to the international boundary. By September 6 the hunters had been thoroughly instructed in the proper methods of hunting and trapping, and the work was turned over to them. . . .

Work on the east side of the park is a straight Biological Survey affair. A large part of the territory to be cleared lies within the Blackfeet Indian Reservation, and this work will benefit local stock interests as well as the park. So long as it remains a breeding ground for coyotes, the animals will drift across the divide into the deer yards of the west slope [of the park]. The game of the east side is not suffering from depredations by coyotes, since deer are not plentiful and mountain sheep and goats are in very little danger. Of other predatory animals there are some lion, a few cats, and, perhaps, some wolves ranging across from the Canadian side.

1919 Annual Report

Introduction by Stephen Mather: Our efforts to reduce the number of predatory animals in the national parks have met with unusual success during the past year, and in several of the bigger parks so many of these animals have been killed that there has already been a noticeable increase in the deer and other species that are usually their victims.

Crater Lake National Park: Cougar, lynx, timber wolves, and coyotes are seen occasionally, and every effort is being made to exterminate them.

1920 Annual Report

Mount Rainier National Park: The reduction of the predatory animals in the park is very desirable in order that the game and wild life may be permitted to increase. This work can best be done by cooperation with the United States Biological Survey in the placing of paid hunters in the park. These men should be adequately paid and devote their time exclusively to predatory animals, without the necessity of trapping fur-bearing animals to supplement a nominal salary. The animals classed as predatory, and whose presence in the park is detrimental to game and other animals, are cougar, bobcat, lynx, coyote, and wolf. The cougar and bobcat are probably the most detrimental in this park. It is estimated that one cougar will kill a deer a week, or 50 per year, and the United States Biological Survey considers this estimate a conservative one. . . .

1922 Annual Report
Introduction by Stephen Mather: The national parks and monuments play a very important part in the conservation of wild life, for in them all animals, with the exception of predatory ones, find safe refuge and complete protection and live unhampered in natural environment.

Mesa Verde National Park: By arrangements completed with the Biological Survey, they will send a mountain-lion hunter in here after the first fall of snow, for the purpose of ridding the park of the deers' worst enemy, and also to control the fast increasing hordes of coyotes and other predatory animals.

Rocky Mountain National Park: A poison campaign directed against coyotes was conducted during January by two representatives of the United States Biological Survey, assisted by park rangers, resulting in nine predatory animals of various kinds poisoned. It is probable that a number of others were poisoned whose carcasses were never found.

Permits were issued last winter to hunters to trap predatory animals. The following animals were killed in the park, or in territory immediately adjacent: Mountain lion, 6; bobcat, 20; fox, 3; badger, 2; weasel, 2; coyote, 8; mink, 6; total, 47.

Glacier National Park: A campaign of extermination was waged against mountain lions the past winter and 31 were killed.

1923 Annual Report
Grand Canyon National Park: In October, 1922, John B. Tooker was appointed predatory animal killer, temporary, and during the winter of 1922–23 he rendered excellent service toward the end of destroying predatory animals that would otherwise prey on the deer, squirrels, rabbits, etc., which it is desired to increase on the south rim of this park. The records show his destruction of predatory animals to have been as follows: 82 coyotes, 14 bobcats, and 1 cougar.

1924 Annual Report
Introduction by Stephen Mather: All the national parks are absolute sanctuaries for wild animals except a few species of predatory ones which are annually reduced by the ranger forces on patrol.

1928–32: Minutes of National Park Service Conferences
Each year, the director of the NPS *and the superintendents of the various parks gathered together to discuss issues of park policy and management. Many of these meetings, commonly called "The Superintendents' Con-*

ference," debated the issue of predator control in the parks. The following excerpts from those conferences show how the NPS director and superintendents viewed predators. This compilation of predator-related comments comes from an undated NPS paper, "Condensed Chronology of Service Predatory Policy."

1928 Conference
At this conference, Stephen Mather, the NPS director, responds to a recently published suggestion by Professor Joseph Grinnell of the University of California at Berkeley, that no predators should be killed in any national park. Mather's statement shows his sympathy to the argument that managers of federal lands have an obligation to help local ranchers by killing predators on public lands.

MR. MATHER: From the standpoint of predatory animals, that brings in a great many problems. In Yellowstone, if Mr. Albright [the Yellowstone superintendent and later, the second director of the NPS] didn't kill off his 200 or 300 coyotes a year it might result in being the developing ground for the coyotes and wolves spreading out over the country and the cattle or sheep men getting much greater losses than they ordinarily would. It does seem we must do a certain amount of that in areas where we have proximity to forests where cattle and sheep are feeding. Otherwise we are in very bad odor with our neighbors. Even in Yellowstone we have no idea of killing off or exterminating.

1932 Conference
During the 1932 conference, the superintendents came to an agreement that they should not seek total extermination of any native species from national parks. These passages from the conference show the close ties the NPS had with sportsmen's associations and the prevailing Park Service view of the predator-prey balance in the parks.

MR. TOLL [Yellowstone Superintendent]: I think everyone is in agreement that no species should be exterminated, whether it is a mountain lion or bobcat, but we have always assumed, whether rightly or wrongly, that the elk and the deer and the antelope were the type of animal the park was for. We have had the support of the game associations only on the basis that the parks would act as reservoirs for the game and the increase would overflow and form legitimate hunting. If we change that policy and say there are to be no killings, coyote will increase to balance the increase of the deer and elk, there will be no hunting and we would have no support whatsoever from the sportsmen's associations of the adjoining States. To me a herd of antelope and deer is more valuable than a herd of coyotes. . . .

MR. EAKIN: As I see it, I do not believe we ought to disturb the balance of wild life when it is proved there is anything near a balance, but if you do not keep the coyote down you will have no deer or antelope.

MR. ALBRIGHT: I am convinced that if we did not have intensive coyote control there would be no antelope in Yellowstone today. From 1908 to 1920 their numbers dropped from 2,000 to less than 200, and we instituted very strong coyote control, took the fences down, and they increased something over 600. But they are not making much more headway than that. I think we have got to get down pretty near the point of eliminating the last coyote in that section or we cannot expect much of an increase.

Horace Albright's anti-coyote statement represented the old style of NPS wild-life management. Park Service documents reprinted in Chapter 8 show that the agency eventually made dramatic revisions in its predator policy.

Chapter 6

The Outlaw Wolves

"He's dared me to come at him . . ."
Bill Caywood, USBS trapper

During the war against the wolf, the vast majority of wolves were killed through the use of traps, guns, poison, and the destruction of pups at the den. A few individuals survived this onslaught—they had learned to recognize traps and poisoned bait, and if they found a mate, they only denned in the most remote wilderness areas. These animals became masters at survival; they possessed the intelligence and cunning to overcome any adversity that humanity put in their path. Certain wolves seemed to howl out a scornful challenge to their enemy: "You'll never get me." If they choose to raid the stockmen's pastures, they did so as unseen phantoms, impossible to catch. Legends developed about the seeming supernatural powers of these outlaw wolves. Some said they were in league with the devil. I prefer to think that they were being advised by the Trickster character that appears in so many Native American stories.

Trappers of ordinary abilities had no chance of capturing these elusive renegades. In the last days of the wolf, epic duels occurred between master trappers and master wolves. A rich literature developed from these hunts. Many of the most popular stories presented the wolf character in a heroic light—he or she was the last of the breed, valiantly fighting overwhelming odds but doomed to certain defeat at the hand of the enemy: the human race.

The real exploits of these outlaw wolves and the stories, fiction and non-fiction, written about them caused many people to see the wolf in a new light. Americans love stories about courageous loners, fighting for a rebel cause, fated to ultimately die, but dying a good death. Slowly, our culture, like the Native American culture, began to think of the wolf as an animal that deserved our honor and respect. This respect for a fellow species would form the foundation for a radical reevaluation of our national policies toward the wolf.

1894: "Lobo: The King of Currumpaw," Ernest Thompson Seton

In his day, the late 1800s and the first half of the 1900s, Ernest Thompson Seton was one of the most popular writers in North America. He was born in England, grew up in Canada, then returned to England to attend the Royal Academy of Painting and Sculpture. His animal stories, especially the ones about wolves, reached millions of readers and greatly influenced public opinion. More than any other contemporary author, Seton presented the wolf as a hero. This story, the tragic tale of Lobo, the "King of the Currumpaw," appeared in the November 1894 issue of Scribner's *magazine, just ten months after the wolf's death. It is especially poignant because of Seton's personal involvement in Lobo's fate.*

In 1898, Seton published a collection of animal stories, Wild Animals I Have Known, *that included the Lobo article. The book was hugely successful: nine printings were ordered in the first eighteen months. The book's popularity led to a series of lecture tours throughout the United States and Europe. Seton's talk on Lobo deeply touched his audiences and gave them a totally new perspective on wolves.*

In his introduction to Wild Animals I Have Known, *Seton wrote, "These stories are true. Although I have left the strict line of historical truth in many places, the animals in this book were all real characters. They lived the lives I have depicted, and showed the stamp of heroism and personality more strongly by far than it has been in the power of my pen to tell." Speaking of Lobo, he added, "Lobo lived his wild romantic life from 1889 to 1894 in the Currumpaw region, as the ranchmen know too well, and died, precisely as related, on January 31, 1894."*

As you read Seton's tale, note his subtle reference to feelings of guilt over the way he lured Lobo to his fate. Seton's tragic encounter with Lobo and Blanca radically changed his attitude toward wolves.

I

Currumpaw is a vast cattle range in northern New Mexico. It is a land of rich pastures and teeming flocks and herds, a land of rolling mesas and precious running waters that at length unite in the Currumpaw River, from which the whole region is named. And the king whose despotic power was felt over its entire extent was an old gray wolf.

Old Lobo, or the king, as the Mexicans called him, was the gigantic leader of a remarkable pack of gray wolves, that had ravaged the Currumpaw Valley for a number of years. All the shepherds and ranchmen knew him well, and wherever he appeared with his trusty band, terror reigned supreme among the cattle, and wrath and despair among their owners. Old Lobo was a giant among wolves, and was cunning and strong in proportion to his size. His voice at night was well-known and easily distinguished from that of any of his fellows. An ordinary wolf might howl half the night about the herdsman's bivouac without attracting more than a passing notice, but when the deep roar of the old king came booming down the cañon, the watcher bestirred himself and prepared to learn in the morning that fresh and serious inroads had been made among the herds.

Old Lobo's band was but a small one. This I never quite understood, for usually, when a wolf rises to the position and power that he had, he attracts a numerous following. It may be that he had as many as he desired, or perhaps his ferocious temper prevented the increase of his pack. Certain is it that Lobo had only five followers during the latter part of his reign. Each of these, however, was a wolf of renown, most of them were above the ordinary size, one in particular, the second in command, was a veritable giant, but even he was far below the leader in size and prowess. Several of the band, besides the two leaders, were especially noted. One of these was a beautiful white wolf, that the Mexicans called Blanca; this was supposed to be a female, possibly Lobo's mate. Another was a yellow wolf of remarkable swiftness, which, according to current stories had, on several occasions, captured an antelope for the pack.

It will be seen, then, that these wolves were thoroughly well-known to the cowboys and shepherds. They were frequently seen and oftener heard, and their lives were intimately associated with those of the cattlemen, who would so gladly have destroyed them. There was not a stockman on the Currumpaw who would not readily have given the value of many steers for the scalp of any one of Lobo's band, but they seemed to possess charmed lives, and defied all manner of devices to kill them. They scorned all hunters, derided all poisons, and continued, for at least five years, to exact their tribute from the Currumpaw ranchers to the extent, many said, of a cow each day. According to this estimate, therefore, the band had killed more than two thousand of the finest stock, for, as was only too well-known, they selected the best in every instance.

The old idea that a wolf was constantly in a starving state, and therefore ready to eat anything, was as far as possible from the truth in this case, for these freebooters were always sleek and well-conditioned, and were in fact most fastidious about what they ate. Any animal that had died from natural causes, or that was diseased or tainted, they would not touch, and they even rejected anything that had been killed by the stockmen. Their choice and daily food was the tenderer part of a freshly killed yearling heifer. An old bull or cow they disdained, and though they occasionally took a young calf or colt, it was quite clear that veal or horseflesh was not their favorite diet. It was also known that they were not fond of mutton, although they often amused themselves by killing sheep. One night in November, 1893, Blanca and the yellow wolf killed two hundred and fifty sheep, apparently for the fun of it, and did not eat an ounce of their flesh.

These are examples of many stories which I might repeat, to show the ravages of this destructive band. Many new devices for their extinction were tried each year, but still they lived and throve in spite of all the efforts of their foes. A great price was set on Lobo's head, and in consequence poison in a score of subtle forms was put out for him, but he never failed to detect and avoid it. One thing only he feared—that was firearms, and knowing full well that all men in this region carried them, he never was known to attack or face a human being. Indeed, the set policy of his band was to take refuge in flight whenever, in the daytime, a man was descried, no matter at what distance. Lobo's habit of permitting the pack to eat only that which they themselves had killed, was in numerous cases their salvation, and the keenness of his scent to detect the taint of human hands or the poison itself, completed their immunity.

On one occasion, one of the cowboys heard the too familiar rallying-cry of Old Lobo, and stealthily approaching, he found the Currumpaw pack in a hollow, where they had rounded up a small herd of cattle. Lobo sat apart on a knoll, while Blanca with the rest was endeavoring to 'cut out' a young cow, which they had selected; but the cattle were standing in a compact mass with their heads outward, and presented to the foe a line of horns, unbroken save when some cow, frightened by a fresh onset of the wolves, tried to retreat into the middle of the herd. It was only by taking advantage of these breaks that the wolves had succeeded at all in wounding the selected cow, but she was far from being disabled, and it seemed that Lobo at length lost patience with his followers, for he left his position on the hill, and, uttering a deep roar, dashed toward the herd. The terrified rank broke at his charge, and he sprang in among them. Then the cattle scattered like pieces of a bursting bomb. Away went the chosen victim, but ere she had gone twenty-five yards Lobo was upon her. Seizing her by the neck he suddenly held back with all his force and so threw her heavily to the ground. The shock must have been tremendous, for the heifer was thrown heels over head. Lobo also turned a somersault, but immediately recovered himself, and his followers falling on the poor cow, killed her in a few seconds. Lobo took no part in the killing—after having thrown the victim, he seemed to say, "Now, why could not some of you have done that at once without wasting so much time?"

The man now rode up shouting, the wolves as usual retired, and he, having a bottle of strychnine, quickly poisoned the carcass in three places, then went away, knowing they would return to feed, as they had killed the animal themselves. But the next morning, on going to look for his expected victims, he found that, although the wolves had eaten the heifer, they had carefully cut out and thrown aside all those parts that had been poisoned.

The dread of this great wolf spread yearly among the ranchmen, and each year a larger price was set on his head, until at last it reached $1,000, an unparalleled wolf-bounty, surely; many a good man had been hunted down for less. Tempted by the promised reward, a Texan ranger named Tannerey came one day galloping up the cañon of the Currumpaw. He had a superb outfit for wolf-hunting—the best of guns and horses, and a pack of enormous wolf-hounds. Far out on the plains of the Pan-handle, he and his dogs had killed many a wolf, and now he never doubted that, within a few days, old Lobo's scalp would dangle at his saddle-bow.

Away they went bravely on their hunt in the gray dawn of a summer morning, and soon the great dogs gave joyous tongue to say that they were already on the track of their quarry. Within two miles, the grizzly band of Currumpaw leaped into view, and the chase grew fast and furious. The part of the wolf-hounds was merely to hold the wolves at bay till the hunter could ride up and shoot them, and this usually was easy on the open plains of Texas; but here a new feature of the country came into play, and showed how well Lobo had chosen his range; for the rocky cañons of the Currumpaw and its tributaries intersect the prairies in every direction. The old wolf at once made for the nearest of these and by crossing it got rid of the horsemen. His band then scattered and thereby scattered the dogs, and when they reunited at a distant point of course all of the dogs did not turn up, and the wolves no longer outnumbered, turned on their pursuers and killed or desperately wounded them all. That night when Tannerey mustered his dogs, only six of them returned, and of these, two were terribly lacerated. This hunter made two other attempts to capture the royal scalp, but neither of them was more successful than the first, and on the last occasion his best horse met its death by a fall; so he gave up the chase in disgust and went back to Texas, leaving Lobo more than ever the despot of the region.

Next year, two other hunters appeared, determined to win the promised bounty. Each believed he could destroy the noted wolf, the first by means of a newly devised poison, which was to be laid out in an entirely new manner; the other a French Canadian, by poison assisted with certain spells and charms, for he firmly believed that Lobo was a veritable 'loup-garou' [werewolf], and could not be killed by ordinary means. But cunningly compounded poisons, charms, and incantations were all of no avail against this grizzly devastator. He made his weekly rounds and daily banquets as aforetime, and before many weeks had passed, Calone and Laloche gave up in despair and went elsewhere to hunt.

In the spring of 1893, after his unsuccessful attempt to capture Lobo, Joe Calone had a humiliating experience, which seems to show that the big wolf simply scorned his enemies, and had absolute confidence in himself. Calone's farm was on a small tributary of the Currumpaw, in a picturesque cañon, and among the rocks of this very cañon, within a thousand yards of the house, old Lobo and his mate selected their den and raised their family that season. There they lived all summer, and killed Joe's cattle, sheep, and dogs, but laughed at all his poisons and traps, and rested securely among the recesses of the cavernous cliffs, while Joe vainly racked his brain for some method of smoking them out, or of reaching them with dynamite. But they escaped entirely unscathed, and continued their ravages as before. "There's where he lived all last summer," said Joe, pointing to the face of the cliff, "and I couldn't do a thing with him. I was like a fool to him."

II

This history, gathered so far from the cowboys, I found hard to believe until the fall of 1893, I made the acquaintance of the wily marauder, and at length came to know him more thoroughly than anyone else. Some years before, in the Bingo days, I had been a wolf-hunter, but my occupations since then had been of another sort, chaining me to stool and desk. I was much in need of a change, and when a friend, who was also a ranch-owner on the Currumpaw, asked me to come to New Mexico and try if I could do anything with this predatory pack, I accepted the invitation and, eager to make the acquaintance of its king, was as soon as possible among the mesas of that region. I spent some time riding about to learn the country, and at intervals, my guide would point to the skeleton of a cow to which the hide still adhered, and remark, "That's some of his work."

It became quite clear to me that, in this rough country, it was useless to think of pursuing Lobo with hounds and horses, so that poison or traps were the only available expedients. At present we had no traps large enough, so I set to work with poison.

I need not enter into the details of a hundred devices that I employed to circumvent this 'loup-garou'; there was no combination of strychnine, arsenic, cyanide, or prussic acid, that I did not essay; there was no manner of flesh that I did not try as bait; but morning after morning, as I rode forth to learn the result, I found that all my efforts had been useless. The old king was too cunning for me. A single instance will show his wonderful sagacity. Acting on the hint of an old trapper, I melted some cheese together with the kidney fat of a freshly killed heifer, stewing it in a china dish, and cutting it with a bone knife to avoid the taint of metal. When the mixture was cool, I cut it into lumps, and making a hole in one side of each lump, I inserted a large dose of strychnine and cyanide, contained in a capsule that was impermeable by any odor; finally I sealed the holes up with pieces of the cheese itself. During the whole process, I wore a pair of gloves steeped in the hot blood of the heifer, and even avoided breathing on the baits. When all was ready, I put them in a raw-hide bag rubbed all over with blood, and rode forth dragging the liver and kidneys of the beef at the end of a rope. With this I made a ten-mile circuit, dropping a bait at each quarter of a mile, and taking the utmost care, always, not to touch any with my hands.

Lobo, generally, came into this part of the range in the early part of each week, and passed the latter part, it was supposed, around the base of the Sierra Grande. This was Monday, and that same evening, as we were about to retire, I heard the deep bass howl of his majesty. On hearing it one of the boys briefly remarked, "There he is, we'll see."

The next morning I went forth, eager to know the result. I soon came on the fresh trail of the robbers, with Lobo in the lead—his track was always easily distinguished. An ordinary wolf's forefoot is 4½ inches long, that of a large wolf 4¾ inches, but Lobo's, as measured a number of times, was 5½ inches from claw to heel; I afterward found that his other proportions were commensurate, for he stood three feet high at the shoulder, and weighed 150 pounds. His trail, therefore, though obscured by those of his followers, was never difficult to trace. The pack had soon found the track of my drag, and as usual followed it. I could see that Lobo had come to the first bait, sniffed about it, and finally had picked it up.

Then I could not conceal my delight. "I've got him at last," I exclaimed; "I shall find him stark within a mile," and I galloped on with eager eyes fixed on the great broad track in the dust. It led me to the second bait and that was also gone. How I exulted—I surely have him now and perhaps several of his band. But there was the broad paw-mark still on the drag; and though I stood in the stirrup and scanned the plain I saw nothing that looked like a dead wolf. Again I followed—to find now that the third bait was gone—and the king-wolf's track led on to the fourth, there to learn that he had not really taken a bait at all, but had merely carried them in his mouth. Then having piled the three on the fourth, he scattered filth over them to express his utter contempt for my devices. After this he left my drag and went about his business with the pack he guarded so effectively.

This is only one of the many similar experiences which convinced me that poison would never avail to destroy this robber, and though I continued to use it while awaiting the arrival of the traps, it was only because it was meanwhile a sure means of killing many prairie wolves and other destructive vermin. . . .

At length the wolf traps arrived, and with two men I worked a whole week to get them properly set out. We spared no labor or pains, I adopted every device I could think of that might help to insure success. The second day after the traps arrived, I rode around to inspect, and soon came upon Lobo's trail running from trap to trap. In the dust I could read the whole story of his doings that night. He had trotted along in the darkness, and although the traps were so carefully concealed, he had instantly detected the first one. Stopping the onward march of the pack, he had cautiously scratched around it until he had disclosed the trap, the chain, and the log, and then left them wholly exposed to view with the trap still unsprung, and passing on he treated over a dozen traps in the same fashion. Very soon I noticed that he stopped and turned aside as soon as he detected suspicious signs on the trail and a new plan to outwit him at once suggested itself. I set the traps in the form of an H; that is, with a row of traps on each side of the trail, and one on the trail for the cross-bar of the H. Before long, I had an opportunity to count another failure. Lobo came trotting along the trail, and was fairly between the parallel lines before he detected the single trap in the trail, but he stopped in time, and why or how he knew enough I cannot tell, the Angel of the wild things must have been with him, but without turning an inch to the right or left, he slowly and cautiously backed on his own tracks, putting each paw exactly in its old track until he was off the dangerous ground. Then returning at one side he scratched clods and stones with his hind feet till he had sprung every trap. This he did on many other occasions, and although I varied my methods and redoubled my precautions, he was never deceived, his sagacity seemed never at fault, and he might have been pursuing his career of rapine to-day, but for an unfortunate alliance that proved his ruin and added his name to the long list of heroes who, unassailable when alone, have fallen through the indiscretion of a trusted ally.

III

Once or twice, I had found indications that everything was not quite right in the Currumpaw pack. There were signs of irregularity, I thought; for instance there was clearly the trail of a smaller wolf running ahead of the leader, at times, and this I could not understand until a cowboy made a remark which explained the matter.

"I saw them to-day," he said, "and the wild one that breaks away is Blanca." Then the truth dawned upon me, and I added, "Now, I know that Blanca is a she-wolf, because were a he-wolf to act thus, Lobo would kill him at once."

This suggested a new plan. I killed a heifer, and set one or two rather obvious traps about the carcass. Then cutting off the head, which is considered useless offal, and quite beneath the notice of a wolf, I set it a little apart and around it placed two powerful steel traps properly deodorized and concealed with the utmost care. During my operations I kept my hands, boots, and implements smeared with fresh blood, and afterward sprinkled the ground with the same, as though it had flowed from the head; and when the traps were buried in the dust I brushed the place over with the skin of a coyote, and with a foot of the same animal made a number of tracks over the traps. The head was so placed that there was a narrow passage between it and some tussocks, and in this passage I buried two of my best traps, fastening them to the head itself.

Wolves have a habit of approaching every carcass they get wind of, in order to examine it, even when they have no intention of eating of it, and I hoped that this habit would bring the Currumpaw pack within reach of my latest stratagem. I did not doubt that Lobo would detect my handiwork about the meat, and prevent the pack approaching it, but I did build some hopes on the head, for it looked as though it had been thrown aside as useless.

Next morning, I sallied forth to inspect the traps, and there, oh, joy! were the tracks of the pack, and the place where the beef-head and its trap had been was empty. A hasty study of the trail showed that Lobo had kept the pack from approaching the meat, but one, a small wolf, had evidently gone on to examine the head as it lay apart and had walked right into one of the traps.

We set out on the trail, and within a mile discovered that the hapless wolf was Blanca. Away she went, however, at a gallop, and although encumbered by the beef-head, which weighed over fifty pounds, she speedily distanced my companion who was on foot. But we overtook her when she reached the rocks, for the horns of the cow's head became caught and held her fast. She was the handsomest wolf I had ever seen. Her coat was in perfect condition and nearly white.

She turned to fight, and raising her voice in the rallying cry of her race, sent a long howl rolling over the cañon. From far away upon the mesa came a deep response, the cry of Old Lobo. That was her last call, for now we had closed in on her, and all her energy and breath were devoted to combat.

Then followed the inevitable tragedy, the idea of which I shrank from afterward more than at the time. We each threw a lasso over the neck of the doomed wolf, and strained our horses in opposite directions until the blood burst from her mouth, her eyes glazed, her limbs stiffened and then fell limp. Homeward then we rode, carrying the dead wolf, and exulting over this, the first death-blow we had been able to inflict on the Currumpaw pack.

At intervals during the tragedy, and afterward as we rode homeward, we heard the roar of Lobo as he wandered about on the distant mesas, where he seemed to be searching for Blanca. He had never really deserted her, but knowing that he could not save her, his deep-rooted dread of firearms had been too much for him when he saw us approaching. All that day we heard him wailing as he roamed in his quest, and I remarked at length to one of the boys, "Now, indeed, I truly know that Blanca was his mate."

As evening fell he seemed to be coming toward the home cañon, for his voice sounded continually nearer. There was an unmistakable note of sorrow in it now. It was no longer the loud, defiant howl, but a long, plaintive wail; "Blanca! Blanca!" he seemed to call. And as night came down, I noticed that he was not far from the place where we had overtaken her. At length he seemed to find the trail, and when he came to the spot where we had killed her, his heart-broken wailing was piteous to hear. It was sadder than I could possibly have believed. Even the stolid cowboys noticed it, and they said they had "never heard a wolf carry on like that before." He seemed to know exactly what had taken place, for her blood had stained the place of her death.

Then he took up the trail of the horses and followed it to the ranch-house. Whether in hopes of finding her there, or in quest of revenge, I know not, but the latter was what he found, for he surprised our unfortunate watchdog outside and tore him to little bits within fifty yards of the door. He evidently came alone this time, for I found but one trail next morning, and he had galloped about in a reckless manner that was very unusual with him. I had half expected this, and had set a number of additional traps about the pasture. Afterward I found that he had indeed fallen into one of these, but such was his strength, he had torn himself loose and cast it aside.

I believed that he would continue in the neighborhood until he found her body at least, so I concentrated all my energies on this one enterprise of catching him before he left the region, and while yet in this reckless mood. Then I realized what a mistake I had made in killing Blanca, for by using her as a decoy I might have secured him the next night.

I gathered in all the traps I could command, one hundred and thirty strong steel wolf-traps, and set them in fours in every trail that led into the cañon; each trap was separately fastened to a log, and each log was separately buried. In burying them, I carefully removed the sod and every particle of earth that was lifted we put in blankets, so that after the sod was replaced and all was finished the eye could detect no trace of human handiwork. When the traps were concealed I trailed the body of poor Blanca over each place, and made of it a drag that circled all about the ranch, and finally I took off one of her paws and made with it a line of tracks over each trap. Every precaution and device known to me I used, and retired at a late hour to await the result.

Once during the night I thought I heard Old Lobo, but was not sure of it. Next day I rode around, but darkness came on before I completed the circuit of the north cañon, and I had nothing to report. At supper one of the cowboys said, "There was a great row among the cattle in the north cañon this morning, maybe there is something in the traps there." It was afternoon of the next day before I got to the place referred to, and as I drew near a great grizzly form arose from the ground, vainly endeavoring to escape, and there revealed before me stood Lobo, King of the Currumpaw, firmly held in the traps. Poor old hero, he had never ceased to search for his darling, and when he found the trail her body had made he followed it recklessly, and so fell into the snare prepared for him. There he lay in the iron grasp of all four traps, perfectly helpless, and all around him were the numerous tracks showing how the cattle had gathered about him to insult the fallen despot, without daring to approach within his reach. For two days and two nights he had lain there, and now was worn out with struggling. Yet, when I went near him, he rose up with bristling mane and raised his voice, and for the last time made the cañon reverberate with his deep bass roar, a call for help, the muster call of his band. But there was none to answer him, and, left alone in his extremity, he whirled about with all his strength and made a desperate effort to get at me. All in vain, each trap was a dead drag of over three hundred pounds, and in their relentless fourfold grasp, with great steel jaws on every foot, and the heavy logs and chains all entangled together, he was absolutely powerless. How his huge ivory tusks did grind on those cruel chains, and when I ventured to touch him with my riflebarrel he left grooves on it which are there to this day. His eyes glared green with hate and fury, and his jaws snapped with a hollow 'chop,' as he vainly endeavored to reach me and my trembling horse. But he was worn out with hunger and struggling and loss of blood, and he soon sank exhausted to the ground.

Something like compunction came over me, as I prepared to deal out to him that which so many had suffered at his hands.

"Grand old outlaw, hero of a thousand lawless raids, in a few minutes you will be but a great load of carrion. It cannot be otherwise." Then I swung my lasso and sent it whistling over his head. But not so fast; he was yet far from being subdued, and, before the supple coils had fallen on his neck he seized the noose and, with one fierce chop, cut through its hard thick strands, and dropped it in two pieces at his feet.

Of course I had my rifle as a last resource, but I did not wish to spoil his royal hide, so I galloped back to the camp and returned with a cowboy and a fresh lasso. We threw to our victim a stick of wood which he seized in his teeth, and before he could relinquish it our lassos whistled through the air and tightened on his neck.

Yet before the light had died from his fierce eyes, I cried, "Stay, we will not kill him; let us take him alive to the camp." He was so completely powerless now that it was easy to put a stout stick through his mouth, behind his tusks, and then lash his jaws with a heavy cord which was also fastened to the stick. The stick kept the cord in, and the cord kept the stick in so he was harmless. As soon as he felt his jaws were tied he made no further resistance, and uttered no sound, but looked calmly at us and seemed to say, "Well, you have got me at last, do as you please with me." And from that time he took no more notice of us.

We tied his feet securely, but he never groaned, nor growled, nor turned his head. Then with our united strength were just able to put him on my horse. His breath came evenly as though sleeping, and his eyes were bright and clear again, but did not rest on us. Afar on the great rolling mesas they were fixed, his passing kingdom, where his famous band was now scattered. And he gazed till the pony descended the pathway into the cañon, and the rocks cut off the view.

By travelling slowly we reached the ranch in safety, and after securing him with a collar and a strong chain, we staked him out in the pasture and removed the cords. Then for the first time I could examine him closely, and proved how unreliable is vulgar report when a living hero or tyrant is concerned. He had *not* a collar of gold about his neck, nor was there on his shoulders an inverted cross to denote that he had leagued himself with Satan. But I did find on one haunch a great broad scar, that tradition says was the fang-mark of Juno, the leader of Tannery's wolf-hounds—a mark which she gave him the moment before he stretched her lifeless on the sand of the cañon.

I set meat and water beside him, but he paid no heed. He lay calmly on his breast, and gazed with those steadfast yellow eyes away past me down through the gateway of the cañon, over the open plains—his plains—nor moved a muscle when I touched him. When the sun went down he was still gazing fixedly across the prairie. I expected he would call up his band when night came, and prepared for them, but he had called once in his extremity, and none had come; he would never call again.

A lion shorn of his strength, an eagle robbed of his freedom, or a dove bereft of his mate, all die, it is said, of a broken heart; and who will aver that this grim bandit could bear the three-fold brunt, heart-whole? This only I know, that when the morning dawned, he was lying there still in his position of calm repose, his body unwounded, but his spirit was gone—the old King-wolf was dead.

I took the chain from his neck, a cowboy helped me to carry him to the shed where lay the remains of Blanca, and as we laid him beside her, the cattle-man exclaimed: "There, you *would* come to her, now you are together again."

In a section of his book entitled "Note to the Reader," Seton draws a moral from his tales of Lobo and other heroic animals. This moral, as expressed in the following passage, deeply influenced great numbers of Seton's readers in their personal ethics toward animals:

The fact that these stories are true is the reason why all are tragic. The life of a wild animal *always has a tragic end.*

Such a collection of histories naturally suggests a common thought— a moral it would have been called in the last century. No doubt each different mind will find a moral to its taste, but I hope some will herein find emphasized a moral as old as Scripture—we and the beast are kin. Man has nothing that the animals have not at least a vestige of, the animals have nothing that man does not in some degree share.

Since, then, the animals are creatures with wants and feelings differing in degree only from our own, they surely have their rights. This fact, now beginning to be recognized by the Caucasian world was first proclaimed by Moses and was emphasized by the Buddhist over two thousand years ago.

In the spring of 1994, exactly one hundred years after the deaths of Lobo and Blanca, I visited the Currumpaw region of northeastern New Mexico. Currumpaw is an Indian word meaning "wild or isolated," but the country is no longer wild or remote. The only animals I saw were cattle and a single raccoon.

I wanted to do something to commemorate the lives of Lobo and Blanca so I stopped my van near a group of cattle and played a tape of wolf howls. The cows stared back at me with blank expressions on their faces, saliva dripping from their mouths as they chewed their cuds. These animals did not recognize the sound of a wolf howl. Lobo and his race had been forgotten by the livestock that now dominated his former range.

I stopped in Des Moines, the small town just west of the Currumpaw, to talk with local residents about Lobo and Blanca. No one had ever heard of them. A few old timers had vague recollections of wolves bothering the ranchers' livestock, but like the local cattle, none knew of Lobo. The situation seemed like the fulfillment of a curse from Old Testament times: "May you die at the hand of your enemy and may your name be forgotten by all."

In researching Seton's life, however, I discovered that Lobo's story does live on in a nearby section of New Mexico. Seton's widow donated his files and possessions to the Ernest Thompson Seton Memorial Library and Museum at the Philmont Scout Ranch near Cimarron, New Mexico. Included in the thousands of items was the pelt of Lobo, King of the Currumpaw. Generations of boy scouts have filed past the glass case containing Lobo's hide and tried to imagine what it must have been like to have lived during Lobo's reign.

🐺 1890s: "Wosca and Her Valiant Cub or The White Mother Wolf," Ernest Thompson Seton

In 1937 Seton published a collection of animal stories entitled Great Historic Animals: Mainly About Wolves. *In his preface, he comments on the preponderance of wolf stories in the volume: "This seems to be mostly a book of famous wolves. It is so because my sympathies and my studies have led me chiefly to that field."*

According to Seton, the story of Wosca and Shishoka took place during the 1890s in the Badlands of the Dakotas and in portions of Montana and Wyoming. To introduce the tale, he wrote, "Those who know the wolf only as a hateful thing, a destroyer of stock, a bandit on the ranges, may be surprised and informed if they ponder the story of 'Wosca, the Cody Wolf,' which is founded on well-authenticated incidents. My personal acquaintance with the fierce creature was limited to one or two hunts after him near Medora, North Dakota. But the episodes set forth are sponsored by many men whose names will carry weight; though, of course, it is certain that not one, but many different wolves, are compounded in the central figure."

Our traditional picture of the wolf presents an odious creature, a monster of cruelty and destruction; actuated by nothing higher than a gluttonous appetite for food.

Yet I have seen wolves that were dainty as deer in matters of diet. I have learned of wolves whose master trait was wisdom.

I have known wolves whose animating force was the spirit of adventure. I have been told of wolves whose strongest motivation was revenge.

I have met many a wolf whose overwhelming motive was the love of its little ones. I have seen wolves whose master passion was devotion to a dearly loved mate. I have heard of wolves who made a brotherhood pact, an affectionate alliance with some wholly different animal.

And I have knowledge of one wolf at least whose chiefest binding urge in life was loving devotion to his blind and helpless old mother.

Ye who would hear the tale as I got it from hunters and the sage-brush clan of the far North-west, listen now to the story of Wosca and her valiant cub Shishoka.

I

About 1890, there lived in the valley of the Little Missouri a well-known white wolf, a female, a pest among the cattle. Though not of large size or remarkable speed, she was endowed with such superlupine cunning that she was known and feared from Sentinel Butte to Palanata, and from Deadwood westerly to Powder River—ten thousand square miles of the finest cattle range in the West.

She never killed sheep or big steers; but showed a marked partiality for yearlings, preferably of the blooded stock; for about this time, the white faced Herefords were beginning to displace the old-time longhorns of the range.

She was identified by her white color, her punched left ear, and the lack of the outside toe on each front foot, whether a natural deformity or the result of accident is not known.

Wolves pair for life, and commonly hunt in couples—a good example of team play in perfect partnership.

The white wolf's mate was never identified, and it is believed that he was killed while she was yet young, and that thenceforth she lived alone except for the company of her latest brood.

Among the most impenetrable and forbidding of the Badlands west of the Little Missouri, a wolf hunter named Bud Dalhousie found a den of young wolves. He got a glimpse of one old one, the mother he believed; but she was too shy to come near. She was nearly pure white; and later, when he examined her track, he noted that there were but three pad-marks for each front foot, which settled her identity.

He crawled into the den, found five pups. Of these, he killed four, with a view to the bounties; but saved one vigorous 'little rascal' for bait to catch the mother, or possibly both parents. This one was ashy grey like the others, but its head and face were washed over with a reddish ochre tint; for which circumstance he called it the Red-headed Pup.

From the rocky lair down the gulch and over the fierce rifts which he crossed on foot, he left a trail by dragging one of the dead pups. Then having got back to his horse, he trailed the body at the end of his lariat to his ranch-house, some five long rugged miles away.

There was not much left of the wolfling's body when he got there, but enough to claim the five-dollar bounty.

Now he prepared for the inevitable visit that the mother would make that night. A quarter-mile form the ranch house in a bare open spot with clumps of Spanish bayonet, he prepared his trap. On the neck of the red-topped pup, he put a collar with a stout dog-chain, and fastened this to a stake well driven in.

Just beyond reach of the chained pup, he buried four strong wolf traps, buried with the consummate art of an experienced trapper, buried them so there was not the slightest hint of a buried trap so far as the eye could detect. Then he threw bits of cactus carelessly between the traps, leaving a clear smooth place on and over each fateful pan. No wolf will tread on cactus; to shun that is an early lesson in their training.

All was now set for the visit that the bereaved mother would certainly make that night to rescue her baby. Every precaution had been taken to make the snare succeed; but there is one sense that the wolf has in perfection, and which it is nigh impossible to fool. That is, scent; the scent of iron is very slight to us, but to a wolf it is as strong as it is fearsome. Even when hidden in the ground, and masked with diverse potent smells, the old wolf would surely smell the iron. But, on the other hand, the sight and smell of her little one would drive her to any desperate length, might make her throw all caution to the winds. And so it was.

The night wind was blowing starkly when the heart-hungry mother wolf came galloping down the trail that the wolver had laid. Craftily he had lulled suspicion by settling his bait and snare in the level open. The mother wolf approached up-wind. Her easy gallop slowed to a trot, to a walk as she came on the scene; and the captive cub, sensing his mother's approach, raised his baby voice in a succession of vigorous squeals and whines.

Curbing her mother instinct to rush direct to him, she circled the place with nostrils near the ground. She made appraisal of every scent and object. The baby's chain was but six feet long, so that as he circled round his stake, he was describing a twelve-foot ring, outside of which were the four great grim-jawed traps in perfect hiding, waiting, biding the time when they should do their work, and prove their mighty power.

But the scent of iron was there; and, as the mother went around, she was thoroughly informing herself. Why the cub did not run to her was puzzling. But she could go to him.

With a long, quick bound, she covered the distance from her safe outer circle, over the hidden traps, into the safe inner circle by her cowering pup. She seized him as a she-wolf or a cat is wont to seize, by the scruff of the neck. But in this case, by good luck, the scruff was covered and protected by the leather collar. Setting off with the pup in her mouth, she meant to bound far away over the hidden menaces about her. She put her strength into that bound. But, at the end of the chain, she was stopped with a fearful jerk that threw her to the ground. It might have killed the pup; but, luckily for him, the chain and collar bore the brunt, and the stake in the ground was so wrenched that on her second spring, the stake came up, and the mother wolf went off with the rescued little one in her teeth and the chain and stake trailing after.

She went at her best speed for the three miles that covered the open plain. Then, reaching the coulées with their brushwood, she went more slowly; and, in a sheltered place, lay down to nurse the pup. And much he needed it. Yet his joy in the solace of his belly-hunger was small compared with the joy she had in her heart-hungry consolation.

Here she left him for her nightly food quest. And here he was curled up alone, when with the sunrise came the wolver. He had gone forth at dawn to see the result of his trapping. The tell-tale footprints gave him all the record of the night; and speedily he, with his trailing hound and some fighting dogs, was hard galloping on the track of the escaping mother and child.

They went direct to the hiding-place of the young pirate.

At the very same time, the mother was returning with a jack-rabbit in her jaws. The wolver's hand flew to his gun, a ball whizzed past the mother's head. She sprang over a near ridge and wholly disappeared.

Of one thing chiefly is the wolf afraid; that is, guns, the thunder that kills from afar. Never will they face it. And the mother wolf was gone.

The dogs easily found the red wolf cub. He tried to run, but he still was bound with collar and chain, and these to a heavy stake which caught in the bushes, and held him so that Bud Dalhousie had no difficulty in retaking the cub.

In an hour, he was securely held in a chicken-wire cage at the ranch, and offered cow's milk and chicken heads, both of which he sulkily refused.

2

All attempts to capture the white wolf continued to be utter failures. Apparently she had lost track of where her little one was held; or perhaps gave up as hopeless all plans of rescue.

She herself continued on the range. The yearling heifers, hamstrung and throat-cut, with one meal taken out of the ham, combined with the sinister track—two forefeet, each lacking a toe—and on one or two rare occasions in the firelight when a white wolf was seen with a punched left ear, all kept the world of cattlemen aware that the old white devil still was on their range.

Meanwhile, the red pup grew. Once he learned to lap milk from a pan and gorge himself on chicken heads and beef scraps, he grew apace. At three months, he gave promise of being a monster.

Then, one day came a-riding one Colonel Cody, better known as

Buffalo Bill. And when he saw the big lubberly wolf pup with the auburn hair, he was possessed of a desire to own him that resulted in the wolver's collecting double bounty money; and Bill went off with the pup.

On the Cody ranch, he continued for a year; and it was here that an Indian scout dubbed him Shishoka, the Red-head.

During his ranch life, he learned many things that were vastly useful to him in his after life, and which could not have been learned on the open range: such as the comparative danger of man, woman, and child; the unpleasant compulsion of a chain; the value of lying low in a hollow when observation promised to be more helpful than escape; the meaning of a turkey vulture making for a slaughter-house; the message conveyed by a cowhorn blast; and above all, the deadly menace of the strychnine smell.

During this period, the red wolf had been kept on a chain, with a kennel for weather; but he seemed so thoroughly dog-like and tame that Buffalo Bill decided to give him a larger measure of liberty. One day, he unsnapped the chain from the wolf's collar, and let him run. The delight of freedom possessed the big wolf. He gambolled around like an overgrown puppy; but was easily decoyed within reach when meal-time came with a big beef bone. Once or twice the experiment was repeated, but each time the wolf was harder to recapture. Then, one fine day, during the absence of the boss, the cook turned loose the big wolf, which quietly walked off, in spite of whistles and savory meat invitations from the cook. And that was the last seen of the Cody wolf in that section of the West.

Under the urge of some inherited impulse, he travelled slowly northward, resting all day at times, but ever northward, till at length, his sense of at-home-ness was satisfied when once more he was in Butte County, Montana, with its dimly remembered buttes and rivers, its well-remembered smells.

3

All men who hunt or study wolves know that they have the country marked at every mile or less with some prominent object that serves as an information bureau. It may be a conspicuous boulder, a buffalo skull, a fence corner, or even a clod where two trails cross. The tell-tale musk is usually left at the place with the kidney product as a medium. This musk varies with every individual, and is quite distinctive; while the foot scent of the caller shows whence he came and whither he went.

With such a system of signal and record, what wonder is it that Shishoka, the Cody wolf, soon found a kind companion. Whether he knew and recognized his old mother is doubtful; but certainly he accepted her as a hunting partner, and very shortly afterwards, the night herders were made aware that the white she-devil—Wosca in Indian phrase—had hooked up with another wolf, a giant with a reddish head and something on his neck that looked 'powerful like a collar'.

Now there was a new and stronger combination—her many years' experience and superlative cunning, combined with his youth, strength, speed and knowledge of man's tricks when at home.

Yarns detailing their incredible sagacity were the theme of nightly fires. One of their tricks was wholly new to the ranchmen. The smaller wolf would sneak to a barnyard, and seize some noisy animal like a pig or a chicken, and hold it, loudly squealing, till all the dogs and men were headed that way on murder bent. Then, as their onset promised danger, she would release the victim, and disappear in the night, followed for a while by noisy dogs. Meanwhile, the big wolf attacked the calf corral, scared the crazy brutes so they burst through wire and picket fence and all, and scattered; which gave the wolves the chance they sought to select and feast at leisure.

And one more crafty policy they had to baffle all reprisals; that is, never come a second time to the same kill, never kill twice in the same locality.

Another trick was observed by a range rider who swears it happened just as he said. From a look-out butte, he was scanning the range with field-glasses, when on a distant flat he saw a wolf—a big one—lying dead. In the grass some fifty yards away, a smaller—a white one—watching. Sailing above was a turkey buzzard, always keen-eyed for carrion. The buzzard sailed over, then around and lower, and deftly lighting near the carcass approached the head, for the eyes are easy meat. But in a flash, the corpse became alive, the buzzard was chopped, and the white wolf from the look-out came trotting to share the unusual feast.

But quite the most diabolical of the plots planned by this wolf team was triumphantly put over one evening after sundown. The wolver of the Angle-bar Ranch had secured an immense female Great Dane, expressly trained to follow and fight female wolves. For oftentimes a male dog declines to pursue with deadly intent a female wolf, whereas the female Dane is even more hostile on account of the other's sex.

The white wolf had deliberately circled the corral, and left a mark of scorn on the saddle that lay by the gate. Then she howled the soft and high-pitched howl of the she-wolf. The wolver seized his gun, and at the same time unchained the furious Juno.

Away they went, the dog racing hard and mouthily baying. Away went the wolf at easy bounds, and silent, headed straight for the wolver's set; that is, four heavy traps around a beef head. She circled these adroitly, for her nose indicated the exact spot of each. But the blundering dane rushed in, and was caught in two; then, as she thrashed around, the other two traps were sprung and she lay on the ground, perfectly help-less, and at the mercy of—what? A huge grey wolf with reddish head, and a collar on his neck. She had no chance at all. It was chop, chop— and her screaming yell of terror was cut short. There, in the morning, the wolver found her carcass, and studied the tracks in the dust. A huge wolf, and with him a smaller one with mutilated feet, had been on the spot—therefore——

4

For ten years, this levy on the beef continued. Then all the cattlemen gathered for a wolf roundup. The Eatons, the Ferrises, the Myers, the Roosevelts, the Petersons, all of them with dogs galore, and horses enough; and they swept the open valley of the Little Missouri, and killed not a few coyotes and one or two grey wolves.

But the Badlands were impassable to this invading army. Here the riders were stopped, and their dogs that ventured in without support came back right soon—or never came at all.

The hunters did not see the great wolf; but that very morning, the Eaton children on their way to school were startled to see, watching them from a near bank, the unmistakable head and the collared throat of Cody's wolf. He looked at them with mild curiosity—no sign or move of menace.

These boys were used to guns, and next day came prepared. But no sign of the wolf did they see, nor the next, nor for a week. Then the guns were left behind; they were needed elsewhere. And the very next day, the wolf was on the bank again.

Whence got he such forewarning? Where do the wild things get such supersensile information? No one knows. The fiction of the An-gel of the Wild Things has been invented to explain. Who knows? This only is sure: they get the warnings if they heed them. And ever the great wolf kept his sense nerves keenly atune [*sic*].

One fact came slowly to the knowledge of the cowmen now. The big wolf was alone; the crafty white one had departed. No one knew when or how. The bounty, three times doubled for her head, was never claimed. They only knew she was gone. And this strange variant in the wolf's mode of life was seen: he still killed cows, but more often lambs; and when he killed a lamb he took it clean away.

5

Of all the weird fantastic uplands in the West, the Badlands are the strangest freaks that ever Nature upheaped in a mood that like madness, in frenzy of unmeasured power—castles, bogs, cathedrals, cloud-capped towers, rainbow-tinted rocks, hell-holes, sinks, endless caverns, death-traps, gas-holes, underground fires, glimpses of little fairylands, forbidding crags, infernos, and fairy dells, mixed, jangled, interspersed and fenced with incredible cliffs of treacherous deadly clay.

The scientist and the adventurous explorer perhaps, or the hunter, visits the Badlands as far in as he can go; the cowboys rarely, for cattle cannot enter. The wolf hunter at times makes an arduous entry at least beyond their outmost confines.

Dalhousie the wolver was more than a wolver. He was a game sport. Nothing inspired him to some wild attempt more than the assurance that it had many time been tried, but never yet accomplished. And when he learned that that thread of smoke across the sunset gold came from some strange subterranean fire that no one yet had seen or even approached, he said: 'That settles it! I'll cook my coffee over that to-morrow noon.'

This was the immediate reason for his venture into the fascinating beauties and horrors of the 'Land of Gehenna'.

He left his horse in a little gulch where the fantasies in clay began. Here was grass and water. Then, with his grub-kit on his back, and his rifle in his hand, he made for the place where the fire was supposed to issue forth. He wandered in devious trails, and slid down dangerous banks; but ever he seemed cut off by impassable gulches from the land of the mystery smoke. Noon came and passed, and still he struggled on. It was indeed near sunset when he realized that he was yet far from his smoky goal.

In a quiet spot, he made a fire with sage-brush and cooked a much needed meal. Then, as he prepared to spend the night, his eye caught a moving object in the next clay gulch. A cautious approach, a long study with his glasses, and he recognized the grey Cody wolf, hanging from his mouth a new-killed lamb.

The wolf was travelling, that is, going somewhere, and knew just where it was he would go. He was carrying that lamb much as a she-wolf will carry home her kill. Yet this wolf was known to be a male; and at this season, autumn, there are no young that need feeding in the den.

Dalhousie followed as far as he could, but soon lost sight of the travelling wolf. Noting the red-topped butte that marked the place, the wolver settled in his blankets for the night. Next morning, he hurried back to his horse and made for home. The fact of the underground fire was interesting, but the fact that the much-sought Cody wolf had a den in the hills was vital.

To find that den was the big impelling motive in his thoughts, for surely this would end with a scalp on Dalhousie's saddle, and the ten times blood-gold in his bank.

This was why Dalhousie and his partner set out that day, with an unusual equipment for a hunt. Guns and grub—yes. Spades and picks—yes. But also a long pole with a wolf-trap tied on the end, and one small dog, a beagle of doubtful ancestry, and rejected from a blooded pack because he *would* run mute.

Fast travellers and keen hunters though they were, it was afternoon before they got to the foot of the red butte where Bud Dalhousie had seen the wolf the night before. Coming to the very spot, they encouraged the dog to take the trail: 'Hya—hya—Dummy, fetch her! Fetch!'

The scent was cold now, and not easily followed. Besides the dog had no mastering desire to overtake the creature who evidently had left it. However, there was no grass on the place, and the clay dust between the scattering sage enabled the men to do some trailing.

Yes, there it was—the huge imprints of a wolf, the largest kind of wolf. The men tracked for half a mile, and then it seemed a new track had joined on, either another large wolf or else a second trail by the same wolf.

Now for the first time, Dummy the beagle seemed to take an interest. The scent was strong, and evidently this was what his master wished him to do. So he raced along the trail, loudly sniffing but giving no tongue; so fast he went that the men were badly blown in following him. But they managed to keep him in sight, and after half an hour they came to one of those strange formations called sinks or volcanic blow-holes. At the edge, they were stopped, for it was fifty feet deep, somewhat funnel-shaped and formed at the bottom by perpendicular walls of varying height. It held no vegetation except some scrubby willows in the centre, but numerous crannies and hollowed banks afforded shelter from sun and weather. In the centre was, as is common with the sinks, a drainage pond, clearly at some seasons much larger; but now though down to the size of a blanket, it was the sufficient watering-place of sundry birds.

The big wolf's track led here. Evidently he leaped down into the sink. But the bank was sheer and six feet high, so the hunters circled round to seek out an easier entry.

They sought in vain, for at all other points the bank was higher and steeper. They were cautiously crawling around the farther side, when Dalhousie saw something that fairly made his hair stand up.

Here, threading his way through the hills by different approach, was no less than a giant grey wolf, the very one he sought; and held high in his powerful jaws as he trotted on was a half-grown sheep. The men crouched behind the nearest rocks.

With unerring sense of place, the wolf came straight to the sink, and to the very spot, the six-foot drop, whither they had tracked him before.

Arrived at the place, and without a moment's hesitation, the wolf leaped down; then, placing the sheep on the ground, he gave one or two low whining calls.

In response, there issued from a near-by cave, not a brood of little wolves, not a joyous young mother wolf, but a worn-out, weak and crawling old wolf. They saw her happy tail wag as, with a growl, she seized the dead sheep. They saw the big wolf's greeting of the venerable old she-one. He licked her face, she licked his face, and he sat couchant by, while she, uttering the happy little growls that are part of a blood-feast, fell on the sheep, and feasted, and blood-licked, and feasted.

The giant wolf did not eat. Even the wild hunters were thrilled by the touching spectacle they had witnessed; but they were not here for sentiment, they were here to kill that wolf.

Both rifles were up in line. But from this point the wolf was partly screened by jutting rocks. They waited, hoping he would move; but he laid his head on his paws, and seemed content to lie and watch the old one's feast.

At length the men tried to crawl to a better spot for aiming. A pebble rolled and rattled into the sink. The big wolf sprang to his feet, looked this way and that, and made for the six-foot bank. Both rifles rang— bang! bang!

But the wolf was racing, the men were hasty, the fire went wild. And with one mighty bound, the big wolf cleared the bank, out of the sink, and disappeared in the rugged hinterland.

The old she-wolf, sensing big trouble, though she could see nothing, dragged the rest of her feast away as she backed into the near-by cave.

6

'Well, we've got her!' exulted the wolvers; 'and I guess we'll soon get him.'

And then they pieced together the various scraps of light they had on the strange situation. Here was the old white wolf, the old she-one! Yes, there was the ball-hole through her left ear. Here she was, trapped in this sink-hole, the only way out the perpendicular leap far beyond her power. Here she had water and shelter—but what about food? That was clear; for in and about the cave were bones of sheep enough to prove that for a whole year she had been a prisoner here, and had been fed for all that time by her devoted companion.

To kill the old she-one would have been easy, or even to take her alive, for their plan had been to spread open the wolf-trap that was tied to the long pole, push it into the den, then the wolf would surely set foot in that and be easily dragged out.

But no! The bigger, better plan was to use her as a decoy, and so ensnare her faithful follower. She could not get out of the sink in any case.

That was why Dalhousie and his pard set off as fast as they could for home, and returned without resting, with six huge wolf-traps whose jaws of steel were heavy enough to hold a lion in their grip.

They set this trap under the six-foot drop, the only place where the sink-hole might be entered. They rubbed their own feet as well as the traps with fresh sheep blood to kill the smell of iron. They buried the traps with the consummate art of their calling. They had brought a small ladder so they could climb out at another place. And, as a finish, they swept the dust above the traps with fragments of the lamb skin.

There was no human trace; there was no sign of traps, no smell of traps at the six-foot height above. The setting was perfect.

The hunters climbed the cliff elsewhere, removed the ladder, and hied them to their camp a mile away.

7

They knew it to be quite unlike the big wolf if he came back the very next night. Yet they must not lose a chance.

The hunters camped, and all day waited. At dusk, they came cautiously to a view-point. But the traps were untouched; there was no sign of disturbance and no sign of the old she-wolf.

The second and third day passed. By this time the old one in the cave was gnawing bones that once had been rejected.

On the third day, the men were casting about for helpful signs, when in a dry arroyo they found the perfectly fresh track of a very large wolf.

Without waiting for nightfall, as had been their custom, they went swiftly and silently to the sink-hole. They found the big track again — and fresh. As they neared it, they heard the unmistakable clank of iron chains. The men rushed forward, and here in the grim and deadly clutch of at least three traps, was Shishoka, the big red Cody wolf — wrenching, writhing, champing the wicked iron with his bloody jaws, heaving with strength that might have wrecked a single trap. But he was held in three.

And, whining, wailing, cowering by, was the old white Wosca wolf, distraught, helpless, crazy to help, but helpless. She champed her blunted teeth on the trap that was lying out, empty but sprung. She ran aimlessly about, she chewed her own front paw, she grovelled in the dust and wailed to the skies.

The men rushed forward, guns in hand. The big wolf knew his foes. He strained, he raved, to get at them. The old wolf, too, despite her ancient fear of guns, howled defiance, and crowded up close to the big one who had loved her.

The rifles rang — and down they went together riddled through, gripping the steel, gripping the dust, each with their last defiance. And two big animal souls — big, strong, heroic souls — had fled.

The men leaped down the bank, and stood beside the quivering bodies. They turned them over, they knew the marks that could identify — the pierced left ear, the missing toes. They knew the big red head and the brazen collar on the neck. They knew the records and the stories that they told.

'Gods! What a wolf! What a fight! this is the old Cody wolf all right, and the one that he died for was — not his mate! Oh, my God! He died to save his helpless blind old mother.'

1920: "World's Greatest Animal Criminal Dead," Dixon Merritt

The Custer Wolf was the most famous of the legendary outlaw wolves. A $500 bounty was offered for his head, a sum roughly equal to twenty months' wages for a cowboy. Despite the tempting reward, no one was able to capture the outlaw, and for nine years he virtually ruled a 2,600-square-mile region surrounding Custer, South Dakota. Eventually, most ranchers gave up trying to destroy this unstoppable renegade — they just wrote off their losses as "boarding expenses" for the wolf and waited for him to die of old age.

The U.S. Biological Survey (USBS) ordered one of its best hunters, H. P.
Williams, a man who had killed more than eleven hundred wolves, to pur-
sue the wolf and destroy him, "no matter how much time was required."
Williams finally killed the Custer Wolf in October 1920.

On January 17, 1921, the U.S. Department of Agriculture (USDA) issued
a press release by Dixon Merritt on the life and death of the Custer Wolf.
With the headline "World's Greatest Animal Criminal Dead," the press
release called the Custer Wolf "the master criminal of the animal world"
and a "criminal genius." Merritt went on at great length to describe the wolf
in legendary terms, including a comparison to the werewolves of medieval
Europe.

The USDA press release hints at the sense of admiration that many people
secretly felt toward this outlaw who, for such a long time, successfully avoided
all attempts by humanity to destroy him. Like Bonnie and Clyde and John
Dillinger, other outlaws who were treated as heroes, the Custer Wolf be-
came a symbol of defiance toward authority and law. His death was truly
the death of a legend.

"The Custer Wolf is dead."

He was the master criminal of the animal world.

Throughout the region around Custer, S. D., that day, the telephone lines were busier than they were on the day the armistice was
signed.

For nine years this wolf had lived as an outlaw—the cruelest, the
most sagacious, the most successful animal outlaw that the range country had ever known. His cruelty was surpassed only by his cunning. He
killed with the refinement of animal ferocity. Here to-night—to-morrow night he devastated a range half a hundred miles away.

He loped through every kind of danger and spurned them all. He
sniffed at the subtlest poison and passed it by. The most adroitly concealed trap was as clear to him as a mirror in the sunshine. Old hunters, unerring shots, drew the bead on him and saw him glide away un-
harmed. The price on his head was $500. Bounty hunters sought him
for profit. Sportsmen put forth every device to slay him for reputation's
sake. And still the old wolf went unscathed about his work of destruction.

Credulous people said he was a charmed thing. Others attributed
his immunity to a wisdom greater than beast ever before possessed. Still
others said he escaped by plain luck—the mysterious thing that ad-
heres to some animals as to some men. In whatever way they explained
his uncanny elusiveness, everybody feared him—perhaps not con-

sciously, very rarely openly but there was no man throughout that region who did not feel a shiver run down between his shoulders blades when, alone or in the dark, he thought of this gray devil of the desert.

All kinds of stories got abroad. This thing, they said, was not a wolf—not merely a wolf. They believed that nature had perpetrated a monstrosity, half wolf and half mountain lion, possessing the craftiness of both and the cruelty of hell. In public opinion he had all the qualities of the Were wolf of Old World legends.

No wonder that the telephones hummed when the word went out that a hunter sent by the United States Department of Agriculture to protect the live-stock industry, had killed the criminal wolf. That word ended a nine years' reign of dread, during which the stockmen around Custer had paid tribute to this wolf to the extent of $25,000 worth of live stock. And mere money loss was not the whole of the horrible toll he took. When he killed for food he took only the choicest animals, but sometimes he killed in atrocious ways for the mere sake of killing. Often he wounded cattle, breaking their legs, biting off their tails, mutilating them in unspeakable ways.

Four years ago his mate was killed. He never took another and many people suppose that he devoted himself to revenge for her death. Later on, he attached to himself two coyotes, not as equals, but as servants. He never permitted them to come near him, and they could feed from his kills only after he himself had finished. They traveled far out on his flanks, giving him warning of ambush or approaching danger and added to the atmosphere of mystery that surrounded him.

After a bounty, reached by stages from $100 to $500, failed to bring in the old criminal's scalp; after private trappers and sportsmen hunters had given up the quest; after poisons and dogs had failed—the stockmen tried a round-up. Having, as they thought, located the wolf, a large number of riders started in a great circle and closed up. This, like all the other devices, was unsuccessful. Some of the stockmen, in resignation, announced that they would have to board the wolf for the rest of his life. Others decided to send for a Government huter. Therefore, in March, 1920, the Bureau of Biological Survey, United States Department of Agriculture, sent to Custer, H. P. Williams, one of its best hunters, with instructions to stay after the wolf until he was taken, no matter how much time was required.

Williams went. He took with him a bunch of traps, but, as the old wolf was known to be trap-wise, he expected to depend mainly on his rifle. As things turned out, he required both the trap and the rifle to get the wolf when he was finally taken on October 11, 1920.

Since there is involved in this story the reputation of two geniuses — the criminal genius of the wolf and the protective genius of Williams — it may be just as well to let the account proceed in the language of the predatory-animal inspector who reported the facts to the Biological Survey. It was a long time coming. Like most outdoor men, he did not want to talk in heroics. Here is the story from the time Williams went to Custer until he brought down the criminal.

"When Williams first went into the country where the wolf ranged, he tried to find fresh tracks, but without success. He asked some of the men who had lost stock just where the wolf made his headquarters in their section. They said the wolf may have had quarters anywhere within a district 40 miles wide and 65 miles long. They told him to wait there a few days and the wolf would be sure to pay him a visit. Contrary to their advice, Williams went into the hills west of Pringle and found that the wolf was staying around some old dens in the Pelgar Mountains.

"Williams scented up the soles of his shoes and started stringing out his traps. The wolf got on his trail that night and showed signs of great excitement at what he thought to be the presence of a possible mate in his neighborhood. He followed the scent entirely around the line and then, returning to Pelgar Mountains, cleared out two old dens and make a new one which ran back into the hill for about 50 feet.

"On April 1, Williams had his first glimpse of the wolf, but was unable to get a shot at him. The coyotes were acting as bodyguards, traveling from 100 to 200 yards on the flanks of their master. They would warn him of danger by taking flight. For a while, Williams did not shoot the coyotes, hoping that he would get a chance at the wolf without having to give him warning by the shots that would be necessary to dispatch his bodyguard. Finally, realizing that there was no chance of getting at the wolf unless the coyotes were killed, Williams shot them, hoping that he had them in a clear field. In this he was greatly mistaken. The wolf played hide and seek with him. After making a kill, he would go on some distance, back trail for a few rods to a point where he could keep under cover and watch the hunter on his trail. Though this is a common habit of a bear, I have never before known a wolf to do it. It was on April 26 that Mr. Williams first found the wolf was doing this. At other times the wolf took to fallen timber and so could not be tracked.

"Twice during May the wolf stepped on the jaws of traps, and on the night of July 3 he rolled into or lay down on one and had a lot of his hair pulled out. This gave him such a scare that he left the country for a while. No sign could be found of him near Custer until the night of August 1, when he made his presence known by killing several head of cattle and wounding several more. Williams found some of these cattle, took the trail of the wolf, and followed him all day on a fresh track. This led up to the mouth of a canyon, and, knowing that the wolf would be taking a sleep after his big feed, Williams tied his horse and started in. Just then two horsemen came up, riding at breakneck speed and calling to Williams that they had found a yearling steer killed by the wolf. Williams motioned them to go back, but they did not understand what he meant and he was forced to return to meet them. Thus, he lost the best chance he ever had of getting the wolf with a rifle. When he returned to the trail, he found the place where the wolf had bedded down to sleep. The noise made by the horsemen had given him the alarm and he had gone back down the canyon very close to the hunter and escaped.

"Early in September the wolf stepped on a trap and was caught slightly by one foot. Apparently the trap had tipped so that it caught only one side of the foot and the wolf was able to pull loose. He left some hair in the trap. This happened again in the early days of October.

"Williams finally got the wolf on October 11. Here is his own account of it:

"'He stepped into a trap in the morning and it got a good grip on him. He ran with it about 150 yards when the hook caught on a tree, but that did not seem to stop him at all. He broke the swivel of the trap and ran on with it on his front foot. I trailed him 3 miles and got a shot at him and got him. He has been so lucky that I expected the gun would fail to shoot, but it worked O.K. He is smaller than the average male wolf, weighed 98 pounds and measured just 6 feet from tip to tip; 11 inches from toe to hock, and had a tail 14 inches long. His teeth would be good for 15 years longer. He broke some of them off on the trap, but aside from that they were in good condition. He is an old wolf, with a fur that is almost white.'"

In that simple fashion does the man who outwitted the cleverest of animal criminals tell his story.

The USDA press release included Williams's description of the wolf's capture and death but avoided any comments on the trapper's personal attitude toward the animal. Years later, Williams made the following statement about the Custer Wolf in an article in the September 24, 1961, Denver Post entitled "The Custer Wolf—Greatest Killer": "I tell you I'd built up such re-

spect for the old devil that, if he hadn't had a trap on one foot, I might not have killed him. I really think I might have let him go."

🐺 1921: "Duel in Colorado: Caywood Versus the Wolf," Rick McIntyre

While researching my first wolf book, A Society of Wolves, *I became fascinated with the legendary story of a USBS predator hunter named Bill Caywood and a renegade Colorado wolf called Rags. They conducted an epic duel, man and wolf, that symbolized the end of the era of wild wolves ranging freely across the Rocky Mountains.*

My version of the story, "Duel in Colorado: Caywood Versus the Wolf," is based on interviews Caywood gave to his USBS supervisor Stanley Young, to writer Arthur Carhart, to The Rocky Mountain News, *and to his hometown newspaper,* The Delta County Independent. *Carhart and Young published the earliest version of the story in the January 1928 issue of* The Red Book Magazine. *The following year, they printed a slightly longer version in their book* The Last Stand of the Pack. *Additional information from Caywood appeared in Carhart's article "World Champion Wolfer" (Outdoor Life, September 1939), and Young's 1946 book,* The Wolf in North American History.

Like other outlaw wolf stories from this period, the tale of Rags and Caywood quickly acquired a mythic dimension that added many layers of embellishment to the original facts. With all the main characters now dead, it is impossible to discern the facts from the embellishments. Legends and myths are often the best way to convey the underlying truth of a subject. I think this tale captures the complex feelings federal wolf trappers had toward the wolves they were assigned to kill.

Building on that information, I included in my retelling some of the things I've learned about USBS wolf trappers and about renegade wolves. I also tried to imagine what the final confrontation with Rags must have meant to Caywood.

Bill Caywood, known as "Big Bill" to his friends, had worked as an independent wolf trapper before joining the Biological Survey. In 1912 and 1913 he killed 140 wolves in northwestern Colorado. The local stockmen's association paid him a $50 bounty on each of those wolves. The $7000 in rewards, an enormous sum at the time, enabled him to buy a ranch, horses, along with plenty of equipment and supplies. His experience and skills caused the USBS to hire him as one of the very first federal predator control agents in 1915.

On Caywood's retirement as a federal predator control agent in 1935, the Denver paper, The Rocky Mountain News, *said he was the "greatest*

Colorado wolfer of all time," then added: "He is a typical man of the open country, a friend of all animals and regretul executioner of those outlaws who must die that other wild creatures and domestic animals may live." Writer Arthur Carhart, who interviewed Bill on many occasions, gave him the title: "World Champion Wolfer." He was probably the most successful wolf trapper who ever worked for the USBS

The men who signed on as predator control agents with the U.S. Bureau of Biological Survey became mythic, larger-than-life figures to their contemporaries in the old West. No agent better fit this description than Bill Caywood. He was judged to be the toughest, smartest, and most experienced wolf killer by his fellow trappers and by his boss, Stanley Young. In the words of a Colorado cattleman, "He knows more about wolves than they know about themselves." During his long career, Caywood killed many legendary outlaw wolves. The death of one of those renegades, a shaggy-coated wolf named Rags the Digger had a pronounced effect on the trapper.

Rags, deemed by stockmen to be the toughest, craftiest, and most experienced wolf in the Colorado and Utah region, never stayed in one location for long. He ranged over a two-state kingdom that covered ten thousand square miles. Ranchers said he killed at least $10,000 worth of livestock. This master wolf, for fourteen years, had survived endless trapping and poisoning attempts. No human could touch him.

The wolf had plenty of reasons to hate people. His first mate had died in a steel trap set for him. He later found another mate and had a litter of pups with her. While Rags was out hunting for his family, a trapper found the den and killed the female and entire litter. Local people believed that the psychological effects of finding his slaughtered family pushed Rags to new heights of vindictiveness against humanity. Destruction of livestock served as his preferred method of retribution.

Legend grew around the wolf. Stories were told that Rags loved to demonstrate his innate superiority over people. Whenever he found a wolf trap hidden in the soil he would carefully dig it up, then flip it out of its hole so that it could be plainly seen by all who passed by. He could accomplish the whole operation without tripping the delicate spring on the deadly trap. This flagrant display of contempt enraged ranchers. Banding together, they brought in the greatest wolf hunter who ever lived to challenge this outlaw wolf to mortal combat.

Caywood, a big man with leathery, weatherbeaten skin, was over fifty at the time, with over three decades of wolf trapping experience.

He drew on his vast experience to set out masterfully concealed traps in places where Rags might travel. These traps, buried a fraction of an inch below the surface, were undetectable to man or beast. Looking at his handiwork, Caywood felt the pride of accomplishment that only an artist or master craftsman can experience. Throughout his long career, the government man had never failed "to get his wolf": Rags would be no exception.

Then the day came when Caywood found one of his traps dug out by Rags and disdainfully deposited on the trail. The trapper had never seen anything like this. Caywood readily deciphered a message: "He's dared me to come at him if ever a wolf's dared a man."

This defiant challenge only made Caywood try harder. From then on, it became a personal duel between man and wolf that could only end with the death of one or the other. Despite his best efforts, Caywood continued to come up short. Local ranchers began kidding him about his failure. "You've met your match," one cattleman told him. "Rags is your equal, Bill. He's outguessing you." Caywood taciturnly replied, "I'm not sayin' when I'll get him, but I will."

The fruitless attempts to trap Rags taught Caywood a few things about his adversary. The government agent's thoughts dwelled on the wolf's namesake habit of digging up traps. Then one day, the way to catch Rags came to Caywood. He rode out, found a likely place that Rags would travel through, and set a trap in a deliberately amateurish manner. No wolf, especially one as experienced as Rags, could miss it. Behind the initial trap, Caywood set two additional ones, muttering, "Here's a surprise for you, old timer," as he worked.

The renegade was hunting sheep in Utah at the time. On returning to Colorado, Rags trotted right up to the trap that Caywood had so sloppily set. With more contempt than usual, Rags began digging up the deadly steel mechanism. To uncover the far side, the wolf had to step over the trap. The instant he put his paw on the ground, a second, well-hidden trap sprang shut around his foot! Caywood had used the obvious trap as a decoy: the real traps were placed just behind it, where the wolf was sure to step if he tried to dig out the decoy. As Rags struggled to free himself, a third trap leaped up and grabbed another foot. Brilliantly, Caywood had used Rags's own arrogance to settle the score. Although two traps held the wolf, his personal duel with Caywood was far from over.

When Caywood checked his traps the next morning, he saw that two had been sprung and dragged off. He knew he had caught the wolf, but experience taught him not to celebrate victory until he had the dead animal in hand. Following the injured wolf's trail on horse-back was easy. The heavy chain and drag hook attached to the two traps left a trail the newest of greenhorns could follow. As he pursued the wolf, Caywood couldn't help admiring Rags's courage and deter-mination. The iron hook frequently had caught on branches and the trapper could see where Rags had yanked the chain until it pulled free. Caywood cringed when he thought of the intense pain the violent jerking would have created in the wounds, still encased in sharp steel.

Coming to the top of a one-hundred-foot cliff, Caywood lost the trail. Looking over the edge, he spotted Rags's tracks at the bottom of the cliff. The wolf had simply jumped to the bottom and continued on, still dragging the traps, chain and hook. As he circled around the cliff, the predator control agent wondered if anything could stop this wolf's valiant attempt to gain freedom.

The climax to the pursuit came a few minutes later. Directly ahead, Caywood spotted Rags in a narrow arroyo. At first the wolf continued on, then he stopped and stared back at his nemesis. Drawing his rifle, Caywood dismounted and walked toward his quarry. Wolf and man stared at each other, seventy-five yards apart, both knowing the duel was about to end. Then Rags did something unexpected—he started walking toward Caywood. The dragging traps slowed him, but he moved steadily forward, straight for the trapper.

Caywood, never having been stalked by a wolf, froze. He was dumb-founded that a wolf with such serious injuries would still have any fight left. With regret at having to destroy such an admirable spirit, Caywood raised his rifle, aimed at Rags's head and pulled the trigger. Nothing happened. He tried firing again but the gun jammed a second time. As he fumbled with the rifle, Rags continued to close the gap between them. When he was thirty feet away, Caywood couldn't resist looking up at him. The wolf had an expression on his face that, despite Caywood's decades of experience with wolves, was completely unread-able. Suddenly the trapper remembered how a rancher had warned him about Rags: "Whatever you do, Bill, don't let that old devil catch you on foot without a gun . . . he'd make mincemeat of you in forty seconds." Was the wolf coming to kill him or to acknowledge, as one wolf might concede to another wolf, that his enemy had beaten him in a fair fight? Mesmerized by the force of the wolf's personality, Caywood stood still with the useless rifle hanging at his side.

Something, perhaps the sound of the clanking metal, broke the spell and Caywood tried the gun again, but it once more failed. Rags now was fifteen feet away and still coming. When they were ten feet apart, a revelation suddenly struck Caywood. Could the wolf be coming to him so that he could remove the traps from the animal's paws? This possibility shook the hardened trapper to his very core. Rags now was almost close enough to touch. Caywood had no idea if the wolf would leap at him and tear out his throat or simply hold out the entrapped paws. Frozen in place, the master predator control agent waited for the wolf to play out his hand. Then, from deep inside Caywood, a lifetime of experience in wolf killing took over his body, severing it from the befuddled mind that had rendered that body helpless. He raised the rifle one last time, aimed at Rags's chest and pulled the trigger. The gun fired and the wolf, just eight feet away, slumped to the ground.

Caywood instantly knew the bullet had gone through Rags' heart. Holding the gun, he stood silently as the life drained out of his courageous adversary. Waves of regret passed through him; he didn't know if he had done the right thing. As he tried to sort out his feelings, Rags opened his eyes and looked up at Caywood.

Now thoroughly spooked, the trapper stared in disbelief as the wolf painfully struggled to his feet and, still dragging the two traps, stumbled forward, gasping for air. Again incapable of any action, Caywood watched the wolf apparition inch closer and closer. Then, for the first time, Rags's indomitable spirit failed him and his lifeless body collapsed to the ground. The wolf's nose landed a fraction of an inch from Caywood's foot. "You poor old devil!" the trapper cried as he bent down and stroked the wolf's fur. "You poor, lonely old murdering devil!"

A rancher once asked Caywood if he got a kick out of killing a wolf. The old trapper replied:

"Oh, yes and no. I've just got a lot of love and respect for the gray wolf. He's a real fellow, the big gray is. Lots of brains. I feel sorry for him. It's his way of livin'. He don't know better. And I feel sorry every time I see one of those big fellows thrashin' around in a trap bellowin' bloody murder. Guess I'm too much a part of this outdoors to hold any grudge against animals."

The same rancher wondered what would become of Caywood in the years to come: "Ever since I can remember you've been around here wagin' war on the wolves. What you goin' to do when they are all gone?" The question proved to be prophetic, for Caywood himself later killed the last wolves in his part of Colorado. After thinking hard about the matter, Caywood told the cattleman:

"Don't know. Guess I'll dry up and blow away like a tumbleweed. I couldn't no more go into town and live, settle down in some store or something like that, than I could fly on horseback. Guess it's in my blood, this outdoors. My daddy and mother started me out on this career. They come across the plains in an ox-drawn prairie schooner when I was only three years old. I've lived in the outdoors, near the ragged edge of what we call civilization, ever since. It's meat and drink to me. No chance for me reformin' and settlin' down so long as I can navigate on horseback."

Government predator control agents like Bill Caywood believed they were doing honest, honorable work in exterminating the wolf from the western United States. These predator control agents were master outdoorsmen who used their hard-earned knowledge of wildlife and trapping skills to carry out government policy as best they could.

Nearly always, when expressing their feelings about the way the West was becoming "civilized," they spoke of their respect for the wolf and the way it had lived free and wild on the open range. The passing of the wolf meant that the time of the wolf hunters had also passed. These tough men had made the West "safe" for civilization but realized that they could never fit into this new order, nor would they want to. In the end, they admitted that they admired the old outlaw wolves far more than they admired the human society that had ordered their destruction.

After writing the story of Rags and Caywood, I came across a 1985 research paper written by Professor Stephen Kellert of Yale University entitled, "Public Perceptions of Predators, Particularly the Wolf and Coyote." In polling the opinions of over three thousand people around the country, Kellert discovered that professional trappers were twice as likely as the general public to view the wolf in a positive light. As was the case with Ernest Thompson Seton, H. P. Williams, and Bill Caywood, constant contact with wolves had given these men a deep respect and admiration for the animal.

The last known Colorado wolf was killed in 1945, but in the near future wolves may once again live in Rags's home state. In 1992, Congressman David Skaggs, elected to represent the Boulder area, shepherded a bill through Congress that directed the USFWS to study the feasibility of reintroducing wolves to Colorado. The first phase of the study, completed in mid-1994, found that the western part of the state could support as many as 1,128 wolves. In the second phase, researchers at Colorado State University conducted a scientific public opinion poll of Colorado residents. That survey, released in December of 1994, found that 71 percent of state residents supported the reintroduction of wolves to Colorado.

Chapter 7

Native Americans
and the Wolf

"We are brothers, after all."
"When Men and Animals Were Friendly," traditional Blackfeet story

Too often, people who are not Native Americans write about Native people and attempt to describe their beliefs, feelings, and attitudes. For this chapter, I vowed that all authors would be Native Americans so that they could speak with authority and experience about their view of the wolf.

The traditional stories and contemporary poems and essays in this chapter illustrate an attitude toward the wolf that sharply contrasts with the views that appear earlier in this book. In the words of Joseph Marshall of the Sicangu Lakota: "For centuries, the Wolf and the Native American shared time, space, and life in North America. They also shared the same fate. The European newcomer . . . drove the Wolf and the Native American from ancestral homelands, disrupted their lives, and upset their balance. Life was never the same." This shared fate has caused many Native people to join the fight to restore the wolf to its traditional homeland.

1983: "Who Speaks for Wolf," Paula Underwood, Oneida
Over two hundred years ago, a Native American woman named Tsilikomah (Bright Spring) was born into the Oneida Nation, one of the six nations of the Iroquois Confederacy. The Oneida lived in what is now New York State and western Pennsylvania.

Tsilikomah learned a vast oral tradition from an Erie elder who had earned the title "Keeper of the Old Things." Blessed with an extraordinary memory, she eventually mastered the extensive Iroquoian oral history and learning stories that he shared with her.

Around 1800, Tsilikomah saw that her Oneida community had decided to abandon their ancient traditions. She voluntarily left her village and sought out a new home in Illinois where she could stay true to the traditions and principles revealed in the oral teachings she had committed to memory.

In the original language, she passed on those stories to her grandson, Oliver Perry Underwood (Gray Wolf Walking), who in turn gave responsibility for them to his son, Perry Leonard Underwood (Sharp-Eyed Hawk). Leonard taught all this to his daughter Paula (Turtle Woman Singing), who later wrote these learnings down in English "as a gift to all of Earth's children with Listening Ears."

The following Iroquoian story, "Who Speaks for Wolf," is thousands of years old. It conveys a Native American view of the wolf in clear and memorable terms. Most importantly, the story shows how one Native community resolved a conflict that developed between themselves and a community of wolves. The wisdom of their resolution contrasts dramatically with the final solution white society instituted against the wolf.

"Who Speaks for Wolf," like most Native stories, is designed to be read out loud. Find someone to share it with. Pass on the message and truth that Tsilikomah saved.

LONG AGO
    Our People grew in number so that where we were
        was no longer enough
    Many young men
        were sent out from among us
            to seek a new place
                where the People might be who-they-were
    They searched
        and they returned
            each with a place selected
            each determined his place was best

AND SO IT WAS
    That the People had a decision to make:
        which of the many was most appropriate

NOW, AT THAT TIME
    There was one among the People
        to whom Wolf was brother
    He was so much Wolf's brother
        that he would sing their song to them
            and they would answer him
    He was so much Wolf's brother
        that their young
            would sometimes follow him through the forest
            and it seemed they meant to learn from him

SO IT WAS, AT THIS TIME
   That the People gave That One a special name
   They called him WOLF'S BROTHER
      and if any sought to learn about Wolf
      if any were curious
            or wanted to learn to sing Wolf's song
               they would sit beside him
                   and describe their curiosity
                      hoping for a reply

AS I HAVE SAID
   The People sought a new place in the forest
   They listened closely to each of the young men
      as they spoke of hills and trees
          of clearings and running water
          of deer and squirrel and berries
   They listened to hear which place
      might be drier in rain
      more protected in winter
      and where our Three Sisters
          Corn, Beans, and Squash
              might find a place to their liking
   They listened
      and they chose
   Before they chose
      they listened to each young man
   Before they chose
      they listened to each among them
          he who understood the flow of waters
          she who understood Long House construction
          he who understood the storms of winter
          she who understood Three Sisters
     to each of these they listened
         until they reached agreement
         and the Eldest among them
            finally rose and said:
               "SO BE IT—
                   FOR SO IT IS"

"BUT WAIT"
   Someone cautioned—
      "Where is Wolf's Brother?
         WHO, THEN, SPEAKS FOR WOLF?"

BUT
> THE PEOPLE WERE DECIDED
>> and their mind was firm
>> and the first people were sent
>>> to choose a site for the first Long House
>>> to clear a space for our Three Sisters
>>> to mold the land so that water
>>>> would run away from our dwelling
>>>>> so that all would be secure within

AND THEN WOLF'S BROTHER RETURNED
> He asked about the New Place
>> and said at once that we must choose another
>> "You have chosen the Center Place
>>> for a great community of Wolf"
> But we answered him
>> that many had already gone
>> and that it could not wisely be changed
>> and that surely Wolf could make way for us
>>> as we sometimes make way for Wolf
> But Wolf's Brother counseled—
>> "I think that you will find
>>> that it is too small a place for both
>>> and that it will require more work then—
>>>> than change would presently require"

BUT THE PEOPLE CLOSED THEIR EARS
> and would not reconsider
> When the New Place was ready
>> all the People rose up as one
>>> and took those things they found of value
>>> and looked at last upon their new home

NOW CONSIDER HOW IT WAS FOR THEM
> This New Place
>> had cool summers and winter protection
>> and fast-moving streams
>> and forests around us
>>> filled with deer and squirrel
>> there was room even for our Three Beloved Sisters

AND THE PEOPLE SAW THAT THIS WAS GOOD
> and did not see
>> wolf watching from the shadows!

BUT AS TIME PASSED
> They began to see —
>> for someone would bring deer or squirrel
>>> and hang him from a tree
>>> and go for something to contain the meat
>>> but would return
>>>> to find nothing hanging from the tree
>>>> AND WOLF BEYOND

AT FIRST
> This seemed to us an appropriate exchange —
>> some food for a place to live

BUT
> It soon became apparent that it was more than this —
>> for Wolf would sometimes walk between the dwellings
>>> that we had fashioned for ourselves
>>>> and the women grew concerned
>>>>> for the safety of the little ones
> Thinking of this
>> they devised for awhile an agreement with Wolf
>>> whereby the women would gather together
>>>> at the edge of our village
>>>> and put out food for Wolf and his brothers

BUT IT WAS SOON APPARENT
> That this meant too much food
>> and also Wolf grew bolder
>>> coming in to look for food
>>>> so that it was worse than before
> WE HAD NO WISH TO TAME WOLF

AND SO
> Hearing the wailing of the women
>> the men devised a system
>>> whereby some ones among them
>>>> were always alert to drive off Wolf

AND WOLF WAS SOON HIS OLD UNTAMED SELF

BUT
> They soon discovered
>> that this required so much energy
>>> that there was little left for winter preparations
>> and the Long Cold began to look longer and colder
>>> with each passing day

THEN
    The men counseled together
        to choose a different course

THEY SAW
    That neither providing Wolf with food
        nor driving him off
                gave the People a life that was pleasing

THEY SAW
    That Wolf and the People
        could not live comfortably together
                in such a small space

THEY SAW
    That it was possible
        to hunt down this Wolf People
                until they were no more

BUT THEY ALSO SAW
    That this would require much energy over many years

THEY SAW, TOO,
    That such a task would change the People:
        they would become Wolf Killers
    A People who took life only to sustain their own
        would become a People who took life
                rather than move a little

IT DID NOT SEEM TO THEM
    THAT THEY WANTED TO BECOME SUCH A PEOPLE

AT LAST
    One of the Eldest of the People
        spoke what was in every mind:
        "It would seem
                that Wolf's Brother's vision
                        was sharper than our own
    To live here indeed requires more work now
        than change would have made necessary"

NOW THIS WOULD BE A SIMPLE TELLING
 of a people who decided to move
    ONCE WINTER WAS PAST

EXCEPT
    that from this
        THE PEOPLE LEARNED A GREAT LESSON

        IT IS A LESSON
            we have never forgotten

FOR
    At the end of their Council
        one of the Eldest rose again and said:
            "Let us learn from this
                so that not again
                      need the People build only to move
            Let us not again think we will gain energy
                only to lose more than we gain
            We have learned to choose a place
                where winter storms are less
                    rather than rebuild
            We have learned to choose a place
                where water does not stand
                    rather than sustain sickness

LET US NOW LEARN TO CONSIDER WOLF!"

AND SO IT WAS
    That the People devised among themselves
        a way of asking each other questions
            whenever a decision was to be made
                on a New Place or a New Way
    We sought to perceive the flow of energy
        through each new possibility
            and how much was enough
            and how much was too much

UNTIL AT LAST
    Someone would rise
        and ask the old, old question
            to remind us of things
                we do not yet see clearly enough to remember

"TELL ME NOW MY BROTHERS
    tell me now my sisters
        WHO SPEAKS FOR WOLF?"

*Paula Underwood is the executive director of The Past is Prologue Educa-
tional Program (PIP), which is based on a learning tradition handed down
in her family for five generations. PIP is used from pre-kindergarten through
corporate training to encourage consensus building, inductive reasoning,
problem solving, reflective thinking, and a creative respect for the Earth,
the same principles taught in Paula's story, "Who Speaks for Wolf."*

*In 1993 Paula completed a fifteen-year project of recording a written
version of her people's oral history.* The Walking People: A Native American Oral History, *along with the full version of* Who Speaks for Wolf: A
Native American Learning Story, *including artwork by Frank Howell, are
available from A Tribe of Two Press, Box 913, Georgetown, TX 78627.*

1995: "Sungmanitu Tanka Oyate: Wolf Nation," Manuel Iron Cloud, Oglala Lakota

*In fall of 1993, shortly after beginning my job at Big Bend National Park, a
Native American walked into the visitor center I was staffing. Somehow the
subject of wolves came up, and he proceeded to tell me a truly amazing
story about his grandmother and a wolf.*

*He introduced himself as Manuel Iron Cloud, an Oglala Lakota, who
was born on the Pine Ridge Reservation in South Dakota. He had just
arrived at Big Bend for a job in the maintenance division. That meant we
would be co-workers and would frequently see each other in the coming
months.*

*Throughout that fall, winter, and spring we often talked about wolves.
In one conversation Manuel told me how his grandmother had taught him
to think of wolves as being a nation or tribe. Just as the Oglala Nation had
a right to a homeland and hunting grounds, his people believed that the
Wolf Nation deserved similar rights.*

*Manuel agreed to write the following article about the things he learned
about wolves from his grandmother. The Lakota words in his title can be
translated as either "Wolf Nation" or "The Big Dog From the Wilderness
People."*

Sungmanitu Tanka Oyate, the Big Dog From the Wilderness People,
were a nation long before human beings realized and declared themselves a nation. For all creatures which possess the breath of life, whether
they be plants, animals that walk or crawl on the earth, fish that live in
the water, or birds that fly in the air, are the children of one father and
one mother, that being the Great Spirit and the Earth. All of their offspring are nations unto themselves, and all deserve recognition as nations with full rights to live and move, as they have been established to

do so by the spiritual laws that govern the universe.

When people study and reflect upon the life of the Wolf, they can see that his ways are similar to those of human beings. Family seems to be important to the Wolf, as he not only feeds and protects his own and the pack, but he nurtures and cares for them as well. Perhaps, like the Lakota, he tells his children and grandchildren the ways of the grandfathers who have gone before, ways that would enable them to live in harmony not only with their own kind but with other nations as well. For it is within the confines of the family that the ways of life are passed on, and in doing so the nation not only survives, but is made stronger.

Growing up as an Oglala Lakota, one learns very early on in life that the Great Spirit, also known as the Creator, is most important in all things. To communicate with Him, whether it be through ritual, ceremony, or by conscious awareness throughout everyday life, is important to family and national unity. When growing up in this manner, one can comprehend the wholeness and the relationship of all things. As children, our first awareness is that of father and mother, and from there all other relationships come into focus. And in the course of everyday life, teaching and learning takes place, with most of it happening unconsciously. To hear stories of the Wolf, the Bear, the Eagle, or any other creature, is to hear of them, not as creatures lesser than ourselves, but as our equals, as relatives, as members of one family much larger than our intellects can comprehend. So we just accept that the Creator knows the origin and the outcome of all things, and that it is our duty to seek out ways of living together in a way that is good for all peoples.

My maternal grandmother Obizita Wakan Win (Sacred Swallow Woman) possessed the ability to communicate with animals. When I was seven years old, she told me this story. When she was a young woman and just married to my grandfather, they built their home out in the wilderness, miles from the nearest neighbor. Grandpa had a job at the agency, also miles from their home, and so he was gone for a major part of the day.

One day when my grandmother was home alone, a Wolf came up from the nearby creek and began speaking to her. The Wolf told her that he had come to deliver a message from her nephew, who was a soldier in the first world war somewhere in Europe. The Wolf told her that the boy had been wounded and was in a great deal of pain, and that the army authorities would soon contact her with this same news. However, the Wolf continued, because the army did not know, they would be unable to tell her that in spite of his wounds he felt hope and was strengthened by his prayers to the Great Spirit, and that they shouldn't worry too much.

My grandmother immediately contacted Grandpa to tell him what had happened. In turn, he got in touch with the army. When he talked to the officer in charge, the man was amazed that Grandpa knew about what had happened as he himself had to investigate to find out what Grandpa had told him. He confirmed that the boy had been wounded in action, but that was all he would tell them.

And so my grandparents left for home, feeling relief and giving thanks that the Great Spirit had watched over their loved one. But my grandmother made a special effort to give thanks to the Wolf who had brought the message in the first place. When she got home she prepared a gift of meat and went out into the wilderness to find the messenger. She stood on a hill overlooking the creek and called to him. She was a little irritated with herself for not having asked him his name, but eventually he heard the call and came to her. She gave him the gift and thanked him for putting their minds at ease with the words that he had brought. And then she asked him how he came to receive the message.

The Wolf told her that the boy had been wounded in battle near a forest where there were other Wolves. When the boy saw them, he had called to them. Because he spoke in a way of respect and recognition, the wolves were more than glad to help him. And so the message was relayed by the Wolf Nation across the miles of frozen wilderness that lay between Europe and the small house on Potato Creek on the Pine Ridge Indian Reservation.

When Grandma finished telling me this story she said "So when you see a Wolf don't be afraid of him, instead talk to him—he might have something to say to you."

It has been thirty-one years since Grandma told me that story, and it has been many years since she herself has gone on to the spirit world to be with her relatives, but in the time since I heard that story I have come to appreciate the beauty and strength the Oglala Nation have gained from our relative and ally, Sungmanitu Tanka.

In speaking with Manuel about his grandmother's beliefs and teachings on wolves, I was reminded of Ben Corbin's book, Corbin's Advice or the Wolf Hunter's Guide. *Corbin would have been a contemporary of Manuel's grandmother. Both individuals lived in the Dakotas around the turn of the century. There is no greater contrast in attitudes toward the wolf than that of Manuel's grandmother and Ben Corbin.*

1995: "A Blackfeet Song of Brotherhood," Jack Gladstone, Blackfeet

In Paula Underwood's story, "Who Speaks for Wolf," a Native man is called Wolf's Brother. In modern times, the Native American who most deserves that title is Jack Gladstone, a Blackfeet singer and storyteller. I first met Jack in the spring of 1991, when he gave a performance for the new ranger staff at Glacier National Park. During his program, Jack told several traditional Blackfeet wolf stories then sang his own composition, "Wolf."

Since that first meeting, Jack and I have spoken often about wolves. I always come away impressed with his passion for his brother, Makuyi, the wolf. As he travels throughout America and Europe, performing the traditional role of storyteller, Jack truly "speaks for Wolf."

My Indian name is Mataksoowoo. Translated from my native tongue into English, this means "never quits." I am *Nizitape*, a part of the real people. To the government of the United States we are the Blackfeet Indian Nation. I am the great-great grandson of Mekaisto, known to the world as Chief Red Crow, leader of the Blood Division of the Blackfeet Confederacy from 1870 to 1900.

For thousands and thousands of years my people lived upon the northern plains and mountains in an area now recognized as Alberta, Canada, and Montana, USA. From the dawn of our spiritual and psychological being our closest relative in the wild has been Makuyi. In English, Wolf.

As a child, my grandfather Red Crow received his training for adulthood from his grandfather Two Suns, his father Black Bear, his uncle Big Plume, as well as his uncle's best friend, White Wolf. The training of a chief included not only the technical aspects of hunting, horse capturing, and warfare emphasized but also tribal mythology and lore, which served to lay a foundation for cultural values, beliefs, and behavior. The parameters of proper behavior, respect, and relationship with the universe were defined and reaffirmed in the communication of these stories. In contrast to the imported Dark Age European mythology, where the wolf is regarded as a satanic manifestation, the parables of the Blackfeet taught our people to recognize the wolf as a sacred medicine animal, coming to the aid of people in the long-ago time, sharing of itself and its powers to the point of merging identities. My favorite among the wolf stories told by my elders is called "When Men and Animals Were Friendly."

When Men and Animals Were Friendly

In the long-ago time, at the end of the green-grass season, our Blackfeet people were breaking into smaller groups, preparing for the winter. Some traveled west toward the mountains, some east farther out onto the plains, still others ventured south; but White Eagle and his family went north, assuming that in this direction there would be little competition in the never-ending quest for game.

The snows came early that fall before White Eagle had the chance to kill and store much surplus meat and soon sparse reserves led to the beginnings of starvation.

From a ridgetop overlooking the valley where White Eagle and his family were camped there scouted the sons of Big Wolf, Coyote, Red Fox, and Black Fox. "Oh," they lamented to themselves, "see the human persons below. They are weak and will surely starve to death unless we do something. Let us ask permission from our fathers to invite them into our camp, the camp of the meat-eaters, the camp where there is always enough to eat." So, this was done after the fathers of the four meat-eating animals had granted their permission. White Eagle and his family, when approached by the four sons, were terrified at what might befall them, but decided to risk accepting the invitation because staying where they were would undoubtedly mean death by starvation.

At the winter camp of the meat-eaters, excitement was in the air as into the center White Eagle, his wife, and his son were led by the sons of Big Wolf, Coyote, Red Fox, and Black Fox. Cougar, Bobcat, Badger, Weasel, and Skunk all stared at the humans, as did the fathers of the four sons.

Just then, Big Wolf spoke up: "Attention, please. I know all of you wonder why I have invited these human persons into our camp today and for this winter. It is because I feel it is about time that they got to know us better and we animal persons came to know them. We are brothers, after all."

During the course of this long-ago winter, White Eagle and his family camped with each of the meat-eating animals, spending time in each one's lodge learning the songs and secrets of their sacred power. Of all the stays in the various lodges, none was more impressive than the stay with Big Wolf.

Big Wolf was the head chief of the camp. When White Eagle entered his lodge he was addressed in this way: "I welcome you, my friend. This is my lodge I give to you and also my songs, my sacred songs." White Eagle stayed with Big Wolf for some time, visiting about many

things, including the importance of responsibility, sharing, cooperation, and discipline within one's family and society. The bond of brotherhood was born and fully realized in this visit between the two.

When finally the green-grass season was upon the plains and the
long winter nights were over, the camp of the meat-eating animals broke
up and White Eagle and his family prepared to leave.

Big Wolf presented, upon departure, a surprise gift to White Eagle.
"Here," said Big Wolf, "my son, as well as the sons of Big Coyote and
Black Fox, will escort you to your people and assist you for a while in
your hunting needs." Once back with his Blackfeet people, White Eagle
introduced his new friends to the rest of the camp. The people liked
these visitors and were friendly and hospitable toward them. During
the late spring and summer, the animal sons visited the lodges of the
various families within the human camp. They hunted, lived, and traveled alongside the human beings as brothers.

At the end of the green-grass season, Coyote and Black Fox, lonesome and restless, prepared to return to their own kind and tried to
persuade Big Wolf's son to do the same. After some thought and a long
silence, son of Big Wolf replied, "Go on without me and tell my father
that I love him but cannot return, for my duty is to remain with White
Eagle, who I also regard as a father. I shall remain with him and keep
his family well supplied with food."

This is the way that Big Wolf came to stay with White Eagle and his
people. While Coyote and Black Fox returned to the animal camp, Big
Wolf chose to stay and assumed human form. Eventually, he took a
fine woman as his wife and had many children by her. He was loved
and respected and lived to an old age. In the long-ago time this happened.

* * *

In this story, as well as others in our Blackfeet mythology, the wolf
exhibits positive personal and social traits, including compassion, gen-
erosity, and a genuine concern for the relationship between its kind
and human persons. A concept of reciprocity also emerges from this
myth when the people accept the sons of Big Wolf, Coyote, and Black
Fox into their summer lodges upon White Eagle's return. The closing
element of the story pictures the son of Big Wolf choosing to stay
amongst the Blackfeet as a son, a brother, and an ally to our people.
The metaphysical message from this final act is: "We are relatives. We
are one."

* * *

An enormous human and environmental holocaust occurred when

Euro-American culture invaded the northern plains. My wild brothers, the beaver, the grizzly, the buffalo, and the wolf, were victims alongside my human ancestors, the Blackfeet people. Countless Indian peoples, as well as animals species, were reduced or eliminated as a result of the corrosive doctrine of Manifest Destiny upon the natural environment. In the winter of 1980, in an effort to convey the feelings of an Indian heart about persecuted brother, I wrote the primary verses to "Wolf." Then, in a shift of key, tempo, and character, I wrote an American bounty hunter's waltz to counterpoint this song of brotherhood.

Wolf

Wolf, you were free, you were hunting in the sun.
Long before man arrived, you were nature,
   you were young.
Then we came and survived, we were brothers
   side by side.
In the days of the arrow, in the days of the bow.
In the days of the spirit, not too long a time ago. . . .

Wolf, you were seen, by the fathers of our dream
And the hunt you engaged was the blueprint for our age.
Then we learned and we burned with desire to know more
In the dawn that was man's, they hunted o'er the plains.
Still the wolf pack set the pace, when the fire was
   just a flame. . . .

   As plows turn the plains, we ranch on the range.
   The bison are gone now, the wolf packs remain.
   In search of the killers of our sheep and our cattle herds,
   The stockmen are helpless, they request our aid.
   Defending the rangelands, are we in our roles,
   To kill thousands of bountiful wolves is our goal.

Wolf, where are you in the lower forty eight?
Once you ran through the woods of the eastern
   seaboard states!
Now you're gone from the woods, from the mountains
   from the plains;
They are filled with the still of a vanishing frontier,
They are broken by the blade, tilling all we once held dear. . . .

So load on your planes, get a permit for game
We'll sweep o'er the tundra, and muskeg terrain.
In search of the killers of our moose and our caribou
And all that are helpless; the weak and the lame.
Protecting the wild, are we in our roles,
    blasting those bountiful wolves down below.

Wolf, you were free, you were hunting in the sun.
Long before man arrived, you were nature,
    you were young.
Then we came and survived, we were brothers
    side by side
In the days of the arrow, in the days of the bow.
In the days of the spirit, not too long a time ago. . . .

In the days of the arrow, in the days of the bow.
In the days of the spirit, not too long a time ago. . . .
* * *

When the memory of brotherhood between humans and wolves is revived
and nurtured, the healing process can begin.
    Onye . . . I have spoken.

*When Jack testified in favor of wolf reintroduction in Yellowstone at the
August 1992 hearing in Helena, Montana (see Chapter 8), he made a strong
impression with both pro-wolf and anti-wolf individuals. Later, as he traveled through Montana, performing his songs and stories, Jack discovered
that the posters advertising his appearances were being defaced. Scrawled
across his photograph was the phrase "wolf lover." The label was intended
to be an insult, but Jack took it as an honor to be considered a lover of wolves
by enemies of the wolf.*

*Jack has put out several collections of his songs on compact disc. For a
catalog and information on his performance schedule, contact Hawkstone
Production, Box 7626, Kalispell, MT 59904–7626, 1–800–735–2965*

A video, Wolf: Beyond the Fairy Tale, *that includes a performance of
"Wolf" by Jack is available from Natural Areas Association, Box 3308, St.
George, UT 84771–3308, 1–800–411–1467*

1905: "The Legend of the Friendly Medicine Wolf," Brings-down-the-Sun (Natosin Nepée), Piegan

*Jack Gladstone referred to the wolf as a "sacred medicine animal." The fol-
lowing story, "The Legend of the Friendly Medicine Wolf," was told by a
famous medicine man named Brings-down-the-Sun (Natosin Nepée), who
belonged to the Piegan Division of the Blackfeet Confederacy.*

In the summer of 1905, writer Walter McClintock visited a Blackfeet village at Two Medicine Lake in Montana. Some of the Blackfeet decided to visit their relatives and friends, including Brings-down-the-Sun, who lived just over the border in Canada. They invited McClintock along. One of the Blackfeet, in describing Brings-down-the-Sun, told McClintock, "He is a noted authority upon our ancient customs and religion. . . . We will take you to Brings-down-the-Sun as our friend, and will persuade him to tell you about the old days."

The party found Brings-down-the-Sun and his extended family camped along the Crow Lodge River. The medicine man was "an elderly man with clean-cut Indian features. His hair was gray and the deep lines in his face indicated a strong character, burdened with care and responsibility."

After a few days in camp, Brings-down-the-Sun tells McClintock, "I have been preparing myself to relate to you many things that have happened to my people in former days." McClintock faithfully transcribed the stories, including "The Legend of the Friendly Medicine Wolf" that Brings-down-the-Sun told him, in his 1910 book, The Old North Trail.

The events, which I will now relate, happened many years ago. The Blackfeet were moving camp. They travelled slowly and, when stretched out on the plains, their line extended so far, it was hard for those in front to see the people in the rear. As a protection against hostile war parties, the warriors were divided into two bands, one riding in front and the other in the rear. Between these two bands of warriors were the old men, the women and children. While passing through a hill country, a large party of Crow Indians, which had been hiding in ambush, attacked the line in the middle. Before the Blackfeet warriors came to their defence, the Crows had killed many women and children, and carried away some women prisoners. One of the captured was a young woman named Itsa-pich-kaupe (Sits-by-the-door), the mother of Calf Looking and grandmother of Ap-ai-kai-koa (Little Skunk). She was carried on horseback by the warrior who took her prisoner, over two hundred miles to the Crow camp on the Yellowstone River. There she was presented to one of his friends, who took her to his lodge and gave her into the care of his wife, an older woman. Itsa-pich-kaupe was so closely watched she could find no chance of escape. Every night the Crow man hobbled her feet, so that she could not walk. He also tied a rope around her waist, and fastened the other end to his wife. One day, when the Crow man was away, and the two women were together in the lodge, the Crow woman conversed with Itsa-pich-kaupe in the sign language, saying, 'I overheard my husband last night say that they intended to kill you. I feel sorry and will help you to escape to-night when it is dark.' That evening the Crow man hobbled Itsa-pich-kaupe as usual and tied her to his wife. When the lodge fire burned low, and the Crow woman knew from his heavy breathing that her husband was asleep, she crawled over to Itsa-pich-kaupe and unfastened the ropes. She then tied the loose end of the waist-rope to a lodge pole, so that if her husband should waken and pull upon the rope, he would not suspect her escape. She loosened the bottom of the lodge covering from the pegs and, giving Itsa-pich-kaupe a pair of moccasins, a flint and a small sack filled with pemmican, pushed her outside. Itsa-pich-kaupe travelled all that night as fast as she could go, away from the Crow camp. When daylight came she hid in some underbrush. The Crows tried to follow her but they could find no tracks and gave up the chase. When she had walked for four nights, and was a long distance from the Crow camp, she began travelling by day also, but her supply of pemmican soon gave out, and there were large holes in her moccasins. One day, when her feet were bruised and bleeding, she saw a large wolf following her. At first she was frightened and tried to run, but her strength was gone and she sank down exhausted. The wolf stood watching her, and then crept nearer and nearer until he lay at her feet. When Itsa-pich-kaupe arose to walk, the wolf followed, and when she sat down again to rest, he lay down by her side. She then besought his aid, saying:

'Pity me, brother wolf! I am so weak for food that I must soon die. I pray for the sake of my young children that you will help me.'

When she finished her prayer, the wolf trotted to the summit of a high butte, where he sat watching. He disappeared, but soon came back, dragging a buffalo calf he had just killed. With the flint the Crow woman had given her, she built a fire. After roasting and eating some of the meat, she felt stronger and started on, but her feet were so bruised and torn she could scarcely walk. When the wolf drew near, she placed her hand on his broad back, and he seemed glad to bear her weight. In this way the wolf helped Itsa-pich-kaupe, hunting food every day and keeping her supplied with food, until he brought her safely home. When they entered camp together, Itsa-pich-kaupe led the friendly wolf to her lodge, where she related to her family the story of her escape from the Crow camp. She besought the people to be kind to the wolf, and to give him some food. But she became very sick, after her return, and, as there was no one to look out for the wolf, the Indian dogs attacked him, and drove him into the hills. They would not allow him to remain in camp. The faithful wolf waited for a long time, watching in vain for Itsa-pich-kaupe. He came every evening to the summit of a high butte, where he sat gazing down at the lodge where she lay. Her relatives continued to feed him, until he disappeared, never to return. The Blackfeet never shoot at a wolf, or coyote, believing them to be good medicine. We have a saying, 'The gun that shoots at a wolf or coyote will never again shoot straight.'

At one time animals and men were able to understand each other. We can still talk to the animals, just as we do to people, but they now seldom reply, excepting in dreams. We are then obedient to them and do whatever they tell us. Whenever we are in danger, or distress, we pray to them and they often help us. Many of the animals are friendly to man. They are able to read the future and give us warning of what will happen.

1992: "Tigin Sutdu'a: Wolf Story," Andrew Balluta, Inland Dena'ina

The theme of the stories "When Men and Animals Were Friendly" and "The Legend of the Friendly Medicine Wolf"—the willingness of a wolf to help a human in distress—is repeated in many other Native American stories.

The inland Dena'ina, an Athabaskan people that live in the Lake Clark National Park region of south-central Alaska, tell a story of the friendship between a boy and a wolf. The wolf serves as a mentor to the boy and teaches him to become a master hunter. When the boy is grown, the wolf warns him that the prey animals will soon make war on him "because I have taught you and you have taken so many of them." The wolf sides with his human friend when the prey species rebel against him. Perhaps this shows one of the strongest ties between wolves and Native people—both were hunters who had to kill game to live—both are natural allies when the game revolts. Hunter and wolf are truly brothers in the hunt.

Andrew Balluta, elder, subsistence hunter, commercial fisherman, hunting guide, and former park ranger, retells the traditional story, "Tigin Sutdu'a: Wolf Story," based on versions he heard as a young man from the elders of his village, Nondalton. Andrew's story appears in the 1992 book, Nuvendaltin-Quht'ana: The People of Nondalton, he wrote with Linda Ellanna, an associate professor of anthropology at the University of Alaska Fairbanks. The introductory paragraphs that precede the story were written by Linda, based on information provided by Andrew and other Dena'ina elders.

The inland Dena'ina considered wolves to be their brothers. Wolves were thought to have once been people, and, as such, they all belong to one of the inland Dena'ina clans—*qqahyi* (raven clan), according to some elders. In the past, when people were short of food and hungry and they heard a wolf howling, they went to where the wolves had been consuming game and took the portion of the meat which had been left behind. The Dena'ina believed that the wolves had notified them by howling that there was food there and had deliberately left part of their kill for their brothers, the inland Dena'ina.

Because of the nature of this relationship, wolves were greatly respected and neither deliberately hunted or trapped. If a wolf were taken in a trap accidentally and not injured mortally, some trappers released it. If it was seriously hurt and had to be killed, the trapper talked to the wolf first. He apologized for trapping the wolf, stating that it had been accidental. The trapper then explained that he had to take the wolf's life.

After killing the wolf in the most humane fashion, the trapper carefully skinned the animal, quartered it, and hung every piece of the wolf in young trees—birch, willow, spruce, alder, cottonwood, whatever was growing in the area in which the wolf had been killed. In this way the trapper was giving every part of the wolf, including his spirit back to nature. The spirit of the wolf was then satisfied and did not bring bad luck to the trapper or hunter. If a man did not treat the remains of a wolf properly or failed to explain and apologize for its unavoidable killing, bad luck resulted and the hunter or trapper was unable to support himself or herself.

Tigin Sutdu'a: Wolf Story

Early one spring a young man and his wife walked up a mountainside far from their village packing a small baby. They made camp near the top. They spent some time making snares out of eagle feathers for snaring ground squirrels. After the snaring started, they were usually gone from their camp most of the day.

One evening they came back late after spending a long day on the mountain. The young man was leading the way with his wife following behind packing the baby. When they reached their brush shelter at camp, the young man held open the skin door for his wife to go inside. When she stood up inside the brush shelter, the young woman was completely taken by surprise. Lying there just in front of her was a large, gray wolf. Her husband was still outside. She didn't know what to do, but she didn't scream or holler. She knew that wolves and people were closely related. She stooped down and laid the baby right beside the wolf. "Here's your little brother," she said to the wolf. "We just found him."

The wolf started licking the baby's face. When the young man stepped inside, he saw what had happened and he spoke to the wolf. As he talked, the wolf laid his ears back, so the young couple knew he understood what they were saying.

From that time on the wolf stayed with the family and hunted with them high on the mountain. The couple treated him like a son, and the wolf accepted their child as his baby brother. Sometimes he would take the baby from the cradle and carry it out into the woods or off around the mountain for hours at a time. Whenever the father went hunting for the caribou, he took the wolf with him. When they'd spot a herd of caribou, the wolf took however much meat they needed, so the family never went without.

As the boy grew older, the wolf taught him how to hunt. The boy learned fast, but the wolf pushed him harder and harder to hunt better. The wolf made the boy run and work until he was faster and stronger than any boy his age had ever been. The boy was so quick he could catch birds as they were flying in the air.

After a while, the boy's father began to grow jealous of the wolf. The boy was always going after the wolf, and the man's wife was always saying what a good hunter the wolf was.

So one day when the boy's father was feeling mean, he took the wolf out with him to hunt some caribou. It wasn't long before they came upon a herd, and the man sent the wolf off after them. In a few minutes, the wolf had killed four caribou, and the man followed along behind cleaning them.

It had always been the man's habit as he cleaned the caribou to wash off the liver and give it to the wolf. However, this time he left the liver bloody and threw it at the wolf, hitting him in the face. "You're no wolf," said the man. "You're half dog. We don't have to wash everything for you all the time."

The wolf just sat there looking at him. He didn't eat the liver. When the man had finished loading up his pack, he put it on his shoulders and started off for the camp. The wolf still sat there with blood on his face, getting madder and madder. He watched until the man was far off in the distance. Then he leaped up and went off after the man. The wolf caught up with the man and killed him there with the pack still on his back.

When the man didn't come home for supper that night, his wife suspected that something had happened to him. Later that evening, she went to the door and found the wolf lying there with blood all over his face. "I guess the wolf has killed my husband," she thought to herself.

Kneeling beside the wolf, she began washing off his face while she talked to him. "What happened to my husband?" she asked. "Did you kill him?" Both of the wolf's ears twitched forward, so she knew that that was what had happened.

After she fed the wolf, he lay down near the doorway and fell asleep. Later on while the woman was nursing the boy, she started feeling angry about what the wolf had done. "I'll get even with him for killing my husband," she thought.

So while he slept, the woman took her own milk and rubbed it all over the wolf's paws. She knew that after awhile, the milk would make his feet so soft, he wouldn't be able to walk. She didn't want to kill the wolf, but she wanted to make him sorry for what he'd done. When she had finished, the woman began gathering up her belongings in the brush shelter. Soon the wolf woke up and the woman said, "There's no use in my staying around here any more. I'm going back home to my village. You won't be able to come along, of course."

The wolf sensed her bitterness now, and so he turned into a man and explained to her exactly what had happened. As he told his story, the wolf-man stood beside the boy holding on to him. The woman began to feel sorry for what she had done to his feet, but she was afraid to tell him about it.

The wolf said he realized that because he was a wolf, he couldn't come into the village to live with them. He promised that he would still do what he could to care for the boy. "Whenever you fellows are having a hard time in the village," he said, "and you don't have enough food, just listen for a wolf howling. Go to where the sound is, and you will find meat." Then he left them.

A year passed and the young boy and his mother didn't see the wolf again, even once. The following winter, a famine struck the village. The women set snares out all over the forest, but there weren't any rabbits. The men hunted clear back into the mountains, but the country was empty of game.

Then one night as the men returned empty handed from a hunting trip, they heard a wolf howling not far from the village. They thought nothing of it, but the young woman heard them talk about it and she knew what it was.

Early the next morning she rushed out to where the wolf had been heard and found him waiting. "I've brought meat for you," he said.

Then the wolf turned into a man and cleaned the game for her. He hung it up until she could return for it with others from the village.

She took part of the meat with her. When she finished loading up her pack, the young woman said to the wolf, "The men from the village will be coming here after this meat. You'd better not be around or they'll kill you." "I only came to make sure you have enough meat," the wolf said. "I'll be gone before they come." As he turned away, the woman saw that he was limping and she knew that his feet were getting softer. But she didn't know how to tell him what she had done.

That afternoon when she got back to the village, the woman told everyone where the meat was. The men went out to pack it in. There was plenty to last until the hunting got good again, and everyone was happy. Life was better in the village after that, and the winter months passed quickly.

But by spring the people in the village started missing food. Some of the people said they had seen a wolf in the village. Others said it had stolen from them. After much talking, the men said they would hunt it down and kill it

When the young woman heard about it, she ran out to look for the wolf. She knew that she must find him before the hunters did. Finally, after hours of searching, she found him. He walked over to her and sat down. Then he lifted a covering like a hood from his face and turned into a man. "Look at my feet," he said. "They are all raw." He told her that he had been stealing meat from the village. His feet were so sore that he couldn't hunt for himself.

The young woman finally told him what she had done to his feet, but said she was really sorry and promised to help him. She took some pieces of skin out of her sewing kit and put them under his feet. When she spit on them, they stayed on, and the wolf's feet were all right again.

So he put his hood back on again and changed back into a wolf. He was so happy that he forgave the young woman for what she had done. He even told her that if they ever needed meat in the village again, he would still be glad to get it for them.

The woman told him he'd better keep out of sight for awhile because the men were out hunting for him. She also told him he should not take any more meat from the village. "It might be poisoned," she said.

So they split up and the woman went back home to her son. The boy was getting older now, so she told him what had happened, After that, the boy always went along whenever the wolf left food for them.

Sometimes he went out alone to meet with wolf and the two of them went hunting together.

As the years passed, the time came when the boy was no longer a child but had become a man. He married and built a sod and spruce bark house on the shore of the lake not far from his mother's village. It was then that the wolf decided to have a serious talk with him. "I am your brother," the wolf said. "I have taught you a great deal and you have learned well. But now you must go on your own. You are a great hunter. I'm getting old now and you could even outdo me. But one day all the animals will make war with you—because I have taught you and you have taken so many of them—and you cannot outfight them all. So you must prepare yourself for that day. The first thing you must do is make a shelter and cache enough food on an island so you can escape there. Be sure you have a skin boat ready at all times. When the animals attack, you can jump into the boat and row out to the island."

The young man hurried to carry out his brother's instructions. Having lived with the wolf for all those years, he knew that whatever he said was true. Before long, everything was ready.

Then one night when he and his wife were asleep, the young man was awakened by strange noises coming from the woods. He woke her, they hurried down to the beach, and they got into the skin boat. They had barely pushed out from shore when the clearing around his shelter was filled with raging animals.

Among the animals was a large gray wolf. After the man and his wife were too far to hear, the wolf said, "You see! I told you we couldn't catch him. He's too fast." The rest of the animals didn't know that the man was the wolf's brother.

Several nights later, a skin boat moved quietly across the water from the island and landed just below the man's shelter. The man stepped onto the beach, moved quietly up the shore to his house, and peered in through the window. All the animals were inside having a feast on some food which the man had left behind. The leader of the animals sat at the head of the table. Putting an arrow to his bow, the man drew back and shot the animal leader in his heart. He dropped dead.

The shelter was in an uproar. All the other animals jumped up and were moving around. By the time some of them got outside to catch the man, he was already in his skin boat paddling back to the island. Once again the old wolf told them, "You see, I warned you that we could never catch him."

A few nights later, the young man returned in the boat with his wife.

Again he sneaked up to his house. But when he reached the doorway, someone was waiting for him there in the shadows. It was the old wolf. He'd been expecting them. The wolf handed the young man a bear bone club and said, "You may kill them all or let some escape—whatever you want."

The man understood. He pulled down the skin over the entrance and rushed inside, swinging the club left and right. He didn't stop until he had killed every animal he could reach and the house was quiet with death. Only a few had escaped. Finally, when his anger and strength were gone, the man walked outside. The wolf was satisfied.

"The few that got away talked to me before they left," the wolf told the man. "They said to tell you they'd forgive you and that they're going to have a party in two years at the dead leader's house. You and your wife are invited." "What are they going to do?" the man asked. "It's a trick. They are going to try to kill you then," said the wolf. But the wolf said he would be back before the time came to talk with the man about it. "Meanwhile, I'll watch out so that nothing happens to you or your family. You should get prepared for that party. You should take a brown bear and some caribou. Soak the bones in oil to make them strong and save them for the party."

The months passed quickly, summer and winter, and before long the two years were up and the wolf returned. "They're getting all ready now," the wolf said, sitting down. "The party will be in about two days, so you must fix up your equipment and be ready. The animals will be ready for you, but I'll do what I can to help. When you find them, I'll be there."

So the young man hurried to get everything ready. He gathered together the oiled clubs and fixed up his bow with plenty of arrows. His wife was busy sewing waterproof boots and clothing for their trip to the party. When the weapons and clothing were finished, the man and his wife gathered them up and walked to where the party was going to be.

Just before they got there, the young man stopped at the home of an old woman who lived in a foxhole right under the trail. He told his wife to wait outside the door for him. Inside, the old woman was sitting down. She lived all by herself. "Who are you?" she asked. He told her his name. She told him the animals were going to make war on a man by that name. "I'm the one," the man said. "I killed your leader."

The old woman started to scream, but he knocked her down with his oiled club and smashed her throat before she could make any noise. She died. The young man called to his wife as he began skinning the old woman out. Together they waited in the foxhole until night time. Then he put the old woman's skin over himself and picked up her cane and left with his wife for the party. His wife didn't need a disguise, because the animals didn't know her.

Pretty soon they came to the place where the party was being held. It was a little settlement—a village of animal people. When the young man and his wife entered the dead leader's house, the wolf, who was there before them with his own wife, recognized his brother. "That's your brother-in-law," he whispered to his wife. "Go invite them over."

So the young man and his wife went over and sat down with the wolf and his wife. Later in the evening the two brothers left the party together and had a talk outside. "They'll all be starting home now pretty soon," said the young man. "They don't think I'm coming, so I'll have to wait right here by the door in the dark and kill them as they leave."

The wolf told him not to kill all the animals, so they would not die out completely. Then the wolf went back inside and began talking each of the party into leaving, one or two at a time, while the man stood outside, killing some and letting some go. Then the house was about half empty, those left inside sensed something was wrong. They began escaping from the house in any way possible.

The man and his wife went inside and walked all around, taking whatever they wanted. "You're too smart for me," said the wolf. "What do you mean?' asked the young man, turning to his brother. "I thought they would get you. But now there won't be any more war again, ever. I must go now," the wolf said, "for I am getting old. But there is one thing you must always remember. Whenever any animal attacks or charges you, just think of me. I'll be right by your side. None of them will be able to catch you or hurt you in any way."

This agreement between the wolf and the young Dena'ina has been good for many generations of their descendants.

The inland Dena'ina believe that wolves often deliberately left part of their kills for their human brothers. This concept reminded me of statements frequently made by anti-wolf people about wolves wastefully leaving portions of their kills uneaten.

These differing interpretations of similar events show how much Native American culture differs from popular opinion in the rest of the country. Native people would thank a wolf for leaving part of a kill behind, whereas other people would condemn a wolf for the seeming waste and use the incident as justification for extermination of the species.

In my experiences with wolves in Denali National Park, I often saw them cache extra meat from carcasses and come back later, sometimes several days later, to finish it off. As best as I can tell, when a wolf leaves uneaten meat at a kill site, it usually returns to make use of it. Even if the wolf does not come back, the meat will provide food for ravens, eagles, bears, and other animals. Nothing ever goes to waste in a natural ecosystem.

1992: "Wolf Song for Wolf Haven," Paula Underwood, Oneida

After telling "Who Speaks for Wolf" to six pairs of captive wolves at an evening of storytelling at Wolf Haven, a non-profit wolf organization in Washington State, the vivid contrast between then and now, and the chain link fences in the forest, inspired Paula to write "Wolf Song for Wolf Haven."

Heavy metal threads
Twine one about the other
Declaring limitations
To our circumstance
    Freedom
    Lies somewhere else . . .
I hear the movement through the brush
A careful eye and a furred ear
Move toward perception
Watching . . . carefully watching
    Awareness
    Rides the Wind
All the Two-legged
Clustered together
Wonder at this circumstance,
Respecting the nature of Wolf . . .
    Relations
    Are made of such stuff
Yet . . . see the limitations
The space between us
Once was established by Respect
Now metal and air mark the borders
    Freedom . . . still lies
    Somewhere else
Life does not change
Only the way we live it
Twists and bends

In each new circumstance
   Awareness
   Points the way
Respect does not change
Only the relation of circumstance
Draws walls
In the forest air
   Relations
   Transcend barriers
And so we sing our songs
And tell our stories to one another
Painting mind pictures
Of the yet to be
   And freedom . . .
   Is coming . . .

1993: "The Fallen," Linda Hogan, Chickasaw

Linda Hogan, poet, essayist, and novelist, is a member of the Chickasaw tribe. She teaches at the University of Colorado and is deeply involved with wildlife rehabilitation and projects to save endangered species. Her poem, "The Fallen," from her 1993 collection The Book of Medicine, *speaks of two different views the wolf.*

It was the night
a comet with its silver tail
fell through darkness
to earth's eroded field,
the night I found
the wolf,
starved in metal trap,
teeth broken
from pain's hard bite,
its belly swollen with unborn young.

In our astronomy
the Great Wolf
lived in sky.
It was the mother of all women
and howled her daughter's names
into the winds of night.

But the new people,
whatever stepped inside their shadow,
they would kill,

whatever crossed their path,
they came to fear.

In their science,
Wolf was not the mother.
Wolf was not wind.
They did not learn healing
from her song.

In their stories
Wolf was the devil, falling
down an empty,
shrinking universe,
God's Lucifer
with yellow eyes
that had seen their failings
and knew that they could kill the earth,
that they would kill each other.

That night
I threw the fallen stone back to sky
and falling stars
and watched it all come down
to ruined earth again.

Sky would not take back
what it had done.

That night, sky was a wilderness so close
the eerie light of heaven
and storming hands of sun
reached down the swollen belly
and dried up nipples of a hungry world.

That night,
I saw the trapper's shadow
and it had four legs.

1995: "The Wolf as a Fellow Hunter," Richard Baldes, Shoshone

In March of 1994, I gave my slide show on wolves at the Annual Meeting of the National Wildlife Federation, held in Austin, Texas. After the program I met Dick Baldes, a Shoshone Indian who serves on the Federation's board of directors, and talked with him about Native American attitudes toward the wolf. We spoke of the respect and admiration Native people feel toward the wolf, a respect largely based on its status as a master hunter. Many tribes, including the Shoshone, deliberately used wolves as role models and tried to imitate their hunting techniques.

Dick has worked as a fish and wildlife biologist with the U.S. Fish and Wildlife Service (USFWS) since 1971. He is stationed at Wyoming's Wind River Indian Reservation, the place where he grew up. As the USFWS's project leader for the reservation, Dick assists the Shoshone Nation in managing their fish and wildlife resources.

He is also a hunter and has spent much time thinking about the loss of this master predator from reservation lands and the possibility of its return in the near future. Dick's article discusses past and present Shoshone attitudes toward the wolf.

All my youth was spent growing up on the Wind River Indian Reservation in Wyoming. The reservation encompasses 2.2 million acres of land, the same area as Yellowstone National Park. The Wind River Mountain Range forms the western boundary; the Owl Creek Mountains and a portion of the Absaroka Mountains mark the northern boundary. The land ranges from semi-arid sagebrush/grassland in the east/southeastern portion of the reservation, to rugged mountains over twelve thousand feet in elevation in the Wind and Owl Creek mountains.

The Wind River country has always been home to the Shoshone Nation. In historic times, subsistence hunting for buffalo and other big game animals provided the basis for communal life. Fishing and berry and root gathering were also important.

The Shoshone originally roamed throughout a vast five-state area. Frequently, while on hunting excursions to Yellowstone, they would meet their allies, people of the Flathead Nation. By joining forces, the two groups were better able to protect themselves against larger warring tribes such as the Blackfeet and Crow.

Two treaties were signed by the U.S. Government and the Eastern (my ancestor's band) Shoshone. The first one, signed at Fort Bridger in 1863, established the 45-million-acre Shoshone Indian Reservation in parts of Wyoming, Utah, Colorado, Idaho, and Montana. Just five years later in 1868, again at Fort Bridger, a second treaty was signed that established the Wind River Reservation, an area approximately one-twentieth the size of the original 1863 reservation.

In the winter of 1878, the Northern Arapaho Tribe, originally from Oklahoma and Colorado, were temporarily placed by the government on the Wind River Indian Reservation. Although, they were traditional enemies of the Shoshones, much like the Blackfeet and Crow tribes, the Arapaho were given joint tenancy of the reservation with the Shoshones in 1939.

Game animals inhabiting the reservation include bighorn sheep, elk, moose, mule and whitetail deer, pronghorn antelope, black bear, coyotes, fox, and mountain lions. Endangered grizzly bears are occasionally observed. The native sage grouse (chicken), waterfowl, and exotic upland birds such as pheasant and Hungarian and chukar partridge are common, as are many other animals native to plains and mountainous areas.

Sadly, the bison and the wolf, two animals traditionally sacred to Native Americans, no longer roam the Shoshone homeland. The last wolf in Wyoming was killed on the Wind River Indian Reservation in the foothills of the Owl Creek Mountains by a sheep man in 1943.

While growing up on the reservation, my brother and I spent much of our time hunting, fishing, and gathering chokecherries, buffalo berries, currants, and other berries. Fish and game were a substantial part of our family's diet.

I remember when my brother and I first became interested in hunting. Many of our friends were telling stories about shooting jack rabbits and prairie dogs and hunting coyotes. I remember asking my dad to teach us to hunt and to be able to "get in practice" by shooting animals other kids were using as targets.

I still remember Dad's words as if they were yesterday. "No one should kill an animal just for practice. Taking the life of an animal should be for a good reason. Any animal you plan to kill, you should plan to eat." Dad, like most Native Americans, practiced the philosophy that all living things created had a purpose. It was wrong to kill an animal for no reason.

Dad explained to us the consequences of shooting prairie dogs and jack rabbits. He said if prairie dogs are reduced, then animals such as eagles, coyotes, and other predators would have less to eat. With fewer prairie dogs and jack rabbits, the eagles, coyotes, and foxes would have to depend on other food sources such as sage chickens, young deer, and antelope, which the Shoshone need to hunt. He was reaffirming that all animals are necessary in the true natural order of life. Today, biologists refer to this concept as biodiversity. It was practiced by Native Americans hundreds of years ago. As a result of my dad's teaching, when were growing up, my brother and I didn't practice on live targets—unless we were prepared to eat them.

Dad's favorite fishing area was on the South Fork of the Little Wind

River. Every year we would spend about a week around the fourth of July camped in the same spot. We would often see black bears on a sparsely timbered slope above our camp. Even though there were no wolves to be seen, I am sure that Dad would have treated them the same way he treated the bears. He could have hunted the bears but he never did; my brothers and I never have either. According to my dad's philosophy, bears are important because they control other animals and because they are a wonderment to observe. Although we never saw a grizzly, my dad and a friend (Fred Peche, a Flathead married to a Shoshone relative) told stories about how grizzlies helped to keep elk and deer herds healthy by preying primarily on old and unhealthy animals.

Both Dad and Fred had not only an appreciation for wild animals, but also a respect and a deep feeling of connection with them. Fred related stories on the importance of wolves to Native Americans spiritually and how Native people talked to wolves and learned hunting methods from them. He had a singular love for the outdoors, and I remember how adept he was at expounding a story in order to capture our attention.

Like many other Native people, the Shoshone have stories about wolves who helped our ancestors. In one story, "The Wolf Saves the Shoshone," an enormous wolf brings a freshly killed deer each day to a snow-bound camp of starving people. Another tale, "The Brave Wolf Is Given an Indian Burial," tells of a wolf who lived among the Shoshone and fought alongside them when the Sioux, traditional enemies of the tribe, attacked. The wolf fights bravely but finally dies after a great throng of warriors surround him. To honor the wolf, the Shoshone sung the death chant at his grave and placed gifts at the site.

Shoshone legend also says that our ancestors learned to hunt antelope by emulating the wolf, the master hunter of the plains. Elders talked about how a wolf would crouch and move to the top of a hill where he could see the antelope, then wag his tail to draw the antelopes' attention. The curious nature of the antelope would bring them into range to enable the wolf to run one down. The same trick worked for Shoshone hunters, who waved a piece of cloth or hide to draw the antelope within range of bow and arrow.

Sometimes when I'm alone on a remote section of the reservation, I remember the experiences my brother and I had hunting with Dad, and I wonder what it might have been like for earlier hunting parties of fathers and sons. I visualize a scene, hundreds of years ago, of a Shoshone father and his two sons who, while out hunting, hear wolves howling. I

envision them watching as a pack of wolves stalk a small herd of buffalo and made a kill.

The experience with wolves would not be forgotten by the father or
sons. Their feeling about wolves would be based on admiration, wonder, and respect. The wolves were masters at working together as hunters and at sharing the fruits of their efforts. The wolf pack was not unlike the father and sons and their family. The lessons learned from observing how wolves worked together to hunt would be etched in their
memory and emulated by them and their descendants for generation
upon generation.

Wolves have already returned to Montana and will soon be restored
to Wyoming when the National Park Service reintroduces them to
Yellowstone. I find it distressing that many modern hunters seem to
oppose wolf reintroduction. An unscientific survey appearing in the
May 1994 issue of *Outdoor Life* suggest that most hunters are opposed
to reintroduction of wolves to Yellowstone National Park. If this is true,
most modern-day hunters don't understand or appreciate the role of
the wolf as a hunter.

If there ever was a group of people that could have taken an adversarial
role towards wolves, it was the Native Americans. They competed with
the wolf directly for the same food supply—bison, elk, deer, antelope,
caribou. Yet Native people chose not to destroy the wolf. They admired
and respected the wolf for his mastery at hunting and survival and emulated his behavior. Jack Gladstone mentioned the importance of the
wolf to Blackfeet as a sacred medicine animal. There are many other
Native stories that depict the wolf as a sacred animal. As a Native American and as a hunter, I believe that the wolf should to be restored to his
ancestral home in Yellowstone and placed back in the Wind River
Mountains.

My brother and I still hunt together every year the first part of October. For us, it would be the ultimate experience to one day hear wolves
howl in our favorite elk hunting spot. Better yet, to see a pack of wolves
making a stalk on a herd of elk would be a dream come true.

The philosophies about hunting and fishing my brother and I learned
from our dad, and the love he and our family had for the outdoors and
wildlife, led to my selecting the field of biology as a profession. His
respect and admiration for animals was forever etched in our brains,
and I decided to make wildlife management my life's work.

It wasn't until after my formal education and personal experiences
with wildlife and falling back to teachings in my youth that the "big
picture" finally came together. There is a good reason that our Creator

put us on this globe with wild creatures. What would this place be without wild things? I like to hunt, but the older I get, the less important it is for me to take the life an animal. My greatest joy comes from being out among wildlife rather than from making a kill.

Maybe the most important reason for wild creatures is their presence (or lack of presence) as an indicator of the health of our environment. We need only look at the Endangered Species List of plants and animals to understand how poorly we've taken care of our planet.

Evolution of Native American culture could not and can not exist without wild creatures. Legends and beliefs revolve around the interaction of Native people and animals. The Shoshone and all other Native tribes need wild animals just as much as they need a homeland.

I mentioned earlier that the last native Wyoming wolf was killed on the Wind River Indian Reservation in 1943. Leo Cottenoir was working as a sheepherder near the base of the Owl Creek Mountains. Leo is a member of the Cowlitz Tribe in southwestern Washington but married a member of the Shoshone Tribe. Fifty year later, Leo can recall very vividly his experience with the last wolf in Wyoming. He heard coyotes yipping and decided to see if they were bothering his herd of ewes and lambs. He rode his horse on a ridge and looked down on an old reservoir. He saw what looked like an old coyote and two pups. As he got closer to the reservoir, the coyotes took off through the rocks and he shot at them and missed. He then saw the wolf come out of the rocks. He said, "It was a wolf and two full grown coyotes, instead of a full grown coyote and two pups." Taking careful aim, Leo shot and killed the wolf.

Recently, I asked Leo if he realized then that this was the last living wolf in Wyoming? He said that at the time he thought if there was one there were probably more.

Leo is now in his early eighties and despite having worked as a sheep man and a cowboy for most of his life, he thinks that wolves are necessary. He told me: "The wolf is one of God's creatures and has as much right to be here as any other animal. They are a native animal, native to the country and something that has always been there. Why do stockmen think that livestock has more of a right to be here than the wolves? Livestock aren't native, the wolf was. Fact of the matter, man is the worst predator there is anyhow, regardless of the predatory animals."

Leo also told me it was sad to think that was the last wolf in Wyoming and the only one he'd ever seen—and, "I killed him." He expressed regret at having killed the wolf but added this hope: "The wolf should have another chance and should be brought back to the reservation and to Yellowstone."

Bill Nasogaluak, an Inuit artist, once eloquently summed up the Native American view of the wolf. He explains, "In our culture, the wolf is very much admired. Like the wolf, we have to work together in order to hunt successfully. The problems he faces in staying alive on the tundra are the same problems we have confronted for thousands of years. It is pointless to set us apart; we are both Arctic hunters." The Shoshone and the wolf had the same bond: We were brothers in the hunt on the Great Plains.

Because of the strong links Native Americans have with the wolf, many of us are looking at the possibility of reintroducing wolves to the Wind River Indian Reservation. Wolves will soon be back in their historic range in Yellowstone, just northwest of the reservation. If we can also restore the wolf to its former territory on the Wind River Indian Reservation, there would be two viable populations of wolves in Wyoming. As a Native American, I would be proud to play a role in bringing wolves back. They deserve a chance to return to their original hunting grounds.

Dick asked me to donate the money he would have received for this essay to Yellowstone National Park, his ancestors' traditional hunting grounds, to help return the wolf to its traditional homeland.

1992: "The Wolf: A Native American Symbol," Joseph M. Marshall, III, Sicangu Lakota

Joseph Marshall, a member of the Sicangu Lakota tribe, recently gave a talk in Jackson, Wyoming, for The Wolf Fund, an organization dedicated to returning the wolf to Yellowstone. Like Jack Gladstone, Dick Baldes, and many other native Americans, Joseph is committed to bringing the wolf back to its original homeland. In this transcript of his lecture, he offers his thoughts on the similarities between Native Americans and wolves and his hope for the restoration of wolves to Yellowstone.

Sharing a continent for thousands of years enabled generation after generation of Native Americans to observe the Wolf and to come to know him intimately. For the nomadic hunter-warrior societies, the Wolf was an especially important symbol. Hunters imitated the Wolf's hunting tactics, noting that patience and perseverance were the wolf-hunter's most effective weapons. Warriors developed the ability to endure physical hardship, noting that it was one of the wolf-warrior's greatest attributes. The Native American warrior stoutly defended home and family, manifesting loyalty and devotion into fierceness on the field of battle . . . as did (and does) the wolf-warrior.

One of the highest compliments that could be paid to a hunter was to say that he "hunted like the Wolf." Likewise, to say that a warrior "fought like the Wolf" was high praise. This did not mean that one was bloodthirsty or savage. The Native American did not generally perceive the Wolf as enemy or competitor, or even as something less than himself. His perception of the Wolf was a realistic assessment of the Wolf's ability to survive and thrive, to be in balance with his world. Therefore, to be "like the Wolf" was a good thing indeed.

For centuries, the Wolf and the Native American shared time, space, and life in North America. They also shared the same fate. The European newcomer considered both Wolf and Native American the antithesis to all he stood for, never really bothering to look sincerely beyond the obvious differences. He drove the Wolf and the Native American from ancestral homelands, disrupted their lives, and upset their balance. Life was never the same. By the late nineteenth century, wolves were rare below the 48th parallel. By 1900, the Native American population had dropped from several million to 250,000.

The wolf and the Native American will never again have access to this entire continent. Our lifestyles are, and will continue to be, restricted. While we once roamed free over all of North America, the boundaries of our present and future existence can now be measured in scant miles or in a few hours of travel. With that perspective, Indian reservations and national parks have much in common.

Today, both Wolf and Native American still struggle with and under the weight of misconceptions—misconceptions based on myth rather than on fact. It is far past the time for eliminating these prejudices. We Native Americans have made strides in that direction. We can speak for ourselves. But what of the Wolf? Who will speak for him? And, perhaps, a more important question is "Who will listen?" Who will listen with open minds and open hearts when any voice is raised on behalf of the Wolf?

Eons ago Native Americans realized that there was an order to life on this land, a certain balance. All beings, all creatures had an equal role; everyone served a purpose. Therefore, no one was greater or lesser than any other. Everyone is born, lives, and dies. It is the equalizer from which no one is exempt, whether we fly, crawl, walk on four legs . . . or two. Today that basic reality of life is forgotten. We operate from a philosophy of dominance—those with the ability to reason dominating those who supposedly have no such ability. It is this philosophy which is adversely affecting our planet. It is preventing the Wolf from returning to its rightful place in Yellowstone National Park, a place he had before we gave it a name.

With so much out of balance in this world, it is easy to feel overwhelmed by the magnitude of our problems. In order to turn things around, however, we must focus on little steps, on doing what is in our power to do. It is in our power to return the Wolf to Yellowstone National Park. Restoring this great predator would be an act of faith and hope—faith in spite of fears that it will have a negative impact, hope that the positive consequences will not be viewed as coincidence or fluke. We won't know until we try. Theories and fears aside, the only basis for honest assessment is to actually put the Wolf back in Yellowstone. The question is whether we have the courage to lay aside our prejudices.

Even in this day and age there is a place and a purpose for all forms of life. Man must realize that his rights do not supersede those of any other species, and neither are they any less.

In the spring of 1995, a collection of essays by Joseph Marshall entitled On Behalf of the Wolf and the First Peoples *will be released by Red Crane Books.*

Chapter 8

A Turning Tide

". . . my sin against the wolves caught up with me."
Aldo Leopold

Thoreau had been far ahead of his times when, in 1856, he lamented the loss of wolves and other predators from the woods of Concord, Massachusetts. Fifty-eight years later, in 1914, a Pennsylvania newspaperman named Henry Shoemaker published a small book that similarly bemoaned the destruction of wolves in his state. Shoemaker may have been the first writer to seriously propose that wolves be reintroduced into areas where they had been exterminated.

Views of the wolf in America began to change radically in the first half of the twentieth century. The best examples of this trend are seen in papers on predatory animals presented at the annual meetings of the American Society of Mammalogists (ASM). Professional biologists were becoming increasingly critical of the U.S. Biological Survey (USBS) and its predator control policies, and the agency's indiscriminate poisoning programs were repeatedly denounced at the ASM meetings. Biologists from universities and museums came to a consensus that the USBS must replace its policy of "absolute extermination" with a program based on selective control of individual animals proven to be livestock killers.

The National Park Service (NPS) made major changes to its predator policies in the 1930s. In 1931, the agency banned the use of poison on its lands, except for rodent control programs. More importantly, by 1936, the NPS official wildlife management policy called for reintroduction of "any native species which had been exterminated" from a national park.

The evolution of our country's attitudes toward wolves and other predators is best demonstrated by the two final papers in this chapter, both written by Aldo Leopold. Once fully behind the wolf extermination campaigns, Leopold later realized that he had been wrong. He courageously admitted his mistakes and set out to lead his fellow Americans to a better understanding and appreciation of the wolf and its rightful place in the natural world.

1914: *Wolf Days in Pennsylvania*, Henry W. Shoemaker

In 1914, one year before the first Congressional funding of the federal wolf extermination program, Henry Shoemaker, president of the Altoona Tribune *newspaper, published a short book entitled* Wolf Days in Pennsylvania. *Shoemaker wrote about the wolf "from an entirely different point of view." For his time, Shoemaker's statement that the wolf has an "inherent right to life" was revolutionary. Adding a theological argument to his theme, he wrote that God made all animal species for a "purpose"—human destruction of a species such as the wolf implies that we thought God had "erred in creating such animals." After describing the beneficial effects wolves have on prey species and the role wolves play in maintaining the balance of nature, Shoemaker proposed that wolves be reintroduced to Pennsylvania.*

I. Preface

That a new book treating on the much-discussed wolf can be written at all, the animal must be described from an entirely different point of view, else it would be superfluous. Happily the author feels that there is a side, an important one, to the wolfish character, which has been over-looked or perverted. It is a side decidedly favorable to the animal, to its inherent right to live, to be protected by mankind. The wolf of Pennsylvania accomplished much more good than harm. At the time when the Indians ranged the Continent and Nature's balance was perfect, the wolf played an important role. It preyed upon the weak and sickly animals and birds, preventing the perpetuation of imperfect types and the spread of pestilences. It kept up a high standard of excellence among all lesser creatures, was the great preserver of type and perfection. In addition it devoured bugs, insects, grubs and worms of an injurious nature. When the white man appeared on the scene and began killing all living things indiscriminately, the food supply of the wolves was affected. The wolfish diet required meat, and this at times became unobtainable. Crazed with hunger the wolves attacked calves, pigs and sheep, which slow of motion and easily captured, occupied the same relative position to them as had the formerly abundant weak and imperfect deer, grouse, rabbits and quail. Just as some otherwise harmless men commit murder when crazed by lack of food, the wolves played havoc in farm yards that otherwise they would have left unmolested. As the result, bounties were put on their heads, they were hunted unmercifully. The wolves were also useful forest scavengers, cleaning up the neighborhoods of camps and hunters' shambles. No person stopped to reason if the wolves had a useful purpose in the world—man deliberately acted as if the Wise Maker had erred in creating such animals. All living things have a *purpose*; it would be a loss to the world if even the common house flies were completely exterminated. It is an over-production of any one species of thing that carries the germ of trouble. Consequently the panther, the sworn enemy of the wolf, kept that species down to proper numbers; the Indian, sworn foe of the panther, kept the "Pennsylvania Lion" within bounds—but there was no warfare of extermination until the white man came. Most of the early hunters came of peasant stock, unused to carrying firearms in the old country, and with deeply rooted feelings against private parks which preserved game. Once loosed in a new continent, given arms and freedom, they set out to slaughter everything in sight. They wanted excuses for wholesale killing; the wolves' thefts of calves, pigs and sheep gave it to them. If they had killed less of the wolves' food supply no farm stock would have been taken. . . . The early settlers of America were unhampered by game laws, their blood lust knew no bounds. The wolves were starved into criminal acts, and then punished for it. Now after the wolves are gone a more discriminating generation looks over the scene dispassionately and notes that nothing has been gained by their extirpation. In Scotland when wolves abounded no one ever heard of "grouse" disease or "rabbit" disease; the ibex and chamois in Switzerland deteriorated after the wolves disappeared. The ibex exists in Italy where there are wolves, and as long as there are wolves there will be ibexes. In Africa buffaloes and certain antelopes diminish as the lions are killed off. The rinderpest rages in regions where there are no longer any lions, leopards or cheetahs. In Pennsylvania the harm done by the destruction of wolves has been appalling. First of all the increase in insect pests. These were practically unknown when panthers, wolves and foxes were prevalent. Secondly, the race of deer has deteriorated, the larger varieties *Odocoileus Americanus Borealis Miller* is completely extinct. The race of deer is only kept up by frequent introductions of specimens from Western States *where there are wolves*. The grouse are getting scarcer, despite "man-made" game laws; disease ravages them every few seasons. The big hares are gone, rabbits not what they were, the quail are frail; sickly specimens breed now; formerly the wolves prevented that.

XI. Possible Re-Introduction

From the number of hunters who took out licenses in 1913, upwards of two hundred thousand, it would seem that they formed an important part of the population of Pennsylvania. . . . It is to be doubted if five hundred deer were killed in the entire Commonwealth. With such meagre results the time is bound to be at hand when a strong demand will be made to re-stock the forests with game worthy of the name. Civilized men are beginning to find that killing rabbits, quails and squirrels is little better than a barnyard slaughter, that they do not furnish the excitement expected. Intelligent hunters read of struggles with wolves and mountain lions, of coyote coursing, and dispatching grizzlies in the West, and compare it to the feeble pastime of slaying a few mangy rabbits at home, to the disparagement of the home sport. A strong demand will be made to stock the Pennsylvania wilds not with more rabbits, quails, ground-hogs and squirrels, but with savage beasts, such as panthers, brown bears and wolves. Deer and elk are here already, but without the so-called predatory beasts with them, they are sure to deteriorate. Wolf and panther hunting can be made the royal sport of Pennsylvania. Wolves, unmolested except at certain seasons, would soon make themselves at home, and would prove a great benefit alike to sportsmen and to the game animals and birds.

1924: "The Predatory and Fur-Bearing Animals of the Yellowstone National Park," Milton P. Skinner

In April of 1924, at the Sixth Annual Meeting of the American Society of Mammalogists, a former Yellowstone ranger and chief naturalist named Milton Skinner presented a report to the nation's top biologists. Skinner's paper criticized the prevailing anti-predator policies of his former agency, the National Park Service. Later revised and published in a 1927 issue of Roosevelt Wild Life Bulletin, *Skinner's report is an early example of a biologist calling for selective control of problem animals rather than extermination of the entire species.*

In his 118-page paper, Skinner refers to wolves in Yellowstone several times. Drawing on his years of field experience as a ranger, he states that wolves were on the increase in 1914, numbering about sixty, "until severe hunting by the Park Rangers [had] again reduced their numbers to the point of extermination." His wildlife observations in Yellowstone caused Skinner to conclude: "The wolf is of positive value as a scavenger and as a killer of weak and diseased wild stock. There is little doubt that they played their part in developing speed and cunning among many forms of animals and in preventing epidemics."

The following excerpts from Skinner's paper show how a pioneering opponent of federal predator extermination policies framed his proposal for a radical change in the way our country dealt with wolves, coyotes, and other carnivores in its national parks.

Our [original] settlers and farmers were antagonistic to the carnivorous animals. On the farms, man's domestic animals are penned up and peculiarly subject to the attacks of the wild predators; and the destruction that follows is often very serious, indeed. For the farmer destroys the carnivorous animals whenever he can to protect his domestic stock. Furthermore the farmers unwittingly aggravate the attacks on their animals by killing off the rodents that would otherwise furnish food to the predators. In the National Parks in general, and in the Yellowstone Park in particular, there is no obligation to defend livestock; but it has been thought proper without a thorough investigation to kill the carnivorous species in order to have a greater increase of other forms of wild life, apparently considered more important by those who have the authority to order the killing.

It has not been appreciated that we need these predatory and fur-bearing animals alive and living their normal lives, that the situation in the Parks where we believed these animals were preserved is not satisfactory, and that we are slowly losing a valuable possession there. Nevertheless, the Yellowstone National Park is a most logical place to preserve our native animals. It is one of our largest Parks; it has a strong and continuing protector; it has large areas of wild land; and it is better stocked with a representative colony of wild life in an environment approaching primitive, natural conditions. In spite of these favorable factors, there has been little, or nothing, said about the situation and almost nothing has been written to show how unscientific, how careless, we have been in the Yellowstone National Park in the past. There have been no wholly adequate studies made and very little is positively known about the wild life in this Park and the interrelations of the various species of its wild plants and animals. Careful, minute investigations should be made on which a wise general policy for the care of all wild life, and for such control as may be needed, can be based. . . .

Economic and Educational Values of the Predators. That the coyotes, wolves, and their near relatives are exceedingly interesting animals cannot be denied by anyone who has read Ernest Thompson Seton's entertaining stories. And by this, I mean interesting to the unscientific as well as to the naturalist. To the naturalist every animal is keenly interesting—especially ones as highly developed and as diversified in habits as the predatory animals are. It is only by study that we can really know an animal and find out what it eats; whether it is detrimental to man's interests and should be kept under control; or whether the good it does (for every animals does *some* good) overbalances the evil it may do. If it does more good than harm, it obviously should be protected. The animals must be preserved somewhere if we are to study them, and the National Parks are logical places for that preservation. Undoubtedly in a careful study of the predators we are going to find them most instructive as well as entertaining. . . .

In another way, wild life is benefited by the predacious animals which serve us well by removing weak and sickly animals, thus keeping the breeding stock vigorous and free from epidemics. . . .

Mr. A. A. Saunders, also is impressed by . . . their influence on bird life. "The wild enemies of birds weed out from their ranks the weaker individuals, those less fitted for the struggle for existence. If through destruction of these enemies, the weaker ones increase, disease or parasitic enemies may start, and spread from weaker to stronger and do far more to decrease bird life than other natural enemies ever would." . . .

Although I have used birds to illustrate my meaning, it is just as true of mammals that they require predatory enemies to keep them at the top-notch of efficiency. The bison of the tame herd in Yellowstone National Park are subject to hemorrhagic septicemia which breaks out at intervals with tragic results. Since the wild animals do not have the disease, we are beginning to wonder if a few predators would not normally have stopped the disease with the first weakened animal before it could spread to others. I know of an instance back in 1917 where I found a single mule deer infected with actinomycosis, or lumpy jaw. This deer avoided all natural enemies by living near Mammoth where the crowds of people scared off the coyotes that would otherwise have killed him during the early stages of his trouble. But as it was, this deer lingered on for two years more. From that date to 1921, I saw five different mule deer that were infected with this disease although I had never noticed a case among them before. Unfortunately I was not able to trace the disease back from the five mule deer to the one first seen in 1917, but the presumptive evidence is very strong that they contracted it from the first deer. . . .

What we contend is that each species should be studied on its own merits. If we had more time we would go even further and say that each individual should be studied on his own merits, for we are beginning to realize more and more that individual animals differ in their ways just as men do. But such studies are too much to hope for yet, and so if the decision is against a species after we have weighed its merits against its demerits, by all means kill the animals individually responsible, but we should move very slowly indeed when it comes to declaring war against a whole species.

Skinner made a detailed study of NPS reports, both superintendent's annual reports and the annual reports of the director of the NPS, including many of those quoted in Chapter 5. After pointing out several examples of park superintendents calling for extermination of predatory animals, Skinner pleads for a change of policy:

We have disturbed the original balance already, and to regain a new one requires further knowledge; but we are fearful of ill-advised experiments although the authorities are continuing to experiment, often rashly. As the Parks are now operated, each Superintendent decides what animals to kill; overburdened as he usually is with a mass of executive detail, he could not give this subject the careful and judicious care that it needs, even if he were trained to decide on such matters. He yields to the tendency to protect the "big game" at the expense of the other animals. But the right course is to protect *all wild life*, not excluding even those carnivores that may prey on the hoofed mammals. To many persons, a wolf or a coyote is an important as a deer; and surely a bear is as valuable as a rabbit. It is a fact that all are equal in value, else they would have disappeared in the struggle to exist. Therefore, we should do that which will benefit all wild life and not favor the hoofed game. To know exactly the consequences of what we are doing, we must know all about the animals and their interrelations. Most assuredly we do not know that now. . . .

   Control, then, for animals *proved* detrimental to the general good, but not extermination, or we destroy that which we can never replace, and we certainly do not preserve the national parks "in absolutely unimpaired form."

At the end of his report, Skinner summarizes his points and presses his vision for a new management philosophy for predators in the national parks:

The abundance of predacious and fur-bearing animals throughout this continent was astonishing when the first settlers landed. Since then the Americans have been more destructive of this valuable resource than either the Canadians or the Spanish. At the present time, the numbers of these animals is but a shadow of what it once was; extermination faces them everywhere, even in the National Parks, where we once had thought they were safe.

In the Yellowstone Park the diverse topographical conditions and rugged climate are suited to varied and abundant animal life. Although this Park has far too small an area of winter grazing grounds (which condition may be remedied by certain additions at the lower altitudes), it is nevertheless the predominant National Park so far as wild life is concerned. There are three great classes of mammals there: the hoofed game, the predators and the rodents. The Park's mammal fauna has changed greatly since its discovery; the original natural balance was destroyed and has not been reestablished. . . .

With natural conditions outside the National Parks disappearing rapidly, we need these large areas maintained in their nearly original wild state. We must not exterminate any part of the wild life but guard it all carefully, for once destroyed we cannot bring it back. The predators should be preserved in the National Parks as a part of the natural environment, and because of their scientific, educational and recreational interest. . . .

Since the ideal policy would be to preserve the Yellowstone Park essentially as nature has evolved it, the extermination of any species of its wild life is indefensible. A certain amount of control is at times necessary, but this is a very delicate matter, requiring careful study by qualified naturalists whose sympathies are with the primary purpose of the National Parks.

A stable, forward-looking policy must be adopted, for it is dangerous to the maintenance of the native fauna to allow each Superintendent to experiment on his own account. All the wild life should be studied intensively and a policy evolved that will fully protect it. For this purpose a responsible technical staff is requisite in each Park to study conditions and control all activities affecting the wild life and its Park environment. This is the chief hope for the future of our highly prized Yellowstone animals.

1930: "At the Cross-Roads," A. Brazier Howell

The thesis, proposed by Milton Skinner and other biologists, that we should move from a policy of predator extermination to one of selective con-

trol of individual problem animals was a major topic of debate at the Twelfth Annual Meeting of the American Society of Mammalogists, held in May 1930 at the American Museum of Natural History in New York City.

During the four-day convention, a number of USBS men read papers on their agency's progress in predator control methods. These men once could have expected an appreciative audience for their comments. Staff members of the USBS had helped to create the American Society of Mammalogists in 1919, and the Society had been thought of as the professional arm of the agency.

At this meeting, the Survey spokesmen found themselves assailed by other biologists over predator control policies. Dr. Charles C. Adams, of the New York State Museum, one of the earliest biologists to earn an Ph.D. in ecology, read a paper entitled "Rational Predatory Animal Control." Adams clearly stated that the ASM "opposed this extermination policy" of the USBS and added that "we strongly protest the excessive expenditure of public funds for drastic reduction of predatory animals." Throughout his talk and during the open discussion that followed it, the transcript of the conference indicates that attending biologists frequently laughed out loud at the Survey's statements and policies. That laughter was proof that the USBS's position was no longer respected in the professional society that the agency itself had helped to found. One USBS man, Stanley Young, in a letter to his friend Arthur Carhart complained of "the abuse which we have been obliged to take during the past several months from biased and uninformed individuals."

A. Brazier Howell, of Johns Hopkins University, delivered the final talk of the convention, a summation of objections the mainstream biologist had of USBS policies. He concluded with this call to arms to his peers: "Now gentleman, what is your pleasure? What are you going to do about it?"

As many of you know, I became interested in the predatory mammal problem last year, and, with the backing of Mr. Madison Grant and the New York Zoölogical Society, I undertook to make some investigations. This could not be exhaustive, by any means, for I had not the time to devote to such a project but I wished to satisfy myself of the situation that must be faced.

The results, which I present to you today briefly and in as fair-minded a manner as I am able to do, are, to me, extremely significant as indicating the present day trend in wild life matters. No longer is the game hog the chief threat to our fauna, but rather the pseudo-conservationist who agitates for the protection of one or two game species and the eradication of everything else, and vested interests of one sort or another, working through legislative channels and by political pressure for systematized destruction.

For several years there has been expressed by members of this Society, in mild and rather guarded terms, dissatisfaction with certain policies of the Biological Survey. We have all been loath to criticize the Survey openly for it is the veritable shrine of American mammalogy. For a great many years our attitude was, I think, that the Survey was the competent federal guardian of our wild life. If it did a thing or said a thing, that thing was right, for it was the expression of some of our most brilliant naturalists. That spirit, and that for which it stood, *was* the Biological Survey, a heritage of good will slowly erected throughout long years by the integrity of its policies.

Understand me clearly. In what I hereafter say there is no shadow of criticism of Biological Survey biologists. They are, without exception, the salt of the earth. To question the sincerity of their motives would be like stating that the sun rises in the west, and if Survey policies were left for them to determine we would have no cause for complaint.

Unfortunately, however, when we speak today of the Biological Survey we no longer refer to this group of biologists but to the men who are responsible for present day policies. Beginning in 1916, when the present predatory mammal control first started, there has been a steady and increasing appointment to the higher Survey offices of non-biologists, until today only a single one of the major positions is held by a mammalogist or ornithologist of recognized standing in these sciences.

Every one of us concedes, I am sure, that these executives are eminently able men, thoroughly conscientious according to their lights, and I have not the slightest criticism to offer of them personally, but only collectively. We care not in the least who runs the Survey so long as it is run on sound biological principles.

It is clearly evident that to these men our suggestions, based on biological reasoning, are nuisances if not downright impertinences. One of them has told me he considered that there always would be sporadic complaints from sentimental quarters and from cranks about predatory mammal work, and it was just a disagreeable part of the job to bear with these. I do not blame him particularly. But it is all too apparent, from many instances, that objection by biologists is regarded exactly the same as other obstructions, to be gently sidetracked by tactful, soothing ut-

terances, and to be quickly forgotten. I know of many letters lately written to the Survey in this vein by prominent naturalists and always the
attitude in reply has been that the item for complaint was an isolated
instance, that the matter would receive attention, or similar vague statements to quiet the correspondent. Or if the letter were of a more vigorous sort, there has been apparent a resentment at the interference and
a clear implication that the writer was an unreasonable radical and an
obstructionist. Even yet, after my letters and the printed protest signed
by so many of you, the cry is uttered that I am a sorehead, my motives
activated by venom because I am unable to get a high position in the
Survey, that people will sign any protest put before them, that I know
little about the matter, and that few of the protest signers have even
seen a coyote.

What the Biological Survey seems not to grasp is that we have at
heart the welfare of our wild life; that because the Biological Survey is
the agency involved we have been most patient in waiting 14 years for
proof that predatory animal destruction was justified and accomplished
in a wise manner; and that almost without exception there is great dissatisfaction among us over present practices.

All of us, I believe, fully concede that some control of predatory
mammals is necessary. Whatever may be our aesthetic feelings toward
mountain lions and wolves we must admit that they are destructive
and should be kept in check. Coyotes, too, do considerable damage in
certain areas and should be thinned in regions where there are many
sheep. But this should be done with discrimination and moderation
with careful consideration by a trained mammalogist of the local factors involved in each area, and not in the wholesale manner now attempted. Few of you realize, I think, the extent to which wholesale
destruction is now carried. For instance, according to Biological Survey figures there were 140 predatory animal hunters operating last year
in Wyoming alone.

But we have no objection to reasonable control. What ever in our
own minds we would like to see obtaining in wild life conditions we
admit that concessions must be made by pure conservation to the economic exigencies of present day civilization, but we hardly feel that we
should be the *only* ones to make concessions. As the most practical
viewpoint I therefore base my arguments on economic considerations,
and leave the aesthetic side, of equal or even greater interest to me, to
others.

Accordingly I pass over the plight of the mountain lion and the wolf.

You already know it. But I may mention that among the tens of thousands of carnivores killed in 1928 by federal hunters there were only 11 gray wolves. The rest have gone from the far west. In 1926 the Biological Survey said that there were no wolves known to occur in Arizona, and a few years ago that no more than 5 adult wolves were known to occur in Wyoming.

According to the reports of the chiefs of the Biological Survey there have been killed and recovered by federal hunters, since 1916, about 416,000 predatory mammals, with an additional estimated kill of 696,000 coyotes poisoned but not found, at a total cost of nearly 10 million dollars. This averages about $23 per recovered animal. Similarly, picking at random from the mimeographed report of Laythe, leader of predatory animal control in the Colorado district, I find that the cost for killing the 229 reportable animals destroyed was $23.21 each in October 1929. This was computed by allowing $200 per month for Laythe's salary, which I understand is below the actual figure, $150 per month for three assistants (there are now four), a stenographer, and $4 per day for his hunters. A report in 1922 by Miles Cannon, Commissioner of the Idaho Department of Agriculture, showed that properly amended figures placed the cost of predatory animal control by the Biological Survey in that state at least $15 per animal, and that at this time state bounties were paid on 72,182 mammals at a cost of $2.74 each. I cannot go into details here of the comparative desirability of Biological Survey results *versus* the bounty system, but many of us question whether the cost of control in many areas is not considerably more than the damage which predators may inflict.

Howell's next section focuses on coyotes. He places "a high value on coyote services" for their role in keeping rodent populations down and questions the validity of livestock depredation to coyotes by ranchers and the USBS. He ridicules the agency for devoting all of its research to devising better ways to kill predators rather than determining the truth about the diets and life histories for species like the coyote.

But there is another aspect to this matter. Prior to 1916 one frequently encountered in Biological Survey publications statements like the following: "The constant warfare of the coyote upon these rodents has much influence in keeping down their numbers, and the growing abundance of rabbits in some sections of the west has been attributed to the destruction of coyotes as the result of the high bounties offered for them";

and "coyotes perform a valuable service to man," (Lantz, 1905). Also that in parts of the west "it may be wise to encourage coyotes and bobcats within certain limits." Coyotes, "if unmolested will free their premises of rabbits and other crop or tree destroyers." "Many ranchers would almost as soon shoot their own dogs and cats as their wild benefactors." (Fisher, 1908).

Now I have not read all Biological Survey publications word for word, but in a diligent search I have been unable to find any such statements in defense of the coyote since 1916. There are a few feeble admissions that the coyote kills some rodents; and I know that in at least one instance a word in defense of the coyote has been summarily deleted from a Biological Survey manuscript. In other words, baldly stated, the coyote admittedly did a lot of good prior to 1916, but none since appropriations have become available for its control. This leaves a disagreeable taste in the mouth. We vigorously object to the stressing of coyote damage to the amount of $50 per year without any mention at all that this is at least partially offset by beneficial habits. Such half truths issued by a scientific bureau are as deplorable as willful misstatements. We believe that this is a practice of which the Biological Survey could hardly have been guilty fifteen years ago. As it thus becomes clear that the coyote is not being given an impartial deal, we cannot have implicit confidence that other forms of wild life are not being similarly treated, and whether we will or no, we are rendered suspicious of other statements.

The statement is constantly made by the Biological Survey that its policy is not one of extermination but only one of moderate control. Now I strongly object to being assured that the Biological Survey policy is one thing when the policy of the field force is quite different. Thus we read in Biological Survey publications such statements as the following: "If western ranges are ever to be entirely cleaned of predatory animals, etc.", "These men work to get the last individual", and "in Wyoming 2,800,726 acres have been systematically treated to eliminate all rodents and predatory mammals" (Day, 1929). Laythe, 1930, admonishes one of his hunters to "get 'em all, Tom, they are killers". On June 25, 1922, the last prairie dog was killed in Cochise and Graham counties, Arizona (Chief's report, 1922) and in 3 years 5 million of them were killed in this state alone. It was expected that by the end of 1928 the last prairie dog would have been exterminated in Kansas (Chief's report, 1928).

In spite of assurance to the contrary it is inevitable that the hunters should try for extermination. There are doubtless many splendid men among them but they are paid to kill and must be born killers, as are many private hunters, or they would not stay with this sort of job, whose pay, I am told, is mostly about $4.00 per day. They are praised for a big bag of coyotes and the competitive spirit is fostered by praise put out in mimeographed form. When the average hunter will shoot at anything alive that he encounters why should we expect the federal hunter to behave very differently?

Although so many of us doubt the wisdom of killing so many coyotes, I venture to state that hardly one of us would be incited to active protest against the killing of 100,000 coyotes per year, *if* nothing but coyotes suffered. To me, the latter condition is our most serious indictment. Killing is accomplished chiefly by the use of poison—strychnine hidden in small cubes of fat or meat and in 1924 over three and a half million of these baits were used. The claim is made that these are distributed where coyotes only can get them, and that the cubes not immediately taken are recovered. One grows exasperated at having his intelligence so lowly rated. In the first place poison can never be anything but indiscriminate. If an area be thoroughly poisoned for coyotes it is thoroughly covered for everything that will take the bait, and the coyote, being the wariest, is the last to take it. Poison cubes less than an inch square can not be completely, or even largely, recovered from the great open spaces. And are they so carefully placed as we are led to believe? One Idaho hunter ran a poison line 700 miles long covering 5000 square miles. Could this mileage be covered by careful work? The only result possible was that every single carnivore over this area of 5000 square miles was endangered and many of them killed. Two other men in Utah ran a poison line 300 miles long. They were praised for their initiative and others were thus spurred to do likewise.

And still the Survey claims that among the predatory mammals killed only three per cent are beneficial fur bearers. Although the estimate of coyotes poisoned but not found has run as high as 100,000 per year, we would be led to believe that *all* of the smaller skunks, foxes, *et cetera*, *are* found. It is most edifying to encounter at the present day such implicit faith in human nature as the Biological Survey places in its hunters. When Mr. Dixon's experience, which I just read to you, was brought to the attention of the Chief he at first would not believe it, and then admitted that it might be an isolated instance. Its importance has been thus depreciated ever since, and recently, upon my continued solicitation that Mr. Dixon publish his experiences, the request was made that he delay publication still longer as it might embarrass the Biological Survey. Dr. Hall's findings were also called isolated instances as was the similar evidence of Mr. Oliver in connection with the Buena Vista mouse plague. And the cry of isolated instances and irresponsible mischief-makers is raised to heaven when I point out the evidence contained in almost a hundred letters received by the California Department of Fish and Game from despairing trappers, which I read last summer. All these were laments to the effect that a government trapper has just been here and the fur is all gone. One found as many as 8 poisoned skunks in one place, another 8 dead raccoons and 6 foxes; 3 skunks and one badger at one poison station and 4 skunks at two more; 30 skunks along one small stream where a government poisoner had just worked; 20 or 25 dead foxes and raccoons, and 19 raccoons in Pope's Valley; in one week in Payne's Creek district 105 skunks were thrown away by a federal trapper; and so on. We will concede that there is some chaff with the wheat, and that a deal of poisoning, learned from federal hunters, is done by private trappers, but these would hardly have discarded the animals before skinning. But the Survey's stand that the testimony of the private trapper is worthless, while all their own hunters are trustworthy, is hardly convincing logic to a grown man.

This implied attitude of the federal hunter is not to be wondered at. From my experience with the few I have met I cannot agree with the exalted opinion voiced by Mr. Young, in the book which he wrote with Mr. Carhart [*Last Stand of the Pack*], that federal hunters are *"friends of all animals, the compassionate, regretful executioners of animal renegades when such outlaws must die that other wildlings may live."* They are hired to kill and their jobs depend on killing. What is a skunk or badger to them but vermin which gets into their traps and prevents them from taking so many more coyotes! Rather than turn the beasts loose they knock them in the head, that they may be bothered no more!

So common sense tells us that to poison, or even trap coyotes means killing other carnivores wholesale, and we have proof that at least some of the trappers' reports are falsified. We would like to know if this incidental destruction is as great as, or twice as great as, the coyote kill. It may well be the latter figure, for poisoning can never be anything but indiscriminate. But poisoning was started because it is the quickest and cheapest method of killing great numbers, and the Survey would be very loath to change its methods, for some time would be lost. Trapping is almost as indiscriminate as poisoning, and it is impracticable to shoot coyotes by still-hunting. But they may easily be run with hounds and then shot, as I myself have found, and a good man with a few good dogs could without difficulty secure 25 coyotes per month, which I am now informed is the kill per hunter by present methods.

We are told that federal hunters operate only where there has been complaint of damage. This they will do first and then go wherever they think they can catch the most coyotes, often to be run off by an irate rancher. They operate regularly in places in California where they are neither needed nor wanted, and in addition, break the state law. A California law reads: "It shall be unlawful for any person to use poison of any kind in the taking or killing of any fur bearing animal." That means it is against the law to leave poison where a carnivore might eat it. I asked a high official of the California Game Commission why this law breaking by the Biological Survey was tolerated. It is because of the sheep men, he said. If we should clamp down on the Survey the sheep men would see that every conservation measure which we introduced in the state legislature was promptly killed. So there you are.

We got constant evidence from naturalists who have been here and there in the west they have visited areas where poisoners worked and made the region almost a faunal desert. Over large areas of the west carnivores have been practically exterminated and some of them can never come back.

The claim is now boldly made by the Biological Survey that carnivores have little or no effect upon the rodent population. This is fairly breath-taking. Upon what do carnivores subsist in the great stretches of the west where small game has been shot out and where there is no small domestic livestock? I agree with them that carnivores could never eliminate rodent "plagues" entirely, but the evidence to us is strongly suggestive that carnivores and hawks in reasonable numbers are instrumental in reducing the severity of such outbreaks as that in Kern County, California in 1926, two years after a coyote campaign had been waged in the same area, and that of South Dakota in 1928, when the freshly planted grain over 40,000 acres was destroyed. It would take many, many dead sheep to equal this loss. . . .

Just before Dr. Nelson's retirement as chief of the Survey he made financial and other arrangements to have Joseph Dixon investigate the destruction of fur bearers and other unfortunate results of coyote poisoning. Dr. Nelson sincerely wished to see this work done, as I happen to know, and it was upon the actual verge of initiation, when suddenly the whole matter was dropped. We are told that the money was not available, but again it seems odd that the $350 could not be found to complete the fund for learning true facts while ten millions were being spent for destruction; and if the Survey had really wanted the work done we could have helped find the money, as its officials well knew.

Because rodent control is advisable it may be foolish to kill off so many coyotes, but it is folly of the maddest type to kill coyotes by poison in such a way that other carnivores are at the same time destroyed. It is too much like swatting flies with one hand and breeding more flies with the other. I am sure that if the public knew the facts it would not tolerate such folly for a moment. Most of the game has been killed by the hunters, and the Biological Survey field men are after all of the rodents and all of the carnivores. What will remain to us of our faunal heritage but insectivorous song-birds?

For a number of years, now, wild life matters have been going from bad to worse. There have been some reforms, coming almost if not quite too late to save the game, but other evils have newly arisen. We are now faced with the necessity of saving our non-game species. We are told that the porcupine damages the forests and must be killed, the nests of the wood rat constitute a fire hazard and must be eliminated, and badger holes are dangerous to horses and the animals should be destroyed (as were actually 1450 of them in Wyoming by federal hunters in 11 years, and we know not how many more unreported). At any moment there is danger that some one will arise to label some additional species as destructive and successfully demand its elimination.

There are strong indications that we are now at a crisis—at the crossroads of conservation as concerns treatment of our wild life. Conditions have been growing intolerable, but there is clearly evident a gathering storm of resentment that should accomplish many reforms. It rests entirely in the hands of such organizations as this Society to determine just what these results shall be and how soon they shall be accomplished.

We, here, are concerned with mammals. The Biological Survey is potentially the most powerful single factor, for good or evil, that we have in this field. For many years it was the respected and trusted public guardian of our fauna, but whether we will or no, conditions are now such that we are forced to label it not our federal wild life warden, but the guardian of the sheep men and other powerful interests.

I for one, am working for the following points:

A change in the attitude of the Biological Survey toward wild life, involving—

An impartial viewpoint; not stressing damage done by a species and under-rating its benefits, for purpose of policy.

A return to its former policy of recommending control only after adequate research and report.

Insistence that actions of field men conform to stated office policy.

Curtailment of predatory animal control where not clearly needed.

Abandonment of destructive poison operations against predatory mammals (save in an emergency) in favor of a less dangerous method of control.

A sincere effort to control rodents by some other method of poisoning than by the broadcasting of poisoning bait.

If a change should come in the present attitude of the Biological Survey toward wild life, then the other reforms, so sorely needed, would naturally follow.

Now gentlemen, what is your pleasure? What are you going to do about it?

1931: *Report of the Committee on Problems of Predatory Mammal Control*, American Society of Mammalogists

The ongoing conflict between professional biologists and the USBS continued to dominate American Society of Mammalogists meetings. At the Thirteenth Annual Meeting of the ASM, held in Philadelphia in May 1931, a six-member commission (including Milton Skinner) called the "Committee on Problems of Predatory Mammal Control" issued a report on the predator control policies of the USBS.

During the previous year, the committee members, without salary, had traveled over twelve thousand miles in Arizona, New Mexico, Texas, California, Nevada, Utah, Colorado, Idaho, and Wyoming, often in the company of USBS agents, as they investigated the agency's policies and methods. As shown in the following conclusion and recommendation from the report, the committee strongly disapproved of those policies and methods, especially the USBS poisoning program.

CONCLUSIONS TO BE DRAWN FROM THE WORK OF THE COMMITTEE DURING THE PAST YEAR, AND FROM EVIDENCE IN ITS POSSESSION

1. The problem of the control of predatory mammals is so complex that much time will be needed to discover and assemble the facts nec-

essary to a satisfactory analysis of all factors involved, but ample data are at hand to justify the assumption that a crisis confronts our native animals.

2. The gathering of these facts should be the duty of the Biological Survey not only because its policy in the field has precipitated this crisis through premature action but because it has some funds and personnel for such studies. The committee believes the Survey needs more men and money to work along these lines.

3. The Survey should curtail the destruction of wild life wherever possible until such facts are assembled.

4. The theory of control as formulated by the Survey in Washington is often quite distinct from the facts of control as practiced in the field.

5. A major activity of the Survey is along the lines of destruction of wild life and, the committee believes, not in the best interests of conservation.

6. The Survey is deliberately educating the public to seek the destruction of certain species of mammals and is actively disseminating propaganda which tends to create a demand for control where none existed formerly. In a word, the Survey is not a passive agent of destruction but is seeking to expand along the lines of its present-day policy.

7. A majority of the people in the United States who are informed on the subject are not in favor of the present Survey policy of predatory mammal control. Even in the West, the studies of the committee show great numbers of citizens opposed to it. The vociferous supporters of this policy are a small but active minority who are interested only in securing the maximum return from their investment in livestock.

8. There is a rising tide of protest throughout the entire country against the destructive activities of the Survey, and institution after institution is going on record against the continuation of such practices.

9. Claims for destruction of game and livestock by predatory mammals are based too much upon hearsay evidence from prejudiced sources. Incontestible facts upon this subject should be made known to the public.

10. Very frequently destruction of livestock can be traced to individual predators and when that individual is destroyed the destruction ceases. This fact is brought out time and again and admitted by the Survey predatory leaders, but they continue to condemn the innocent with the guilty and to carry control measures beyond the point justified by circumstances.

11. Shiftlessness of herders results in losses which could easily be avoided and strays are charged up to the coyotes. Efficiency in herding would materially cut down losses and weaken the indictment against predators.

12. It has been demonstrated by the testimony of many competent witnesses, numbers of them in the Survey employ, that more coyotes can be taken by traps than by poison, although perhaps at greater expense. Trapping can be made more selective, by use of splints under the pan, than poison.

13. There is little trustworthy data upon the full numbers of mammals killed by poison baits. Many Survey poisoners visit stations so infrequently, often not at all, that Survey statistics on this point are valueless.

14. Considerable poisoning is being done by private parties in some cases with, and in some cases without, the connivance of Survey leaders. The argument advanced by the Survey that the well-being of our fauna is better served by keeping control of poisoning in the hands of the Survey can be effectively answered as follows:

A. Such an argument is an admission that poison is a menace in some instances, and the administration of the Survey policy in the field has not demonstrated that the Survey can or ever will be able to remove that menace.

B. The issue of poison, through Survey leaders, as a special privilege, to certain favored individuals, is a commentary as to how far this argument is effective with those who advance it.

15. The use of poison in the field should be discouraged regardless of who employs it. The fur trade has assured your chairman, through one of its spokesmen, that it will attempt to make it unpopular with their trappers, but the Survey must set a good example.

16. Cooperation between the Survey and the Society, as attempted during the past year, will produce no tangible result as long as the Survey manifests such an interest in intensifying its present policy of predatory control.

17. Far from indicating a desire to cut down on poisoning until in possession of sufficient facts to meet all criticism, the Survey has shown by advocation of the Ten-Year Plan, and by other indications of satisfaction with the present policy of predatory mammal control, that in the future the use of poison is to be increased.

18. The fur trade, from trapper to dealer, is unanimously against this policy of the Biological Survey and believes that the very existence of

the domestic fur trade is threatened. The dollar value of mammals destroyed by poison may equal or even exceed the sums saved to special interests.

19. The executive officers of the Survey have brought about the crisis confronting our wild life and are more directly responsible for it than any other agency. The burden of proof rests upon the Survey and the issue at stake is not for us to prove that it is right. The Society need feel no necessity for digging out those facts which the Survey should seek for itself, but by every dictum of logic and common sense it can call upon the Survey to show full and adequate cause for becoming the most destructive organized agency which has ever menaced so many species of our native fauna.

THE COMMITTEE RECOMMENDS TO THE SOCIETY

1. That the Society strongly urges the Biological Survey that the use of poison as a control measure against predatory mammals be drastically curtailed, with the view of complete suspension of poisoning as soon as it is reasonably possible.

2. That the Society deplores the propaganda of the Survey which is designed to unduly blacken the character of certain species of predatory mammals, giving only part of the fact and withholding the rest, propaganda which is educating the public to advocate destruction of wild life.

3. That the Society asserts the claim of the great nature-loving public to a voice in the administration of our wild life resources, and challenges the right of a federal organization, such as the Biological Survey, to consider only the interests of a very small minority, the livestock interests.

Mr. President, I move that this report be adopted by the Society. This motion was seconded and, being put to a vote, was carried.

It was further voted to continue this special committee for the ensuing year. Its members are: H. E. Anthony (chairman), Lee R. Dice, M. P. Skinner, Charles T. Vorhies, and E. Raymond Hall.

1931: "National Park Service's Policy on Predatory Mammals," Horace M. Albright

In the late 1920s and early 1930s, the NPS received a number of petitions, resolutions, and letters criticizing the agency's predator control policies. Victor Cahalane, an NPS official sympathetic to this viewpoint, listed in his 1939 paper, The Evolution of Predator Control Policy in the National Parks, *some of the groups that condemned the current policy: The ASM, the Wilson*

Ornithological Club, Cooper Ornithological Club, New York Zoological Society, and the Boone and Crockett Club.

Horace Albright, a former superintendent of Yellowstone, had been fully supportive of extensive predator control in the national parks. In 1929, Albright succeeded Stephen Mather as director of the NPS. Pressured by the ASM and the other organizations listed above to revise his agency's policy on predators, Albright issued an NPS directive that he published in a 1931 issue of The Journal of Mammalogy, a publication widely used by ASM members and other biologists.

Albright's memo announced that he was banning the use of poisons on predators within the national parks. More importantly, he stated that predators "are to be considered an integral part of the wild life protected within national parks and no widespread campaigns of destruction are to be countenanced." A copy of this policy statement was sent to every NPS superintendent in the country. This was the action that men like Skinner and Howell had demanded. The anti-extermination forces were winning their battle.

The National Park Service is attempting to put the parks to their highest use. Every policy developed is an attempt to meet the purposes for which the parks were formed; First, the national parks must be maintained in absolutely unimpaired form for the use of future generations as well as those of our own time; second, they are set apart for the use, observation, health, pleasure, and inspiration of the people; and third, the national interest must dictate all decisions affecting public or private enterprise in the parks.

Certainly, one of the great contributions to the welfare of the Nation that national parks may make is that of wild life protection. It is one of the understood functions of the parks to give total protection to animal life. A definite policy of wild life protection is being developed with the result that fine herds of game are furnished as a spectacle for the benefit of the public, and those same herds furnish the best opportunity for scientific study. Many disappearing species are to be found within park areas, so that in some instances we may speak of the parks as providing "last stands."

Of late there has been much discussion by the American Mammalogical Society and other scientific organizations relative to predatory animals and their control. The inroads of the fur trapper and widespread campaigns of destruction have caused the great reduction of some and the near disappearance of several American carnivores. The question naturally arises as to whether there is any place where they may be expected to survive and be available for scientific study in the future.

The National Park Service believes that predatory animals have a real place in nature, and that all animal life should be kept inviolate within the parks. As a consequence, the general policies relative to predatory animals are as follows:

1. Predatory animals are to be considered an integral part of the wild life protected within national parks and no widespread campaigns of destruction are to be countenanced. The only control practiced is that of shooting of coyotes or other predators when they are actually found making serious inroads upon herds of game or other mammals needing special protection.

2. No permits for trapping within the borders of a park are allowed. A resolution opposing the use of steel traps within a park was passed several years ago by the superintendents at their annual meeting.

3. Poison is believed to be a non-selective form of control and is banned from the national parks except where used by Park Service officials in warfare against rodents in settled portions of a park or in case of emergency.

Though provision is made for the handling of special problems which may arise, it is the intention of the Service to hold definitely to these general policies. It can be seen, therefore, that within the national park system definite attention is given to that group of animals which elsewhere are not tolerated. It is the duty of the National Park Service to maintain examples of the various interesting North American mammals under natural conditions for the pleasure and education of the visitors and for the purpose of scientific study, and to this task it pledges itself.

1936: "National Park Policy for Vertebrates," National Park Service

In 1933, the NPS *appointed George Wright, a former field ranger, as the chief of its new Wildlife Division. Wright quickly instituted a broad array of wildlife research projects in the national parks. Convinced that predators played a necessary role in the parks, Wright wrote a proposed revision of the agency's policy on wildlife management. Wright's suggestions became official* NPS *policy in 1936, when the agency published the following statement in* The National Park Supplement to Planning and Civic Comment. *This new policy modernized management practices in the parks and, as seen in point 5, included the first NPS mandate to restore species that had been locally exterminated:*

In the present state of knowledge, and until further investigations make revision advisable, the following policies are applied to best serve National Park Service objectives regarding the vertebrate land fauna.

1. No management measure or other interference with biotic relationships shall be undertaken prior to a properly conducted investigation.

2. Every species shall be left to carry on its struggle unaided, as being to its greatest ultimate good, unless there is real cause to believe that it will perish if unassisted.

3. Where artificial feeding, control of natural enemies, or other protective measures, are necessary to save a species that is unable to cope with civilization's influences, every effort shall be made to place that species on a self-sustaining basis once more.

4. The number of native ungulates occupying a deteriorated range shall not be permitted to exceed its reduced carrying capacity and, preferably, shall be kept below the carrying capacity at every step until the range can be brought back to original productiveness.

5. Any native species which has been exterminated from the park area shall be brought back if this can be done, but if said species has become extinct no related form shall be considered as a candidate for reintroduction in its place.

6. Any exotic species which has already become established in a park shall be either eliminated or held to a minimum provided complete eradication is not feasible.

7. Species predatory upon fish shall be allowed to continue in normal numbers and to share normally in the benefits of fish culture.

8. No native predator shall be destroyed on account of its normal utilization of any other park animal, excepting if that animal is in immediate danger of extermination, and then only if the predator is not itself a vanishing form.

9. The predators shall be considered special charges of the national parks in proportion that they are persecuted everywhere else.

🐺 1938: "A Study in Predatory Relationships with Particular Reference to the Wolf," Sigurd F. Olson

Sigurd Olson, a professor at Ely Junior College in northern Minnesota, and later president of the Wilderness Society, was one the first biologists to study wolves in the field. Olson had the good fortune to be based in an area that still had a viable wolf population. Starting in 1920, he gathered extensive observations and information on wolves and their prey in Superior National Forest. This field research enabled him to draw the following conclusion: "The presence of the timber wolf in the Superior Area, instead of being a hazard, is a distinct asset to big game types. Long investigation indicates that the great majority of the killings are of old, diseased or crippled animals."

As shown in the following excerpts from Olson's 1938 scientific paper, "A Study in Predatory Relationships with Particular Reference to the Wolf," his research proved that the ASM biologists were correct in demanding that the Biological Survey drop its policy of extermination of wolves and other predators. As Olson put it, "The timber wolf is an integral part of the wilderness community, the destruction of which would destroy the fine balance between related forms."

During the past quarter of a century, the American people have heard much in regard to the conservation of animal life, but stress has been largely placed on the saving and protection of herbivores at the expense of predatory forms. The predators, those animals which live perforce upon the herbivores, have not as a rule come under the plan of conservation as outlined, and in many areas attempts have been made to eliminate them entirely with total disregard for the influence these forms might have upon the balance of life in the communities of which they are a part.

Game refuges have often been administered as herbivore sanctuaries, until today there are comparatively few areas in which the original animal population can be said to exist under primitive conditions. The tendency has been one of extermination, particularly for the larger predators, the wolf, the coyote, and the mountain lion, and little scientific investigation has been carried on to determine the exact status of these forms in relation to the herbivores upon which they prey.

The extermination of predators is no longer a strictly economic problem, for other factors have entered in, factors of scientific, recreational and esthetic value. With the fast-growing appreciation of the true meaning of wilderness, we are beginning to question the idea of the total elimination of predators, realizing that, after all, lions, wolves and coyotes may be an exceedingly vital part of a primitive community, a part which once removed would disturb the delicate ecological adjustment of dependent types and take from a country a charm and uniqueness which is irreplaceable. To go into a region where the large carnivores are gone, to see hoofed game with its natural alertness lacking, to know above all that the primitive population has been tampered with, is like traveling through a cultivated estate. Wilderness in all its forms is what the true observer wants to see and with this realization dawns a new appreciation of carnivores and the role they play.

The fact that in 1928, out of tens of thousands of carnivores killed in the West, there were only eleven grey wolves recorded, that in the state of Wyoming a few years ago only five wolves were reported at large, points definitely toward ultimate extinction in those areas. In 1926 the Biological Survey reported no wolves in Arizona, and recent reports from other regions indicate a similar scarcity. In the Middle West and East, only occasionally, is a specimen recorded. In the hinterlands of Canada and in the fringe of wilderness along the borders of the lake states are all the wolves that are left, and at the present rate of depletion, the area encompassed by the Superior National Forest in northeastern Minnesota will soon include most of the remaining animals of the species in the United States.

Any one who has made a study of the life histories of the larger predators knows that the accusations against them are not entirely without grounds. On the other hand, it is not hard to see that many indictments are made without sufficient proof to substantiate them. It is therefore the purpose of this paper to bring out a few outstanding facts regarding the life habits of one of the largest and most maligned of the predators, the timber wolf of the north (*Canis nubilus* Say), in the hope that some day accumulating evidence may grant it the protection and sanctuary which other forms of life now enjoy. I shall also contend that a large wilderness area may harbor a carnivore population without danger of annihilation to hoofed game and that the constant presence of such large animals of prey as the timber wolf may actually prove of benefit to the herd.

All investigations have been carried on within the boundaries of the Superior National Forest, a comparatively primitive area, where the deer (*Odocileus virginianus borealis* Miller), and the moose, (*Alces americana americana* Clinton), are present in fairly large numbers. Although predatory animal control has been exercised for a number of years, it has been done in rather haphazard fashion and with no great diminution of the species in question. Natural conditions prevail over much of the area, so that observations recorded should give a true picture of predatory relationships in an undisturbed situation. A great many observations are the result of a long time study not only by the author but others who are familiar with wilderness conditions. These are conclusions arrived at after many years of experience in the north, unfortunately not always from carefully kept notebooks, but rather in many cases as general conclusions based on personal deductions. This applies to a good many of the points made in the paper under discussion. The writer's experience in this particular region covers roughly the period from 1920 to the present. During this time he has covered thousands of miles, by canoe, on snowshoes, on and by airplane, and feels that he knows the country fairly well. The conclusions drawn are based on incidents and observations, which, had he kept a careful notebook, would be easy to cite, but like those of most other woodsmen, they are the sum total of experiences and general working knowledge for which it is impossible to cite authority accurately. The best the writer can say is that they represent what he considers his most accurate judgment of the problem involved. . . .

Feeding Habits of the Wolf

The entire problem of predatory relationship is based upon the food habits of the carnivores concerned. This is the phase of life history which determines whether or not a species is an acceptable member of any society. Certainly, the most often voiced complaint against the timber wolf is that it is a killer of deer, and that there is a certain amount of truth to this contention stands without question.

The major portion of the food of the wolf during the summer months is grouse, woodmice, meadow voles, fish, marmots, snakes, insects and some vegetation. In fact, almost anything that crawls, swims or flies may be included in its diet. During the winter months, when most of the small animals are in hibernation, the wolf is forced to feed almost entirely upon deer and the snowshoe rabbit (*Lepus americanus* Erxleben). The wolf is never a consistent and regular feeder and can go for long periods without food. When food is scarce, as it often is in the north, three or four meals a month will keep him from starvation.

Close students of wild life in the border country all agree that wolves kill comparatively few deer, and then only in the late winter and early spring periods. While there are instances of individual killers, both in the north and the west, who have slaughtered large numbers of deer, moose or elk during the course of a winter, it is no more true to say that these isolated instances are the normal feeding and killing habits of wolves as a species than it is to say that because a man runs amuck his behavior is an index for the rest of his kind. Like all omnivorous types, the wolf prefers variety in his diet and only takes the big game trails when driven to it by the scarcity of the normal food supply. . . .

Storage Habits

During the period when the pack is moving there is abundant evidence that more deer are killed than it will consume immediately. It is through this habit that the wolf brings upon itself condemnation, for it gives the impression that the members of the pack do not kill for the express purpose of food, but rather to satisfy the blood lust of the race. Each winter usually produces news stories of such killing, abundantly illustrated with pictures of mutilated carcasses of deer or moose. There is hardly a lake of any size in the Superior region which has not at least one carcass to its credit, and some of the larger bodies of water, such as Basswood, Vermillion and Lac La Croix, usually have quite a number. This evidence, to the casual observer, is conclusive that the timber wolf kills more than it needs during periods when food is plentiful and easy to get. Such adverse publicity is responsible for most of the clamor for additional predatory control.

Investigation, however, convinces the unbiased observer that such killing habits are purely storage acts, even though a number of deer may be left where they fell, with no evidence of feeding upon them or of any attempt to return later for that purpose. The habit of storage is deeply seated in all carnivores and is one of the primary laws of survival. There is no reason to suppose that the wolves of the Superior Area have suddenly varied from an age-old custom and kill to-day for an entirely different reason.

The failure to return to their kills can only be explained by the many years of poisoning and trapping which have made them suspicious of every old carcass, even of the animals they have brought down themselves during the course of normal hunting. In other words, wolves kill instinctively as an act of storage and would return to their kills, had not experience instilled in them a fear of every carcass that has turned cold. During the heat of the chase, the old habit of slaughter for storage purposes asserts itself, and as a result many kills are made to-day which are not used. Passing by these same kills a night later, wolves, instead of feeding as they might be expected to do, often give them a wide berth, inhibited no doubt by past experience with poison and trap.

Under primitive conditions of sanctuary, in areas where man has not made his activities felt, it is reasonable to assume that wolves would return to kills sometime during the winter. The fact that very often they are trapped or poisoned by the use of old carcasses substantiates this belief. I am confident that if an area containing a normal population of deer and wolves was left unmolested for a long period, evidence would soon accumulate, indicating that the wolves were returning regularly to their kills. Ability to do this without the danger of being caught or poisoned would soon restore the normal situation in which they would not kill more than needed. At the present time there is no question but that a ranging pack on the hunt, due to the fact that kills are not always utilized, creates an abnormal situation in which there is more actual loss of game than would be the case under conditions of equal sanctuary for both predators and herbivores. . . .

General Conclusions
Proponents of predatory animal extermination base their claims on the numbers of big game animals sacrificed every year as food. To combat and refute these claims it must not only be known how many deer and moose are killed, but how great a drain a herd can stand without serious diminution of its breeding stock. It becomes then a problem in which one set of figures is balanced against another, a problem in which the burden of proof is placed upon those who believe that predators have their place.

Since the total deer population of the Superior Area is in the neighborhood of 20,000 animals, and as authoritative research has estimated they can stand a drain of 20 per cent. without diminution of adequate breeding stock, it means that the deer herd could stand an annual loss of about 4,000 animals. Inasmuch as the deer and moose populations seem to be holding their own and in many parts of the forest actually increasing, it may be inferred that no more than this number are being lost each year. It may also be assumed that at least half of this number can be accounted for either because of old age, disease or the fact that a large number are either killed or wounded as they stray beyond the refuge lines during the biennial hunting season. It has been estimated that wolves are directly responsible for some 1,500 deer killings annually, which comes well below their share of the possible 20 per cent. drain.

Those who hold that wolves will soon mean the complete extermination of deer and moose are still influenced by the oft-quoted estimate that each wolf kills a deer a week. If this were so, and if the wolf population is 250 animals, as estimated, they would exact at that rate a toll of 1,000 deer per month or 12,000 per year, 60 per cent. of the total herd, an absolutely untenable figure.

The presence of the timber wolf in the Superior Area, instead of being a hazard, is a distinct assent to big game types. Long investigation indicates that the great majority of the killings are of old, diseased or crippled animals. Such purely salvage killings are assuredly not detrimental to either deer or moose, for without the constant elimination of the unfit the breeding stock would suffer. Furthermore, the wolf is a natural stimulus to a herd's alertness and injects the primitive element of danger without which most big game animals lose much of their natural charm.

Large wilderness areas such as the Superior Forest demonstrate that sanctuary can be successfully given to both herbivores and carnivores without danger of decimation of the big game types. The timber wolf is an integral part of the wilderness community, the destruction of which would destroy the fine balance between related forms. To eliminate as vital a relationship as exists between predatory forms and the animals they prey upon, to destroy a mutual dependence, means that artificiality has entered the wilderness picture.

1944: *The Wolves of Mount McKinley*, Adolph Murie

My personal involvement with wolves began in 1976 when I accepted a park ranger job at Mount McKinley National Park (later renamed Denali National Park). During my fifteen summers in the park I accumulated well over five hundred observations of wolves. Most of those wolves were members of the East Fork Pack. My earlier wolf book, A Society of Wolves, *was dedicated to the alpha male of that pack, a wolf with a maimed foot.*

The first book I ever read on wolves, The Wolves of Mount McKinley, *was written by Adolph Murie. The Park Service had invited Murie to McKinley in 1939 to conduct a detailed study on the relationship of the park wolves and their prey. Rangers had been killing wolves for years in McKinley, but in light of the new NPS policy on predators, the park now wanted a trained biologist to advise them on wildlife management.*

From April of 1939 through August of 1941, Murie spent thousands of hours watching wolves as they hunted and as they cared for their pups at their den. In 1944, the U.S. Government Printing Office published the results of his study. His book was a milestone in our modern understanding of how wolves interact with their prey. Like Sigurd Olson, Murie concluded that wolves are beneficial to the natural process: "It appears that wolves mainly prey on the weak classes of sheep, that is, the old, the diseased, and the young in their first year. Such predation would seem to benefit the species over a long period of time."

In addition to his scientific analysis of the wolves' impact on prey species, Murie's book also contained his observations of what he called the "routine activity" at the East Fork Pack's den. The following excerpt from The Wolves of Mount McKinley *shows how Murie came to admire the wolves as he recorded those activities. He experienced "an inexhaustible thrill" in simply watching the wolves at their den, as they rested and played with their pups. Comparing the wolf who returned to the den after an exhausting night of hunting to a tired "laboring husband" coming home to his family, Murie enabled his readers to see wolves as fellow creatures whose lives paralleled the activities of a human family. These informal observations, along with his scientific conclusions, influenced many generations of park rangers and wildlife biologists to accept wolves as animals that deserve our respect, as animals that have a right to exist.*

Murie's observations centered on the East Fork Pack, the same pack that I studied intensively in the 1970s and 1980s. The wolves that I watched and described in my earlier book, including the limping alpha male, were likely the direct descendants of the animals that Murie observed from 1939 to 1941.

Many hours were spent watching the wolves at the den and yet when I undertake to write about it there does not seem to be a great deal to relate, certainly not an amount commensurate with the time spent observing these animals. There were some especially exciting and interesting incidents such as the times when the grizzlies invaded, and a strange wolf was driven away. The departure for the night hunt and the reactions of the wolves to caribou were always of interest . . . but the routine activity at the den was unexciting and quiet. For 3 or 4 hours at a time there might not be a stir. Yet it was an inexhaustible thrill to watch the wolves simply because they typify the wilderness so completely.

The periods of watching were sufficiently long to yield behavior data of statistical value. I believe that the routine activity at this den was fairly well known.

Just as a laboring husband comes home to the family each evening after working all day, so do the wolves come home each morning after working all night. The wolf comes home tired, too, for he has traveled far in his hunting. Ten or fifteen miles is a usual jaunt for a hunt, and he generally takes part in some chases in which he exerts himself tremendously. His travels take him up and down many slopes and ridges. When he arrives at the den he flops, relaxes completely, and may not even change his position for 3 or 4 hours. Often he may not even raise his head to look around for intruders. Sometimes he may stretch and yawn, change his position, or shift his bed a few yards. Usually in summer he lies stretched out on his side, but occasionally may be curled up as in winter. Frequently a wolf will move over to a neighbor, perhaps sniff of him, getting for a response only a lazy indication of recognition by an up-and-down wag of the tail, and lie down near him. An animal may move from the point of the bluff down to the gravel bar, or while the overflow ice still remains on the bars, he may lie in the snow for a while. When the caribou grazed near the den a wolf might raise up a bit for a look, but generally a caribou was not sufficient reason for him to disturb his resting. The female may be inside the den, or on the outside, for hours at a time. The five adults might be sleeping a few hundred yards apart or three or four of them might be within a few yards of each other. Of course all the adults were not always at home, one or two might be out for a short day light excursion or fail to come home after the night hunt. That, in brief, is the routine activity at the den.

The first few weeks the gray female spent much time in the den with the pups, both during the day and at night. When she was outside she usually lay only a few yards from the entrance, although she sometimes wandered off as far as half a mile to feed on cached meat. When the rest of the band was off on the night hunt she remained at home, except on three occasions that I know of—June 1, June 8, and June 16. Each time she went off with the band she ran as though she were in high spirits, seeming happy to be off on an expedition with the others. On these three occasions the black female remained through the night with the pups.

The father and the black female were seen to enter the den when the pups were only a couple of weeks old. Later, when the pups were old enough to toddle about outside, the father and the two females were very attentive to them. The two gray males often sniffed at the pups which frequently crawled over all five wolves in their play. Sometimes the pups played so much around an adult that it would move away to a safe distance where it could rest in greater peace.

The attentiveness of the black female to the pups was remarkable. It seemed at times that she might have produced some of them and I do not absolutely know that she did not. But her absence from the den the first 10 days (so far as I know), the uniformity in the size of the pups, and the greater concern and responsibility exhibited by the gray female, strongly indicated that the gray one had produced all the pups. The companionship of these two adults suggested that two females might at times den together, although having pups in one den would be somewhat inconvenient. Rather, one would expect them to den near each other as these two females did in 1941.

Wolves have few enemies and consequently are frequently not very watchful at the den or elsewhere. Often I approached surprisingly close to the wolf band before being discovered. Several times I was practically in the midst of the band before I was noticed. Once, after all the others had run off, one which must have been sound asleep got up behind me and in following the others passed me at a distance of only about 30 yards. These wolves were scarcely molested during the course of the study, so they may have been less watchful than in places where they are hunted. But their actions were probably normal for primitive conditions. When alert their keen eyes do not miss much.

Before the vegetation changed from brown to green the gray wolves, when curled up or when only the back showed, were especially difficult to see against the brown background. But if they were stretched out so as to expose the light under parts they were plainly visible. The black ones were usually more conspicuous but under certain conditions of poor light or dark backgrounds the gray wolves were the more conspicuous. At the den all the wolves were sometimes difficult to see because of slight depressions in which they lay, and the hummocks hiding them. Once when all five adults were lying on the open tundra slope above the den not one could be seen from my lookout. Often only two or three of the five could be seen until some movement showed the position of the others.

The strongest impression remaining with me after watching the wolves on numerous occasions was their friendliness. The adults were friendly towards each other and were amiable towards the pups, at least as late as October. This innate good feeling has been strongly marked in the three captive wolves which I have known.

🐺 1947: Unpublished Foreword to *A Sand County Almanac: Sketches Here and There*, Aldo Leopold

Aldo Leopold, author of two selections in Chapter 4, "The Varmint Question" (1915) and "The Game Situation in the Southwest" (1920), once served as a lobbyist and cheerleader for federal predator control programs. While working as a forest ranger in Arizona, he also enthusiastically participated in the killing of wolves.

Leopold later dramatically reversed his position on predator control. His 1949 book, A Sand County Almanac: Sketches Here and There, *published posthumously, contains a collection of essays on conservation, wildlife management, and the role of predators in ecosystems. In the book's original foreword, which was written in 1947 but deleted from the published version, Leopold speaks of several experiences that forced him to reconsider his fundamental beliefs. In this foreword, Leopold confesses his past sins: "I had . . . played the role of accessory in an ecological murder."*

These essays deal with the ethics and esthetics of land.

During my lifetime, more land has been destroyed or damaged than ever before in recorded history. As a field-worker in conservation, I have seen, studied, and measured many samples of this process.

During my lifetime, the stockpile of scientific facts about the land has grown from a molehill into a mountain. As a research ecologist, I have contributed to this pile.

During my lifetime, the thing called conservation has grown from a nameless idea into a mighty national movement. As a sportsman and naturalist, I have helped it grow—in size—but so far it has seemed almost to shrink in potency.

This concurrent growth in knowledge of land, good intentions toward land, and abuse of land presents a paradox that baffles me, as it does many another thinking citizen. Science ought to work the other way, but it doesn't. Why?

We regard land as an economic resource, and science as a tool for extracting bigger and better livings from it. Both are obvious facts, but they are not truths, because they tell only half the story.

There is a basic distinction between the fact that land yields us a living, and the inference that it exists for this purpose. The latter is about as true as to infer that I fathered three sons in order to replenish the woodpile.

Science is, or should be, much more than a lever for easier livings. Scientific discovery is nutriment for our sense of wonder, a much more important matter than thicker steaks or bigger bathtubs.

Art and letters, ethics and religion, law and folklore, still regard the wild things of the land either as enemies, or as food, or as dolls to be kept "for pretty." This view of land is our inheritance from Abraham, whose foothold in the land of milk and honey was still a precarious one, but it is outmoded for us. Our foothold is precarious, not because it may slip, but because we may kill the land before we learn to use it with love and respect. Conservation is a pipe-dream as long as *Homo sapiens* is cast in the role of conqueror, and his land in the role of slave and servant. Conservation becomes possible only when man assumes the role of citizen in a community of which soils and waters, plants and animals are fellow members, each dependant on the others, and each entitled to his place in the sun.

These essays are one man's striving to live by and with, rather than on, the American land.

I do not imply that this philosophy of land was always clear to me. It is rather the end-result of a life-journey, in the course of which I have felt sorrow, anger, puzzlement, or confusion over the inability of conservation to halt the juggernaut of land-abuse. These essays describe particular episodes en route.

My first doubt about man in the role of conqueror arose while I was still in college. I came home one Christmas to find that land promoters, with the help of the Corps of Engineers, had dyked and drained my boyhood hunting grounds on the Mississippi River bottoms. The job was so complete that I could not even trace the outlines of my beloved lakes and sloughs under their new blanket of cornstalks.

I like corn, but not that much. Perhaps no one but a hunter can understand how intense an affection a boy can feel for a piece of marsh. My home town thought the community enriched by this change, I thought it impoverished. It did not occur to me to express my sense of loss in writing; my old lake had been under corn for forty years before I wrote "Red Legs Kicking." Nor did I, until years later, formulate the generalization that drainage is bad, not in and of itself; but when it becomes so prevalent that a fauna and flora are extinguished.

My first job was as a forest ranger in the White Mountains of Arizona. There I conceived a large enthusiasm for the free life of the cow country, and I admired the mounted cowmen, many of whom were my friends. Through the usual process of hazing and horseplay, I—the tenderfoot—acquired some rudiments of skill as a horseman, packer, and mountaineer. . . .

It was in the White Mountain country that I had my first experience with government predator-control. My friends the cowmen shot bears, wolves, mountain lions, and coyotes on sight; in their eyes, the only good predator was a dead one. When some particularly irksome depredation occurred, they organized a punitive expedition, or even hired a professional trapper for a month or two. But the overall outcome was a draw; the predators were kept down, but they were not extinguished. It occurred to no one that the country might eventually become bearless and wolfless. Everyone assumed that the fewer varmints the better, and within limits this was (and is) true.

Then came the paid government hunters who worked on salary, took pride in their skill, and (in the case of wolves and grizzlies) were often able to trap a given unit of range to the point of eradication. The sum of a dozen local eradications was extinguishment in the state, and the sum of a dozen "clean" states was national extermination. To be sure, there was a face-saving policy about leaving some predators in the National Parks, but the actual fact is that there are no wolves, and only a precarious remnant of grizzlies, in the Parks today.

In "Escudilla," I relate my own participation in the extinguishment of the grizzly bear from the White Mountain region. At the time I sensed only a vague uneasiness about the ethics of this action. It required the unfolding of official "predator control" through two decades finally to convince me that I had helped to extirpate the grizzly from the Southwest, and thus played the role of accessory in an ecological murder.

Later, when I had become Chief of Operations for the Southwestern National Forests, I was accessory to the extermination of the lobo wolf from Arizona and New Mexico. As a boy, I had read, with intense sympathy, Seton's masterly biography of a lobo wolf, but I nevertheless was able to rationalize the extermination of the wolf by calling it deer management. I had to learn the hard way that excessive multiplication is a far deadlier enemy to deer than any wolf. "Thinking Like a Mountain" tells what I know (but what most conservationists have still to learn) about deer herds deprived of their natural enemies.

In 1909, when I first moved to the southwest, there had been six blocks of roadless mountain country, each embracing half a million acres or more, in the National Forests of Arizona and New Mexico. By the 1920s new roads had invaded five of them and there was only one left: the headwaters of the Gila River. I helped to organize a national Wilderness Society, and contrived to get the Gila headwaters withdrawn as a wilderness area, to be kept as pack country, free from additional roads, "forever." But the Gila deer herd, by then wolfless and all but lionless, soon multiplied beyond all reason, and by 1924 the deer had so eaten out the range that reduction of the herd was imperative. Here my sin against the wolves caught up with me. The Forest Service, in the name of range conservation, ordered the construction of a new road splitting my wilderness area in two, so that hunters might have access to the top-heavy deer herd. I was helpless, and so was the Wilderness Society. I was hoist of my own petard. . . .

Ironically enough, this same sequence of proclaiming a wilderness, erasing the predators to increase the game, and then erasing the wilderness to harvest the game, is still being repeated in state after hapless state. . . .

These essays were written for myself and my close friends, but I suspect that we are not alone in our discontent with the ecological *status quo*. If the reader finds here some echo of his own affections and of his own anxieties, they will have accomplished more than was originally intended.

1949: "Thinking Like a Mountain," Aldo Leopold

The classic essay, "Thinking Like a Mountain," is the centerpiece of A Sand County Almanac. *Here Leopold tells in detail the story of his conversion to a more ecological view of predators. Because Leopold had once been such a keen supporter of predator control, this eloquent essay represents a major turning point in the evolution of American philosophy toward predators. This brief essay is the most influential piece of writing ever published on wolves.*

A deep chesty bawl echoes from rimrock to rimrock, rolls down the mountain, and fades into the far blackness of the night. It is an outburst of wild defiant sorrow, and of contempt for all the adversities of the world.

Every living thing (and perhaps many a dead one as well) pays heed to that call. To the deer it is a reminder of the way of all flesh, to the pine a forecast of midnight scuffles and of blood upon the snow, to the coyote a promise of gleanings to come, to the cowman a threat of red ink at the bank, to the hunter a challenge of fang against bullet. Yet behind these obvious and immediate hopes and fears there lies a deeper meaning, known only to the mountain itself. Only the mountain has lived long enough to listen objectively to the howl of a wolf.

Those unable to decipher the hidden meaning know nevertheless that it is there, for it is felt in all wolf country, and distinguishes that country from all other land. It tingles in the spine of all who hear wolves by night, or who scan their tracks by day. Even without sight or sound of wolf, it is implicit in a hundred small events: the midnight whinny of a pack horse, the rattle of rolling rocks, the bound of a fleeting deer, the way shadows lie under the spruces. Only the ineducable tyro can fail to sense the presence or absence of wolves, or the fact that mountains have a secret opinion about them.

My own conviction on this score dates from the day I saw a wolf die. We were eating lunch on a high rimrock, at the foot of which a turbulent river elbowed its way. We saw what we thought was a doe fording the torrent, her breast awash in white water. When she climbed the bank toward us and shook out her tail, we realized our error: it was a wolf. A half-dozen others, evidently grown pups, sprang from the willows and all joined in a welcoming mêlée of wagging tails and playful maulings. What was literally a pile of wolves writhed and tumbled in the center of an open flat at the foot of our rimrock.

In those days we had never heard of passing up a chance to kill a wolf. In a second we were pumping lead into the pack, but with more excitement than accuracy: how to aim a steep downhill shot is always confusing. When our rifles were empty, the old wolf was down, and a pup was dragging a leg into impassable slide-rocks.

We reached the old wolf in time to watch a fierce green fire dying in her eyes. I realize then, and have known ever since, that there was something new to me in those eyes — something known only to her and to the mountain. I was young then, and full of trigger-itch; I thought that because fewer wolves meant more deer, that no wolves would mean hunters' paradise. But after seeing the green fire die, I sensed that neither the wolf nor the mountain agreed with such a view.

Since then I have lived to see state after state extirpate its wolves. I have watched the face of many a newly wolfless mountain, and seen the south-facing slopes wrinkle with a maze of new deer trails. I have seen every edible bush and seedling browsed, first to anaemic desuetude, and then to death. I have seen every edible tree defoliated to the height of a saddlehorn. Such a mountain looks as if someone had given God a new pruning shears, and forbidden Him all other exercise. In the end the starved bones of the hoped-for deer herd, dead of its own too-much, bleach with the bones of the dead sage, or molder under the high-lined junipers.

I now suspect that just as a deer lives in mortal fear of its wolves, so does a mountain live in mortal fear of its deer. And perhaps with better cause, for while a buck pulled down by wolves can be replaced in two or three years, a range pulled down by too many deer may fail of replacement in as many decades.

So also with cows. The cowman who cleans his range of wolves does not realize that he is taking over the wolf's job of trimming the herd to fit the range. He has not learned to think like a mountain. Hence we have dustbowls, and rivers washing the future into the sea.

We all strive for safety, prosperity, comfort, long life, and dullness. The deer strives with his supple legs, the cowman with trap and poison, the statesman with pen, the most of us with machines, votes, and dollars, but it all comes to the same thing: peace in our time. A measure of success in this is all well enough, and perhaps is a requisite to objective thinking, but too much safety seems to yield only danger in the long run. Perhaps this is behind Thoreau's dictum: In wildness is the salvation of the world. Perhaps this is the hidden meaning in the howl of the wolf, long known among mountains, but seldom perceived among men.

In December 1944, Aldo Leopold reviewed Stanley Young and Edward Goldman's book The Wolves of North America *for* The Journal of Forestry. *After quoting a passage from the book that vaguely calls for letting wolves "continue their existence" in "some areas," Leopold proposes that the wolf be brought back to its former home in Yellowstone National Park. As he was in many other issues, Leopold was far ahead of his time on this subject. The NPS reintroduced wolves into Yellowstone in early 1995, fifty years after Leopold's initial suggestion*

Even the national parks offered no protection for wolves. These photographs, taken in Yellowstone in 1916 when the U.S. Army was in charge of the park, show the work of Donald Stevenson and Cruse Black, "two special rangers . . . employed by advice of the United States Biological Survey for the purpose of exterminating carnivorous animals in the park." The photograph on the upper right shows the entrance to a wolf den on Hellroaring Creek where the men removed and killed six pups. The other photos show adult wolves killed in the same area. (From Animal Life of Yellowstone National Park, 1930, by Vernon Bailey)

In October of 1922, Ranger Henry Anderson killed two wolves near the confluence of Pelican and Raven Creeks. They were mounted and later were placed in the Albright Visitor Center at Mammoth Hot Springs. This photo shows the animals outside the visitor center. The wolves are still on display. (Photo from the Yellowstone National Park Archives)

Yellowstone park ranger Henry Anderson found an active wolf den near Hellroaring Creek in April of 1922. He killed the mother, captured the ten pups alive, and brought them back to park headquarters at Mammoth Hot Springs, where they were put on display. The pups were later destroyed. (Photo from the Yellowstone National Park Archives)

Two wolf pups trapped at a bison carcass near Soda Butte, Yellowstone National Park, October 1926. These animals were the last wolves killed in the Park Service's wolf control campaign in Yellowstone. (Photo by Scott Riley, Yellowstone National Park Archives)

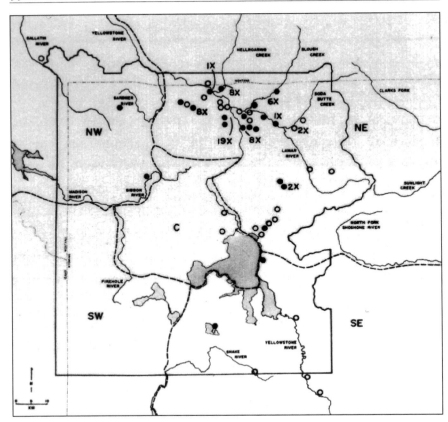

This map shows the location of wolf observations and places where some of the park wolves were killed (x) in Yellowstone and vicinity from 1914 to 1926. Open circles represent sightings of singles or pairs; shaded circles, three or more animals together. In all, a minimum of 136 wolves were killed in this period; eighty of these were pups. (Map from The Wolves of Yellowstone, 1978, by John Weaver. Used by permission of the author)

This model is posing in front of a U.S. Biological Survey display of traps and other weapons used in its war against the wolf, other predators, and rodents. (Photo from the Smithsonian Institution Archives)

A man yanks a trap still attached to the leg of a red wolf. This animal and its pack were captured by U.S. Biological Survey trapper J. B. Woodward at New Hope, Arkansas, in 1929. (Photo from the Smithsonian Institution Archives)

This red wolf was caught in a U.S. Biological Survey trap near Ardmore, Okla-homa, in 1929. As of 1980, red wolves were considered extinct in the wild. In the late 1980s and early 1990s, captive-born red wolves were reintroduced into the Alligator River National Wildlife Refuge in North Carolina and Great Smoky Mountains National Park in North Carolina and Tennessee. (Photo from the Stanley Young Collection, Denver Public Library, Western History Department)

The U.S. Biological Survey set up exhibits at state and county fairs to promote and build public support for their mission of predator extermination. In 1931, the American Society of Mammalogists condemned such exhibits: "The Society deplores the propaganda of the Survey which is designed to unduly blacken the character of certain species of predatory mammals . . . propaganda which is educating the public to advocate destruction of wild life." (Photo from the Stanley Young Collection, Denver Public Library, Western History Department)

At the height of the Roman Empire, conquering generals paraded victoriously through the streets of the capital city. Prior to their execution, defeated enemy officers, chained to carts, followed behind the Roman general as the crowds jeered and tossed filth at the humiliated and vanquished foes. In a similar fashion, the U.S. Biological Survey chained the wolf and bear in this photograph and paraded them through the streets of Douglas, Wyoming, during the 1930 state fair. (Photo from the Stanley Young Collection, Denver Public Library, Western History Department)

This photograph of Aldo Leopold was taken in 1946. As a mature man, Leopold rejected the anti-wolf policies he had once carried out as a forest ranger and regretted the fact that he "was accessory to the extermination of the lobo wolf from Arizona and New Mexico." (Photo by Robert McCabe, Negative #X25 1097, University of Wisconsin–Madison Archives)

Adolph Murie, a pioneering wolf biologist, summarized his lengthy observation of a wolf den in Alaska in the 1940s with these words: "The strongest impression remaining with me after watching the wolves...was their friendliness." Murie's 1944 book, The Wolves of Mount McKinley, *was a milestone in the scientific understanding of wolf behavior. (Photo from the Louise Murie MacLeod Collection)*

Despite the new evidence that was being gathered about wolves, extermination campaigns continued. In 1950, the U.S. Biological Survey, now known as the U.S. Fish and Wildlife Service, sent its agents into Mexico to demonstrate wolf poisoning techniques to local ranchers. By 1958, the New Mexico district of the USFWS reported their that exported poison had achieved "complete control of the wolf" south of the United States border. News of this successful wolf poisoning campaign caused thirty-five other nations to request information on USFWS poisoning techniques. (Photo from the Smithsonian Institution Archives)

Traditional Native American stories reflect a very different view of the wolf from the one espoused by American popular thought and bureaucracy. In 1910, Piegan medicine man Brings-Down-the-Sun told Walter McClintock the story of a wolf who saved the life of a Blackfeet woman. ("The Legend of the Friendly Medicine Wolf," from The Old North Trail *by Walter McClintock)*

Contemporary singer and songwriter Jack Gladstone performing his song "Wolf" at a rally held in Helena, Montana, just before the August 1992 hearing on wolf reintroduction in Yellowstone. During the hearing, Gladstone read a resolution unanimously passed by the Blackfeet Tribal Council supporting the restoration of the wolf to Yellowstone. Part of the resolution read: "The Blackfeet Tribe has long considered the wolf as a sacred medicine animal worthy of respect, imitation, and admiration." (Photo by Rick McIntyre)

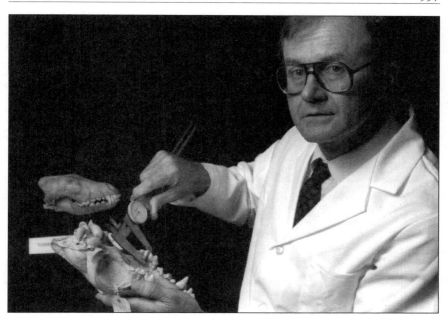

Dr. Philip Gipson measuring wear on teeth in the skull of Three Toes of Harding County, South Dakota, who was killed on July 23, 1925. According to reports at the time, Three Toes destroyed livestock worth more than $50,000 during a thirteen-year period. As he would probably have been at least a year old before he started to attack cattle, he should have been fourteen or older when he was killed. Comparing the wear on the teeth with the wear on teeth from wild wolves of known age, Dr. Gipson and his colleagues Dr. Warren Ballard and Dr. Ronald Nowak estimate Three Toes was no more than six to eight years old when he died. That age estimate casts serious doubt on the accuracy of reports on Three Toes' career. (Photo from the Kansas Cooperative Fish and Wildlife Research Unit)

On some level, it seems, we all are fascinated by wolves. These young children at the Philmont Scout Ranch in New Mexico in the late 1960s listen with rapt attention to the story of Lobo, King of the Currumpaw. Lobo's pelt is displayed in the glass case. (Photo from the Ernest Thompson Seton Memorial Library and Museum)

This rendition of a Native wolf medicine Shield is by Canadian Cree artist Ellen Jorden. According to Jack Gladstone: "Once you've met the eyes of a wolf they will never leave you." (Jack Gladstone Collection. Photo by Rick McIntyre)

Wolf researcher Diane Boyd with three-month-old Son of Sage. Son of Sage was one of a core population of wolves from which dispersing descendants showed up as far south as Yellowstone National Park; as far north as Pouce Coupe, British Columbia, and Banff National Park, Alberta; as far west as Washington state; and as far east as Choteau, Montana. To Diane, Son of Sage represents the wolf species well: resourceful, intelligent, and adaptable. With a little human tolerance, she feels wolves are very likely to successfully recolonize former wolf ranges. (Photo by Diane K. Boyd)

**Do you
want
information
about
or wish to
become
involved in the**

*Yellowstone National Park and Central Idaho
Gray Wolf Reintroduction
Environmental Impact Statement?*

Congress directed the U.S. Fish and Wildlife Service to prepare
an Environmental Impact Statement on the reintroduction of
wolves to Yellowstone and central Idaho, in cooperation
with the National Park Service and Forest Service.

The U.S. Fish and Wildlife Service needs active participation
throughout this 2 year process. If you want to receive information
please write:

Yellowstone National Park & Central Idaho
Gray Wolf EIS
P.O. Box 8017
Helena, MT 59601
(406) 449-5202

This was one of the posters used to solicit citizen participation in the Environmental Impact Statement on the reintroduction of wolves to Yellowstone National Park and central Idaho. The U.S. Fish and Wildlife Service held over 120 public hearings and meetings on the Yellowstone wolf reintroduction issue. (Poster from the U.S. Fish and Wildlife Service, Helena, Montana)

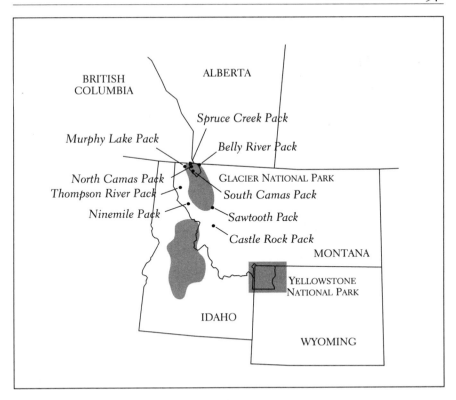

The goal of the 1987 U.S. Fish and Wildlife Service Northern Rocky Mountain Wolf Recovery Plan was "to remove the Northern Rocky Mountain wolf from the endangered and threatened species list by securing and maintaining a minimum of 10 breeding pairs of wolves in each of three recovery areas for a minimum of three successive years." The shading on the map indicates the recovery areas. Montana is currently being recolonized by a population of wolves that entered the state from Canada in 1985. Dots indicate where wolf packs were living in 1994. (Updated from Yellowstone Environmental Impact Statement, U.S. Fish and Wildlife Service, Helena, Montana)

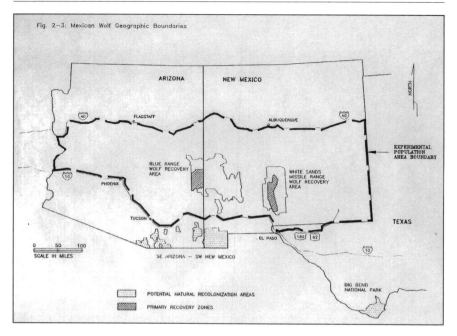

Fig. 2—3: Mexican Wolf Geographic Boundaries

As of early 1995, there were eighty-eight Mexican wolves living in captivity in the United States and Mexico; most experts feel the Mexican wolf is extinct in the wild. The U.S. Fish and Wildlife Service hopes to make reintroductions in early 1997 in the White Sands Missile Range in New Mexico and the Blue Range section of the Apache National Forest in Arizona, historic homelands of the Mexican wolf. (Map from the U.S. Fish and Wildlife Service, Albuquerque, New Mexico)

For most of the history of our country we sought to exterminate the wolf. Since the passage of the Endangered Species Act, our national policy seeks to save the wolf and reestablish the species in some of its former range. (Photo by William E. Rideg)

Anthropologist Carveth Read of the University of London once commented: "Man is more like a wolf . . . than he is like any other animal." Both species share many cultural traits: pair-bonding, extended family clans, group cooperation, communal care of young, leadership hierarchies, division of labor, and social ceremonies. Our society has waged war against the wolf for over three centuries. Now, like Native people, we are beginning to treat wolves as a kindred species deserving of our respect and admiration. (Photo by Rick McIntyre)

Chapter 9

The Wolf
in the Modern World

The passage of the 1973 Endangered Species Act (ESA) was a pivotal event in our country's relationship with the wolf. Prior to that law, American policy usually encouraged the destruction and extermination of wolves. With the wolf now classified as an endangered species, our national policy seeks to save the wolf from extinction. Beyond that, the act legally mandates that federal agencies such as the National Park Service, U.S. Forest Service, and the U.S. Fish and Wildlife Service try to find suitable areas to reestablish wolf populations. The papers in this section report on how wolf recovery has progressed since the passage of the ESA and how our country is reevaluating our view of the wolf.

🐺 1995: "Wolves and Wolf Literature: A Credibility Gap," Philip Gipson

During my transcription of historic accounts of wolves, I frequently came across statistics on livestock depredations that seemed greatly exaggerated. I mentioned this to a USFWS wolf biologist and he suggested that I talk to Phil Gipson, leader of the U.S. National Biological Service (USNBS) Kansas Cooperative Fish and Wildlife Research Unit at Kansas State University. The USNBS is the new scientific arm of the United States Department of the Interior, whose mission includes coordinating research and monitoring of endangered species such as wolves.

In speaking to Phil, I learned that he had formerly been a senior wildlife ecologist in the headquarters of Animal Damage Control (ADC), the federal agency currently responsible for predator control operations, and had studied the wolf/livestock issue for nearly thirty years. Phil told me that he too had come to question the validity of the historic accounts of wolf depredation on livestock. He and two colleagues recently began a detailed scientific investigation into the credibility of those old accounts, including many of the government reports reprinted in Chapter 4.

At this stage of their investigation, the biologists feel that much of the currently accepted information on wolves is based on false and inaccurate historic reports. They hope to set the record straight, and in the process, exonerate many wolves who have been falsely declared guilty of crimes against humanity. This paper is Phil's preliminary report on their findings.

My interest in wolves started during the early 1960s with a class assignment I had as a young student of wildlife ecology at the University of Central Arkansas. One of my introductory ecology classes required each student to write a paper about an important conservation issue. I selected the topic "Controlling damage caused by wolves to livestock and big game." The assignment called for a through review of the literature and interviews with professionals in conservation agencies.

The professor explained that a review of the literature meant searching the library for all of the information that I could find about wolves and their management. He said to include articles from scientific journals, popular magazines, government reports, and books. After spending several days in the university library I had accumulated an impressive stack of documents on wolves and campaigns to control them. The more I read about wolves, the more interested I became.

Two writers impressed me most: Ernest Thompson Seton and Stanley P. Young. Seton because of the colorful details he provided about the lives of predators; Young because of the insight he provided into wolf control strategies and the lives of government trappers assigned to kill wolves. I read many accounts of famous wolves, including some of the ones described in chapters 4 and 6 of this book.

I arranged interviews to talk about wolves and their management with Harold Alexander, supervisor of Wildlife Research for the Arkansas Game and Fish Commission, and Luther Birchfield, state supervisor of Animal Damage Control for the U.S. Fish and Wildlife Service. These two individuals provided me with accounts of their first-hand experiences with red wolves and wolf control in Arkansas. Both biologists indicated that wolves were declining in the state and that coyotes were increasing.

By the time I finished the class paper, I was fascinated with wolves and wolf management. My interest in wolves broadened to include other canids. I became interested in both gray and red wolves, and how they interacted with coyotes and wild dogs. In the mid-1960s I decided to pursue a Ph.D. at the University of Arkansas investigating the ecology of wild canids in sections of Arkansas where there appeared to be red wolves, coyotes, wild dogs, and hybrids between the three species. It was an ideal opportunity to investigate the life histories of wolves and find out how they related to coyotes and wild dogs.

During the second year of my Ph.D. program I realized that the hunting behavior and diets that I noted in wild canids often differed from accounts in early publications. I started to wonder about the validity of literature such as the reports by Vernon Bailey and other Biological Survey documents reprinted in Chapter 4. How could those early field biologists and trappers possibly have known so many details about the lives of individual wolves? They did not have radio-telemetry and most of them had not followed trails of wolves in snow, yet they sometimes reported the number of miles particular packs of wolves traveled between livestock kills and some even logged up the numbers of cattle and deer killed by specific wolves.

At scientific meetings I reported the results of my studies and visited with predator specialists. Topics we often discussed, but never seemed to feel comfortable about, were predation rates of wolves and other canids, and the gap between predation rates reported in early literature and rates noted in recent studies. For example, J. R. Gunson, reporting on wolf predation of livestock in western Canada from 1974 through 1980, described one of the rare documented cases of excessive killing of livestock, where a pack of seven wolves killed or injured twenty sheep. In contrast, Stanley P. Young, describing depredations caused by a lone Arizona wolf known as the "Aguila Wolf" between 1916 and 1924, claimed the wolf had killed sixty-five sheep in one night and forty at another time.

Later, as assistant leader of the Alaska Cooperative Wildlife Research Unit, I conducted research on wolves and advised three graduate students studying wolves. Again, marked differences were obvious between our findings and early accounts about predation. For example, Stanley P. Young and other early writers suggested that hamstringing—cutting the large tendon that connects the hock (the heel in man) with the hip muscles—was a common method used by wolves to disable large prey. One of my graduate students and I published a paper describing the characteristics of wolf attacks on moose in Mount McKinley (now Denali) National Park. We saw no evidence of hamstringing on eleven moose and one Dall sheep that had been injured or killed by wolves. While we were questioning the credibility of early literature about wolf depredations, there was no obvious way to examine the validity of early accounts.

In 1987 I went to work for the Animal Damage Control Program, a branch of the Animal and Plant Health Inspection Service, U.S. Department of Agriculture, at their headquarters just outside of Washington, D.C., in Hyattsville, Maryland. ADC is the modern descendant of the predator control program originally funded by Congress in 1915 and managed by the U.S. Biological Survey until 1940. ADC was part of the USFWS in the Department of Interior from 1940 until it was transferred to the Department of Agriculture in 1986.

I was hired as a wildlife ecologist on a special ADC advisory staff, and later worked as a senior wildlife biologist in the Policy and Program Development Section. One of my first assignments was to review proposals to reintroduce wolves to Yellowstone National Park and other remote areas of the Rocky Mountains. The goal was to provide the best possible assessment of the risk that wolves pose to the livestock industry.

I worked with a team of biologists to obtain and organize pertinent literature. We planned to use historic accounts and papers by modern wolf ecologists to help assess risks to livestock producers and to make recommendations about wolf reintroductions and management. As I read about damage attributed to wolves, I finally realized that some of the early literature simply could not be valid. After eighteen years of working with wolves and other predators, this realization came as a shock to me. I was disturbed as I reflected on the far-reaching consequences of having non-credible accounts of damage by wolves as part of the scientific literature.

One of the most obvious problems related to records about damaging wolves is that losses attributed to individual wolves are frequently exaggerated. Reported depredations were inflated both in terms of the duration of time that particular wolves were reported to have caused damage and in terms of the total amount of damage reported. A number of the famous wolves simply did not live long enough to have caused the damage attributed to them.

Records from captive wolves show that a ten-year-old wolf is very old and sixteen years is about the maximum life span. Information from wild-caught wolves suggests they rarely live to be ten years old, with twelve to sixteen years being the maximum age. Yet, of thirty damaging wolves that I have information about, eleven were reportedly eight years old or older. Stanley P. Young said the Custer Wolf of South Dakota had damaged livestock for nine years before it was killed in 1920. Two other wolves from South Dakota, Three Toes of Harding County and the White Wolf of Pine Ridge, had reportedly been killing livestock for thirteen years when they were killed, and they were both still preying on cattle when taken. Big Foot, a famous wolf from Colorado, was believed to have used a well-established range for seventeen years. One female, the Greenhorn Wolf, reportedly lived near Pueblo for an incredible eighteen years before she was finally died after eating strychnine placed in meat.

Another serious discrepancy exists between reported depredation rates for damaging wolves and the kill rates noted for wolves in recent studies. Shortly before Three Toes was captured in 1925, he reportedly killed sixty-six sheep belonging to one rancher in two nights. Three Toes was credited with killing livestock worth more than $50,000 (in 1920s' dollars). The distinctive tracks of Old Clubfoot, a Colorado wolf, were supposedly sighted about the carcasses of seventy-five freshly killed cattle and horses. His footprint was unique because of an earlier trap injury. These reports are highly suspect when compared with the average numbers of domestic animals killed by wolves in Minnesota and Montana.

Dr. Steven Fritts, currently the USFWS wolf recovery coordinator for the northwest United States, and his coworkers have verified an average annual kill of 29 cattle and 49.5 sheep by wolves in Minnesota. Those figures cover 1979–92, a period when wolf numbers in the state ranged up to 1750 animals. In Montana, Steve calculated that the state's wolf population (currently between sixty and seventy animals) killed an average of 2.4 cattle and 1.5 sheep annually during the years 1987–94.

Questions exist about whether some of the famous damaging wolves may have been wolf/dog hybrids or even wild dogs. The descriptions of some of the famous wolves suggest that they could have been hybrids or wild dogs. The Gray Terror, a notorious Wyoming wolf, displayed a kill pattern more typical of the random slashing and tearing of wild dogs than the more efficient pattern of most true wolves. The behavior of wild wolves usually follows a predictable pattern. This helps experienced trappers capture damaging wolves, even those that have earlier been caught in traps and escaped. On the other hand, the behavior of hybrids and wild dogs is less predictable and they are often difficult to capture. Great efforts were required to kill some of the famous outlaw wolves. For example, USBS hunter H. P. Williams worked from March to October 1920 before he finally captured the Custer Wolf.

This wolf also traveled with coyotes, an almost unheard-of behavior in wild wolves. These factors, along with the animal's small size, suggest to me that the Custer Wolf may have possibly been a coyote/dog or wolf/coyote hybrid.

It is difficult to assess objectively the credibility of popular and scientific literature about damaging wolves. Wolf populations have long been extinct in most areas where damage was reported and animal husbandry practices have changed. So, how can we confirm or disprove claims about the amount of damage done by wolves?

An idea to test the validity of literature about damaging wolves occurred to me while I was reviewing *The Last of the Loners*, a book about famous damaging wolves by Stanley P. Young. I realized that skulls from famous wolves must be available in museums for study. Some of the famous wolves reportedly damaged livestock for eight to fourteen and even eighteen years. If I could locate skulls of famous wolves, I could determine the ages of the wolves at the time they died. Then I would know if they were old enough to have caused the damage attributed to them.

Comparing the depredation rates reported for famous wolves with kill rates determined for wolves in recent years would show if the reported depredation rates were reasonable.

Finally, it would be possible to compare the skulls from damaging wolves to skulls from other wolves taken in the region to be sure the damaging wolves were actually wolves and not wild dogs or wolf/dog hybrids. I have been working with two other wildlife biologists to borrow skulls of famous wolves: Dr. Ronald Nowak (USFWS) and Dr. Warren Ballard (director of the New Brunswick Cooperative Research Unit). We have arranged to borrow skulls of three famous Colorado wolves: the Unaweep Wolf, Three Toes of the Apishapa, and Old Clubfoot; two from New Mexico: Blanca and Lobo, King of the Currumpaw; and one from South Dakota: Old Three Toes of Harding County. We also have the teeth of Lobo, the Killer Wolf of the North from Minnesota, so we can determine how old he was when he died.

Dr. Nowak, Dr. Ballard, and I hope that our detailed investigation of damaging wolves will help to set the record straight about how much damage the famous outlaw wolves might actually have been responsible for and will help eliminate some of the myths about them. The results of our findings will be published soon in a scientific paper.

Credible literature about wolves has always been available, but it was often published along with unreliable literature and it has been difficult to sort out factual accounts from speculation and fabrication. Literature from the 1800s and early 1900s about how wolves relate to their prey is a complex blend of factual accounts, speculative tales, and outright fabrications. A few books stand out as benchmarks of credibility or mythology in the wolf literature. Books published in 1944 and 1970 were particularly important.

Prior to 1944, some of the American naturalist authors, such as Ernest Thompson Seton, wrote both factual and fictionalized accounts about damaging wolves. Seton took care to note when he had taken a "writer's liberty" in ascribing to wolves in his stories adventures that "really belonged to other wolves." Unfortunately, other early writers apparently took similar liberties but failed to note when their accounts were exaggerated or when their conclusions were based on limited information. Later writers relying on published literature sometimes failed to distinguish between factual and fictionalized accounts and simply referred to whatever literature served their purpose.

Two important books about wolves were published in 1944: *The Wolves of North America* by Stanley P. Young and Edward A. Goldman, and *The Wolves of Mount McKinley* by Adolph Murie. *The Wolves of North America*, published as one volume, included two sections. Part I, about natural history and depredations, was written by Young and Part II, about wolf taxonomy, was written by Goldman.

Parts of Young's summary of historic literature about how wolves relate to their prey in Part I of *The Wolves of North America* are speculative and contain erroneous information. An important contradiction in Young's part of the book is his statement, "There still remain . . . areas . . . in which we feel that both the red and gray [wolves] may be allowed to continue their existence with little molestation," when in fact, Young had spent his professional career leading campaigns to extirpate wolves throughout the United States. In hindsight, after working for the modern version of Young's agency and as an extension specialist in predator control, I can appreciate Young's position. As chief of the federal predator control program, Young had to keep livestock producers and supporters of the program happy, yet to be "politically correct," he also needed to say something to placate wolf enthusiasts and other critics of predator control.

A clear distinction should be made between parts I and II of *The Wolves of North America*. Part II, written by E. A. Goldman, was a taxonomic revision of wolves and it was a classic study in mammalian taxonomy. Thanks in part to the expert work of Goldman in Part II, the book, published by the American Wildlife Institute, was widely publicized and generally accepted as the most authoritarian work available on wolves until 1970.

The second book published in 1944, *The Wolves of Mount McKinley* by Adolph Murie, reported the first in-depth ecological study of wolves. Murie provided insight into the role of wolves as predators and their social lives that had only been speculated about before his study. *The Wolves of Mount McKinley* was published in the U.S. National Park Service Fauna Series, but unfortunately, outside of Alaska, the book remained relatively obscure in comparison with the more widely distributed *The Wolves of North America*.

In 1970, as in 1944, two important books about wolves were published: *The Wolf* by L. David Mech and *The Last of the Loners* by Stanley P. Young. *The Wolf* was outstanding. Mech reviewed most of the research about wolves published by 1970. Mech drew upon his research with wolves on Isle Royale and elsewhere, and he brought together the literature about wolves from both North America and Eurasia. This book served as a reference for a new generation of graduate students and natural resources management biologists as they planned and conducted studies of wolves.

The Last of the Loners by Young was a collection of embellished stories about nine "renegade wolves." Young described them as among the last wild wolves in their respective states, yet all nine were presented as notorious livestock killers. This book has clouded the debate about reintroducing wolves. Young failed to point out that the accounts of wolf depredations were highly speculative and, as a result, they leave readers with lingering concerns about the wisdom of reintroducing wolves.

Since 1970 a number of credible books and hundreds of well-researched, objective scientific papers about wolves have been published. These publications have greatly expanded the factual information we have on wolves.

My colleagues and I are examining the validity of early reports of damaging wolves. Our goal is to help set the scientific record straight and dispel myths about damage caused by wolves. In some ways we are acting like a team of defense attorneys representing clients whose civil rights were abused in an earlier era. Our job is to assemble facts about wolves and compare them with the speculative reports that were presented and uncritically accepted years ago.

We are like court-appointed lawyers presenting an appeal on behalf of the wolves. The jury will be the scientific community and the public. It is clear that a great deal of damaging, speculative, and hearsay evidence about wolves was accepted by earlier juries of wildlife managers, ranchers, and the public. We hope, once and for all, to establish which early accounts about damaging wolves are true. Those that are false should be set aside so that development of future wolf management programs is not biased by unreliable literature. We owe it to the wolf and the livestock industry to find out the truth about levels of damage to expect from wolves, especially from reintroduced populations.

After Phil finalized his paper, I spoke with Carter Niemeyer, the ADC *wolf management specialist for the northwest United States, about his experience in investigating cases of alleged wolf depredation on livestock. Carter is the* ADC *agent who immediately responds to every reported incident of livestock suspected of being attacked or killed by wolves.*

Summarizing the results of his work, Carter told me, "I've now examined approximately one hundred cattle, sheep, and other livestock allegedly attacked by wolves. After inspecting those animals, I concluded that only about 5 percent of the attacks could be attributed to wolves."

1994: "Cry Wolf: Tracking Down an Alleged Wolf Attack on a Human," Nancy jo Tubbs

Phil Gipson addressed the issue of the need to critically examine historic accounts of wolf attacks on livestock. In the following article, Nancy jo Tubbs, secretary of the International Wolf Center's board of directors, reports on an investigation of a supposed wolf attack on a human.

In the past, many writers, including such respected authorities as Audubon (see Chapter 1), uncritically accepted secondhand accounts of wolf attacks on people. As Nancy jo proves in her story, such accounts need to be thoroughly examined for proof of the incident. At the present time, I know of no documented accounts in North American history of a healthy wild wolf attacking and killing a human.

This article originally appeared in the summer 1994 issue of International Wolf *magazine, published by the International Wolf Center in Ely, Minnesota.*

There has never been a verified attack on a human by a healthy wolf in the wild in North America. True or false?

Wolf biologists and naturalists say "True," and they rely on the statement in fighting the Big-Bad-Wolf reputation of one of the world's largest but shyest predators. Since wild wolves do not attack humans, the reasoning goes, humans have no reason to fear them. If healthy wild wolves did attack people, proponents would find arguing the case for protection and reintroduction of wolves more difficult.

In August of 1991, a letter writer to the "Readers Comment" section of the *Montana Farmer and Stockman* countered with "False." George B. Knaggs wrote that not only had there been an attack on a child by a wolf in the 1930s, but he had seen its grizzly and emotional aftermath. He was sure that official reports of the incident existed somewhere. Knaggs signed his letter and said he was from Sheridan (but mentioned no state):

> I remember one incident, that took place at Big Rapids [in Michigan on the Lower Peninsula] when I was a kid. My Dad and I went to Big Rapids to move my uncle, who was the Western Union operator of that city, to a new assignment. When we arrived, the "hunt" had just finished. The townspeople were standing around on the street looking over the remains of one helluva big wolf, and the remains of a baby that had been eaten by him. It was a beautiful autumn day, and the young mother had put the child in the buggy and placed it out under the kitchen window, where she could keep an eye on the child. A short time later, she looked out the window in time to see the wolf running off with the child that was in the buggy.
>
> If this was not documented, I find that hard to believe, because the sheriff's department, Michigan State Police, and many other people worked hard and long to bring the wolf in. We just happened to be on the scene, at the moment, so to speak, that the wolf was displayed on the street and was cut open to reveal what he had devoured.

About a year after Knaggs's letter was published, Norman A. Bishop came across a copy. Bishop is a research interpreter for the U.S. Department of the Interior at Yellowstone National Park, and his curiosity was piqued. He set out to find a historian to investigate the incident.

Richard A. Santer, a professor of geography in the Social Services Department at Ferris State University in Big Rapids, Michigan, agreed to go after the facts. Twins Shannon and Shawn Campbell were undergraduate work-study students assigned to Dr. Santer in the fall quarter of 1992. He had them review the decade of microfilmed newspaper records of *The Pioneer,* the Big Rapids daily newspaper, from 1930 to 1940. They noted every story that referred to attacks by wolves, coyotes, or dogs. Dr. Santer followed up by interviewing 10 local residents who had lived in the Big Rapids area in the 1930s.

The newspaper research turned up five relevant headlines between 1930 and 1940. None of them referred to wolves.

August 29, 1931
"Farmers Warned of Raids by Dogs"
August 7, 1939
"Urge Parents to Keep Children Away from Dogs"
August 12, 1939
"Fifth Resident Bitten by Dog in Past Two Weeks"
August 29, 1939
"Man Bitten by Dog at Stanwood"
January 4, 1940
"Wild Killer Dog Tracked, Killed by Paris Hunters"

The first three stories played on page one, the others on pages two and four of the newspaper. One incident took place seven miles south of Big Rapids, another in Green Township, north of the city.

"Given these types of articles and headlines, if a child was 'devoured' by a wolf, it is reasonable to expect that an article would have appeared reporting such a tragedy," Dr. Santer summarized. "No such articles were found."

With the help of the current senior editor of *The Pioneer,* Dr. Santer then came up with a list of community elders available for telephone interviews about wolves in the 1930s. The ten they chose were respected citizens noted for their trustworthiness, local knowledge, and alertness. Dr. Santer summarized their comments. None of them validated the Knaggs letter. Here are notes from several of the interviews:

No wolves. Locals like to tell greenhorns stories.
—*Maxine Sofoulis, director of the Mecosta County Historical Society Museum, long-time secretary for the High School Alumni Association, and daughter of the local Mecosta County Sheriff 1939–49*

Dad was an avid hunter in the area, but never told about any sightings of wolves—bobcat and bear rare once.
—*James Sofoulis, community volunteer since 1936*

Several years there were coyotes in the area. No wolves. I would have known about a wolf if there was one. One recollection about being invaded by coyotes—most hunters and two game wardens hung some dead coyotes—two, three—from Judson's Hardware store awning out front. People took pictures and the like. Never heard [of a] kid hurt.
—*Stanley "Kuie" Longcor, employee Judson's Hardware 1927–70*

Wolves? Farfetched. Rings no bells. A few red fox. Coyotes got into Wheatlakes's sheep once. Wolves—can't be true. Good story, ha ha. No wolves in the area in the 1930s.
—*Norman Mason, former township officer, city mayor, city commissioner, director of the county chamber of commerce*

Never heard of such a thing. No wolves. Coyotes once, a posse hunted them down east of town, west of Burden Lake. They displayed the coyotes. No wolves in the county. Never heard [about the child]. If it happened, I would have known; I'm a curious person. Lynx I vaguely remember.
—*Geneva Gilcrest, lived in the country and her family farmed*

Yes, I remember—wolf, but it's horse manure! All poppycock! I'll tell you the story. It was fall, October or November of 1936, I think—cold, some snow—before deer season. Dad joined the hunt with a bunch of guys. Dad left me and my brothers, we were kids at the time, in the car. Mrs. Leon Totten was chased into her house. Will Totten's mother. He's still alive. Well, anyway, people wanted to back her statement, but they determined later it was a coyote or a vicious dog, a bad dog. Dad, I can remember saying, "Hell, no wolf out there!" I can tell you no wolf! I will sign a statement today to attest to it. If there was a wolf killed, it would have been displayed at Dad's tavern, at Judson's, or the Western Hotel. Never, never!
—*Carly Schuberg, businessman, hunter above the Arctic Circle, descendent of early settlers, lifelong resident, age 78*

Lived in Big Rapids all my life. Talking to me is best. Wolf attacking a child? No such recollection. No, no. Good story!
—*Mrs. Harry Rogers*

Based on the research, Dr. Santer said, it is impossible to confirm George Knaggs's recollection. "Rather," he reflected, "we have a situation of coyotes at times being hunted, killed, and displayed; [of] crowds gathering on the sidewalks with adults having a history of 'telling stories' to greenhorns . . . but no wolves. The one and only time 'wolf' can be traced, it leads to mistaken identity and a desire of the hunters to gentlemanly protect the story of a frightened mother."

What did George Knaggs see? It is hard to say. He clearly believes that wolves attack humans, and from what he believes he saw, he created a powerfully negative attitude about wolves. Anyone who reads his letter might do the same and pass the story and the attitude to others. Myths about white alligators in the sewers of New York and house cats who suck the breath out of babies are spread the same way. Both myth and research shape the knowledge and attitudes about wolves that humans will use to make decisions about the wolf populations of the present and the future. At the end of his letter, Knaggs shares his conclusions:

> I am sure there are many more incidents of this sort, if someone were to do a little research on this subject. Of course, this took place in Michigan, some time in the 1930s, I remember. I was sick when I saw it. So we sure as hell don't need anymore wolves. Let them become extinct; they aren't anymore valuable than the dinosaur was.

In Alaska and Montana, I had at least fifty close encounters with wild wolves but never felt the slightest sense of danger or threat. Since dogs kill an average of twenty people and injure another five hundred thousand annually, they are far more dangerous than wolves.

International Wolf Magazine, the source of this article, is an excellent source of news on wolf issues. For a subscription, contact the International Wolf Center, whose address is listed in the appendix.

1995: "The Return of the Wolf to Montana," Diane Boyd
One of the fringe benefits of working on my first wolf book, A Society of Wolves, was the opportunity to meet a number of wolf researchers and discuss their work with them. In January of 1992, I arranged to rendezvous with Diane Boyd in the North Fork region of Glacier National Park for an interview about her research on wolves. As she drove me around her study area, she told me the exciting story of the Glacier wolf recolonization that had begun in 1985. Diane had witnessed the reestablishment at close range

and had done detailed research on the process.

In the summer of 1993, I volunteered to work for the Park Service in the North Fork subdistrict of Glacier so that I could see the wolf recovery process firsthand. During that time I got to know Diane better and had the privilege of seeing many wolves. Realizing that Diane would be the best person to tell the story of the Glacier wolf recolonization, I asked her to describe her experiences as a witness to the historic process.

The lanky, black wolf frantically tried to escape the approaching human, but was restrained by the trap on its foot. The trapper walked toward the captured wolf slowly, admiring the sleek fur and the wild spirit that flashed in the wolf's gaze as their eyes met. Weapon loaded, the trapper silently approached the frightened animal. As the wolf faced away in a futile attempt to flee, it presented itself for the perfect shot. The trapper quickly poked the wolf in the rump with a jabstick that she had loaded with a fast-acting tranquilizer. The hit was on target, and the wolf was asleep in three minutes.

I have replayed this scene many times since coming to Montana in 1979 to study the ongoing recolonization of Glacier National Park by wolves. Wolves were extirpated from all of the western U.S., including the national parks, during the early 1900s by means of poison, guns, and traps. Ironically, the same basic trap that was used to eradicate wolves is now used by researchers to study them and enhance their recovery. Modern biologists, however, modify the trap to minimize the chance of injury. Captured wolves are sedated, fitted with radio-collars, released on site, and monitored. By instrumenting one wolf in a pack, we can determine the activities of the entire pack by remotely monitoring the telemetry locations of the radio-collared individual. Information collected from radio-collared wolves is used to learn about their movements, food habits, dispersals, pack dynamics, and causes of mortality. This information is then passed along to the public to present an objective picture of the real wolf, an animal quite different from the beast of superstition and legend.

While working on wolves for the U.S. Fish and Wildlife Service in my native state of Minnesota in 1979, I received word in early September of my acceptance into graduate school at the University of Montana. That was on a Tuesday. By Friday I had left in my compact car packed with everything I would need for a two-year master's degree research project in the wilds of the Rocky Mountains—or so I thought. But the one thing I could not possibly have prepared for was the draw of the mountain spirit and its wolves, a draw that would turn my two-year study into a lifetime passion.

Our study was based out of Moose City, an old abandoned homestead ranch situated at the northwest corner of Glacier National Park, a stone's throw south of the Canadian border. Moose City consisted of a large hay meadow and a half dozen log buildings that were losing the inevitable reclamation battle with Mother Nature. The North Fork of the Flathead River rushed by the cabins, fed by high mountain streams from the rugged, snowcapped peaks around me. My new home was also home to numerous grizzly bears, black bears, cougars, lynx, wolverine, coyotes, deer, elk, moose, and one wolf.

I arrived at the tiny customs station on the U.S./Canadian border a quarter mile north of Moose City, in awe of the spectacular wilderness I was about to become a part of. The customs officer, John, was sitting on the porch of the old log cabin that served as his residence, office, and remote outpost. John was tipped back on a chair, feet propped up on the log railing, reading Edward Abbey's *The Monkey Wrench Gang*. He greeted me warmly with a "Hi" and a smile. It was just past noon, and I was the first person to arrive at his port of entry that day.

Having spent twenty-three of my twenty-five years in urban Minneapolis, I realized this venture would require some major lifestyle adjustments. Moose City had no electricity, telephones, or running water, and few neighbors. It was fifty miles of rough dirt road to the nearest town to get groceries or get a flat tire fixed. I soon learned that the few residents of the North Fork were there because they didn't fit in anywhere else. They were quite an opinionated lot—and they didn't care for university-type city folks coming into the country to study their wildlife.

As seasons passed, I learned to run a chain saw to cut my own firewood, dealt with twenty-two flat tires in one year, and got to know many of the local residents. I learned to love the long, snowy winters, the breath-stealing plunges into the chilly river on hot summer days, the frosty morning air year-round (which was hard on my meager vegetable garden), and the encounters with wildlife—ranging from a weasel in my bedroom to charges by perturbed bears. I monitored the growth of the recolonizing wolf population, spending most of my time in the backcountry radio-tracking and following my study animals along their travel routes through deep snow and swift creeks. Above all, I valued my connection with the wolves: be it following their tracks, catching a glimpse of one disappearing into the forest, or hearing their howls echoing off the mountains.

In a surprisingly short time, this foreign landscape and its formerly hostile residents became a welcome home and a community of friends. I knew the transformation was complete when I drove to Minneapolis a couple of years after my exodus to Montana, and felt exposed and vulnerable in the Dakota prairies. The horizon was missing the up-thrust of rock and alpine inhabitants I loved. Worse yet, there was nothing wild and no habitat for large, wild carnivores in the endless sea of cultivated crops. Although I enjoyed visiting my family, I felt restless until I first sighted mountains in Montana upon my return drive. It was after midnight when I pulled into Moose City; from the middle of the meadow I raised my voice in a mournful howl, hoping to elicit a response from a wolf. Only the coyotes yapped a welcome, but I was grateful to hear them again.

Researchers with the University of Montana Wolf Ecology Project radio-collared a gray, adult, female wolf ten miles north of Glacier National Park in April 1979. We named her Kishinena, after a wild creek in the area of southeastern British Columbia where she had been captured. The significance of her presence cannot be overemphasized. Many years of predator control (both federal and private) had wiped out the wolves of Glacier by the 1940s. When wolves became scarce, one enterprising homesteader hung coyote pelts from his cabin rafters with bricks on the legs to stretch their size and was rewarded with bounty money for his "wolf" hides. After the 1940s wolves occasionally wandered south from British Columbia and Alberta into the Glacier area. In 1950, a wolf was shot in Big Prairie in Glacier and the head mounted with a menacing snarl. Another wolf was shot near Polebridge, just outside Glacier's boundary, in 1970. The 1973 passage of the Endangered Species Act and an increased awareness of the value of predators in a balanced ecosystem allowed for Kishinena's arrival. Little did we realize that the arrival of this elusive female wolf would set the stage for wolf colonization in much of Montana, Idaho, Wyoming, and Washington.

Kishinena would be the first wolf to be studied west of the Mississippi River. Our hope was that she would extend her territory south into Glacier Park, find a mate, and perhaps even den there. When I first began my research with the Wolf Ecology Project in September of 1979, Kishinena was the only wolf known to inhabit the North Fork study area around Glacier Park (and all of the western U.S. for that matter). The nearest breeding population of wolves was approximately two hundred miles north in Jasper National Park, Alberta. A few lone individuals may have existed in southeastern British Columbia and southwestern Alberta between Jasper and Glacier, but wolf populations were still recovering from earlier extermination programs in Canada and the U.S.

A black wolf was observed in the North Fork in 1978, but efforts to capture it in 1979–80 resulted only in the capture of Kishinena. During my master's research on coyotes and Kishinena, we observed no evidence of any other wolf in the area. Kishinena's radio-collar failed in July 1980, but we continued to see tracks of a single, female wolf within her territory the following winter and presumed Kishinena was still around. During fall of 1981 and winter of 1981–82, a black, three-toed wolf was seen and his tracks observed within Kishinena's territory. These wolves paired and in the spring of 1982 produced a litter of seven pups in Canada six miles north of Moose City. Those pups would later begin the recolonization of Glacier National Park and, eventually, the northwestern U.S.

The first step of natural wolf recovery got off to a shaky start when the three-toed alpha male was accidentally killed in a bear snare on June 19, 1982. This meant the alpha female (probably Kishinena), without help, had to find enough food to feed herself and seven growing pups—a monumental task. But she was resourceful and all seven pups survived into their first winter. Funding for wolf research was terminated in September 1981, and without any radio-collars transmitting in this first wolf pack, it was extremely difficult to keep tabs on them with chance observations.

On the morning of November 1, 1983, I was writing in my Moose City cabin when a wolf began howling just outside. I sped to the door and opened it slowly to see a gray wolf, nose to the sky, standing on the opposite river bank approximately seventy-five yards away. I grabbed my camera and telephoto lens and snapped a few shots before the wolf slid into the brush and was gone. I had been studying and searching for wolf activity for over three years, covering hundreds of miles and running down reports of phantom wolves, and never seen a wolf as it was howling. I had just encountered the proverbial "wolf at the door" as I was sipping tea inside the warmth of my own cabin. I was thrilled and wishing the moment could have lasted longer.

This was the first of dozens of rendezvous with this wolf, "Kootenay," over the next two months. I often observed him and photographed him within a half mile of my cabin. I say "him" because it became clear from his raised-leg urinations that Kootenay was definitely a male. At the time, I had two very large mongrels named Stony and Max whom the wolf was very interested in. In Minnesota wolves often kill domestic dogs upon encountering them, so I kept my dogs inside as much as possible to avoid a confrontation. However, one morning the wolf came by while the dogs were out. I nervously watched the encounter, but the wolf seemed to be drawn to the dogs out of curiosity rather than hunger. After all, there were darn few wolf-sized canids in the area and breeding season was just around the corner. For the next two months this strange threesome gingerly investigated each other, but never actually had physical contact. Then in January Kootenay went in search of a more likely mate than he could find in my two neutered male dogs. My neighbors to the south and near the hamlet of Polebridge occasionally saw him over the rest of that winter, but he disappeared with the snow in the spring.

We received some funding late in 1984 for more wolf research, which culminated in the capture and radio-collaring of "Sage" approximately two miles from where Kishinena had been trapped. Sage was a gray male, and his movements his first year of transmission approximated those of Kootenay; I believe they were one in the same animal. We learned that Sage was a lone wolf not associated with the resident pack, although he was probably one of the pups born in Kishinena's 1982 litter.

No wolf pups were born in 1983 or 1984 in the Glacier area. In May 1985, grizzly bear researcher Bruce McLelland captured a nearly white wolf, "Phyllis," in his bear snare and fitted her with a radio-collar. Bruce told me the exciting news that she was lactating. I suspect that Phyllis was also one of the 1982 litter. Subsequently, we observed her with her seven black pups and six other adult pack members. At last, six years after we first radio-collared Kishinena, we had an instrumented pack, the "Magic Pack," to follow. We called them the Magic Pack because they seemed to magically come and go and were often difficult to find.

Phyllis proved to be a good mother and whelped litters in 1986 and 1987. The 1986 litter was especially important because the Magic Pack had shifted its territory south into Glacier Park in the fall of 1985 and denned there—the first time a pack had produced pups in the western U.S. in approximately fifty years.

Sage dispersed from the Glacier area and found a black female in November of 1986. They set up a territory in the Wigwam drainage of British Columbia and produced six pups in April of 1987. This was the first documentation of a successful dispersal from the Glacier area. The den of Sage and his mate was approximately twenty miles due west of where Sage was born. We monitored the movements and habits of this growing family throughout the summer. So did the hunting guide who resided part-time in the Wigwam Pack's territory. One pup was legally shot during the 1987 fall big game season by one of his clients. The parents and the five remaining pups survived through the winter; Sage almost did not.

During a routine telemetry flight on December 31, 1987, pilot Dave Hoerner and I located Sage three hundred yards north of the hunting guide's camp. We could see him below us in the willows along the gravel bar looking up at us. But something didn't look quite right—the area was all torn up and broken willow branches littered the snow. We cruised low over the distressed wolf for a better look. Sage got up and tried to leave the site but was followed out of the willow by a log. Closer inspection revealed that Sage's hind leg was in a steel trap connected to a log drag. I felt totally helpless as I watched the wolf struggle against the drag.

We flew back to Kalispell where I contacted my co-worker, Mike Fairchild, and we began planning our rescue of Sage. We headed out about supper time in our four-wheel drive, loaded with two snowmobiles, capture equipment, a new radio-collar, and veterinary advice regarding treatment of frostbitten feet. It was -20° F at Moose City that morning and I feared that Sage's foot would be frozen. We began the frustrating process of trying to reach government officials on New Year's Eve to get permission to turn the wolf loose. We got the go-ahead from a Canadian official at 9:00 P.M. We still had a two-hour drive on snow-clogged backcountry roads followed by a one-hour snowmobile ride to reach the wolf. We reached him shortly after midnight, tranquilized him by moonlight, and wrapped him in my sleeping bag. We carefully unthawed his partially frozen hind foot with the warmth of our hands. We replaced his radio-collar, checked him over thoroughly, and waited quietly for him to shake off the drugs. At 4:00 A.M. Sage stood up, shook off the sleeping bag, and walked slowly out of sight through the frosty vegetation. Quite a New Year's party for all.

Sage limped noticeably for a month or so, but had recovered fully by breeding season. He and his mate produced six pups in April 1988. We accidentally captured two of them, a male and female, that summer while trying to radio-collar another adult pack member. The thirty-pound pups were too small to radio-collar, so we just ear-tagged them and released them on site. The female was legally shot three months later. Sage's radio-collar stopped transmitting in November of 1988. Since the collar was new and unlikely to fail, and since he, as the alpha male, was unlikely to disperse, I suspected that he had been shot and killed. After he vanished, tracks of the other seven pack members were seen through the following April until the start of the spring bear hunting season. The entire pack then disappeared under suspicious circumstances and foul play was suspected. I wondered what became of that thirty-pound "Son-of-Sage" but would have to wait several years to discover his fate.

The rate of wolf recolonization increased after 1986 in the Glacier area, spilling out into adjacent unoccupied wolf habitat . The players have changed, packs splitting, growing, disappearing, but the trend toward recovery continues to this day. Since Kishinena trotted into the country in 1979, we have documented twenty-five litters (as of 1994) born in the Glacier area, containing approximately 140 pups. This natural recovery has been a true success story, with the Glacier population continuing to grow and expand into areas as far as 550 miles from Glacier. There are presently four resident packs in the Glacier area, plus numerous satellite packs up to 150 miles away.

So what became of that lucky Son-of-Sage? In February of 1993, a gray male wolf and a black female wolf were observed mating on the Sun River Game Refuge near Choteau, Montana, southeast of Glacier. The U.S. Fish and Wildlife Service and the Montana Department of Fish, Wildlife, and Parks coordinated their efforts and successfully helicopter-darted the larger gray wolf. The tranquilized animal was examined, radio-collared, and weighed in at 122 pounds. As the biologists were preparing to eartag him, they found he had already been eartagged with #33 and #34 UNIV MONT tags—he was Son-of-Sage. I wondered how he had escaped the demise of his pack and where he had been for the past five years. What gauntlet of mountain passes, highways, cattle pastures, and hunters had he successfully run to end up near Choteau, 150 air miles southeast of where he had been born? In 1979 I couldn't have imagined that Glacier would become the core population from which dispersing descendants would show up as far south as Yellowstone National Park, as far north as Pouce Coupe, British Columbia, and Banff National Park, Alberta, as far west as Washington state, and as far east as Choteau, Montana. To me, the robust Son-of-Sage represents the wolf species well: resourceful, intelligent, and adaptable. With a little human tolerance, wolves are very likely to successfully recolonize former wolf ranges.

A ninety-two-pound male wolf was shot south of Yellowstone National Park in September 1992. Genetic analyses show he was related to wolves in the Ninemile Pack (near Missoula, Montana) and Glacier. A different wolf had been filmed by Busch Productions two months earlier in the Hayden Valley area of Yellowstone. Although this wolf has not been genetically sampled, the odds are very high that it has close ties to the Glacier wolves. A yearling female radio-collared in the Glacier area in 1985 dispersed in December 1986. She was shot in early July 1987, 550 miles north of her last Glacier location. Four wolves radio-collared in the Glacier area have made trips to Banff, and one radio-collared wolf from Banff made forays south into Montana and Idaho. A wolf radio-collared in the Ninemile area dispersed and was found dead six months later in northeastern Washington.

The frequency and distance of these movements strongly suggests that we are dealing with a single wolf population between Jasper and Yellowstone national parks that spans four states and two provinces. Wolf status in this area ranges from a protected endangered species to a varmint legally hunted 365 days a year. Our new understanding of the vast range of this wolf population and the high rate of human-caused wolf mortality has convinced me that it is time to undertake an international ecosystem approach toward integrated wolf management.

As wolves move farther from the protection of the national parks, there is an increased need to identify the necessary elements of successful colonization in other areas. Because parks alone do not contain enough land to maintain viable populations of wolves and other large carnivores, the key to wolf recovery is the increased survival of colonizing dispersers and established wolf packs outside the parks. I am presently conducting my Ph.D. work on three aspects of wolf recolonization in the Rocky Mountains: dispersal, genetics, and habitat selection. I'm eager to unravel the mysteries of recolonization and recovery in mountainous terrain, and am hopeful that this information will be put to practical use in enhancing wolf recovery in other western states. I've had the good fortune to arrive in northwestern Montana at approximately the same time as the first lone successful colonizing wolf. It's been a great privilege to be an eyewitness to the reestablishment of the wolf in the western U.S.

During my fifteen years studying wolves in the Glacier area, the good times have far outweighed the bad. The wolves are constantly teaching me new ideas about their ecology and needs. The challenging lifestyle of a wolf researcher has taught me a lot about myself and strengthened my desire to continue learning about wolves. The biggest problems have come, not from biological issues, but rather from people issues: illegal wolf mortalities, shoestring budgets, politics, and disjointed management.

If wolves were simply a biological problem, wolves would never have been extirpated in the first place. It was politics and misperceptions that resulted in their removal. These obstacles can only be overcome by sound research followed by objective and thorough public education programs. The majority of former wolf habitat is gone; however, there is still much unoccupied wolf habitat out there, containing sufficient ungulate populations and minimal potential for conflicts with humans. I hope through a coordinated effort of researchers, educators, and managers, we will soon see wolves returning to these wolfless places. In the near future, I would like to hear the howls of a wolf pack, perhaps the descendants of Sage's, in the backcountry, far from Glacier Park, but even if I don't experience this personally, it is enough for me to know that they could be there.

In the spring of 1994, one of the Glacier packs dug out a new den site just a short distance from Diane's cabin. In July she howled from her front yard and got an immediate response from the pups and adults. Now in her sixteenth year of documenting the process of the return of the wolf to the West, Diane's ongoing research will be used by many other biologists as they help to reestablish wolf populations in former ranges.

1992: "A Song for the Smokies," Jan DeBlieu

As gray wolves were recolonizing Montana in the late 1980s, the USFWS was attempting to reintroduce the red wolf (Canis rufus) *into its former habitat in the South. Writer Jan DeBlieu, author of* Hatteras Journal *(1987) and* Meant to be Wild *(1991), assisted in the first red wolf reintroduction project at North Carolina's Alligator River National Wildlife Refuge in 1987. In this article, originally published in a 1992 issue of* American Way, *Jan reviews the history of the red wolf recovery program and describes the initial stages of the wolf reintroduction project at Great Smoky Mountains National Park.*

One evening last fall, deep in east Tennessee's Great Smoky Mountains National Park, a federal biologist opened the gate of a pen and released a family of red wolves. During their first two days of freedom, all four animals—a male, a female, and their two pups—stayed close together, making only short forays from the hemlock grove where they had been brought ten months earlier. The wolves had been raised in captivity, and they needed to learn how to live in the wild. Their behavior over the next year would determine if red wolves, which have been exterminated in the wild throughout North America, would be allowed to return to the Smokies.

On the third day, just before dawn, the adult pair suddenly left the pups and moved two miles north, down a hollow and into a grassy, bowl-shaped valley of some three thousand acres known as Cades Cove. Daylight and tourist traffic soon frightened the male back into the mountains. The female, however, settled into a small stand of oaks and poplars and refused to budge, even when a hiker passed within five yards of her. Eleven hours later, she was still there.

I had gone to the release site in a government pickup truck with Christopher Lucash, a biologist for the U.S. Fish and Wildlife Service. A slim, energetic thirty-year-old with an olive complexion and short, dark beard, Lucash has worked with red wolves for five years and understands the species' behavior as well as any scientist on earth. He assembled his radio-tracking gear, a small receiver with headphones and an H-shaped antenna, to study the female's erratic radio signal. The eerie beeping from her collar transmitter showed her to be restless—one minute moving, one minute still—crowded perhaps by a young male coyote in a nearby pasture. Lucash speculated about the possible reasons for the wolf lagging behind her mate. "I'd be worried," he said, "if I thought she was lost or if she'd wandered too far to find her way back to her pups. I think she's just laying low, waiting to see what that coyote does."

He stopped talking abruptly and leaned out the window. "Listen," he said. From a mountain two miles to the south came the ethereal, mournful howl of wolves: the prolonged, low note of the male and high-pitched yaps of the pups. The sounds clashed, an imperfect chorus that bounced across ridges, growing louder and slowly fading, blending harmoniously for a moment as one pup fell silent, then increasing in intensity as each animal howled anew. It was a song not heard in the Smokies for one hundred years.

"I bet they're calling the female, calling her home," Lucash said. Wasting no time, she scrambled toward the plaintive calls. Her radio signal suddenly grew strong, so strong that Lucash hastily pointed a spotlight in her direction in hope of catching a glimpse of her. But the beam washed across empty fields. The thin electronic pulse faded as the wolf picked her way up into the mountains, running for the ridge where her family waited.

For the four red wolves released in the Smokies, each day would bring a slow expansion of their world, a spreading of horizons as they explored the slopes and hollows of the Tennessee mountains. For the species *Canis rufus*, each day would mean a kind of expansion as well, an increase in the chance to win a new life of freedom—but only as long as this first family stayed out of trouble.

The red wolf no longer exists in the wild, except for a small population that has been restored to coastal North Carolina. Though believed to have been a common inhabitant of the southeastern United States two hundred years ago, it was destroyed as a functioning species by human hatred and the destruction of its habitat. By the early 1900s, the red wolf lived only in remote marshes along the Gulf of Mexico and on portions of the Texas, Arkansas, and Oklahoma prairies. Leaner than the gray wolf, it weighed between fifty and eighty pounds, with rich cinnamon-colored fur flecked with gold and black. It generally stayed back in the marshes and bottom-land forests, feeding on raccoons, rabbits, and deer. Occasionally, however, red wolves haunted the edges of farm fields, preying on calves and sheep. As late as the early sixties, the federal government was still running predator-control programs to eliminate the species. Finally, in 1967, *Canis rufus* was listed as an endangered species.

In 1975, biologists from federal wildlife agencies set out to capture the last known red wolves from the mosquito-infested marshes of southwest Louisiana and southeast Texas. By then the wolves had begun to have difficulty finding mates and were interbreeding with coyotes. Over five years, the biologists located only seventeen pure-bred animals, which were flown to a breeding center outside Tacoma, Washington.

To preserve an adequate gene pool for the red wolf, federal biologists felt compelled to take in every pure-bred red wolf they could find, probably eliminating the species in the wild. They could only hope that enough of the wolves would breed in captivity to allow reintroduction to their native habitats. Such a radical approach had no precedent in American wildlife management. The red wolf was the first endangered species in the country to be taken prisoner for its own protection.

It would not be the last. Since 1980, the Fish and Wildlife Service has initiated breeding programs for the California condor and the black-footed ferret, both of which were virtually extinct. Breeding programs are also being conducted for species such as the whooping crane, the Florida panther, and the Puerto Rican parrot, which still roam free in small numbers.

But preserving an animal's genetic purity and preserving its natural behaviors are separate matters. In reintroduction experiments abroad (with, for example, golden-lion tamarind monkeys in Brazil), researchers have found that animals raised in captivity for several generations may lose their ability to survive in the wild. A previous release conducted in North Carolina, however, has given biologists hope that captive-bred red wolves can survive in the Smokies. In 1987, when the number of wolves in captivity reached eighty-six, federal wildlife officials decided to release eight red wolves in Alligator River National Wildlife Refuge, a coastal preserve near the Outer Banks. The reintroduction at Alligator River was considered a watershed in wildlife conservation. No one had ever tried to rebuild a population of wild predators entirely from captive animals. And never before had Americans sought to nurture wolves in the wild, instead of killing them.

I first met Chris Lucash six years ago at the Alligator River refuge, where he worked as a field biologist and I served as a volunteer. In autumn and winter of 1987–88, we tracked the wolves through the coastal swamps, listening through long nights to their fluctuating signals, worrying when at first the animals took to hanging out along roadsides, marveling at their stealth when they finally began to stay back in the woods. Within six months of living on their own, the wolves learned to avoid people and became proficient at hunting. That spring, two pairs gave birth to pups. Only one survived from each litter. The mortality rate for adults was also high; by midsummer, five wolves had been killed by cars, fight injuries, and illnesses. After more were released, the population slowly began to thrive. Some twenty red wolves now live free on the North Carolina coast. The Alligator River refuge had been chosen as a reintroduction site because its physical characteristics reduce the chance that wolves will come into conflict with people. It lies on a sparsely populated peninsula where the animals are contained by natural barriers, and there are no farms in the area where they can develop a taste for killing livestock.

With the captive red-wolf population reaching about 140, the Fish and Wildlife Service was ready to take the next difficult step: releasing the species in an area of the Smokies within range of livestock. The service was gambling that the public's long-standing aversion to wild predators had dissipated. It was also betting that the wolves would live up to their reputation as shy, furtive creatures adept at avoiding people.

The biologists on the project could not have devised a more rigorous test. The Great Smoky Mountains park draws more visitors—some 8.6 million last year—than any other national park in America. But few roads traverse its 516,000 acres, and only one out of the three visitor centers is located in Cades Cove. As a result, every day in summer and fall, thousands of cars travel through the area on an eleven-mile asphalt loop. The attraction is the opportunity to see wildlife as much as the scenic vistas of undulating pastures and the shaggy, surrounding mountains. Bears, deer, raccoons, groundhogs, coyotes, and foxes are often visible from the road, and in the adjacent woods live hawks, owls, and wild boar. The abundance of animals had led federal officials to conclude in mid-1990 that, despite its popularity with humans, the cove was the best reintroduction site in the region for wolves. "It's a great habitat, much better than Alligator River," Lucash says. "Besides the amount of prey, it's easier for the wolves to get around in these mountains than in all the thick brush at Alligator River. I don't think we're going to have problems with wolves bothering hikers and campers.

"They're just too skittish around people. It may be the other way around. It may be that there are so many people in the cove that the wolves get pushed around too much and get stressed out."

At public hearings held in 1990 and 1991, many local residents voiced support for the release, while others questioned predictions that the animals would stay within the bounds of the park, feeding only on wild prey. The northern perimeter of the park abuts farmland where cattle graze, and a rancher leases the grazing rights to the pastures in Cades Cove. Service officials have promised to reimburse stock owners for animals killed by wolves. Nevertheless, the Tennessee Farm Bureau Federation, a powerful lobbying group, objected to the reintroduction program. In strongly worded letters to the park superintendent and to Tennessee Congressman James H. Quillen, who opposes the wolf release, the Farm Bureau Federation complained that stock owners should be able to shoot wolves that threaten their animals. The federal regulations written for the reintroduction allow stock owners to shoot *toward* menacing wolves or use any other means to scare them off, as long as the wolves are not harmed. "From what we know of how shy these wolves are, just shooting at them will get rid of them in a hurry," Lucash says. "But it's hard to convince ranchers of that."

Biologists have resigned themselves to the likelihood that the wolves will occasionally prey on livestock. Partly for this reason, the first release is considered experimental. Before the wolf family was freed, the father underwent a vasectomy to prevent the adults from breeding in the wild this spring. If they avoid people and do not kill many cattle, another family could be released in the fall, shortly after the first family is recaptured. Over the years, as many as eighty red wolves could be established in the Smokies, until the population becomes self-sustaining.

"We've always seen this first release as a test," Lucash said. "We're dealing with a completely new kind of habitat in a completely new region. We can't say for sure how the wolves will react around cattle. There was no way to find out without letting them go."

At six o'clock on a cool Saturday evening, four days after the wolf release, Lucash parked his pickup in a field near the Cades Cove Visitors' Center and set up his radio. Once again, he and I would sit up with the wolves until midnight. All day the family had stayed on the wooded ridge near their old pen, as if the adults were worn out from exploring. If they were going to move that evening, Lucash predicted, they would move early, then settle down and sleep during the deepest hours of the night. Although red wolves hunt nocturnally, they tend to be most active at dawn and dusk. "My guess would be that they're not going anywhere tonight," Lucash said. "We put a deer carcass outside the pen right before we released them, and they've probably caught some small animals on their own. I don't think they'll be good and hungry for a couple of days."

To the east, a half-moon was rising; its pale, white light silhouetted the saw-toothed ridges and peaks rising as high as five thousand feet, sheltering the cove. In the dimly lit pastures I could see the bulky forms of cattle, and occasionally the slighter shapes of deer. Somewhere nearby a small animal screeched once, then hissed and panted loudly. Lucash swung his spotlight toward the sounds, but we saw no sign of life, only darkness. "Something just got killed, probably by an owl," he said.

We sat in silence, listening to the sporadic noises of the night, envisioning the animals that might be moving around us. What must it have been like, I wondered, to be a settler in the cove two centuries ago, living among the bears and wolves? The park is now a vestige of wilderness, much tamer than it was in the eighteenth century. Lucash and I could seek encounters with wild predators; we did not have to fear them.

This effort to settle four wolves in a vast chain of mountains is a token beginning, an almost laughable attempt to restore an independent population of wolves to a region depleted of the species. But that is the hope of biologists—to build a thriving, self-sufficient population of red wolves through the park and the million-and-a-half acres of national forest to the south and east. It is an immense task. Yet captive wolves have adjusted quickly to freedom at the Alligator River refuge. Researchers have every reason to think they will adjust well in the Smokies, too—if the human population lets them.

Lucash tuned his receiver to the frequency of two coyotes that had been trapped and fitted with radio collars several months before. Coyotes are not native to the Appalachian Mountains, including the Smokies, which bolster the range's southern extremes. They arrived in the park during the mid-eighties, migrating from the south and west and taking over the predatory niche originally filled by wolves. Some biologists speculate that red wolves released in the park will begin to breed with coyotes, as the last wild wolves did in Texas and Louisiana. But Lucash disagrees. "I don't really think that'll be a problem," he says. "The wolves that mixed with coyotes in Texas and Louisiana probably couldn't find others to breed with. If we can't put red wolves out where there are coyotes without them interbreeding, we're in trouble. There aren't many big pieces of wild country left, besides Alligator River, that haven't been taken over by at least a few coyotes."

The coyotes' signal was distant and spotty, so he tuned in the frequency for the wolves, which still showed no sign of activity. A thin layer of fog settled over the pastures. Although the temperature was in the low forties, the night seemed warmer in the moonlight. What were the wolves feeling, I wondered. Were they content with their new freedom, or besieged by conflicting emotions: caution, curiosity, fear?

Lucash drummed his fingers on the dashboard of the truck and sighed. During his four years of work at Alligator River, he had spent hundreds of nights like this, monitoring wolves that were probably asleep. In the Smokies he would spend many nights the same way.

Breaking the silence, I asked Lucash if he still liked working with wolves. He grinned. "Exciting, isn't it? Sitting out here, trying to stay awake. Yeah, I still like it—most days. I want to keep working with predators. I won't tell you it's glamorous; you know better. Sometimes I worry that I'm wasting my time. If nothing else, though, I'm helping people get used to the idea that having wolves out in the wild is okay, that it's nothing to get upset about."

That was all. The silence descended again, and without a blip of activity registered by the wolves, we left before midnight.

At seven o'clock the next morning, as the sun's first rosy fingers reached through the smokelike haze for which these mountains were named. The two adult wolves descended from the ridge and trotted through a field near the west end of Cades Cove. Radio trackers Barron Crawford and Melissa Pangraze, hearing strong signals, caught sight of them. As they watched, the animals picked up pace and disappeared over a small hill. "It was incredible, especially in that early morning light," Pangraze says. "It was like something out of a movie."

Over the next two months, the wolf family settled into a predictable pattern of behavior, hunting in the cove at dawn, then disappearing into the hills when cars began appearing on the loop road. The pups began ranging farther and catching small prey: rabbits and rodents. The animals were seen only occasionally by the trackers and even less frequently by the public. One day, however, a wildlife photographer surprised the two adults feeding on a six-point buck on the edge of the cove. It might have been the first deer killed by red wolves in the Smokies in one hundred years, but from what remained of the evidence, project biologists could not be sure whether the wolves had been hunting or just scavenging.

In late January the male was seen in the backyard of a farmhouse in Happy Valley, a small community about a mile south of the park boundary. He killed two turkeys on the property and refused to return to the park despite efforts to frighten him away from human settlement. Reluctantly Fish and Wildlife Service officials agreed to return him to captivity permanently. At the age of ten, the male was apparently too old and too used to people to adjust to life in the wild. The seven-year-old female did not seem to share his tolerance for people, and she and the pups remained free.

Spring has brought calving season, and with it heightened concerns about wolves preying on livestock. "Sooner or later there's going to be a situation where a mother's not paying attention to a newborn, and a wolf's going to get the calf," says Gary Henry, the coordinator of the red wolf-recovery program at the U.S. Fish and Wildlife Service office in Asheville, North Carolina. "We're set up to provide compensation in that kind of case. The real problem is going to come if the wolves start killing cattle all the time. We couldn't handle something like that. For one thing, we couldn't afford it."

Regardless of whether a thriving population of red wolves eventually inhabits the Smokies, the release of the species will draw attention to the way Americans have historically treated wild animals and their habitat. One clear advantage of the release at Cades Cove is that the Fish and Wildlife Service, through a public-education program, has been able to teach area residents and park visitors about the thoughtlessness with which predators have been exterminated. "We're going to have to work with the farmers, the park visitors, and everybody else if we're going to put wolves out in any numbers," Henry says. "It's going to take a lot of compromising and trust."

Chris Lucash told me there were seven red wolves living in Great Smoky Mountains National Park in the late summer of 1994. The NPS hopes to release additional red wolves into the park soon.

1993: "Wolves for Yellowstone," Rick McIntyre

For A Society of Wolves: National Parks and the Battle Over the Wolf, I researched the issue of reintroducing wolves into Yellowstone National Park. Since the primary objection to reintroduction comes from ranchers, I looked at other areas that currently have wolves living near livestock so that I could analyze the potential for conflict in the Yellowstone region. The following excerpt from my book shows that modern documented levels of wolf predation on livestock in Minnesota, British Columbia, and Montana are far lower than ranchers have traditionally claimed.

For millions of years, wolves and their ancestors roamed the area we now call Yellowstone National Park. The wolf became the dominant predator of such wildlife as elk, deer, bison, and moose. To cope with the presence of wolves, those species evolved ways of escaping predation. Some acquired the speed to outrun wolves, others grew big enough to fight off a pack, and all developed the alertness to sense danger. More than any other factor, the wolf shaped those species into their modern form.

The traits we so admire in deer and elk and other wild game — speed, grace, agility, and alertness — are conspicuously absent in domestic animals like cows and sheep. Thousands of years of domestication and protection have devolved those species into soulless caricatures of their wild ancestors. If the wolf and their prey are allowed to compete, we end up with species like deer and elk. Spiritless animals who have the disposition of cows and sheep are the end-product of wolf-free ecosystems.

To survive as a species, the wolves also had to evolve and adapt. Improvements in speed, intelligence, and group-hunting techniques served as counteradaptations to the advantages possessed by their target prey. With these skills and traits, the wolves could catch the more vulnerable members of the wildlife community. So it went in Yellowstone for unknown millennia. Wolves and their prey both thrived in this arena of coevolution.

A few decades after the area became a national park, the managers of Yellowstone exterminated the wolf, one of the ecosystem's major players. According to current National Park Service policy, the primary function of Yellowstone is to preserve the area's original ecosystem and the dynamic, natural processes that perpetuate that system. Yellowstone, without a wolf population, fails to truthfully represent that natural state. Like a complicated machine with a vital component missing, the Yellowstone ecosystem will never function properly until that missing element, the wolf, is restored to its rightful place. Robert Barbee, the current superintendent of Yellowstone, made this point in a 1986 statement: "We all here in Yellowstone believe that biologically the case is clear—the wolf is an important missing link and it should be here."

The NPS has understood this truth for some time. Going back at least as far as the 1960s, Yellowstone rangers and biologists have spoken out for the need to reestablish wolves in the park. The importance of wolf restoration in Yellowstone escalated when wolves became a protected endangered species in 1973. The 1987 *Northern Rocky Mountain Wolf Recovery Plan* proposed releasing wolves back into their original range in Yellowstone. If the reintroduction meets the goal of the Recovery Plan (a minimum wolf population in the Yellowstone area of at least ten reproducing pairs for three consecutive years), wolves would be considered recovered and could be removed from the local endangered species list.

Biologically, there is no question that wolves belong in the Yellowstone ecosystem. Politically, the proposal to restore wolves has set off great controversy. The debate over wolves and Yellowstone has raged for years and will continue to do so for many more.

Of the groups opposed to Yellowstone wolf reintroduction, the livestock industry is the most vocal. To the people in this business, wolves threaten economic hardship and symbolize big government interference in their lives. With the specter of government-released wolves killing cattle and sheep haunting their minds, most Yellowstone area ranchers resist reintroducing wolves into the park.

Some wolves probably will stray beyond the recovery zone, and a few of them may kill sheep and cows. To make an intelligent prediction on the possible scale of wolf predation on livestock, it is worth looking at the experience of other areas where wolves and domestic animals live in proximity.

The wolf population in Minnesota is approximately 1,550 to 1,750. In an average year, Minnesota wolves kill cattle, sheep, and turkeys on about one out of every three hundred farms located in wolf range. The level of predation amounts to around one-hundredth of 1 percent of the local cattle and one-fourth of 1 percent of nearby sheep. Although these wolf predation rates are extremely low, the state of Minnesota has set up a compensation and control program to aid any land owner who experiences problems with wolves: Livestock owners receive reimbursements for documented losses to wolves and depredating wolves are captured and relocated or killed by federal agents.

In British Columbia, the province's 6,300 wolves kill about one-fiftieth of 1 percent of neighboring cattle and one-twentieth of 1 percent of local sheep each year.

The recovering Montana wolves' rate of predation on livestock is well below the previous figures. They kill an average of just three cows and two sheep annually, a rate that translates to roughly one out of every 25,000 cows (1/250th of 1 percent) and one out of every 5,500 sheep (1/50th of 1 percent) available to them.

Biologist Steve Fritts helped investigate and compile the surprisingly low rates of wolf predation on livestock in Minnesota and Montana. Steve theorizes that wolves are programmed with a search image for the wild natural prey of their area. Since cows and sheep don't match that search image, most wolves pass them by and continue to seek out other targets that do fit their mental image of what prey should look like: deer, elk, moose, beaver, rabbits, hares, and squirrels.

To put these wolf predation numbers in perspective, look at the number of domestic sheep killed by loose dogs in Montana. According to the Montana Agricultural Statistics Service, state ranchers reported a total of 3,500 sheep killed by loose dogs in 1991. As just mentioned, wolves kill an average of just two sheep per year in Montana. Based on those figures, sheep in Montana are 1,750 times more likely to be killed by a dog than by a wolf.

Some people oppose wolf reintroductions because they fear wolves would kill pet dogs. Approximately 34,000 dogs live in the portions of Minnesota that have wolf populations. In recent years, just three dogs per year (about one in 11,000) have been taken by wolves. Any Minnesotan wolf proven to be a dog killer is captured and relocated or destroyed. During my fifteen years in Alaska, our local community had two to three hundred pet dogs and sled dogs. These dogs lived and often traveled through wolf territories, but as far as I know, none were ever killed by a wolf.

Experts expect the Yellowstone wolf population to eventually stabilize, perhaps twenty years after the initial reintroduction, at a level of about 150 animals, far lower than the Minnesota or British Columbia wolf densities. The numbers of cattle and sheep that graze near the Yellowstone boundary are only a small fraction of the livestock that live near wolves in the other areas. Because grazing on Yellowstone area public land takes place mainly in the summer, the period of livestock exposure to wolves would be much shorter than in Minnesota where many animals are left outside all year.

Lack of natural wild prey would not be a problem for Yellowstone wolves. Wolf expert L. David Mech described Yellowstone by saying, "I've never seen an area with a denser prey base." Based on current wildlife population numbers, Mech estimates there will be as many as three hundred big game animals for every wolf. That ratio of prey per wolf is among the highest known to wolf researchers. . . .

Before any wolves are released into Yellowstone, a well-defined system of dealing with problem wolves will be delineated. A special provision of the Endangered Species Act allows reintroduced animals, such as the wolf, to be classified as "experimental populations." This option, if selected, could provide the necessary flexibility to manage wolves that create conflicts.

Under the experimental population designation, any wolf that leaves the park and preys on livestock will be immediately targeted by federal or state wildlife managers. The offending wolf will be captured and relocated to an area without stock. Under some circumstances, the targeted wolf will be destroyed or kept in permanent captivity.

Quick action in dealing with problem wolves will, in the long term, increase public support for reintroduction programs. Problem wolves, if allowed to continue to prey on livestock, would cause embittered members of the public to feel justified in shooting any wolf they see. For the good of the recovering wolf population and the safety of nonoffending wolves, any livestock-killing wolves must be removed promptly. Pro-wolf groups must accept this as part of the cost of return-ing wolves to Yellowstone.

To summarize the wolf-livestock issue, it first must be emphasized that wolves in other areas kill very few domestic animals. The Yellow-stone wolves will live in an area with a very high density of wild prey. Numbers of livestock near the park boundary are low. Since any wolf known to be a livestock killer will be either removed or destroyed, and economic losses suffered by ranchers will be reimbursed by Defenders of Wildlife, it seems reasonable solutions exist to minimize any prob-lems that reintroduced wolves may cause ranchers.

Public opinion polls have documented substantial support for the Yellowstone reintroduction program. A number of polls conducted in the states surrounding Yellowstone show that substantially more people in Montana, Wyoming, and Idaho are for wolf reintroduction than against it. A survey conducted in Yellowstone found 82 percent of visi-tors felt wolves deserved a place in the park. During the summer of 1992, Defenders of Wildlife gave Yellowstone visitors a chance to vote for or against wolf reintroduction in the park. At the end of the season, the "yes" votes accounted for 97.3 percent of the total ballots cast.

In the fall of 1991, Congress authorized the preparation of an Envi-ronmental Impact Statement (EIS) on the reintroduction of the wolf into Yellowstone and central Idaho. Part of the EIS process involves extensive opportunities for the public to comment on the issue and possible actions. Assuming the final document, anticipated in May 1994, recommends reintroduction, wolves could be in Yellowstone by late 1994.

What would be the significance of returning wolves to Yellowstone? First, it will fulfill the mandate of the Endangered Species Act to re-store an endangered species to the range it lost through the adverse action of humankind. Second, wolves will help restore Yellowstone's ecosystem to a condition that more closely resembles the way the sys-tem originally functioned. A critically important missing component, a large predator, will be reinstated to its rightful place in Yellowstone. With wolves again roaming the park, visitors to Yellowstone will experi-ence a natural, complex ecosystem that is essentially complete. The idea of the national park—now evolved to mean conservation of the integrity of the original ecosystem—will be closer to reality.

Once wolves return to Yellowstone, natural interactions between predators and prey also will be restored. The wolves, as Adolph Murie found in Alaska, will selectively target the weakest and most vulnerable members of the populations of deer, elk, bison, and other wildlife. Such a selection process will enhance the health and vigor of the park's prey species.

The successful return of wolves to Yellowstone will be symbolic of a new attitude toward wolf society by human society. It was our species that exterminated the wolf in Yellowstone and from 99 percent of its original range in the lower forty-eight states. Now, many in our society have come to understand the value of allowing nature to work out its own balance in at least a few protected areas. Yellowstone, the first and most famous national park, with wolves again roaming within its boundaries, will be the proof that our species has finally learned to share the earth with a kindred species.

As of mid-1994, the livestock depredation rate of Montana wolves had dropped to an annual rate of 2.4 cattle/year and 1.5 sheep/year. There is an obvious discrepancy between these low modern figures and the high wolf depredation statistics cited by livestock industry spokesmen and USBS officials in chapters 3 and 4. Phil Gipson has already commented on the credibility of the old statistics. To supplement his remarks, I've often wondered if wolf control campaigns might have selectively killed off the genetic lines of wolves who preyed on livestock. The wolves that survived control programs in the United States and Canada may have been mostly non-livestock killing individuals. The modern descendants of those survivors, wolves that are now repopulating former wolf ranges in the lower forty-eight states, seldom bother livestock.

🐺 1992: Public Hearing on Wolf Environmental Impact Statement, Helena, Montana

In August of 1992, at the height of the controversy over the possibility of reintroducing wolves into Yellowstone, the USFWS held a series of wolf hearings in a number of cities across the country. That summer I was working as a park ranger at Glacier National Park, so I decided to attend and testify at the nearest hearing, held at Helena, Montana, on August 18.

Of the 450 people who attended the eight-hour Helena hearing, 142 testified. My own testimony was scheduled for the last hour of the session, so I sat through all of the pro-wolf and anti-wolf speeches given throughout the day. Listening to those comments was an in-depth education on the vastly divergent, and frequently conflicting, views of wolves held by the citizens of our country. Jack Gladstone, representing the Blackfeet Nation, called the wolf an "elder brother," whereas a hunting guide referred to the same ani-

mal as "hazardous waste." To convey the atmosphere of the hearing, I have selected twenty representative statements—ten pro-wolf and ten anti-wolf—from people who spoke or turned in written statements that day.

MR. JACK GLADSTONE: Good afternoon. I come here today as a spokesperson of the Blackfeet Indian Nation. I have a resolution to read to you initially.

Whereas, the Blackfeet Tribe, from time immemorial, has inhabited and hunted in the geographical area now known as the state of Montana, including Yellowstone National Park, and

Whereas, the Blackfeet Tribe recognizes as an intrinsic part of this ecosystem the predator-prey relationship involving the bison, elk and wolf, and

Whereas, the Blackfeet Tribe has long considered the wolf as a sacred medicine animal worthy of respect, imitation, and admiration for its social prowess, and

Whereas, the wolf has been eliminated from its original range and habitat within the area now known as Yellowstone National Park,

Therefore be it resolved: The Blackfeet Tribal Business Council supports wolf reintroduction into Yellowstone National Park.

The traditional perspective of looking at an animal like the wolf in conjunction with nature is to view the wolf as an elder brother. The wolf preceded our Blackfeet people being here for thousands and thousands and thousands of years. Our Blackfeet people, our Indian people in this state, in living and coexisting with the wolf, we have learned how to do it. We learned the language of respect.

I see the buttons, and I see the wolf and the X through the wolf. I think the buttons, or the buttons depicting a circle, can be very useful in examining this whole issue because in Yellowstone National Park and in the Yellowstone ecosystem, we have a circle. We have a circle that was broken in 1920 when the wolves were removed. Wolves belong as part of the sacred circle of Yellowstone National Park. They do not belong outside the park killing ranchers' cattle and sheep. We are in agreement about that. However, it's that sacred circle that must be respected if we are to possess a national park worthy of handing down for future generations. This issue is not an issue that must be contained just within ten or twenty years. We have to think about generations to come in order to grasp a mature perspective of what we are facing today. [Here Jack Gladstone sings his song "Circle of Life."] [The wolf is] worthy of respect and worthy of finding a small place[to live in] the lower 48 states.

MR. LEN SARGENT: I thank you for letting me speak here today. Incidentally, I hate written statements; but you are lucky because if I was just going to be talking, we'd be here a long time.

I'm Len Sargent, born in Baltimore to a Navy family, graduate of Princeton University, math and science teacher and ice hockey coach for 30 years, including 4 years in World War II. While I don't claim to be a native or I have no Indian blood, my parents honeymooned in Yellowstone by carriage; and a relative, Nathaniel P. Langford, was one of the Bozeman businessmen who conceived not only the idea of a national park, but contrived to make Yellowstone the first one in the world, and Langford became its first superintendent. I bought my ranch just north of Yellowstone after several years of fishing, hunting and camping, from Mexico to Canada. I thought then that it was the best place; and 30 years later, I still do.

I'm here today to testify in favor, and I repeat in favor of the reintroduction of wolves in Yellowstone, either naturally or by transplanting. Wolves have a necessary place in the natural cycle of this area and are critically needed to return here. We have the same wildlife on our ranch, largely, as does Yellowstone; and in 30 years we may have lost one cow to a grizzly and between the four ranches in this basin in the same 30 years, no one has lost a calf, sheep, goat, chicken, pigeon, pig or pet rabbit to the many coyotes in our area. That's possibly some luck—(Interruption by crowd). It's true. That's possibly some luck, but mostly it's because we haven't poisoned or shot all the predators' natural prey. Natural prey. In turn, they keep the level of ground squirrels, mice, grasshoppers, and so forth, at a reasonably low level, a good example of a natural cycle.

With specific regard to wolves in this area, one of my neighbors, now in his 80s, remembers working as a boy with his father in Yellowstone. In those days, the Park ran numerous cattle in order to supply the various lodges; and although there were numerous wolves in the Park, my neighbor said they never bothered the cattle, most probably because there was plenty of their natural food, as I'm sure there still is today.

HEARING OFFICER: Mr. Sargent, your time is up.

MS. CATHERINE T. BUSHWAY: My name is a Catherine Bushway of Potomac, Montana, and I believe the wolf should be reinstated to its one-time territory in the Greater Yellowstone Ecosystem. This is not a desire or a dream. This is the law. In accordance with the Endangered Species Act, this should already be done. This meaningless and unnecessary hearing, and others like it, are delay tactics by big-money politicians. It is a last-ditch effort to delay the fulfillment of the law and the wishes of most Americans in hopes of revoking one of the best laws this country ever enacted.

What we need most is to stop wasting so much time, energy and money fighting over what is already the law. Zealots on both sides need to stop ranting and start listening. A good compromise will cost a lot less and put Canis Lupus back in its rightful place in the Greater Yellowstone Ecosystem.

The wolf may need a little help from man to get started, but even then, they should be fully protected by the Endangered Species Act. There will be no immediate hordes of wolves leaving Greater Yellowstone to prey on domestic cattle. There is sufficient space and prey to keep them in the ecosystem. When or if problem wolves do stray out of the designated area, the individual wolves should be investigated by a pre-determined government agency and humanely destroyed only if there are not other ways to solve the problem. This and the Defenders of Wildlife reimbursement fund should protect ranchers if they will only give it a chance. It has been proven to work in Minnesota, where wolves and ranchers live together. It can work in Yellowstone, too.

In closing, I would like to mention that there is now filmed documentation of a possible female wolf in Yellowstone. It would serve both sides right if, while the bureaucratic machine stumbled and fumbled along, Canis Lupus has found its own way home to Yellowstone. Thank you.

MR. DAVE WITT: I am a third generation rancher from Jordan, Montana. It's sad when a small minority can dictate to the majority how we are to live and what we have to live with. This is the approach of Communism. This isn't just an issue of introducing wolves into the Greater Yellowstone. It's the issue of taking of private property rights guaranteed by our Constitution.

These environmentalists and special-interest groups will keep working on our private property rights until we have no more left. It doesn't matter if it's the wolf, the water, the salmon or the spotted owls. It's all the same.

I find it real disturbing in Congress as well as the people on the wolf committee. As far as I can tell, there's very few that work for a living.

They either are government, state or private parasites living off the tax-payers. These are the people that are telling us that we are going to live with wolves in harmony. On our ranch, we lose from ten to one hundred lambs every year to coyotes. Anybody that's never seen a lamb chewed up by a coyote is really missing a pleasant sight. They are nice. Nobody in their right mind would introduce the wolf, which is a far worse predator than a coyote.

We in agriculture will protect our livestock and our private property from all predators, whether they have wings, four legs, two legs, by any means possible. No wolves, nowhere. Take the taxpayers' dollars wasted on the study and go clean up the environment in the inner city.

MR. TRIEL CULVER: Good afternoon. I'm from Bozeman, Montana. I've been a resident of this state for 26 years. Both my parents were born and raised here. My great grandparents homesteaded outside of Stanford, Montana. Even though I have spent most of my life here in Montana, I've traveled outside of the state and it's interesting to see how misinformed a lot of people are about what Montana is all about. Many people have this romantic illusion that there are bears and wolves running around everywhere across the state. The sad fact is that this isn't true. I spend most of my time hunting and recreating in the great outdoors here, and I've never been even remotely close to any wild wolf or any wolf signs, even though I avidly look for it.

With all the abundant resources that this state has to offer, I think we in Montana often forget that some things simply don't grow back. Once they disappear, they are gone forever. That's certainly the case with wolves. I don't want Montana to be just a romantic illusion in people's minds, but a real place with all the diverse wildlife habitat that once roamed this great state. Even though I've never had a chance to see a wolf while I was growing up here, I'd like to be able to give my kids that opportunity.

I have very strong feelings about this state, and I understand and recognize the strong feelings that other people have about it. I feel as though it's one of the last wild places left. We've made some mistakes in the past by trying to eliminate wolves, and I believe it's time to rectify those mistakes. The wolves want to come back. I want them back. Thank you.

MR. KEN KERSHNER: I'm Ken Kershner from Stevensville. I've lived my life in Wyoming and Montana and I knew some oldtimers in Wyoming and Montana who had lots of experience with wolves, and their experiences were very much alike, and I feel that their information they have given is very authentic. One of the things about wolves that most agree on is they're probably the most cruel animals in the world. They kill for sport as well as for something to eat. A rancher in Sweet Grass County, Montana, lost 18 cows one night from wolves and the wolves did not eat the animals at all. They just had them down and they were still alive when they found them. They had to be destroyed. The wolves did that just before.

I think the money spent to reintroduce the wolves is a waste of money. There's plenty of expenses in this country, and it's just a waste of our tax money.

One thing, if it so happens the wolves are reintroduced, I think we should by all means have the right to protect our property from wolves, by whatever means we feel is necessary. Thank you.

MR. CHAD SHEARER: My name is Chad Shearer. I'm a resident of Great Falls, Montana. I'm a licensed professional hunting guide and I have taught Montana hunter safety for five years. I guide 45 miles from West Yellowstone, and I oppose the reintroduction of wolves to any-place.

Why do people want wolves in Montana, anyway? I am amazed that the same people who want to reintroduce wolves to the northwest are the ones who opposed the issue of bringing hazardous waste to Ringling, Montana; but I have a certain doubt in my mind about those people. They protest one type of hazardous waste, but they want to bring an-other type of it in. I consider the gray wolf to be a hazardous waste. They are trying to dump wolves in our state, which has an adverse effect on wildlife and livestock populations. Not only are they doing this, but they are trying to make us look like villains who don't enjoy Yellowstone's beauty, and they try to make us feel guilty for wanting to keep wildlife numbers high all around.

I enjoy Yellowstone and Glacier all year round because I live in this great state called Montana. Let me paint you a picture in your mind. It's getting late in the fall. The snow begins to fly and the temperature starts to fall. The snow starts to get deeper and deeper. The deer and elk and buffalo are finding it harder to find food in Yellowstone. So what do they do? They migrate to places like Jackson Hole, Wyoming, and the Paradise Valley just north of Gardiner, Montana, where they can find food.

Now let me add another dimension to this picture. When the Environmental Impact Statement ordered by Congress came out last year, it called for bringing in 100 mated pairs of the Canadian gray wolf in

1993. That's 200 wolves, or shall I say 200 wolves too many. Now let's look at this picture again. What is going to happen when the elk and other wildlife start to migrate out of the Park? Are the wolves going to stay in the Park and feed on trees and shrubs? I don't think so because they are carnivores, not herbivores. Maybe we should put up chain-link fences so the wolves will stay within the boundaries because I really don't think they can read the sign that says, "You are now leaving Yellowstone National Park."

I want my future generations to be able to enjoy Montana where the elk, deer, buffalo and other wildlife species, excluding wolves, are plentiful, because if you introduce wolves, you'll be lucky to see a calf elk frolicking in a stream next to its mother, because if wolves are reintroduced to Montana, you might as well look forward to seeing numerous cow elk missing calves. That is, you'll be lucky to see vast numbers of elk if wolves are reintroduced.

Like I said earlier, we Montanans who love wildlife don't want to see the hazardous waste species, the gray wolf, reintroduced. Therefore, I oppose any reintroduction of wolves to anyplace in the northwest. Thank you.

MR. JOHN MURPHY: My name is John Murphy, and I'm the President of the Montana Woolgrowers Association. I am opposed to the reintroduction of wolves to any part of Montana, Idaho or Wyoming. The Montana Woolgrowers Association has approximately 2,900 members. We have a resolution stating no wolves in Montana and surrounding areas.

There are between 50,000 and 60,000 wolves on the North American Continent. They are not an endangered species and should not fall under the Endangered Species Act. An endangered species is one that is about to become extinct on this earth. Wolves certainly do not fit under this category.

I am concerned about the ranchers who live next to any area where wolves are introduced. The predator losses are already causing a hardship on these people and wolves would just make it worse. These wolves will not stay in the Park or high mountain wilderness areas, but will follow the wildlife, which they prey on, down into the valleys where domestic livestock is raised, and it is much easier to prey on domestic livestock than it is wildlife. The presence of wolves will also reduce the animals which hunters can hunt and greatly restrict outdoor activities such as skiing, snowmobiling, hunting or hiking in the surrounding areas.

I feel the state is in enough financial difficulties without putting some of the ranchers out of business. The farms and ranches in this state are a business just like the shops on Main Street, the gas station, grocery store, parts store and so on. When any business has to quit, the State and school districts suffer. Not only will it affect the ranchers, but also the townspeople who live next to an affected area. Anything that has blood in its veins will be a target for wolves. When the weather turns minus thirty and the snow is deep in the mountains, these animals need meat every day and will travel anywhere and attack anything to get something to eat.

In the early 1900s, the ranchers and rural people found that they could not live with wolves and they were removed. It is no different now. I don't think the ranchers and the people of Montana should have to deal with all the extra problems that these wolves would cause. Thank you.

MR. LEROY KEILMAN: I am Leroy Keilman, and I'm from Billings, Montana. I was raised on the Judith River in Central Montana. My father had both cattle and sheep. I've watched these young people with stars in their eyes get up and talk about wolves. How many of them have lived in the days of the wolf? Well, I'm in my 80s, and I have lived in the days of the wolf, and I mean wolves. Have you ever seen what a wolf can do to cattle or sheep in a short time? They are in a hurry to not only kill to eat, but to have fun and kill extra so that they have plenty and, remember, they like fresh kills. They may not eat for several days, but when they want to eat, they kill and kill lots; and they have found that it's much easier to come out of the mountains and kill cattle and sheep that are penned up. Calves, especially, they like.

Have you ever seen your pet horse hamstrung by a wolf and eaten alive while it's still screaming? That's what a wolf will do. How many of you have ever seen a wolf in the wild? How many have ever killed a live wolf? How many of you have any idea what it costs to get and capture one killer wolf? It took a government trapper, and one of the best in Montana, three years. Think of the cost. Three years to get that one wolf.

In the 1920s, three of us high school boys spent a week at Yellowstone Park, and we didn't see the wolves, but they had them. They had them back out of the way. We didn't get to see all those nice animals. Well, folks, just think of the cost for something we don't need. For our budget, the state and national is way overdrawn. Why spend more? We've done well in 70 years without wolves. Why do we need them now?

Thank you.

MR. BRENT MITCHELL: My name is Brent Mitchell. I live in northwest Montana, and I am one of the dirty-hands people. I'm a blue-collar worker. I deal with building maintenance, fix boilers and plumbing work, pull toilets and do carpentry work. I weld. I'm basically brilliant.

I favor wolf reintroduction. I think it's important enough to take time off work to testify at these hearings today. I am a hunter. I am a competitive shooter, a life member of NRA and the Montana Rifle and Pistol Association. I'm also a certified firearms instructor and the past vice-president of the Whitefish Rifle and Pistol Club. I guess if I wanted to take a wolf, it wouldn't be that difficult.

Many hunters are worried about wolves competing with them for game, the deer and elk and antelope. They are concerned that the sport and ability to provide meat for their families will be diminished. We need to address this concern with education and facts.

Minnesota has lots of hunters. Minnesota has lots of wolves. The same worries, fears and arguments we hear in Montana about the wolf's impact on game populations were expressed in Minnesota by sportsmen. They did not materialize. Today Minnesota has healthy big game populations, healthy wolf populations and healthy hunter populations.

We are talking about reintroduction of the wolves in Yellowstone. What could be a benefit of that reintroduction? We have major problems with migrating bison and elk herds in and around Yellowstone National Park. We have excluded hunters from reducing both of those populations. Ranchers are worried about disease and livestock loss. The rangelands are getting pounded in the Park, and so the bison and elk are moving out along with the elk.

We need to restore the natural balance in the Yellowstone area. The wolf will help control overpopulations of bison and elk in the Park where hunters have been excluded. The wolf will not significantly reduce the hunter's opportunity to take big game anywhere in the state of Montana. Again, check Minnesota's experience. They still have good hunting and lots of hunters.

Man is a hunter, a predator, and well-equipped with firearms, skill and determination to out-compete any wolf. In my opinion, we need to do three things. Number one, restore the balance in Greater Yellowstone ecosystem by reintroducing the wolf; number two, educate hunters, let them know they won't be displaced by wolves; number three, reassure stockgrowers that problem wolves will be dealt with immediately.

As I said earlier, I am a hunter and an ordinary working stiff. I am also a conservationist and the president of Flathead Audubon Society, a 450-member chapter covering all of Northwestern Montana. Thank you.

MS. CAROL TAYLOR: Greetings, Ed Banks and company. My name is Carol Taylor, from Fort Benton, Montana. I still can't believe you are still actually pursuing this wolf recovery nonsense. But since you are, let me tell you how it looks to the rest of the world. I recently sat next to two young German travelers on the plane. They spoke fluent English. I told them about the Endangered Species Act and said to them, "Do you realize it's against the law here to shoot a wolf, even when he's killing your own animals?" The two Europeans gave me a funny look and simply said, "How illogical." They were even more amazed when I explained your idiotic plan to dump even more wolves out here. This was when I realized that we Americans and our deaf-and-blind government are the laughing stock of the whole world.

I am for the no-wolf option, period. We can warn you and plead with you until we turn blue, and we probably will, but you'll go on and push wolf recovery anyway. That really proves your ignorance and insensitivity. This issue also boils down to your job or mine, Ed. Being a bureaucrat, you probably think your job is safer; but at least in my job, I try to help, not destroy, other people's lives. More and more thinking people will come around to my side, which reminds me, here is a copy of my article that appears in the new issue of *God's World Today*, published in Asheville, North Carolina. This is going out to 600,000 American school children right now. It tells about the many good things cows do for mankind. Cows are a life-enhancing species, not a life-destroying species.

You can have this copy, Ed. The White House will be getting a copy, too, and all the Senators. I just want everyone to know what a valuable resource you're going to be throwing to the wolves.

Also, here are a few hundred signatures, 551, against wolves from my friends, the Hutterites. There are two letters, one from Max Baucus and one from Ron Marlenee, and two from the Hutterite Colony with all these signatures. All 3,000 of them want me to tell you in no uncertain terms "no wolves." That's my Environmental Impact Statement, and my son has something to say.

YOUNG TAYLOR CHILD: I don't want any wolf to kill a person or animal or adult with a will to live.

SECOND TAYLOR CHILD: I don't want a wolf to harm a dairy cow, a beef cow or any other important farm animal, including a pig. It can even kill a horse, probably even your favorite horse. That's why wolves, I don't want wolves returned to Yellowstone National Park. Thank you.

MS. LILY ALVES: Hello, my name is Lily Alves, and I'm a sophomore at Hellgate High School in Missoula. I will be old enough to vote in two years, but that doesn't mean I'm going to wait around to deal with the mistakes of my elders. I will inherit your problems. Yellowstone Park represents one of the last areas of wilderness in the Lower 48 to the American people. It is incomplete in the absence of the wolf. Wolves have been depicted in movies and literature as the epitome of evil. That the hysteria has continued this long can only be attributed to closed minds on the part of superstitious people. Wolves keep herds strong by killing the weak and old. Tales of mass killings by wolves are simply folklore.

What gives humans the right to condemn any one creature? All living things play a part in the world. We have disrupted the ecosystem in Yellowstone by removing wolves. It is our responsibility to correct this mistake.

Shrinking habitats are forcing us to all get along. If people cannot find a way to live with wild animals in their habitat, then the problem is not animals, it's people. We need to look at the whole picture and not just our own needs. Wolves have a place in Yellowstone, and I support their reintroduction. Thank you.

MR. MONTE FITCH: Thank you. The only option I can support is the no-wolf option. I'm Monte Fitch from Jordan, Montana, and we farm down there, raise sheep and cattle in Garfield County.

Let's not disregard the wisdom and firsthand experience of our fathers and grandfathers who, with full assistance of the U.S. Government, rid this area of wolves in the first half of this century. This was not done just because someone did not like wolves, but because of the savage nature of wolves. Let's not expose our abundant wildlife and domestic livestock in Idaho, Wyoming and Montana to being eaten alive or, if they are lucky, killed by these savage predators.

Do not be fooled into believing the wolf will stay in the Park. When deer, elk, bighorn and buffalo leave the Park boundaries in the winter in search of food, the wolf will follow. Wolves den at elevations less than 7500 feet; Yellowstone averages 8500 feet. Wolves won't return to the Park in the spring voluntarily.

Also consider the large amount of tax dollars that it will take to reintroduce the wolf to the Park. With over 50,000 to 90,000 wolves in North America, it is time to delist the wolf from an endangered species and return him to the predator list where he belongs. Thank you.

MS. GLORIANN KLEIN: Hi, on behalf of the Defenders of Wildlife, I fully support the reintroduction of the wolves. We have been in the Park in Yellowstone and surrounding communities since the beginning of June taking public-opinion polls. We have over 25,000 votes, 97 percent in favor of wolf reintroduction. We also are bending over backwards by putting our money where our mouth is in terms of offering a $100,000 compensation fund fully reimbursing ranchers for the losses of any livestock that do occur. That potential loss is only half of one percent; and in the last five years, we have only paid out less than $12,000 for loss. In addition, we have a $5,000 incentive program for ranchers with wolves on their land to assist them in terms of wolves and in successfully raising wolf pups to the age of adulthood.

We have bent over backwards to try to work with the ranchers, who have not budged an inch in terms of meeting us halfway or three-quarters of the way. Think of the number of livestock the wolves take. It's very minimal. They will only take livestock when there is nothing else available. We were there after the wolves. We took their habitat away from them first. They have a right to exist. Creatures on this planet have been able to cohabitate without us. They should be able to cohabitate with us.

Those of you who are so fearful of wolves attacking people, I testify, having worked with captured wolves, that wolves shy away from people. They do fear people and they do avoid us like the plague. You would have to seriously provoke a wolf in order to have one come after you. There has never been a documented case of a wolf attacking a person in North American history.

To Ron Marlenee's testimony about having only a small minority in favor, again, I assure you that we talked to visitors from all over the world, especially in the tri-state area, and the majority of the people favor wolf reintroduction.

I urge you to work with us on behalf of all groups, agencies and the public to have the wolf brought in successfully and give it the right to restore it to it's natural balance, especially in the Yellowstone area. And, again, there are plans being made for when the wolf does leave so that people can feel successful in terms of raising the livestock and allowing the wolf to range in its habitat. Thank you.

MR. SCOTT DREBLOW: My name is Scott Dreblow of Bozeman. Like most Montanans, I support restoration of wolves to the Greater Yellowstone Ecosystem. A friend of mine from Bozeman just asked me to turn in a list of 450 names that he collected in about eight hours in Bozeman of people that are actively supporting the reintroduction of the wolf.

Restoration of the wolf in the Greater Yellowstone ecosystem is required by the mandate of the National Park Service, by the Endangered Species Act, and supported by majorities of the U.S. Congress and of the American public. Therefore, we are here today to discuss how to manage, to allow the recovery of the wolf in the Greater Yellowstone.

Preventing wolf recovery is not an alternative, nor is abdicating this responsibility to state legislators or game and fish officials.

Wolves were a vital part of the Greater Yellowstone for thousands and thousands of years. As people in Minnesota have known for a long time, as people in Northwest Montana are learning, wolves will not wipe out the hoofed species on which they prey. We know this based on observation of wolves all around the world where they exist. We know this from science. This is not based on any family history or personal anecdotes.

Humans, including livestock producers, can thrive and prosper in this region, as they have done, after wolves are returned to our wild lands in this area. I say this as someone who has lived and worked on two beef ranches in Teton County, Wyoming, and made my living with horses in Gallatin County, Montana.

Wolf predation on livestock in the Greater Yellowstone will occur. It will be on a small scale, and it can be managed. We know this from the experience in northern Minnesota and northern Wisconsin, and elsewhere, and the details can be worked out as part of this EIS process.

Let us move forward now, without hysteria, without irrational fears of the unknown, and bring gray wolves back to the Greater Yellowstone. We and our children and grandchildren will all be richer in a sense and wiser for it, and this wildness is why we live here and why we are willing to fight to protect this area. Bring back the wolf. Thanks.

MS. SANDY MALCOLM: Hi, my name is Sandy Malcolm. I'm a 16-year-old. I attend school at Gardiner High School, north of the Park.

If God wanted wolves in the Park, they would be there. As it is, they are not there so we don't need to put them there. People are seeing more and more wolves farther south each year, and by south, I mean closer to the Park. Nature will fix the messups we, the people, have ever made. As it is, the wolves will move on their own to a place they like, and there's no way we can put them where we want to put them and make them stay.

Wolves are a vicious animal that will kill anything from a house dog to a moose calf. If wolves get reintroduced into the Park, they will kill little children's' pets, if not the child, himself. Wolves will be a constant threat to people who live in the Park and the tourists that come to the Park. The people who want wolves back in the Park have never seen a wolf in action because if they had, they would never want that wolf anywhere near their family or them.

We have to consider the people that live where the wolf will be put. They have a right to their lives just like anyone else. They will have to stop going alone into the back country or carry a weapon to defend themselves. If the people who want wolves in the Park don't know the way a wolf behaves, it is up to us to save them from their own ignorance. Oftentimes when riding young colts, we put the colt and ourselves in a dangerous position without even knowing it and the young colt will save us by saving himself. This goes on without our even knowing it; therefore, like the colt, we must save you from this dangerous position.

We have to stop and consider the after-effects of this move. What will an eastern gentleman or woman do when they see the wolf bringing down the mother deer in front of their eyes? They will worry about the fawn and if it will survive; and chances are, the fawn will die within two days unless a miracle happens. They will also think it inhumane to purposely put the wolves in the Park to kill the animals. After the wolves have mauled, injured, or killed somebody, people won't want to take the risk of getting themselves killed or hurt to see these animals that they can see in a zoo or in a more favorable habitat.

Also think of the lawsuits against the Park because their registered toy poodle that won Grand Champion in the National Dog Show three times in a row got killed by a wolf. Pretty soon the wolf will be the bad guy and the Park will be in up to their necks to kill off the wolves so the danger level or traveling through the Park is down to earth so these people that have come a thousand miles or from Europe can see the baby moose and deer again.

Wolves, like any other predator, will go toward the easy stuff first. One of the first things they will hit will be the deer, the wild sheep, the moose calves, the antelope and the smaller animals that roam around the Park. After they are all gone, the wolves will move to another place, and that place will be out of the Park—

HEARING OFFICER: Sandy, your time is up.

MR. RICK BASS: I'm a first-generation Montanan, a fifth-generation Texan and, as somebody was telling me, thirteenth-generation American. I live up in Yaak, surrounded by federal wildlands, and I'm angry at having to be here today to even jack with this. I appreciate the Fish and Wildlife Service's work that they've done with wolves in the state.

I had the fortune to work on this book about these wolves [*The Ninemile Wolves*] that came down into the Ninemile Valley and hung out in a cow pasture. I'm angry at the political manipulations that have pulled this meeting together, not for spreading information but for trying to count votes and get elected. In the Ninemile, as I hope everybody knows, three steers were killed over a period of three years by wolves. The wolves, if anything—I've been talking to the rancher, the only living rancher I know of that's watched wolves den on his property, and it would be worth everyone's while to talk to him—those wolves are kind of scared of the cows. The cows are big and the wolves had never learned to hunt them and they didn't want to hunt them. We've got all these myths of these old cow-killing wolves of the previous century from when we came in and killed all the buffalo and brought the cows in their place. We didn't have the big deer herds and there was nothing for the wolves to hunt but cows, and all the wolves that turned out to be the bad killers were three-legged wolves with names like "Old Three Toes" and "Old Three Leg" and "Old Devil" and "Old Crip," wolves that have been wounded in traps. That's not the story of modern wolves. The story of modern wolves, and this is borne out by facts in Minnesota, Alaska and Montana, they are going to kill about one cow for every 10,000 available, and that cow will be compensated for.

I think that's a heck of a deal. I've done about every bad thing there is. I'm an environmentalist, but I'm an oil and gas geologist, I'm a hunter, my family raises cattle in South Texas, these big Brahmans that would probably kill the wolves. I've even cut wood in the woods, so I'm not one of those raving lunatics that I'm accused of by the politicians; and I get angry that the politicians play us against the middle, just to take the votes that come off the top.

I think that's just a heck of a deal, that environmentalists are trying to work with the ranchers. We respect ranchers. We respect all wild things, and ranchers are wild. They are out in the open all day. They work all day. They are not lazy. I understand the fear that a lot of them are operating under; but again, I'm angry at being jerked around by unnamed politicians that are just trying to continue their short-term aspirations. It's not good for the long-term feature of Montana, and I hope everybody will continue looking at the facts, not the myths.

MR. JACK SULLIVAN: My name is Jack Sullivan. I've got a ranch over in the Twin Bridges area. I've listened to these people sit here and say their reasons for reintroducing wolves into the Park. Not one of them, not one of these people is going to lose one nickel in wages or salary. They aren't going to lose one head of livestock. Half of them were hired by the Sierra and these other rich clubs to come and protest at these meetings. Most of the people are living on food stamps and Welfare. They are not going to lose a thing. Typically, they do not want mining, ranching, livestock grazing, hunting, anything on these grounds.

There's no way in the world they are going to keep them wolves in the Park. My grandparents came from Michigan in about 1910, and my parents. They had wolf problems back there then. They had wolf problems when they came to Montana. If the wolf is so popular, why did they get rid of them? There wasn't a livestock producer that could survive at all with losing their stock. The wolf isn't going to add one nickel to the economy. The people that are working for a living and paying the taxes are the only people that are going to be hurt by these wolves, which is the logger, the miner and the rancher. They aren't going to help the ecosystem. Isn't there a place in this ecosystem for man? Everybody says the circle has to be complete, but not one of these people has said man is in this circle. It's just the wolf.

This ecosystem has gone along for 70, 80, 90 years without a lot of wolves. If they want to learn about the wolves, let them go to Canada and find out about the problems they are having, or let them go to Minnesota. One lady says, "Well, we haven't paid out hardly anything for killed livestock with wolves." Of course not. They don't have wolves here yet; but you wait until the wolves get as thick as coyotes and the government trappers can't do anything with the coyotes because the wolves are there, and then it will be like the Minnesota fund. They went completely, flat broke trying to pay for the killed livestock.

The only people here that are for the wolves are the people that are getting big donations from the rich. The young people that haven't got into the world life yet, they don't know what real life is yet; but when they get there and have to earn a living, it's going to change a lot of their minds on these wolves. There's no way that the wolf is going to help this country, the ecosystem or anything else by introducing him because when they introduce him into that park, where are they going to introduce him next? The Tobacco Roots, the Highlands? They are going to put him wherever they want.

MS. MARJORIE ROBINSON: Thank you. I'm Marjorie Robinson from Melville, Montana, which is exactly a hundred miles north of the Park border, so I'm sure within two or three years I would have wolves on my place. I'm a widow. I run 60 cows and 100 sheep, so I don't think that qualifies exactly as one of these rich ranchers that you are so busy beating on.

There's four things. This is an artificial crisis. We've said so all afternoon. Wolves are not endangered; but what I really came to talk about, I don't think you are thinking about the animals, the animals that these wolves are going to chew on. I don't raise my cattle to be killed. I'm not so interested in the money. I just don't want them eaten up.

These kids that think they want to love the wolves, do you have a pet? Sooner or later, and it's not a myth, it's in *Reader's Digest*, the wolves are taking pets out of the yards in Minnesota. That's in *Reader's Digest*.

This one man alluded to hearing a baby deer or something scream. Well, something we don't hear about is horses. You look around Helena Valley here. Every pasture, there's two or three horses. Well, if you get wolves, some day you are going to look out there and one of your horses is going to be carrying a leg because he was run through the wire. One of them is going to be caught in a cattle guard with a broken leg and one of them is going to be laying there dead. That is what is going to happen if you bring the wolves back.

As they said, the people, so many that are for it, they are the ones that don't have any money at stake. If we put up — if we have to have wolves, every single one of them should have one of these recapture collars. You blow your money on everything else. Put it on something useful, on these recapture collars.

I do appreciate the people who realize and are willing to pay the ranchers, but you can never find all of them and you can never be compensated for all your time hunting wolf kills; and the people who have said guard dogs or Llamas or donkeys to guard your sheep, they are going to be just eaten up. They would be no protection. They would have no chance against a wolf. You'd just end up with one more dead pet. Thank you.

MR. JOHN FREDERICK: My name is John Frederick. I live in Polebridge,

Montana, in the North Fork of the Flathead River Valley since 1979. I am representing the North Fork Preservation Association and its 200 plus members.

There are wolves in the North Fork, lots of them. I can document that wolves have been there for twenty years. Wolves in the North Fork are well behaved. There have been no wolf depredations in the North Fork on livestock although the numbers of wolves have increased in the last ten years.

I'd like to mention that I hunt. Every year I've gotten a deer during hunting season except the year before last when I missed a shot. There is plenty of game in the North Fork for hunters. I have never seen as many white-tail deer as I have this year despite the number of wolves.

I have owned goats, rabbits, chickens, horses, dogs and a cat in the North Fork. I have had horses for eight years. I have had a wolf in with my horses. My horses are *not* nervous around a wolf. A week ago from last Friday, my two horses were within several hundred yards from a wolf and they showed no fear. A friend (a biologist) saw a wolf chasing a deer through some cows in the North Fork while the wolf showed no interest in the cows. I have had no problem with wolves. Many people in this room have complained about the dangers of wolf depredations without having seen wolves or even having been around them. The paranoia around wolves is unwarranted. The hundred-year-old stories of wolf depredations are greatly exaggerated through the passage of time.

Wolves are going to enter Yellowstone National Park on their own or people are going to place them in Yellowstone. Wolves belong in Yellowstone and the sooner the better. Wolves are largely a non-problem as far as people and livestock are concerned. Let's worry about significant problems instead of wolves.

Because several people inaccurately referred to the endangered species status of the wolf, I need to clarify this issue. The Endangered Species Act applies to wildlife species on a regional or state-by-state basis. Since the wolf was once a native animal in Wyoming but was exterminated, it is legally considered an endangered species in the state. According to statistics published on the day of the hearing by USA Today, the estimated population of wild wolves in the lower forty-eight states, outside of Minnesota, is 117 to 124.

🐺 1995: "Wolf Hysteria: Reintroducing Wolves to the West," Ed Bangs

Ed Bangs is a wildlife biologist with the USFWS *stationed in Helena, Montana. In an earlier incarnation (the U.S. Biological Survey), his agency had been given the mission of exterminating the wolf in the lower forty-eight states. The passage of the Endangered Species Act gave the* USFWS *the primary responsibility for reestablishing wolf populations in former habitats. In most cases, it was the Biological Survey that exterminated the last of the wolves in those areas.*

In 1988, after working with wolves in Alaska for twelve years, Ed moved to Montana to become the USFWS *project leader for wolf recovery in the state. In 1991 he was asked to be the project leader for the Environmental Impact Statement for wolf reintroduction in Yellowstone National Park and central Idaho.*

Ed gave me a great deal of help while I was researching my first wolf book. As I got to know him, and as I attended public hearings on wolves—including the 1992 Helena hearing discussed in the previous selection—I was increasingly impressed with his ability to handle the extreme stress associated with the Yellowstone wolf EIS. *I asked him to write the following article on what it was like for a biologist to be thrown into an extremely controversial public policy arena and live to tell the tale.*

Wolves and their management have almost nothing to do with reality, which makes working on any wolf issue hard on biologists, who are trained as scientists and not as psychologists. There is a saying among some of us in times of stress: "It isn't the wolves—it's the loons."

"I hate the government stealing my money to do things like this—we ought to shoot all the wolves, then the government biologists!" As the man presented his reaction to the U.S. Fish and Wildlife Service's plan to reintroduce wolves to Yellowstone National Park and central Idaho, I thought back four years to an unfortunate event that occurred just after my arrival in Montana—I had had to shoot a wolf because of a capture-related infection. A vet had bandaged a trapping wound but gangrene had set in and I had to destroy him. He was part of a pack that had killed livestock in another part of Montana and the entire pack had been moved to Glacier National Park. I was still in the field monitoring the other members of the pack when the calls from "wolf lovers" to my family began: "Wish you would move the hell back to Alaska where murderers are tolerated!" No matter how we handled the wolves, it seemed we couldn't win.

In the course of my work, people often ask me how I personally feel about wolves. Wild animals and wild spaces define both my personal and my professional life and many of my fondest childhood memories involved the outdoors. I remember fishing in Wonder Lake at Mt. McKinley National Park (now called Denali) when I was fifteen years old. It was after midnight and both my parents were asleep. The howl of a lone wolf echoed across the lake. Seconds later it was joined by two or three others. I quickly fished my way back toward camp and went to bed. Even though it has been nearly thirty years, I can still vividly hear that sound. Today, I appreciate wolves in the wild in the same way as I appreciate other wildlife. To me, all wildlife species are equally important.

Sometimes I don't like wolves. It was 1:00 A.M. in the summer of 1990 when the phone rang. Shirley Hager was very upset. She was crying and talking about a wolf killing her dog, Bear. She had held her dog one last time and his blood was still on her hands. She and her family had just pulled up to their front yard after a late dinner at friends. A wolf had Bear, their thirteen-and-a-half-year-old chow/shepherd mix, by the throat and was dragging him across the driveway. Bear, who had recently had a stroke had been spending most of his time on the front porch. It was much worse than just that as Bear, for reasons I won't discuss, had been a living memorial within her family. On the other end of the phone Shirley was now worried about the safety of her husband and son as they recovered Bear's body. As I tried to reassure her that humans are in no danger from wolves, I could clearly hear the pack howling in the background. My words suddenly seemed hollow. I couldn't go back to sleep for quite awhile. I knew Shirley to be a decent and kind woman who had liked having wolves living nearby. She certainly did not deserve such pain. An empathic USFWS biologist, Mike Jimenez, appeared at first light and helped bury her dog, now wrapped in a blanket.

Other times I like wolves. In 1990, a male and female wolf were raising their six pups and minding their own business when someone (trying to "solve" things with a gun) illegally killed the female, leaving the male and pups on their own. I was walking along an old logging road with a couple of the wolves' young neighbors—a boy about twelve and his young uncle. We were trying to locate the rendezvous site to see if the pups needed any help when we spotted fresh wolf tracks on the road near a small spring. I stopped and howled. Not fifty yards in front of us the grass moved. Black plump furballs scurried away and began barking, their mini-howls—"D-a-a-a-d-d-d!" About seventy-five yards away, the brush snapped and charging toward the pups came the male, howling deeply, then barking. I only hoped I could be that kind of father for my children. I will never forget the look on the faces of those young men. Only if you have heard wild wolves howl can you ever begin to understand the pure exhilaration I saw. We quickly left the area so as not to disturb the family further, but we were almost giddy with excitement as we returned to for a session of milk, cookies, and story sharing with the younger boy's parents. Two months later this male wolf killed Bear.

I started working with wolves in 1976 as a USFWS biologist on the Kenai National Wildlife Refuge in Alaska. I was younger then and had lots of fun trapping wolves and darting them from helicopters for radio-telemetry studies. I also accidentally killed wolves in the process and felt badly about screwing up. On the other hand I would have been prepared to shoot wolves with bullets instead of darts if that had been the only way to resolve a specific problem, such as depredation on domestic animals. While I enjoyed seeing and hearing wild wolves in Alaska and Montana and I liked working on wildlife management issues that involved predator/prey interactions, I prefer projects that involve controversy and people. Wolves, with their high profile and ability to raise conflicting emotions in people, give me the opportunity to do work that is personally challenging—sometimes too much so. But wolves are about us, not about me.

Our past is woven into our future, and so it is with wolves. Ecologically speaking, wolves are important. But what were "brothers in the hunt" to Native Americans became "creatures of wanton destruction" to early settlers. I believe it is because wolves and people are so alike in social structure and behavior (both packs and tribes have strong family ties and defend territories) that we place such high expectations on wolves and feel such deep emotional ties to them. We expect wolves to live up to our image of them, either good or evil, and because they are just wolves and do wolf things, they usually disappoint us. We take our frustrations out in many ways—usually on the wolves or anything near them—sometimes acting inhumanely. So it has been with people and wolves since Columbus stepped ashore.

Regret appears to be solely a human burden. Just as no elk has ever wished it had caught a rifle slug in its chest rather than die from wolf bites, I doubt if any wolf's last thoughts have ever been: "I would rather have been killed by a neighboring pack or a swift kick from a moose than a poison bait or airplane-delivered shotgun blast." Likewise, I suspect that a wolf is not all that embarrassed by being led around on a leash or by receiving a daily meal that isn't going to try and stomp it into the forest floor. Most aspects of wolf management have little to do with wolves or any feelings they may have, and everything to do with people and their hopes and fears. The process of developing a plan to restore wolf populations to the northern Rocky Mountains of the United States, therefore, is a story about people.

In the fall of 1991, the seventh in a long history of scientific groups was called in by Congress to wrestle with wolf-recovery issues. I was part of that group, and our job was to produce an environmental impact statement (EIS) on reintroducing gray wolves to Yellowstone National Park and central Idaho. The final act in the war on wolves had occurred about seventy-five years previously when Congress had directed federal biologists to exterminate all large predators from the West. The extirpation of wolves, which was completed by the 1930s, was the most successful part of that campaign.

Few seriously considered the wisdom of that act until about World War II, when a slowly growing chorus of wildlife biologists began to reflect openly on whether wolves might be needed in areas like Yellowstone National Park to restore some semblance of a naturally functioning ecosystem. In 1944, Aldo Leopold wrote: "Probably every reasonable ecologist will agree that some of them [areas with wolves] should lie in the larger national parks and wilderness areas: for instance, the Yellowstone and its adjacent national forests."

After the idea of wolf restoration was finally brought into the open, talk turned to action. In the 1960s, the state of Alaska and several Canadian provinces started wolf restoration programs. In 1973, Dr. Robert Ream from the University of Montana, began the Wolf Ecology Research Project, discovering and radio-collaring a wolf in 1979 who was living near the U.S./Canadian border. Then in 1986, a pack denned in Glacier National Park. In 1973 the Endangered Species Act (ESA) was passed and mandated "that all Federal departments and agencies shall seek to conserve endangered species and threatened species and shall utilize their authorities in furtherance of the purposes of this act".

In 1974 the USFWS formed one of the first endangered species recovery teams under the authority of the ESA. That team, led by the state of Montana, completed their recovery plan for the northern Rocky Mountain wolf in 1980. Shortly thereafter, the recovery team began work on a revised wolf plan. It was signed in 1987 and recommended an EIS on an experimental reintroduction of wolves into Yellowstone National Park and possibly central Idaho. Wolf recovery was defined as "a minimum of 10 breeding pairs in each of three recovery areas for a minimum of 3 successive years," a total of about three hundred wolves in the northern Rocky Mountains on the U.S. side of the border. By this time the human sides of the wolf recovery issue were firmly established, sharply polarized, and politically organized.

In 1988–90 Congress specifically prohibited funding for an EIS. Instead it directed the National Park Service and USFWS to answer basic questions about the potential impacts of wolves in the Yellowstone system. In 1990 Congress, again prohibiting an EIS, established a Wolf Management Committee (composed of federal, state, and special-interest group representatives) to develop a plan for wolf restoration in Yellowstone and central Idaho. That plan was not enacted. Finally, in late 1991, work finally began on an EIS began, but with a congressionally mandated short time frame—with the draft version due by May 13, 1993.

As some people are aware, the EIS process is legally defined, thorough, and tedious. Being appointed to an EIS team is often said to be a punishment for wildlife biologists who appear to enjoy their work too much. At the time Congress passed the EIS directive, I had been the USFWS project leader for wolf recovery in Montana for four years. When the USFWS regional director began a conference call about producing an EIS with the statement: "Ed said he wanted the EIS project leader job—or were you lying to us, Ed?" I almost felt the trap snap shut. My predicament was motivated by the most basic of sins—curiosity and ego. Like any drowning person, my first reaction, once I had agreed to be the project leader, was to start looking for others to cling to—and the interagency EIS team was formed.

The team comprised a core group of USFWS, National Park Service, Forest Service, Idaho Department of Fish and Game, and University of Montana representatives who would actually do the analysis and writing; a primary coordinating team of representatives from fish and game agencies in Wyoming and Montana, Animal Damage Control people, and members of the Wind River and Nez Perce tribes who would provide ideas and data, help with meetings, and review draft materials; and a larger team representing a wide variety of agencies that manage wolves throughout North America or might be affected by any decision about wolf recovery in Wyoming, Montana, or Idaho who would be kept apprised of the project and would formally review the draft EIS. In

402 / WAR AGAINST THE WOLF

addition, a specialized "skills" team provided legal, procedural, and technical advice, since legal challenges were almost certain. Fortunately, all members of the team had been involved with previous wolf recovery efforts. Most carried scars and none carried illusions of grandeur. The goal from the beginning was to simply produce a professional document.

It was obvious that the most productive thing the team could do was to provide the public with accurate information about wolves and the EIS process. After twenty years and many other plans (and dozens of mauled biologists), few of us believed that the EIS would be the final chapter in wolf restoration. We resolved, if nothing else, that everyone would be a little bit better informed when the EIS was completed. We hoped that any future public discussions of wolf recovery would then be more sane and less political than they had been before.

In early 1992 the EIS team was finally formed after I had negotiated my way through a maze of bureaucratic necessities such as internal planning documents, cooperative agreements, memoranda of understanding, funding transfers, federal register notices, and modifications in state law (Idaho law prohibited the Department of Fish and Game from any involvement with wolves, except their control, without special legislative permission). Carol Tenney, who provided administrative support, and I were the only full-time employees dedicated solely to the EIS team. In a process as uncertain and politically driven and with as short a time frame as this EIS, the fewer permanent employees involved, the lower the chance that good people would be left twisting in the wind.

The start of public involvement in the EIS process officially began in March, when a letter and poster were sent to about 2,500 groups and individuals already interested in wolf recovery, informing them of the EIS process. It was also announced in the news media and people were invited to place their names on the USFWS's mailing list. The rock had been kicked off the mountain, and there would be no rest for the wicked.

In April 1992 we produced a brochure to describe a little about wolf biology, the EIS process, and to solicit public comment on which issues (livestock losses, ecosystem completeness, etc.) needed to be addressed. A series of thirty-four open houses were planned for April. At these open houses, the public could watch a continuously playing ten-minute video of me describing the EIS process (the team referred to it as the "hostage video" because it was just a talking head staring into a camera—a scene reminiscent of Iranian footage from 1980), obtain brochures, look at posters and maps, and question team members. The meetings were designed to be informal and reduce the risk of any confrontation or violence and they were widely covered by the news media. Over 1,730 people attended and nearly 4,000 people gave us about thirty general issues they would like to see discussed. No meetings were seriously disrupted, there was only one bomb threat, and only one team member (Wayne Brewster from Yellowstone National Park) was threatened with being "shotgunned in the back." With nothing much more than follow-up letters to elected officials asking for the heads of those involved with "this stupid wolf thing," things were turning out better than I had hoped for.

The meetings, however, were hard on team members. Because we were on such a tight schedule, each of the three teams did a meeting a night. Towns out in the West can be a long ways apart. Laird Robinson (U.S. Forest Service) and Steve Fritts (USFWS) finished their meeting in Thermopolis, Wyoming, and had one in Missoula, Montana, the next day. They left Thermopolis in a snowstorm and at midnight were stopped on a maze of oilfield roads somewhere in northwestern Wyoming, (a supposed shortcut) hoping for a break in the clouds so they could catch a glimpse of the North Star to orientate themselves. At 4:00 A.M. they arrived at their motel in Bozeman, Montana, only to discover that their rooms were not theirs anymore. After refueling (gas, coffee, and donuts) they made it to Missoula by 7:30 A.M.

By June 1992 we had printed a report describing what the public had told us and had sent it to the nearly 16,000 people on our mailing list. In August, we produced a new brochure on wolf-management options and another hostage video. Several Congressmen and Senators had requested we also hold a new series of public hearings in addition to the twenty-seven open houses we had planned to hold in Wyoming, Montana, and Idaho. Our brochure discussed five ways that wolves might be dealt with, from managing for no wolves to managing primarily for wolves and invited public response on these options. This brochure would be handed to people attending the next set of hearings, and we also inserted it into a Sunday edition of the two largest newspapers in Montana, Wyoming, and Idaho, which between them had a circulation of about 250,000.

By August 3rd, when we began the new round of open houses and hearings, virtually no complaints about our brochure had been received. The April meetings had gone well but normally as a high profile EIS progresses, it becomes more controversial and the political tactics become nastier. In anticipation of this, we added a meeting facilitator (a person who knows how to calm things down) to each team to help run the meetings and to give team members more time to answer questions. My confidence was building—Big Mistake!

At my team's first meeting there were about twenty people in the audience. They had watched the video a couple of times and glanced over the brochure. I decided to move to the front of the room, turn off the video, and answer questions. I should have just stuck a pistol in my mouth. The first comment came from a stout Native American who said, "Why don't you just do it?" I hoped he was just quoting a Nike advertisement, but my stomach knotted as several cowboys leaned forward in disbelief. I choked out, "Well, not everyone thinks it is such a good idea," as I moseyed toward the side of the room. A cowboy then said, "You obviously don't raise stock." The cowboy and the Native American began a livelier discussion.

As the facilitator, Cory Thompkins of the U.S. Forest Service, wedged her way between them smiling, nodding, and saying, "This is good that you can discuss differences of opinion with each other," Carter Niemeyer and Reg Rothwell, my two traveling companions, and I moved closer. Carter is a U.S. Department of Agriculture animal damage control wolf management specialist who also just happens to be six foot five and weighs 260 pounds. Being team leader has some advantages and I got first pick of a "buddy."

The ending salvo came when the cowboy said, "I care about hunting and the elk, which you obviously must not." To which the Native American replied, "You guys killed off all the buffalo, wolves, and Indians to make room for your cattle. Why don't you leave the elk alone and eat your damn cows. . . . When there were wolves and buffalo they [Native Americans] could make it rain, man!" As the man turned to walk out the door, the cowboy said, "What's your name? I think I know you.". Turns out the two men were cousins who hadn't seen each other since they were in their teens. I relaxed as they acted embarrassed and shook hands. Just then a heavyset bearded man in red suspenders with a *big* revolver in his waistband walked through the door. Cory, Carter, Reg, and I resembled deer caught in the headlights. He stared in at the complete silence for a second and then sauntered into the adjoining bar. I didn't stand up front anymore.

The next day we were driving toward the next town, listening to the local radio station. The night before a young reporter, with parts of questions on scraps of paper, had interviewed me on tape. The on-the-air question now being read live by the announcer was "Will wolves kill excessive numbers of deer and elk?" The tape clicked and my casual response was, "Absolutely, we are planning on it. That's what wolves do for a living." We all howled with laughter. Actually, I had been asked "Will wolves eat deer and elk?" I would like to believe it was just a simple mistake that the question I had responded to in person was not the one the radio audience heard. The lesson was clear. Get a thick skin and be prepared to be burned once in a while. News is a business and does its best, but almost any message can become garbled. Wolves will sell an otherwise nothing story, and resorting to them for hype does nothing to help the public distinguish myth from reality.

Fall 1992 was an election year, and hearings were held in several cities at the request of local congressmen and senators. Both sides were making a play for media attention. In Helena, we rented the civic center which could hold a thousand people. Luckily, the civic center didn't know what the meeting was for or they might not have let us in. We arranged for six police officers and two USFWS special agents to ensure public safety, and we had people at the entrances with bright yellow-and-black signs that read "OFFICIAL FEDERAL HEARING. No Alcohol. No Signs. No Weapons. No Animals." At a Wolf Management Committee meeting a year before, wolves had killed a steer two days before the hearing. Turnout and emotions were running high, prompting the local SWAT team to be put on alert. Nothing bad happened then, thank goodness, but the difference between a crowd and mob can be seconds. This time I wanted to be prepared.

Pro-wolfers had rented the park across the street from the civic center for a rally before our hearing. Famous people made statements, songs were sung, and a captive-born wolf made an appearance. The anti-wolf folks had had to rent the park down the street. They gave a couple of "the environmentalists are out to get you" speeches and then marched down to the civic center. After instructions from the hearing officer that demonstrations from the crowd would not be tolerated, the news cameras began rolling and the testimony began.

The first speaker, a congressman's aide, called for the crowd to stand and cheer for "No Wolves." Nearly half did and then quickly sat down. This prompted the next speaker to ask for a show of pro-wolf support and the other half of the audience briefly stood. After the second warning from the hearing officer, that was about it. The rest of the hearing was very polite and there were absolutely no problems. I felt a little foolish about having the police there, but I consoled myself with the thought that at least the emotional level seemed to be waning. About time, the issue had been going on for at least twenty years.

Attendance at the August open houses was very low, and the hearings were dominated by pro-wolf opinion. Nearly two thousand people attended meetings, and nearly five thousand provided wolf management alternatives they wanted considered. This new round of meetings appeared to have been successful, although holding the hearings, which we hadn't planned on, set our schedule back a month and cost us $40,000 we hadn't allowed for. In November, a report about what the public told us was mailed to the nearly thirty thousand people now on the mailing list.

In July of 1992 what appeared to be a black wolf was filmed in the middle of Yellowstone National Park feeding on a dead buffalo. Although we had considered the possibility that wolves would be found in the park before the EIS process was completed, we were still taken aback by the public reaction. The media screamed, "They're baaaacck!!" and the public on both sides of the issue questioned why are we still doing this EIS thing about reintroduction since the wolves seemed to be taking matters into their own hands. The scientifically correct response, and the one urged by the USFWS, was caution. The newcomer could either be a released captive wolf or a lone wolf who would soon disappear again. The media pictures totally overwhelmed words, however, and our response was interpreted by many as a classic bureaucratic delaying tactic.

Then, late that September, just outside the park's southern border, a man reportedly mistook a ninety-two pound black wolf for a coyote and shot it. He reported the shooting to authorities—and the public went nuts. He received both congratulations and harassing phone calls at home. He was also the butt of "slob hunter" jokes: "This is a picture of Mr.— with something he shot to find out what it was. It turned out to be a) his horse; b) a wolf; c) his hunting partner." The man was not prosecuted, and he ended up making thousands of dollars off a poster of him holding a rifle and wolf pelt, with the words: "The government says there are no wolves in Wyoming. Clinton won't raise your taxes. Elvis lives in Jackson Hole."

The USFWS tried to determine if it had been a wild wolf or not, which turned out to be nearly impossible. What distinguishes wild wolves from dogs is their behavior— they can live and reproduce in the wild. Dead captive wolves or wolf/dog hybrids and dead wild wolves act just the same—*dead*. Six months later the USFWS was faced with a

skull analysis that indicated possible doglike or captive animal characteristics, whereas the DNA analysis indicated that the wolf was likely a
recent descendant of the wolves in Montana. This episode taught me
not to expect more from scientific inquiry than it can deliver. My reaction to everyone was: "I have a recent update on the wolflike canid shot
near Yellowstone National Park this fall. It is still dead." Since then
monitoring has not located any wolf pack activity in either Idaho or
Yellowstone, but many of the pro-wolf public continued to ride a wave
of false hope.

The draft EIS was written between December and May 1993. From
public feedback we had received during the process, it was obvious
that there was a lot of inaccurate or misinterpreted information about
wolves out there. My favorite example was a young man who said: "You
really had to watch those captive wolves and wolf/dog hybrids around
people with any type of disability. . . . You know wolves, they can sense
when something is wrong, and then their instincts take over and they
attack trying to cull out the sick and weak." When some joked that this
theory explained why some western politicians are so fearful of wolves,
the hysterical laughter quickly brought an embarrassed grin to the man's
face and an end to that story.

To address the problem of misinformation, we published a Gray Wolf
EIS Planning Update Report in April to let everyone know where the
EIS process stood and, most importantly, to provide basic accurate information about wolves and their management. We mailed the report
to the nearly forty thousand people on our mailing list, which by now
represented people from all fifty states and over forty countries. To my
great surprise, we received virtually no flak about the content of that
report. Either we were making headway, no one was reading anything
we were writing, or everyone was just holding their fire so they could
really blast us later.

In July 1993, the draft EIS was released. The 408-page document was
mailed to hundreds of special interest groups and put in public libraries throughout Wyoming, Montana, and Idaho. The summary was
mailed to everyone on the mailing list (by now over 43,000) and was
inserted into the Sunday edition of the six largest newspapers in Montana, Idaho and Wyoming, with a combined circulation about 280,000.
The comment period, originally until October 15, was later extended
until November 26, 1993, at the request of several anti-wolf groups and
legislators. Overall reaction to the release seemed mild. Briefings in
Washington D.C. to bureaucrats, legislators, the media, and special

interest group representatives went well. Maybe there was a chance that this EIS was close to finalizing the issue of the wolves in Yellowstone, as a taxpayer I certainly hoped so. Since 1973, nearly $6 million had been spent in a stream of seemly endless studies and committees.

In August and September, sixteen public hearings were held. Four in each affected state and four elsewhere. To everyone's great surprise turnout was light and fairly reserved. Neither the pro- or anti-wolf groups made a concerted effort to rally the troops for the hearings, although they did urge their members to provide written comments. Between them over 160,200 people provided some form of comment on the draft EIS, primarily in the form of votes for or against, the largest public response ever received on a federal EIS.

Once the comment period on the draft EIS began and it worked its way toward being a final EIS, positioning for media attention by the variety of special interest group began in earnest. Those that feel they are "losing" start pulling out all the stops, which often entails crossing the fuzzy line between American hardball politics and unethical behavior. This is the stage of the EIS process, that I have the hardest time dealing with personally. Even when you know what's coming, biologists are still people and have the same aspirations and feelings as other humans (or so we tell each other). Being attacked on a personal and professional level and being held responsible for every tiny aspect of wolf recovery by both sides is very trying. As a consequence, the carcasses of "wolf" biologists and managers are littered throughout North America. Some become bitter, some lose perspective, some burn out, some end up alone, and others have to do something else. Professional Darwinism at the top of the food chain means very few thrive.

I had started working on the EIS with pain in my heart, so memories of it often bring a touch of sadness. In March 1992, four months after I was appointed to the EIS team, the kindest and most giving person I ever loved, and my biggest fan, my mother, died after a nearly year-long struggle with cancer. While in the short term the high workload associated with the EIS helped me deal with that battle and loss, it also provided an unhealthy escape from the natural grieving process. A person commenting on the draft EIS wrote, "Ed, love your mother and return the wolf to her arms." It was the most powerful message I received, and it fortified my resolve to do the best possible job I could.

Knowing what I know now, I don't know if I would do anything differently or if I would even do it over. Today I seriously doubt if it was personally "worth it." In early November 1993, while the draft EIS was still in review, my best friend for nearly twenty years unexpectedly told me she had fallen in love with someone from the health club where she worked and was leaving our marriage. I was devastated. I felt in my very soul an anguish such as only a loved and trusted friend can inflict. At the time, I believed it was beyond human endurance. I blamed myself for being too consumed with work, for traveling too much to notice the subtle changes in her behavior, for not letting her know often enough how honored I was to be her companion, for not showing that it was only the support and love of my family that made it possible for me to endure all the pressure, for not being able to recognize and fulfill her "new" needs. Despite my depression, loss of hope, sense of failure and helplessness, and horror, the EIS, the media, the public interest, and the politics went on—oblivious to real life or me.

When it gets really bad, you want to tell your detractors (at that point nearly everyone) about you as a person, about your personal experiences with wolves, about your love of the outdoors and about the sights you have seen, but then you "get real." The public's reactions to something as symbolic as wolves can't be solved by a single individual or by a single event. With that you double your resolve to do a professional job that you personally know is the best you can do. That way, when it is all said and done, you can hold your head up with pride, have few regrets, and get on with the really important things in life, in my case, my two young daughters, my remaining family, my friends, and sticking to my core values about honesty, empathy, and living a meaningful life. As my Great-Aunt Millie (now eighty-nine) told me, "Eddie, do all you can in your short time. Some day when you are old and feeble, all you will have left are your memories and family. You will make the final judgment of the worth of your life by them." The key to working on an EIS process on something as emotional as wolves is to act like a wolf—simply be yourself, fulfill your role in the scheme of things as best you can, and try to survive.

The final EIS recommended that, if naturally occurring wolf packs could not be located before October 1994, wolves from Canadian populations be reintroduced to both central Idaho and Yellowstone National Park as nonessential experimental populations under section 10(j) of the Endangered Species Act. Reintroduction would result in wolf population recovery within about eight years and the experimental designation would resolve nearly all the concerns of local residents about the potential effects of wolves on livestock, big game populations, land uses, economics, and federal government interference with local citizens. It was a moderate approach that was bound to upset everyone. Only time will tell if all this latest planning will actually result in real wolf populations having the opportunity to play out their natural role in the northern Rocky Mountain ecosystem.

When I am sixty-five, I plan to take my grandchildren to Yellowstone National Park. We will go out late at night under a full moon, and I will howl up a pack of wolves. Over a midnight snack, and perhaps a glass of fine red wine for Grandpa, I will tell my grandchildren about what it took to provide them with the opportunity for that experience, all the good people and friends that were involved, and all the funny and interesting stories that occurred before, during, and after my part had been played out. I'll also remind them how their bloodline had some small part in restoring the immortal relationship between predator and prey in this special place. I'll promise, God willing and if the creeks don't rise, to spend a similar night with their children. I hope that they will always remember that night with fondness and pride.

The final EIS *was released in May 1994. On June 15, 1994, Bruce Babbitt, the Secretary of Interior, approved the Yellowstone wolf reintroduction plan recommended in the* EIS. *The Yellowstone wolf plan, in its final version, included regulations that would allow a rancher to kill a wolf on his or her private property if it was caught in the act of attacking livestock. The death would have to be immediately reported and the subsequent investigation would have to find evidence verifying the need to kill the wolf.*

The Yellowstone wolf EIS, *headed by Ed Bangs, is a model of how well the political process can work in resolving a controversial issue such as wolf reintroduction. Every individual and group had numerous opportunities to express their opinions on the subject. Based on available research data and on the input of the public, Ed's team chose reintroduction as the best way to fulfill the legal mandate of the Endangered Species Act on wolf recovery. The details of their plan strike a rational balance between the need to reestablish the wolf and the concerns of local communities and residents.*

Ed Bangs asked that the payment for his article be donated to the American Lung Association.

1995: "Supply-Side Environmentalism and Wolf Recovery in the Northern Rockies," Hank Fischer

When the story of the successful return of the wolf to Yellowstone is written, historians will give a great amount of credit to Hank Fischer for helping to make wolf reintroduction acceptable to many groups and individuals who otherwise would have opposed the plan.

Since 1977 Hank has been the northern Rockies regional representative for Defenders of Wildlife. Based in Missoula, Montana, he has effectively reached out to ranchers and other groups that other environmental organizations traditionally ignore. One of his most innovative programs has been Defenders' Wolf Compensation Fund. In explaining the theory behind the program, Hank has said, "Our goal has been to shift any economic burden associated with wolf recovery away from the individual livestock producer and onto the willing shoulders of the millions of wolf supporters around the country." This refreshing attitude of cooperation has won over many former opponents to wolf recovery in the northern Rockies.

Back in the frontier days, entertainment consisted of placing a bear and a buffalo in the same arena and watching the ensuing fracas. We in the West occasionally engage in similar sport today, only instead of bears and bison, the combatants are environmentalists and ranchers. One of the favorite jousting topics for this spiritual, almost ritualized, warfare is wolf restoration. The only common ground ranchers and environmentalists seem to find is the dirt they fling at one another.

"We need wolves like we need another drought," say many ranchers, reinforcing many environmentalists' view that ranchers are selfish and hate wildlife. "Wolves should be restored and cows should be removed," say some wildlife activists, reaffirming the view of many ranchers that environmentalists are selfish and hate people. Meanwhile, the media are mesmerized by this spectacle of ranchers and environmentalists whacking and hacking away at one another — cowboy hats versus Patagonia jackets; new culture versus old. Newspapers and TV cameras are drawn to this tiresome conflict the way some people are drawn to car crashes.

But doesn't it seem like a country smart enough to send men to the moon should be able to figure out a way for wolves and humans to coexist? All it takes is a willingness to place the spiritual warfare aside and look at the real issues. Most would agree that the single strongest argument against wolf restoration is that it *might* cause economic hardship for livestock producers. While environmentalists can argue accurately that industry-wide livestock losses to wolves are only a fraction of 1 percent, they cannot deny that losses to individual producers will occur, and that in some cases they will be significant.

This is the backdrop Defenders of Wildlife faced in the mid-1980s, when wolves were recolonizing northwestern Montana and initial consideration was being given to reintroducing wolves to the Yellowstone National Park area and central Idaho. Did we really want to adopt the uninspired strategy of trying to convince livestock producers that their losses to wolves weren't really going to be *that* bad? I'd rather try and talk a prairie dog into climbing a tree.

The idea for a private wolf compensation program was suggested to Defenders in 1985 by the director of the National Park Service, William Mott. Defenders, with Mr. Mott's assistance, had arranged to bring the Science Museum of Minnesota's "Wolves and Humans" exhibit to Yellowstone Park that year. At a meeting prior to the opening of the exhibit, Mott told Defenders that the single most effective action a conservation organization could take to advance wolf recovery would be to create a program to compensate ranchers for verified livestock losses to wolves. He felt strongly that their argument about potential economic hardship was the only significant impediment to wolf restoration.

It took a dose of reality to understand the wisdom of Mr. Mott's advice. During the summer of 1987, Montana experienced its first wolf-caused livestock losses in nearly fifty years. Over a period of two months, three ranchers lost of total of ten sheep and five cows worth slightly more than $3,000. The reaction from livestock producers was extreme. What had been a popular and widely reported successful recovery effort in northwestern Montana quickly began to unravel.

The losses initiated a spiral of anti-wolf sentiment. Ranchers were not only angry that they couldn't control problem animals themselves, they were upset that they had to bear the costs of wolf recovery. Anti-wolf feelings were escalating rapidly. There was little doubt that negative attitudes would result in illegal wolf killing and a shoot-on-sight local mentality. What about law enforcement, you might ask. There aren't enough police in all of New York City to prevent wolf killing if that is what people decide they need to do.

Defenders watched this unfold with a helpless sensation; it was a no-win situation for everyone. The wolves killing the livestock were removed by government control agents, yet local ranchers were still not satisfied because they had lost money. If the existing level of polarization over wolf recovery continued, it was clear that wolves wouldn't have a chance. So we decided to take Mr. Mott's advice. Defenders contacted its members and supporters in Montana and asked them to pay for these livestock losses. We reasoned that if wolf supporters could assume some of the economic responsibility for wolf recovery, it might take some of the sting out of losing livestock. The response from our supporters was terrific—we raised the $3,000 in less than forty-eight hours. Once we paid the ranchers for their losses, media interest seemed to wane and the controversy dissipated.

This initial experience convinced us that wolf compensation was an essential part of any wolf recovery program. We realized that for such a program to be effective, it had to be seen as substantial, dependable, and long-lasting. Therefore, in 1990 Defenders announced that it would create a permanent $100,000 fund to compensate ranchers in the northern Rockies for all verified livestock losses to wolves.

The centerpiece of the campaign to create this compensation fund was a Yellowstone wolf poster created by Montana artist Monte Dolack. Entitled "Restoring the Wolf to Yellowstone National Park," it was Dolack's colorful vision how wolves might appear if reintroduced to Yellowstone. Defenders' Wolf Compensation Fund also received a substantial boost from a benefit concert given by recording artist James Taylor. Finally, donations from our members and supporters put us over the top. We reached our $100,000 goal in 1992.

Since 1987, Defenders has paid more than $15,000 to approximately fifteen different ranchers. On a case-by-case basis, Defenders has also assisted some ranchers in working with non-lethal predator prevention techniques, such as electric fencing and livestock guarding dogs. The program has proven very successful. Wolf recovery in northwestern Montana is no longer particularly controversial. In every circumstance where a livestock producer has lost livestock, the wolves have been controlled and the rancher has been compensated at market value. While illegal wolf kills have occurred, they haven't been significant enough to keep wolf populations from increasing steadily. As of 1994, it was estimated that five packs of wolves numbering approximately sixty-five individuals live in northwest Montana.

Here's how the Wolf Compensation Fund works. Defenders compensates livestock producers at market value for all verified livestock losses to wolves. Federal animal damage control experts have been primarily responsible for verification, although we accept reports from state and tribal officials or the U.S. Fish and Wildlife Service. These officials inform the producers they are eligible for compensation, and then report verified losses to Defenders. We then contact the livestock producer, get his estimate of the livestock's value, compare that to current market reports and local auction prices, and then send the producer a check. If there's a significant difference between our estimate of the livestock's value and the producer's, the local county extension agent makes the final determination. Defenders does not pay over $2,000 for an individual animal and does not compensate if producers have insurance policies or any other means of indemnification. If experts are unable to verify a loss, but have compelling evidence that wolves were responsible, we compensate producers at a rate of 50 percent.

The response to Defenders' wolf compensation program has been overwhelmingly positive. It has been featured in dozens of publications, including the *Smithsonian*. The *Wall Street Journal* called it "enterprising and imaginative"; the *Chicago Tribune* "innovative"; and the *Missoulian* "a responsible approach." According to U.S. Fish and Wildlife Service wolf biologist Ed Bangs, "This program should be a model for others who want positive solutions for complex environmental issues. The livestock compensation program certainly made wolves much more tolerable to livestock producers, the endangered species recovery issue more rational, and has made wolf recovery more easily attainable."

At the same time, there are detractors. Some are anti-wolf advocates who argue that the purpose of the program is to facilitate wolf recovery (they're right). Others are wildlife advocates who argue Defenders' compensation program is a subsidy to ranchers that places the burden of recovery on wolf advocates.

Defenders doesn't worry or care about whether or not the compensation program is a subsidy. We simply view that meeting the legitimate concerns of livestock producers is the most effective way to get what we want: wolf restoration.

To the charge of wanting to assume responsibility for wolf recovery, we plead guilty. We are convinced that the more we can shift economic responsibility for wolf recovery away from individual livestock producers and toward the millions of people who support wolf recovery, the more likely we are to succeed. When ranchers alone are forced to bear the costs of wolf recovery, the result is both ill will and dead wolves. Once wolf supporters assume economic responsibility for wolf recovery, opponents have no reason to say no.

In 1992, through Hank Fischer's leadership, Defenders established a wolf reward program that awards landowners $5,000 if a litter of wolf pups is successfully reared on their property. This "supply-side environmentalism" enables pro-wolf individuals to pay property owners to supply wolf habitat.

The brilliance of this program is that it transforms wolves into financial assets rather than liabilities for landowners. These innovative programs developed by Hank Fischer and Defenders of Wildlife demonstrate that conservation groups can provide effective, workable solutions to complex issues. To make a contribution to Defenders of Wildlife's wolf projects, write to: Defenders of Wildlife, 1244 19th Street NW, Washington, D.C. 20036.

🐺 1995: "The Story of Wolf 5105," Steve Fritts

Steve Fritts works out of the same USFWS office in Helena, Montana, as Ed Bangs. Involved in wolf research and management for over twenty-two years, Steve is the USFWS wolf recovery coordinator for the northwestern states. His primary responsibility is to facilitate wolf recovery in the states of Montana, Idaho, Washington, and in Yellowstone National Park. Like all of the other wolf biologists I have met over the years, Steve deeply admires the wolf. Despite that, he understands the necessity of killing or relocating individual wolves who have become proven livestock killers. He is convinced that for the good of wolf recovery programs, and for the good of wolves that avoid livestock, problem wolves have to be controlled.

While doing wolf research for his Ph.D. at the University of Minnesota, Steve became well acquainted with a female wolf known to him as 5105. Years later, when 5105 began killing domestic sheep, Steve had to deal with her. In the following article, he describes the emotions that a wolf biologist experiences when he must resolve a conflict created by a problem wolf.

I could hardly believe my eyes. Here we were again—face to face—like old friends and old nemeses at the same time. However, the setting and circumstances were so different. This time I was standing in the shaded street outside my apartment in Grand Rapids, Minnesota, peering into the end of a canvas-draped wire cage in the back of a government pickup truck assigned to wolf control technician Tom Meier. The truck made sharp popping sounds as the engine cooled from a 175-mile drive across northern Minnesota that hot July afternoon. Is it possible she remembered me? Although I am one of the first to denounce anthropomorphizing about wolves, I could not help but perceive a sense of guilt in those sad eyes that complemented her graying fur and added to an already dejected appearance. So much had changed since our paths last crossed, and my mind raced through the past few years and happier times in our unique relationship.

It had been almost four years since I had personally laid eyes on this wolf, and five since she last had the opportunity to view me close up. By all rights, she should have been dead by now. The last time I saw her was from the cramped rear seat of a circling Piper Supercub as my feet froze, despite wool socks and Sorrel boots, and my headphones blared out the steady beep-beep-beep signal from her radio collar. I was in the final days of field work in a four-year graduate study of wolf ecology in northwestern Minnesota, a place where the forests and bogs begin to intermingle with the fields and pastures of the flat agricultural region of the state. Lake-of-the-Woods dominated the far horizon to the north.

It wasn't a particularly beautiful area, but I had grown to love it anyway. There were lots of old grown-over homesteads left from the early part of the century when the government had promoted an ill-fated land boom there. Wolves had never been studied in the area before. For several decades few wolves had managed to survive there, despite an abundance of white-tailed deer. The Endangered Species Act of 1973 changed all that, and my study was able to document a fairly rapid increase in the local wolf population, as well as provide some new information on how young wolves explore new areas and start new packs. The life story of 5105 was a major piece of information that went into my Ph.D. dissertation at the University of Minnesota's Department of Ecology and Behavioral Biology.

Wolf 5105 was one of the few wolves I had followed for the entire study. She had been one of about five pups born to the Clear River Pack in 1972. Renowned wolf trapper Bob Himes had captured her 105-pound father and three of her littermates for me in August of 1972 as my study got underway. We knew from watching the Clear River Pack from the air that her mother was a white wolf (the white color phase was quite rare in Minnesota). I first captured 5105 in July 1973, estimated her to be a yearling, and fitted her with a radio collar. She was the first wolf that I had personally trapped in that area. The ear tags that I placed in her left and right ears were numbered B5105 and B5106. My wife, Diana, who was along for the capture, developed an instant fondness for her and named her Rhoda. (Diana gave all the study wolves a name, although I stubbornly insisted on referring to them by the number inscribed on their eartags.) In future research my colleagues and I would locate this female over two hundred times and observe her from a circling airplane on more than eighty occasions. The very first time I saw her from an aircraft she was playing with at least three pups at the Clear River Pack's rendezvous site, while the white mother of the pups rested and looked on from nearby.

Like many yearlings in that newly protected and increasing population, 5105 did not stay with her pack. The maturing wolves seemed to realize that there was plenty of unused space and food available to start their own packs. She dispersed from the Clear River Pack's territory in October 1973 and checked out an area of mixed spruce, jackpine, aspen, and marsh that was immediately to the southwest of the territory where she grew up—and also at the very edge of farmland. It took only two weeks for her to join up with a radio-collared adult male wolf (No. 5051) who had left a pack elsewhere in the forest. Diana named that wolf "Hector."

We came to think of Hector as the Casanova of the study area, but that's another story. Warden-pilot John Parker and I, with the help of local biologists Phil Watt and Bill Berg, watched 5105 and 5051 several times during the winter of 1973–74 through the window of the state's Cessna 180. One cold March morning my study of 5105 almost came to an untimely end when the plane's motor sputtered and died as we were flying toward her signal. Fortunately, John was able to get the engine going again before our glide ended in a thick stand of jackpines.

Although 5105 remained in that same 110-square mile area for over two years, that particular male separated from her and became part of another pack. Number 5105 was joined by another male prior to February 1974, but the pair produced no pups that year. Whether she gave birth to pups in 1975 was quite a mystery. She dug a den under a pile of old boards and later frequented three locations that could have been rendezvous sites. Howls were induced from what seemed to be a pup at one of those locations, but no pups were ever observed and I was certain that none survived into autumn.

The female had to be recaptured for replacement of her faulty radio collar in June 1975, which tested my trapping skills to the maximum. After being initially trapped, most wolves get much harder to catch the second and third times. It took several weeks for her to step into one of my traps set along the sandy roads and trails in her territory, and that happened only after tracks indicated she had carefully detoured around several of them. On one occasion, it was clear she scooted to a quick stop about five feet from a trap buried in the center of an old logging road. She then bypassed it on the extreme edge of the road before getting back into the wheel rut after a distance of several yards.

The fresh radio collar allowed us to resume tracking her and to learn that her second mate disappeared in November 1975 during the deer hunting season, when there were a high number of hunters in their area. I was amazed that she survived. When flying above the forest, we were astounded at all the blaze orange below us in this wolf's territory. It was not unusual to see a hunter within a hundred yards of her location without his or her being aware of the wolf's presence. During the winter of 1975–76 it appeared 5105 was forced to move westward by two large packs just to her east, as both were found deep within her territory at about the same time her mate disappeared. (One of these was her former pack with her sister as its alpha female; the other had her former male associate 5051 as its alpha male).

Almost immediately, 5105 began drifting west, which brought her outside the Beltrami Island State Forest and into a mixture of forest and farmland. While gradually settling into that area, she seemed to have a two-month relationship with another wolf before finding a mate near the 1976 breeding season. That summer she, at the age of four, and her dark-colored mate, raised seven pups in a mosaic of woods, brush, and farms. That was the first year that I was certain she had produced pups, and by this time her count of possible male companions was up to four (so much for monogamy in wild wolves). In December 1976 I reluctantly left this old friend behind forever—or so I thought—realizing I owed her a great deal for all the data she had provided. As our plane broke out of what I knew was its final pass over this wolf and sped off to find others, I mumbled a brief lecture to her to stay away from livestock.

Fond memories of individual wolves and carefree days of field work faded into long months of number crunching and writing. After completing my Ph.D. thesis (*Dynamics, Movements and Feeding Ecology of a Newly-Protected Wolf Population in Northwestern Minnesota*), I was hired on by the U.S. Fish and Wildlife Service in 1979 to conduct its new program for controlling wolves that preyed on livestock in Minnesota. In addition, my assistant Bill Paul and I were assigned the task of monitoring wolf populations in western portions of the state.

I felt relieved to have a real job. Although I had spent all those years working on a Ph.D. on wolves, I had by no means been sure that gainful employment was at the end of the tunnel, especially work directly involving my favorite animal species. I must admit to having some apprehension about working on the depredation control program. Dealing with angry farmers while environmentalists looked over our shoulders would be no bed of roses. Having to kill wolves that kill livestock was something I knew I could handle, but not something I would enjoy. I was realistic enough to know that the control of individual problem wolves had a valid and necessary place in the well-being of the species as a whole, and with more wolves in Minnesota there would be more depredation and more problem wolves to deal with.

The control program in Minnesota had recently undergone several lawsuits and hardly anyone seemed happy with it. When the wolf was placed on the federal list of endangered species in 1973 it was not legal to kill problem animals, so federal control personnel relocated them to remote areas of the state. Some of those wolves returned to their place of capture and caused additional problems or got into trouble elsewhere. That situation changed in 1978 when wolves were downlisted to "threatened" in Minnesota, allowing wolves that killed livestock to be euthanized by the U.S. Fish and Wildlife Service.

At that time, another point of contention with controlling problem wolves was how much documentation of a depredation was needed before a wolf would be captured and euthanized. Our new program, under the direction of Dave Mech, took the view that some remains of the livestock carcass would have to be seen by our personnel, there would have to be hard evidence that wolves were the cause of death or injury (for example, tracks or other wolf sign near the kill site), and there would have to be the potential for further losses. Our goal was to control wolves only in the event of proven depredations and to take the minimum number of wolves necessary to solve depredation problems. Moreover, we would try to solve problems with non-lethal methods as much as possible. Such methods include scare devices, taste aversion conditioning, and improved livestock husbandry.

It turned out that only about half the reports we received of wolf depredations turned out to be the real thing. On-site detective work often failed to turn up a piece of the alleged animal killed, or determined that death was from disease, accident, or some other predator, for instance, coyotes, dogs, or black bears. One example of an alleged wolf depredation on a milk cow comes to mind. The farmer had found his cow fairly well decomposed but with skeleton and skin mostly intact, lying in a ditch a few hundred yards from the farmhouse. Technicians Tom Meir and John Burch had trapped two wolves at the farm a month earlier. There were a few tears in the skin, which were interpreted by the farmer to be slash marks made by wolves. When Tom and John investigated the alleged depredation, they lifted the dried hide off the skeleton and found all four of the cow's legs stuck straight down in mud. The cow had become mired in mud to the point where she could not escape and died there, likely of dehydration, without any predator being involved. Of course, we investigated many other reported wolf depredations where a wounded or partly consumed carcass was found and abundant evidence of wolves at the site indicated their guilt.

By now, you may have figured out the awful predicament that this wolf and I were in. In summer of 1980, at age eight, wolf number 5105 was preying on domestic sheep. She and her pack killed lambs that summer and may have killed others the previous summer. Our investigation of the kill sites left no reasonable doubt. Why did she do it? I don't know. Certainly, being forced into an agricultural area by other wolves may have been a factor, but I knew of other wolves that had lived next to livestock for years without killing them. Strange as it sounds, it seems that most wolves do not immediately recognize livestock as prey.

I've speculated that wolves form a search image for the prey they grow up eating (mostly deer in Minnesota), and they have to learn to prey on anything that doesn't fit this image. I found it interesting that wolf 5105 apparently had lived at her new location for three to four years without killing sheep or other livestock. Maybe she got her start by feeding on dead sheep, thereby learning that sheep were food. Availability of natural prey did not seem to be a factor. When we were locating her from the air, there were times when we saw as many as eighty deer near her. Our personnel spent a total of fifty-two days trapping near her depredation site in summer 1980, but we didn't know until we caught 5105 that she was still alive or that her pack (we called it the Thief Lake Pack after a lake nearby) was the cause of the current sheep losses.

The overall problem of wolves killing livestock was slowly increasing in Minnesota, although it took several additional years to be sure of that trend. The wolf population was increasing and beginning to fill in areas of habitat that had not seen wolf packs for over half a century. Wolf 5105 and the Thief Lake Pack were but one example of that trend. Then, as now, a small percentage of farmers in the wolf range (less than 1 percent) suffer depredations from wolves. Although that percentage is extremely low, individual farmers may have to put up with substantial losses within a given year. Wolves that started killing sheep seemed particularly prone to repeat the action and sometimes killed several in a short period, a behavior known as "surplus killing." Experience had taught us that killing the problem wolf was the best solution.

Half a decade earlier, as I had watched this wolf move her home range to the agricultural fringe, I had wondered what the future held in store for her. As I stared into the eyes of this old acquaintance, a complex mixture of feelings welled up inside me. I felt a sense of indebtedness to her for the data she had provided me. There was sorrow for her if her livestock killing spree had in any way come about because she could not find enough wild prey to support her young. There was a touch of anger that she had done this thing and put the two of us in this predicament. There was admiration and respect for her, perhaps akin to the feelings that old-time government trappers had toward the famous outlaw wolves they were assigned to track down and kill. And there was regret—intense feelings of regret—and pity. If only she hadn't. . . . If only we could have. . . . Although there was never any real doubt that I would carry out 5105's inevitable fate, doing so was one of the most unpleasant tasks I have had in some twenty years of working with wolves. Her life ended in a lab at the edge of town later that same day by my own hands, but with as little pain to her as possible.

The loss of wolf 5105 would not have any lasting impact on the local wolf population. At the age of eight, she was an old wolf by the standards of the wild. She certainly had lived a full life and done her share toward wolf recovery in that part of Minnesota. I suspect she had produced five litters of pups. Wild animals seldom die peaceful deaths, so hers must have been relatively easy. Despite knowing all that and being able to rationalize her end, I still felt a deep sadness about her for a long, long time.

Experiences such as this bring into sharp focus the fact that wildlife researchers and managers have feelings for their subjects that sometimes make their jobs exceedingly difficult. Doing what must be done can be very painful, yet it still has to be done. The role of wolf controller is never easy for those of us who admire the species so much. Maybe this ordeal would have been easier had I disliked wolves. Every once in a while a wolf comes along that affects you for as long as you live. For me that happened with Rhoda.

1992: "Lonesome Lobo," Charles Bowden

The native wolf of the Southwest, known as lobo or the Mexican wolf, once lived in Texas, New Mexico, Arizona, and Mexico. Not a true desert-adapted species, the Mexican wolf preferred habitats above 4,500 feet in elevation, areas where cooler temperatures and increased rainfall enabled prey populations to reach higher densities than in nearby deserts. This subspecies of the gray wolf may now be extinct in the wild.

Charles Bowden, a freelance writer based in Tucson, wrote a 1992 article on Mexican wolves for Wildlife Conservation *that sums up the wolf situation in Arizona and discusses the possibility of reintroducing wolves in Arizona and New Mexico.*

The wolves are parked like idle hunting dogs in a cyclone-fenced run at the Arizona-Sonora Desert Museum in Tucson. They get about 15,000 square feet of the Southwest; we get the rest.

Sixteen years ago, the Mexican gray wolf was placed on the U.S. endangered species list. Fourteen years ago, seven wolves were captured in Mexico for a breeding and release program in the United States. Ten years ago, the U.S. Fish and Wildlife Service (USFWS), to fulfill the requirements of the Endangered Species Act, produced a reintroduction plan. But a fight over where the wolf release should take place, or if it should take place at all, has dragged on and on and now involves three states (Arizona, New Mexico and Texas), a fistful of state and federal wildlife agencies, pro-wolf coalitions, and anti-wolf ranchers' and cattlemen's associations, and has generated bushels of papers with analyses, charges and countercharges.

In Mexico, perhaps 10 Mexican wolves live in zoos and 60 (maybe more, maybe fewer) survive in the Sierra Madre. In the United States, none run free. There are 29 wolves in captivity in seven U.S. facilities all descended from four of the original seven animals. Breeding the wolves for release under the 1982 plan proved to be embarrassingly easy. Within a year, breeding had to be halted for lack of space, and since then, the program has lurched from active to shut down to active again. "From a biological point of view," says Peter Siminski, curator of mammals at the Arizona-Sonora Desert Museum and a participant in the captive-breeding program, "the breeding program is very orderly. But from a human point of view, it is very political." Siminski confesses he does not understand the world of politics. He is not alone.

Siminski is disturbed by descriptions in the press that compare the canids' behavior in bondage to what they might do if they were free. "In captivity," he explains, "you can go in a pen with any wolves, for the most part, and they just curl up and lie there. They know when they've been had."

I go up on the roof of an adjacent building to watch the museum's breeding pair without disturbing them. They are both sitting on the ground, staring out through the cyclone fence. Their enclosure is largely barren; the last litter of pups devastated the landscape. The adults remain motionless by a large doghouse, which they do not use except for occasionally sitting on the roof. The female is in heat and with luck she will conceive. The male sits right behind her. In stir, they get a pound and a half to two pounds of dog chow a day. They see very few humans, are allowed no visitors. How long they will emain here is anyone's guess.

Four Arizona sites are being assessed for the release; the most likely candidate at the moment is the White Sands Missile Range in New Mexico—the same place chosen for testing the atom bomb. White Sands encompasses an isolated mountain range surrounded by hard desert that wolves will not like to cross, missile-impact zones that wolves will not like to camp on, gunnery ranges that wolves may find a bit noisy. Because of the activity on the base, there are no cattle on its 3,152 square miles There also is no evidence the wolves ever used the White Sands region historically.

There are 40 million acres of federal land in New Mexico and Arizona alone. Though the American pblic is entranced with rhetoric about the wild and woolly West, apparently the 996 square miles of habitat deemed suitable for 30 to 40 wolves in White Sands is all that can be spared for carnivores whose ancestors roamed North America when the first humans arrived. The missile range may be the best deal we are willing to offer the Mexican wolf as it dodges both cages and extinction.

We don't know much about the Mexican gray wolf, *Canis lupus baileyi*, the smallest and southern-most subspecies of the North American gray wolf. (There were once 24 subspecies, five in the Southwest.) In 1988, James Bednarz, a University of New Mexico biologist, studied the Mexican wolf under the auspices of the USFWS, and glumly concluded, "Data dealing with the behavior, ecology, and other aspects of the biology f the Mexican wolf essentially do not exist."

We killed them all before we had a chance to observe them. Early settlers shot them on sight and dug up dens and killed the young. The Forest Service slaughtered them for the benefit of its clients—ranchers. The final campaign was run by the Predator and Rodent Control section (PARC) of the U.S. Biological Survey, the ancestor of today's Fish and Wildlife Service. Funded by Congress in 1914, PARC obliterated the breeding populations of the Mexican wolf in Arizona, New

Mexico, and west Texas by 1926. It was not a terribly big job; in 60 years, PARC bagged only 600 wolves in the region (the agency killed 24,000 gray wolves in Montana, Wyoming and Colorado).

Estimates of the original Mexican wolf population vary from 600 for the species' entire range to anywhere from 300 to possibly 1,500 in New Mexico alone. The area lacks large herbivores such as elk and caribou, which could sustain big packs, and in many places is too arid or rugged to be good wolf habitat. After 1926, the only wolves in the Southwest were lone lobos that drifted up from Mexico, and for decades, PARC diligently guarded the border with various traps and poisons. In recent years, as Mexico has exploited the Sierra Madre, even this seed stock of wolves has nearly vanished. The only bright spot, according to trapper Roy McBride and Mexican ecologist Julio Carrera, may be the current boom in growing marijuana, which is more profitable than raising cattle. Marijuana fields are well guarded and could be inadvertently providing sanctuary for the few remaining wolves.

The men who killed the Mexican wolf kept records; and from this strange set of documents, mined by the Arizona biologist David E. Brown for his 1983 book, *The Wolf in the Southwest: The Making of an Endangered Species,* we can glimpse the animal. True, the PARC records are a bit like a history of the Jews as Hitler might have written it. But still, reading this record is worthwhile.

The obvious observation is that there was never any effort to control or manage the wolf. From the beginning, it was a genocidal campaign — the final solution. The founder of PARC, J. Stokely Ligon, headed the campaign. But he was also among the first to point out the devastating effects on wildlife of overgrazing by cattle. His colleague in the Forest Service, Aldo Leopold, cheered Ligon on. At that time, conservationists, who were responsible for saving much of the wildlife of the West, drew the line at the wolf, the grizzly, and the mountain lion. (Years later, Leopold changed his mind about the relationship of man to the land and today is regarded as one of the first American environmentalists.)

With a budget of $100,000 and some 30 hunters, PARC killed 359 wolves in the first year. Officials justified the killings by citing estimates of the enormous sums of money saved by preventing cattle losses — figures no one questioned then or, for that matter, until very recently. According to government records, the last wolf in Arizona was killed in 1960, the last one in Texas in 1970, and the last one in New Mexico in

1976.

A second observation can be made from the PARC records In the early part of the century, wildlife populations in the Southwest were, thanks to the lusty appetites of settlers, at their lowest known ebb. The region was being raped by livestock and doubtless any wolf not committed to vegetarianism was taking some calves and sheep. There were not many choices left. According to PARC records, stomach analyses of 41 dead wolves showed that about 45 percent contained livestock remains (the stomachs of almost all the rest were empty). PARC itself doubted the accuracy of these numbers because, according to a 1918 Ligon report, "many trappers fail entirely to report stomach contents, while others are careless, and records that are made by them have little value." Also, the trappers focused on stock-killing wolves—assuring a kind of self-fulfilling prophecy. Whatever the flaws, these numbers are now regularly put forth by stockmen's groups as proof of the economic threat posed by wolf's introductions.

Against these numbers we have more-recent figures on wolves vs. livestock in British Columbia Alberta, and Minnesota, where the canids' appetite for beef seems greatly diminished Alberta, with 5,000 wolves, averages about one stock killing er year for every 93 wolves. British Columbia has 6,300 wolves and estimates livestock losses at about $60,000 per year. In a scat study in Minnesota—with a population of 1,200 wolves—3 percent contained evidence of livestock. Apparently, wolves prefer traditional prey, such as deer, rodents, and hares, to new-fangled dishes like livestock. None of this, however, may influence the wrangling over reintroduction of the Mexican wolf, a debate in which questionable data from 70 years ago collected by a hit squad still seem to hold center stage.

The final thing to be recognized from the PARC records is our deep-rooted feelings about wolves. The PARC extermination program went on for years after cattle losses had ceased and after breeding populations of wolves had been wiped out. And until quite recently, say the past 10 years, very few humans disagreed with this agenda. You never hear scary stories about people being transformed into spotted owls or snail darters, but tales of werewolves make great copy. Centuries of folklore have kept the wolf a slavering beast at our door.

What wolves actually were like in the Southwest can be surmised only from observations of other North American gray wolves: probably 60 to 90 pounds in weight, living as mated pairs or in small family groups of four to six, dining lagely on deer and rabbits, inhabiting forested high ground where the terrain was not too broken (wolves need fairly easy slopes to chase down their prey). The pre-settlement Southwest was a world in which coyotes dominated the lower deserts, wolves took the transition zones of oak and pine, and mountain lion clung to the ragged peaks. Wolves were most likely nocturnal, shy, and secretive, their presence revealed more by their periodic howling than anything else. From all we can gather from living wild wolves, humans scared them to death. North America is noticeably scant in authentic records of wolves attacking people. And there were probably never very many Mexican wolves anyway.

Small family ranches are almost as endangered in the Southwest as the wolf, though they persist without a captive-breeding program. The ranchers, too, are predators—top predators—and what they have seized is most of the land. Their ancestors literally helped wipe out the wolf and the grizzly and they do not welcome them back. I once interviewed a rancher who had a pedigree in his canyon five generations deep. He told me two things. He had been in on the kills of 249 mountain lions and was keen for number 250; and he couldn't abide the thought of living in an Arizona bereft of lions. He also said, with almost a tip of his hat, that he believed that lions kill only the very finest bucks (an enduring fantasy about the skills of predators). In short, he saw the lion as a peer.

The wolf arouses deeper feeling, I suspect. The wolf may not be a peer; rather, it may be a superior out there howling mockery in the night.

An Arizona game ranger helped put the matter of the ranchers' power in perspective. I asked him how such a tiny group could, with waning economic power, have such clout. He smiled and told me I did not understand. At night, he said, "The ranchers are like the Viet Cong—they own the countryside, they are out there."

Any wolf reintroduction that ignores ranchers faces a lot of dead animals, a common problem in some other wildlife releases. In a letter to the Fish and Wildlife Service, Wayne D. Klump of Bowie, Arizona, captured the hard feelings of many cowmen: "The intent of the government and the Bureau of Land Management is to manage, control, steal, acquire, and take our private property. . . . This is to serve notice on the government or anyone that might turn loose or plant any animal or predator within a 500-mile radius of Bowie, Arizona, that they are responsible and liable for any and all damages that said animal or predator might do."

Phil Harvey, of New Mexico, is a calmer voice in the wolf reintroduction debate but just as dedicated to stopping the idea. He is a member of the third generation to operate the family's 33-section ranch (one section equals one square mile)—a small operation by regional standards—and the ranch is 95 percent patented rather than leased public land. (Patented land is land that has been deeded to the owner, for eternity, by the federal government.) His ranch abuts Holloman Air Force Base, which borders the proposed White Sands Missile Range release area. Harvey is puzzled why the federal government, after decades of exterminating predators, now wants to return them to the land. And he is skeptical that, once released, the wolves will stay put. "It's ridiculous," he says, "to want to put them out there, because they're not going to stay. They're going to go into the Gila River, the Sacramento Mountains, and so forth. They're going to go where the livestock is plentiful." He argues that any wolf knows cows are a better deal than "chasing skinny old deer for miles."

Harvey is skeptical as well of compensation plans for rancher losses. Kill verification is difficult on huge ranges where ranchers don't see their stock for days or weeks at a time and other predators and scavengers can muddy the facts about what originally killed an anmal. Besides, he thinks the compensation funds will run out, as they once did in Minnesota. He cites the federal animal-control studies of the early 1900s, those dubious stomach analyses of the wolves that revealed the remains of lots of sheep and cattle.

Deep down, Harvey harbors the anger that a man who lives on the land holds for the notions of people who live in cities. The wolf proponents have "an emotional, esthetic reason for reintroduction. They want the satisfaction of knowing if they go out they might hear a wolf howl. And there's no question these wolves are ferocious carnivores. Wolf advocates go to the schools and show how soft and cuddly these wolves are." This he cannot abide. His father fought the wolf, his grandfather fought the wolf, and "wolves are about 10 times worse than coyotes." A federal study estimates the worst livestock loss resultig from the White Sands release at one cow and two sheep per year, but this does not sway Harvey. It is his ox that may be gored.

His assertions cannot be completely denied. The friends of the wolf tend to live far from the animals' former haunts. There would be no need for wolf coalitions if these creatures *were* soft and cuddly. It isthe very aura of wildness and ferocity and independence that has pitted people against the wolf since Aesop spun his fables.

Harvey is a serious breeder of registered Herefords, and beyond the possibility of economic loss—one cow can cost $2,000 to $10,000, a decent bull $10,000 to $20,000—there is the matter of creativity. For Harvey, a fine calf is the result of generations of breeding, a work of art he has created through wit and luck and lots of effort. A perfect meat machine. To go out one morning and find it torn to shreds is like "losing one of your kids." His passion for maintaining genetic potential is similar to the passion one hears in the voices of the various biologists dedicated to maintaining the genetic purity of the Mexican wolf in captivity.

For Harvey, wolves are not endangered. He has seen them in zoos and that is where they should stay. Family ranchers are, on the other hand, almost extinct, and he believes the wolf may be the straw that breaks their backs. For wolf advocates, Harvey is a serious opponent; articulate, in command of his facts, willing to debate, and with a vested interest in the result. He sees the wolf for what it may actually be, a potential competitor for the surface of the Earth. And he will fight for his ground, as possibly the wolf once did against interloping mountain lions and coyotes.

David Parsons is Mexican Wolf Recovery Coordinator for the Fish and Wildlife Service. He has a small one-windowed cell in the downtown Albuquerque federal building facing the parking lot. On the wall are two charts that capture the current world of the Mexican wolf. One is a procedural flow chart. Neat lines connect more than 20 boxes and steps that start with "Captive management program" and end with a small box labeled "Wolves released." The other chart is a felt-tipped-pen creation showing a row of circled numbers with arrows trailing and intertwining below. The numbers identify the six wolves trapped for the breeding program by Roy McBride in Mexico's Sierra Madre during the 1970s. Plus one. The six original captives included only one female, which was pregnant. Thus the seventh number identifies a possible unknown male, one that remained wild and free (at least for a time), and whose genes may be represented in the program.

The Mexican wolf is not a biological problem. Not a true land problem. With the wolf, we dip into the potent waters of human emotions, those parts of our being we can feel but not always recognize or name. How else can one describe an issue in which none of the parties have ever seen a Mexican wolf in the wild? In which we are discussing releasing a tiny band—maybe forty wolves—in a region that quite possibly never had more than six hundred anyway. And if the wolves are actually released in White Sands, no one will ever see them, except for an occasional biologist monitoring the pack. For this beast, 300 people show up at hearings in Las Cruces and Tucson. For this beast, 100,000 people attend an exhibit at the New Mexico Museum of Natural History, in Albuquerque.

Parsons took command of the wolf program in October 1990, late in the fray. The recovery plan (figuring, at that time, a release of 100 wolves in 5000 square miles) was a done deal in 1982, and captive breeding was halted a year later, when the number of pups overwhelmed the facilities. Between 1982 and '86, the project stalled because the Fish and Wildlife Service budget for endangered species was small, there were many projects, the wolves, because of their reputation, presented a big problem. At one point in the '80s, USFWS seemed to give states veto power over wolf reintroduction by suggesting the department would not do it if a state did not want it.

But wolf advocates spurred USFWS into asking Texas, New Mexico, and Arizona to propose sites. By 1987, USFWS had focused on White Sands. The military, however, balked at hosting an endangered species and risking having unhappy neighbors. In frustration, Michael Spear, Southwest regional director of USFWS, announced in September 1987 that the Mexican wolf reintroduction program had been "terminated," a word he says he later regretted using. In response to the situation, New Mexico conservationists founded the Mexican Wolf Coalition; another group, PAWS, sprang up in Arizona; and The Mexican Wolf Coalition of Texas was born. In April 1990, the New Mexico coalition sued the Department of Interior and Defense for violating the Endangered Species Act. Within months, Parsons found himself with a new job—coordinator of the Mexican wolf recovery program.

"I was given a simple charge," he explains. "My job is to get those wolves back in the wild. And it's been so intense."

We go upstairs to the man who makes the decisions, Mike Spear. His office is large, with a stuffed bear in one corner. After years of being a kind of whipping boy in the wolf controversy, Spear is eager to talk. To a rancher like Phil Harvey, Spear is biased because he publicly announced that his job under the law is to reintroduce the wolf. Conservationists have described him in various newsletters as a patsy of cattle interests and state game and fish departments. In person, he is friendly and plainspoken.

When the military denied him access to White Sands in 1987, he says he shut down the program because "that left us with no place to go." As for the lawsuit against the government, he says he's got very little money to work with and is supposed to preserve and/or reintroduce 110 to 115 endangered species. In his eyes, the wolf at the door was a bad investment with small prospect for a return on the money. What the lawsuit *did* do was stimulate the government to take action again.

When protesters milled in front of his building last fall, Spear went out to talk to them and announced that wolves would be released in April 1992—which stunned wolf advocates and which some feel may be too fast for a good release. As Spear says, "The fact that there are enough people that care to make a fuss about it does make a difference. Reintroducing a large carnivore required the right political climate." Apparently, the climate remains right; Spear is adamant, given a good crop of pups, that the release will take place in April, or, at the latest, this summer.

Spear is obviously pained at being castigated as some kind of demon by conservationists. "These are people out there," he patiently explains, "who think the feds can do anything they want. It doesn't work that way." He has to cooperate with the states on many matters. He takes a long view, one that sees full wolf reintroduction at multiple sites—a task taking 10 years, 20 years.

Critics say his agency did little for the wolf in the early and mid-1980s, and he agrees. "The do-nothing charge is pretty close," he admits, "but it was not conscious. . . . We had no money but we kept the wolves alive. It was a kind of benign neglect." But now, he says as he warms to the subject, "we have window of opportunity. We didn't have it around '84 or '85." Hunters are no longer strongly opposed. The wolf coalitions are growing like mushrooms. Public education in the schools and elsewhere is having an effect. Spear sinks back in his chair and adds, "Some of these things take an ungodly amount of time." For example, USFWS started a captive-breeding program for the critically endangered whooping crane about 30 years ago and now looks for that species' recovery sometime around the year 2150.

I ask Spear if I'm going to be back in his office in five years asking him why he hasn't yet released Mexican wolves from captivity. He bluntly says no. The question now is *where*—White Sands? a site in Arizona? Texas?—not *when* or *if* but simply *where*. He insists that the Mexican wolf will return to the Southwest soon.

The exhibit on the Mexican wolf at the new Museum of Natural History, in Albuquerque, is busy on my weekday visit. This is the twenty-second institution in which it has been displayed and it will leave soon for permanent exhibition in a museum dedicated to the wolf in Ely, Minnesota. At the exhibit entrance, large type on the wall sums up the wolf controversy: "Wolves and humans evolved along parallel lines in the Ice Age environment of the Northern Hemisphere. Both were intelligent social animals that lived in small groups and hunted large prey animals. Both shared food and cared for young within their social group. Both communicated with other group members. . . . When humans began domesticating . . . herd animals, livestock became the helpless prey of wolves. . . ."

Some of us have learned to live with wolves. Wild wolves still hunt within 60 miles of Rome, where peasants hate them but share ground with them. Some of us have not learned to live with them. Witness the genocidal policies of North Americans. Now wolves are returning—packs in Montana, a new pack discovered in Washington State in the Cascade Range, wolves in Minnesota, a reintroduction in North Carolina, and finally, a good chance for their return to the Southwest.

They are coming back because we have changed . . . a little bit. Bobbie Holaday heads Preserve Arizona's Wolves (PAWS) in Arizona. She is a systems analyst who has spent much of her life in towns and large cities. She learned the plight of the Mexican wolf, started PAWS in the summer of 1988, and now heads an advocacy group of about 500 members. She likes progressive-minded ranchers, wants a good compensation program (the Washington, DC–based Defenders of Wildlife has announced it will start such a fund in Arizona), and is careful to avoid "rancher bashing." She thinks we need to learn how to share, share part of the Earth with wolves.

She wears wolf pins, wolf earrings, a wolf cap, has a wolf key chain, and wears a wolf T-shirt. A couple of times a week she talks to students or other groups about wolves. She is one of the forces that helped to open Mike Spear's window of opportunity. When I meet her, she is manning a table at a street fair in Tempe, Arizona, surrounded by people peddling sand candles, wood carvings, mirrors, paintings, and hundreds of other things no one needs in order to survive. She is selling the idea of the wolf and people stop by to get literature and to buy T-shirts.

About her passion for the Mexican wolf, Holaday says, "The Southwest has millions of acres and yet the real essence of wilderness, the howl of the wolf, is gone. The Mexican wolf deserves to be returned to its native habitat, where it can resume its role as top predator in an ecosystem that is poorer without it." She has never heard a Mexican wolf howl, but she wants to someday.

But what kind of wolf will it be? To start with, one with a radio collar (those too young for collars will get radio implants). And under a 1982 amendment to the Endangered Species Act that authorizes an experimental-nonessential classification for some endangered species, the released wolves will be "surplus" animals. In other words, if they die, it will not threaten the gene pool. Throwaway wolves that can be monitored and recaptured repeatedly if they stray.

This Robo Wolf transmitting radio signals into the heavens will not be some bizarre creation of berserk scientists. He will be the product of all our hands. He will not be the fault of the federal government. He will be the creation of our will as expressed through wildlife agencies. Apparently, this is the only wolf we will allow at the door. We cannot bring ourselves to set aside a nice chunk of ground where wolves will eat whatever they knock down and we will have little to say about it. A place where wolves may not be convenient for us, a place we will have to give up and one whose upkeep will cost us money. We cannot imagine a wolf we do not manage . . . and a managed wolf isn't much of a wolf at all. One night, I go to a spot on the outskirts of the Arizona-Sonora Desert Museum and wait. Peter Siminski told me how he found this site. He was walking through the picnic area when he discovered people sitting in rows on the tables, facing the hidden cage of the Mexican wolves. None of the people spoke or made a sound. He wondered if he had stumbled upon some weird religious cult. Suddenly, the coyotes in the desert museum started singing, and yelps and barks of wild coyotes could be heard from neighboring peaks. Then the wolves began howling, a kind of sonic lightning bolt rising up from the center of the coyotes' mild efforts.

And still none of the people on the benches made a sound.

But their ears grew very large.

The howling.

I want to believe that what I'm hearing is the call of the wild.

But sometimes I think the weird haunting sound erupts becaus the wolves know what we have done in the past and have some kind of intuition of what we plan to do in the near future.

Welcome home, Robo Wolf.

According to David Parsons, there are eighty-eight Mexican wolves living in captivity in the United States and Mexico, as of early 1995. No known Mexican wolves exist in the wild.

After a series of delays, the USFWS is now proposing their Mexican wolf reintroduction for early 1997. White Sands Missile Range in New Mexico and the Blue Range section of theApache National Forest in Arizona will be the likely release sites.

The Blue Range, part of the White Mountains, was the probable location of Aldo Leopold's confrontation with the wolf who died "with a fierce fire in her eyes." Based on Leopold's story of his encounter with that wolf in "Thinking Like a Mountain," I think he would be pleased to know that wolves will soon be back in the Blue Range.

1995:"Aqui No Hay Mas Lobos," Rick Lobello

Rick Lobello, currently the executive director of the Carlsbad Caverns/Guadalupe Mountains Association, is a great example of an activist working to restore wolves to his local region. In 1990, while running the natural history association at Big Bend National Park, Rick cofounded the Mexican Wolf Coalition of Texas, a group that has made significant progress in raising the issue of wolf reintroduction in the state. In this article, Rick discusses the history of Mexican wolves and describes his hopes for their return to Texas and other parts of the Southwest.

Nearly sixteen years have passed since I first came face to face with the legendary lobo or Mexican wolf. I was working at Big Bend National Park and had driven the hundred miles to Alpine on my monthly grocery shopping trip. Friends of mine, Roy and Jere McBride, had invited me to stop by to see one of the wolves Roy had captured in Meico. I remember being surprised in learning that wolves still survived in northern Mexico and not far from my Chisos Mountains home in Big Bend. At the time I knew very little about Mexico except for the food I had tasted at bordertown restaurants across from Presidio, Texas, in Ojinaga and at Juarez across from El Paso. Like many Americans today, I had never heard of a Mexican wolf.

Roy was a well-known wolf and mountain lion trapper who was under contract with the U.S. Fish and Wildlife Service (USFWS) to capture endangered Mexican wolves for a new U.S./Mexico captive breeding program. He had been making trips into the Sierra Madre of northwest Mexico for years, many of them wolf trapping ventures for ranchers wanting to kill off wolves interfering with cattle operations.

In March 1980, Roy completed a status and distribution report on the Mexican wolf for the USFWS. The illustrated report summarized over twenty years of his wolf hunting trips, mainly in the Mexican states of Chihuahua and Durango. On one such trip Roy went after Las Margaritas, a famous Durango wolf with two toes missing from the center of his left front foot. Las Margaritas roamed over a large territory along the Zacatecas-Durango border, killing steers and avoiding all efforts to kill him with poison and traps. After eleven months of intensive efforts,Roy finally caught Margaritas with a steel trap on March 15, 1971.

If anyone knew where to find wolves in Mexico and how to capture them, Roy was the man. It was ironic that after playing a part in helping to bring the species to the brink of extinction, he was now being asked to help save it.

One of the last wild endangered Mexican wolves known to science glared at me from inside a large enclosure on McBride's small ranch. I can still picture its shaggy gray-and-rust-colored coat and how out of place it looked from behind the wire fence. A three-minute 8mm movie film refreshes my memory of that haunting day. My heart is filled with sadness at the thought that to save the species we had to capture the last known survivors and keep them and their descendants in pens until the time that it will be safe to release them back into the wild.

I had first met Roy in the fall of 1974 when I moved to Alpine as a graduate student at Sul Ross State University. One of my advisors, Dr. James F. Scudday, suggested that I contact Roy for some insight and advice concerning my interest in studying pronghorns for my Masters thesis. Roy and his wife, Jere, lived on a small ranch in the Sunny Glen area just west of Alpine. They had three young children, a few cattle, a half dozen or so hound dogs specially trained to hunt mountain lions, a pair of ocelots, and at least one mountain lion. From the first day we met in the driveway outside his small house surrounded by peach trees, it was obvious that this rugged West Texan was closely connected to the natural world around him. I soon discovered that he was a walking encyclopedia on the natural history of nearly all of West Texas and a good part of Mexico, an attribute that I would eventually try to emulate when I was hired as a park ranger at Big Bend the following summer.

I had just spent four years working on my B.A. degree in biology at William Jewell College in Missouri, and Roy and his young family helped me to adjust to my big move to Texas. Our friendship was bolstered by not only our shared love for wild animals but also by our shared Christian faith. To this day I have many fond memories of long conversations with Roy about mountains lions, wolves, bears, and Christian values. He had such a powerful influence on my life when I was a young man in my early twenties, I will always be grateful for the time we shared.

Less than a year later, while I was undergoing a minor financial crisis as a graduate student, Roy and Jere welcomed me to their home, where I stayed for little over a month. Roy was finishing up his Masters thesis on mountains lions and I had numerous opportunities to gain firsthand knowledge from a man whom many in Alpine and at Sul Ross already considered to be a living legend. To say the least I was honored to be Roy's friend and when he invited me to accompany him on a road trip, I jumped at the opportunity. Roy often had captive mountain lions on his ranch and was planning to take two adult lions to a private ranch in south Texas. He said that the rancher wanted lions to help control his white-tailed deer herd. Roy was curious to learn how well a transplanted West Texas lion would adapt to a new habitat. Twenty years later, biologists in Florida would ask this same question when studying the possibility of bringing closely related Texas mountains lions to south Florida to help save the endangered Florida panther. Roy was involved in many of the early trapping surveys in the Everglades when the USFWS declared the Florida panther an endangered species.

I consider myself fortunate to have spent the past twenty years living and working in three of our great national parks: Big Bend in Texas, Yellowstone in Wyoming and Montana, and Carlsbad Caverns in New Mexico. The natural world is truly a splendid and wonderful place. To be caught up within the concrete jungles of our cities and urban areas is to miss out on some of life's greatest treasures. It is here in the natural world that one can experience life as it was really meant to be, our ancestral homeland, the land of our pioneer forefathers and Native American peoples.

I was a twenty-two-year-old rookie when I took on my first park ranger assignment at Big Bend. I loved wearing the gray-and-green uniform and the broad brimmed "Smokey Bear" hat of the National Park Service. What a joy, what a privilege to have such a opportunity and get paid for it at the same time! My life has been enriched abundantly.

For years after seeing Roy's captive Mexican wolf, I shelved the idea of working to help return the wolf to the park that I had grown to love so well. Suddenly in 1988, NPS Director William Penn Mott, Jr., called upon the agency to launch a massive education effort focusing on species extinctions and the restoration of the wolf. A Wolf Task Force was established and Big Bend received a number of memorandums and educational materials highlighting the dilemma of the wolf, especially in Yellowstone. At the time I was executive director of the Big Bend Natural History Association (BBNHA), a non-profit organization helping the NPS with many of the educational needs at Big Bend National Park. I had convinced my partner in education and Association liaison person, Bob Rothe, who was NPS chief of interpretation at Big Bend, to allow me to write an article about wolves in Big Bend for the park's newspaper *El Paisano*. A year later, in 1989, the Association sponsored a seminar on wolf ecology taught by Dr. Jane Packard of Texas A&M University. Packard has spent time with famed wolf biologist Dave Mech studying the white Arctic wolves of Ellesmere Island. As seminar participants learned about wolf survey techniques along the trail to Grapevine Hills, everyone wondered whether the howls of the wolf would ever be heard in the national park again.

One of the inquiries I received about the seminar program was from Elizabeth Sizemore of Richardson, Texas. Elizabeth wanted to do something to help bring back the wolf to Texas and I encouraged her to contact Defenders of Wildlife in Washington, D.C., for assistance and advice. Defenders sent her a mailing list of Texas activists, and in February of 1990 I joined Elizabeth and others in forming the Mexican Wolf Coalition of Texas.

I would never have encouraged Elizabeth to start up a wolf advocacy group in Texas if it hadn't been for a Big Bend area rancher whom I had talked with in 1989 about the BBNHA wolf seminar program. I asked him how he would feel about wolves being returned to Big Bend if they were contained within the park and if the interests of ranchers were protected. He responded that he would support reintroduction and then told me why. Many ranchers consider wildlife to be an important asset to the value of their property. If you have mule deer, pronghorn, and mountain lions on your land, you can be sure that their presence will increase the value of the ranch. Many of the people buying up ranches in West Texas are looking at the land more as an escape from suburbia rather than as a place to raise livestock. These potential buyers also love wildlife, including those that many ranchers hate, like coyotes, eagles, and mountains lions. If you had wolves on your land, it would be worth that much more.

I wish my rancher friend would speak out on this issue, but there's another force here that has helped to impede the return of the wolf—peer pressure. If you're in the ranching business or a supporting business, you don't want to anger your neighbors when it comes to certain issues, such as predators. Unfortunately, while there are many ranchers and other local people who would support the return of the wolf in Big Bend, few if any are willing to speak out. For example, imagine that you were the owner of one of the two feed stores in Alpine, Texas. How long do you think you would stay in business if your customers knew you were pro-wolf? What if you owned a gas station or a small grocery store on the edge of town. How long do you think you business would last if you lost the patronage of people working in the livestock industry?

One Big Bend friend who always spoke her mind was Hallie Stillwell. Pioneer ranchwoman, named by two Texas governors as the "Yellow Rose of Texas," former schoolteacher along the border during the days of Pancho Villa, and simply a great lady with a lot of spunk at age ninety-five, Hallie has had many a conversation with me about returning wolves to Big Bend. Despite her reputation for speaking out against predators, especially mountain lions, even Hallie Stillwell has a small soft spot for wolves way down deep in her heart. One day she wrote me a letter thanking me for a birthday gift that included a set of wolf postcards and candy mints: "The wolf pictures are so beautiful, I think I can love those wolves and not want to kill a single one of them."

The Mexican Wolf Coalition of Texas was organized to support the preservation of the Mexican wolf, to provide education on the plight of the wolf, and to assist with reintroduction efforts of the wolf into its native habitat in Texas and other parts of the Southwest. Since 1990 the Coalition has been instrumental in rallying support for the Mexican wolf in Texas and across the United States. Coalition efforts have been vital in soliciting support from other conservation groups, including the Lone Star Chapter of the Sierra Club, Defenders of Wildlife, the National Audubon Society, and the National Parks and Conservation Association. The combined efforts of hundreds of volunteers have helped to convince the USFWS, the NPS and Texas Parks and Wildlife Department (TPWD) that there is a lot of public support for the Mexican wolf including support of an experimental release of the wolf in Big Bend National Park. Coalition efforts have also helped to alert Americans across the country to the plight of the Mexican wolf by means of magazine and newspaper articles, national and regional television news stories, radio talk shows, school programs, fair exhibits, petition drives, and speeches at public forums and hearings.

Wolves have been known to the West Texas area of Big Bend for over one hundred years. In 1901 Vernon Bailey reported that "the lobo is common over most of the plains and mountain country of West Texas. . . . On many of the large ranches a special bounty of $10, $20, or sometimes $50, is paid for every wolf killed." Early NPS planners had hoped that wolves survived in large enough numbers in the nearby mountains of Mexico to naturally repopulate the new national park. But by the time Big Bend National Park became a reality in 1944, viable wolf populations across the Rio Grande had already experienced a major decline.

The last confirmed record of a wolf in the Big Bend area was documented by Dr. James F. Scudday of Sul Ross State University in a 1972 issue of the *Journal of Mammalogy*. In 1970 one wolf was shot from the Cathedral Mountain Ranch south of Alpine and one was trapped from the Joe Neal Brown Ranch located at the point where Brewster, Pecos, and Terrell counties meet. According to Cathedral Mountain rancher Ralph Meriwether, the last wolf shot in West Texas was killed by a deer hunter. Although no one knows how long the wolf was on the ranch, Meriwether reports that he was unaware of any wolf depredations.

In 1993 friends of mine from the State of Chihuahua learned of my interest in the Sierra Madre and invited me to a ranch in the very area where nearly twenty years earlier Roy had searched for Mexican wolves for the USFWS. Since 1980 no one has been able to verify that the Mexican wolf still survives in the wild. There have been plenty of reports on both sides of the border, but no indisputable photographs, dead or living animals, hides or skulls. McBride made a rough estimate of fifty wolves left in Mexico when he finished his capture work in 1980. God only knows if any still endure in the wild today. The only known surviving Mexican wolves are the descendants of six wolves he brought into captivity as of 1980.

I would like to think that a wild population still exists somewhere in the mountains of Chihuahua, Durango, or Coahuila. But my hope quickly fizzles away when I recall conversations I have had with rural and ranching people living in the three Mexican states. For example, when I visited the Sierra Madre in 1993 I asked a number of people living on ranches if they knew of any wolves. Their response was always the same: "Lobos? Aqui no hay mas lobos. [There are no more wolves here.]"

After a nearly four-hour drive from the main highway running from Juarez to Chihuahua City, my friends and I reached the ranch where we were to spend the weekend. On Saturday morning we hiked to the top of a high mountain ridge that reminded me of my former home in the Chisos Mountains of Big Bend. When we got to the top, without hesitation ceremoniously, I howled like a wolf, hoping to get some kind of response. A few seconds later, there in a pinyon pine-oak-juniper woodland at over seven thousand feet, a coyote returned my call. Although I was a little surprised to hear a coyote I knew that coyotes historically lived in the lower elevations of the Chihuahuan Desert and that when the wolf disappeared they moved into former wolf territories. Yes, sad but true, it looked like wolves no longer lived in this part of Mexico.

For over twelve thousand years, long before the coming of the first Spanish explorers, the Mexican wolf lived in harmony with the land and Native Americans in what today we call the southwest United States and northern Mexico. Rarely killed by man, the wolf was viewed as having power and mystery. For nearly four hundred years European cattle raisers who had settled in the region managed to live with the wolf. Although wolves were often killed on sight along with other predators such as grizzlies and mountain lions, the wolf was just another natural force to be reckoned with, a part of nature accepted as unavoidable as drought, flash floods, and soaring heat. But all that would change during the late 1800s when a campaign to eradicate the species was initiated by ranchers and supported by federal, state, and local governments.

In the late 1970s, in response to the Endangered Species Act, the USFWS asked Roy McBride to mount a last-minute rescue effort to capture the last wild Mexican wolves in northern Mexico. The wolves he captured became the founders of a captive breeding program geared to produce wolves for eventual reestablishment back into the wild. After the captive population reached sufficient numbers, wolves would be released into former habitats where they could be protected in both the U.S. and Mexico. As of early 1995, the population of captive Mexican wolves stood at eighty-eight animals.

The descendants of those wolves survive within fenced enclosures at a small number of zoos and rare animal breeding centers in both countries. Unlike the dilemma facing most endangered species, saving the endangered Mexican wolf is more of a political problem than a biological one. Wolf restoration funds have been withheld by politicians more sympathetic to those who oppose restoring the species, even though prime habitat awaits wolf restoration across large expanses of the Southwest.

When I first started working at Big Bend National Park, I remember many long conversations with Roy McBride concerning the future of the Mexican wolf. Roy was never very optimistic and years later I have a much clearer understanding why. Back in the 1970s and nearly twenty years later in the mid 1990s, the direction and policies of the USFWS are still too closely tied to politics. No matter how good a law like the Endangered Species Act may look on paper, unless those individuals working for the government have the full backing of political leaders, carrying out conservation mandates can be very difficult. Up until 1993, for example, this fact of life was one of the main stumbling blocks preventing USFWS staff in the Southwest from implementing the Mexican Wolf Recovery Plan of 1982. There was simply not enough money set aside for Mexican wolf recovery in the budget.

When I was attending graduate school in Alpine, Roy was finishing up his Masters thesis on mountain lions. On the weekend we released a couple of captive lions at a private ranch in south Texas, Roy and I talked a lot about predators including wolves and bears. We joked about driving to Mexico, catching a few wolves, and bringing them to Big Bend. But we knew that such a scheme would have little chance of success without careful planning and long-term commitment.

Why not put the wolf back in Big Bend? Whenever I brought up the subject to not only Roy but also to Dr. James Scudday, my former advisor and professor at Sul Ross State University, the discussion always ended the same way: Big Bend area ranchers would simply never allow it.

Years later Roy served for a short time as an advisory member of the Davis Mountains Trans Pecos Heritage Association (DMTPHA), a West Texas ranching organization formed in 1989 to protest federal and state land acquisition actions in West Texas. Since Roy had allegiances to both groups, as a trapper for ranchers and as a trapper/wildlife biologist for the USFWS and the NPS, it was often difficult for him to please all parties.

One day in late 1991, Roy visited me at my office in Big Bend when I was executive director of BBNHA. I could see that things had changed between us. He wasn't very happy with my involvement with Mexican wolf education, especially the idea of promoting the possibility of bringing back wolves to Big Bend. Since one of the leaders of the DMTPHA group was regularly on my case concerning the subject, I suspected that he was sent to the park to try to change my mind about giving the wolf a chance to return to Big Bend.

When I asked him if the DMTPHA had sent him, he denied it and he said that he hadn't expected to find me still working in Big Bend. Although I had left the park for a few years to work with a youth ministry during the early 1980s, I returned to Big Bend with the BBNHA in 1986 and had talked by phone with Roy on a number of times since then. We had also met at the Arizona Wolf Symposium in March of 1990. I found it very hard to believe that after five years he was not aware that I was working in the park.

Roy wanted me to know that he thought that I should divert my pro-wolf efforts to other areas such as New Mexico and Arizona, where we both agreed there were much larger tracts of potential wolf habitat. I argued that Big Bend could support a small wolf pack and that the main factor that would keep them in the park was an adequate prey base of javelina, white-tailed deer, and mule deer. Once the wolf numbers increased beyond the carrying capacity of the park's prey base, the extra wolves could be captured and released in other areas or included in the captive breeding program.

Roy countered my remarks with the unsubstantiated premise that there wasn't enough of a prey base in the park to sustain wolves and that the park was not big enough for a wolf population. He believed that released wolves would not stay in the park and would immediately head north toward private lands.

I told him that until a habitat study was conducted and wolves given a chance to reinhabit the park, his theory couldn't be proven. To strengthen my point that his views weren't always infallible, I reminded him of our earlier conversations concerning mountain lions in Big Bend. As the preeminent mountain lion expert in West Texas, Roy often told me that he doubted the reliability of visitors' mountain lion reports in Big Bend. His basic premise was that after over twenty years of hunting lions, he had only seen one in the wild without the aid of his lion hunting dogs. How could so many visitors see mountain lions on short trips to the park when he had only see one on his own in twenty years?

After over fifteen years of working in Big Bend I alone had seen lions on eleven different occasions and had complete faith in most of the reports turned in to the Park Service. To this day I doubt that Roy wants to admit that he could be so wrong about the hundreds of sightings on file in Big Bend.

Although I can't really explain why his attitude about wolves was now so negative, compared with our conversations years earlier, I did have the opportunity to remind him where many of my ideas and values about predators originated—from Roy himself, one of strongest influences in my life during my early years in Big Bend.

I am sure that it hasn't been easy for Roy to work with park managers and environmentalists, helping to save endangered species like the wolf and mountain lion, while at the same time helping ranchers to control many of these same animals thought to be killing their livestock. Roy tries to be a good politician to both sides of the controversy. You can't blame a guy for trying to make a living.

I told Roy about a credibility problem I and others had noted about him when it came to riding the fence on Mexican wolf issues. My words must have had some effect for he called me lter that week to inform me that he was having his name removed as an advisor for the DMTPHA. I will always have a lot of respect for the man that I too would agree is a living legend when it comes to his knowledge of predators in the Southwest and in many other parts of the world, including Mexico, Central and South America, and Africa. I sincerely believe that, if given the chance, he would jump at an opportunity to help save the Mexican wolf from extinction.

The International Union for Conservation of Nature and Natural Resources (IUCN) announced in May of 1991 that its Wolf Specialist Group considers Mexican wolf recovery the highest priority need for wolf conservation the world over. The group, chaired by David Mech, the world's leading wolf authority, urged the USFWS to follow through with recovery efforts in light of recent research identifying the Mexican wolf's unique genetic makeup. With all the international attention afforded the Mexican wolf, one would think that other government agencies in the United States would join hands with the USFWS in giving Mexican wolf recovery full support.

Spirited delegations of Mexican wolf supporters have spoken out every year at Texas Parks and Wildlife Department Commission hearings since 1990. In 1992 Texas governor Ann Richards issued a news release in support of giving wolf restoration a careful look. Longtime Big Bend naturalist and former chief scientist of the NPS Roland Wauer was bold enough to say in an interview with the Dallas *Times Herald* that he felt Big Bend would be ideal habitat for the Mexican wolf. "There's probably nowhere else in the southern United States where the restoration of a species like that would work biologically," said Wauer. "There's a lot of food for animals, there's adequate space. There's a 99% chance it will work."

Late in 1992 the Mexican Wolf Coalition of Texas presented TPWD with petitions containing over five thousand signatures calling for the agency to work jointly with the USFWS and the NPS in conducting an Environmental Impact Statement for Mexican wolf restoration in the Big Bend area. Despite growing support among the general public, from political leaders like the governor of the state, and from members of the scientific community, TPWD has continually chosen to either ride the fence or take a very negative outlook when it comes to any discussion of wolf restoration in Texas. Many Coalition members are hoping that when the day comes that wolves are successfully restored to New Mexico or Arizona, or both states, TPWD will have a change of heart and choose to support wolf restoration in Texas.

Today, when you visit Big Bend National Park you can experience a nearly complete Chihuahuan Desert ecosystem. Mountain lions, bobcats, coyotes, gray and kit fox, Mexican black bear, eighteen species of bats, over four hundred species of birds, including peregrine falcons, zone-tailed hawks, and Colima warblers, fifty-five species of reptiles, over four thousand species of insects, and eleven hundred species of plants make the flora and fauna of the region one of the richest assemblages in any national park, richer than most people would imagine in a desert ecosystem.

And yet, despite our knowledge that most of Big Bend's original pre-European settlement biodiversity is still intact, I am ardent in my frustration over the missing pieces. We're missing not just Mexican wolves but also desert bighorn, opossum, prairie dogs, Montezuma quail, and Aplomado falcons.

In 1993 Roger Kennedy, the new director of the NPS told employees at a meeting in Santa Fe, New Mexico, that they have an obligation to speak out for the preservation of the nation's natural and historic treasures. In strongly supporting the reintroduction of the wolf to Yellowstone National Park, and anywhere else the animal once lived, Kennedy came to the ranks of the NPS with a evangelical spirit that has been sadly lacking since the days of William Penn Mott, Jr.

Secretary of the Interior Bruce Babbitt is adamant in his commitment in making the Endangered Species Act work. "American's cannot credibly ask Chinese to save tigers, for example, if they cannot save species in the United States."

Restoring Mexican wolves to Big Bend National Park could help to bring the park into ecological balance for the first time in over seventy years. The return of wolves to this vast wilderness area of Texas would restore an important predator with the capability of filling an important ecological niche left void when wolves were exterminated from the area in the early 1990s.

As I sit back writing the final words to this essay in 1995 and look southward across the vast Chihuahua desert from my home in the Guadalupe Mountains, I think back to my experience in 1978 when I saw what was one of the last wild Mexican wolves in the world. I hope that someday, and very soon, descendants of that animal will be running free in places like Big Bend and other former habitats in New Mexico, Arizona, and perhaps even Mexico. The Mexican wolf is an important part of our natural heritage. It has a right to return to its ancestral home.

Free El Lobo!

1994: "Wolf Medicine," Brenda Peterson

Brenda Peterson grew up in the home of a forest ranger who later became the chief of the U.S. Forest Service. Living close to wild areas and wild animals her whole life, Brenda has developed a special understanding of issues that affect the natural world. She has written three novels and two collections of essays, including Living By Water: True Stories of Nature and Spirit, *a book about life in the Pacific Northwest. This article will be part of Brenda's forthcoming book,* Wolf Medicine. *A portion of this essay also appeared in the September/October 1994 issue of the* New Age Journal. *Brenda requested that a portion of her payment for this article be donated to wolf organizations.*

I was raised under the steady, clear gaze of animals I believed were my babysitters: The doe's dark eyes fondly followed me as I crawled, barebelly against the itchy rag rug in our Forest Service lookout cabin high in the Sierra Nevadas. An elderly elk witnessed my first steps and when I slept, a young buck right above my crib kept a watchful eye over me.

It never occurred to me that these animals who stood such patient guard were themselves dead. They were simply my guardian animals who never left the cabin or me alone. I did not know I was separate and different from these animal heads mounted on the cabin walls. Their eyes were so intent, dark, and luminous—no more blank than window glass that reveals another world. Inside these animals was still spirit, the aliveness that always stays with it own skin, and bone, and muscle.

Sometimes my young father, whose office was the forest, would lift me up to run my hands over the tanned fur of these familiar faces, touching black lips, long slope of jawbones and sensitive snouts, the pricked ears and tuft at the top of their heads. Most amazing were the antlers—I expected I would grow my own someday. Long before I could talk, I understood that these animals who guarded me also fed me with their own bodies. They nurtured me with their meat the way my mother had first nursed me with her milk. My father explained that the animals in our cabin had each given their lives so that we might eat. Himself part Swede, Seminole, and French Canadian Indian, my father taught us to say thank you to the animals sacrificed so that we could survive; but before every meal we said grace to God, not the animals. I assumed God, like my father, must be a hunter.

One night when I was sleeping in my first real bed, my father woke me up. "Listn," he shushed me. "Do you hear that?" Thin wavering howls through tall trees, almost like wind crying. "No wolves around here for years, but still . . ." Again, those haunting, high-pitched calls. Not the yip-yip of coyotes, but the full-throated singing of wolf pack. "No, can't be . . ." my father shook his head and tucked me back in bed. "Maybe wild dogs got some wolf left in them."

Then my father told me the story of the wolf, who once lived in these forests alongside us, who also hunted game to survive. "They have families, like us," he told me. "But they're all gone now." He laughed, "I can tell you, if there were wolves still round these parts, even our mounted deer heads might just run away."

I looked up at my animal guardians and felt a sudden, sharp sorrow, a loss. What would I do without their company? If the wolf drove them away would I go hungry? Would I be all alone?

My father reassured me, it was the other way around. The wolves couldn't take our game because we'd driven them away, so far away that few wolves had been seen in all the lower forty-eight states or any other part of the world for that matter. "Go to sleep, honey," he said. "There's no more Big Bad Wolf. You'll never go hungry. I'll see to that."

And I haven't. Every year my father has sent his children moosemeat, elk, deer—whatever he hunted that season. Not only did I grow up eating game, I have continued to eat the sweet, lean meat of wild animals since childhood. But in 1993 everything changed. That fall, along with receiving the frozen Alaskan caribou meat my father sent me, I also accepted another of his gifts—an airline ticket to join him at the 1993 Wolf Summit in Fairbanks, Alaska.

My father's free ticket to the Summit surprised me. I had wanted to go, both as a nature writer and environmentalist. My father was officially attending as an impartial observer in his role as director of International Fish and Wildlife Agencies. For decades now my father and I have argued about wilderness, wildlife, and other environmental issues, most often finding ourselves on opposite sides. But here was an opportunity to come together on a subject as wild and controversial as wolf management—a subject as primal as hunger and hunting.

So we found ourselves, my father and I, at the Wolf Summit, warily circling each other (when we were not walking familiarly, arm in arm). In the early morning darkness of that Alaskan land where winter daylight waits until nearly noon to show its slight glow, we walked a plowed path between six-foot snow banks and pickets carrying signs: "Wolf Management, not Wolf Worship!" "Iraq—Want Some Wolves?" "Eco-Nazis Go Home!" Many of the wolf-control proponent picketers were dressed head-to-toe in bear, fox, a few wolf skins as they passed out bright arm bands to crowds already clothed in orange hunting vests and hats. Far fewer in numbers were the signs, "Don't Kill Wolves on My Public Land," "Respect the Wolf!" and several sled dogs bearing signs, "The Wolf is my Sister."

The Wolf Summit had been called by Governor Walter Hickel supposedly to reach a politically acceptable compromise on wolf control. Hickel had fended off a massive tourism boycott by canceling the original Alaska Game Board's plans for aerial shooting of wolves by state employees in three management units north of Anchorage. The Summit was set against an international outcry over aerial shooting that seemed to pit Alaska against the rest of the lower forty-eight. Outside the Fairbanks ice rink, scene of the Summit, the angry crowd's mood was white-hot—though I still shivered inside my parka against the sub-zero Arctic temperature.

My father and I had happened to share a ride from the hotel with a Game Board member who was also a vet, in favor of wolf control. Amidst the yelling crowd, the Game Board member glanced around nervously. He seemed awestruck, still startled at the media glare, the outrage from the lower forty-eight and the Alaskans' own feisty resistance to any kind of control, wolf or otherwise. "It's a circus," he marveled, "not a summit." He and my father entered the Summit; I stayed outside with my tape recorder to listen to the crowd.

A bearded man wore an entire wolf skin, its sleek, glossy snout atop his head, its pelt fully embracing his back. He seemed to speak to me from within the animal, but what he said was, "You people from the lower forty-eight just don't understand that we've got plenty of wolves up here. What we don't have is enough caribou. And if we let you goddamn eco-outsiders take over our state, we won't have any game to eat at all!"

"I eat game," I told him, unable to take my eyes off his wolf-head hat. "Sometimes."

Caught up in that crowd of hunters outside the Wolf Summit I found myself confused, uncomfortable. What was I doing here anyway? I wondered. I wasn't a wolf person. My nature writing had been devoted mostly to marine mammals, not wolves. I'd spent the last decade swimming with dolphins and studying whales. Aside from my father's invitation to join him at the Summit, the only inkling I'd had of why I was here was a Nootka Indian legend which taught that when the orcas go walking on land, they do so as wolves.

Holding my tape recorder high like an antennae in the darkness, my face chafed and frozen, I realized I was the only woman among these fur-clad hunters. It was not the moment to remember the chilling statistics I'd recently read: that Alaska leads the nation in incidences of rape; that a white woman has double the chance of being a homicide victim here than in any other state. Even though I was afraid, I also felt my fear mirrored in these protesters. Clearly, they believed themselves victims, terrorized by outsiders who would change their lives and traditions.

Approximately one thousand wolves are annually killed in Alaska by traditional methods of gun, snare, or iron trap. The proposed aerial shooting plan would have resulted in the additional deaths of three to four hundred wolves in the targeted areas during the first year of the five-year plan. The Game Board's stated goal of their proposed winter 1992–93 wolf control program was to increase the caribou population for hunters. In response, the Alaskan Tourism Marketing Council (ATMC) had expressed dismay over the Game Board's program, which coincided with mid-winter tourist bookings for summer travel. The ATMC discovered that within a fifteen-day period (Dec. 15–29, 1992) the negative effects on Alaska tourism had been profound: postponement of travel was up by 200 percent, cancellations up 50 percent, and reconsideration of travel plans increased by 75 percent. Based on their own survey of potential Alaska tourists, the ATMC estimated that the state would have lost over $85 million in tourist spending due to the boycott. There was also the independent survey of Alaska residents that found that only 8 percent of Alaskans supported an increased wolf take over current levels (10 percent among subsistence Native hunters). The hunters and Game Board members attending the Wolf Summit had every reason to feel themselves under siege of public opinion.

And yet they still held the power. That was obvious in the attendance of the Summit. Just as I was the only female in the crowd outside the ice rink, I found upon entering that 90 percent of those officially attending the Summit were male, with only three out of the some thirty-odd speakers female. In the bleachers around the rink, hundreds of orange-clad hunters booed and hissed whenever a speaker spoke out against wolf control. The atmosphere was much like a sports event with few fans for the wolf.

All day long, various biologists and wolf control proponents offered their evidence pro and con on wolf control. Sometimes it seemed the presenters spoke different languages. First, there was the biologists' dialect of population densities and distribution, of "predator pits" and prey collapses, of ungulates (hoofed mammals such as caribou and moose) and habitat conservation; then there was the language of the wildlife managers who spoke of "harvesting the wolves," of "caribou calf crops," of "wolf control."

Listening to the professionals from Fish and Game agencies, almost exclusively male, I heard beneath the language of "control," "lethal management," and "sustainable yield" this subtext: Our traditions train us to fear the wolf as evil, that our human need to control nature for our own purposes comes from some ancient, at times religious, terror of the "chaotic" and "destructive" animals and world around us. It's as if some part of our psyche were still entrenched in the world view that we are little humans, victimized by a brutal, uncaring natural environment. We humans try to control what we believe is out of control—whether it's nature or her wild animals.

When Renee Askins, of the Moose, Wyoming-based Wolf Fund made a poignant appeal to stop the wolf hunting, she was met with raucous catcalls and boos. It struck me then that what we might need at this Wolf Summit and in our attitude toward animals in general, was self-control, not wolf-control. Askins compared the wolf control to a war against this much maligned animal.

In the lower forty-eight states, wolves lost 99 percent of their original range. At the time of the Pilgrims, there were as many as two million wolves in what would become the contiguous states. By the time we got through with them there were just a few hundred survivors, a tiny remnant of a once-numerous race.

Later that night, as Wolf Summit attendees filled the bars and restaurants of this off-season Alaskan town, I found myself following my father into casual meetings with Fish and Wildlife employees. Again, the company was all men, mostly wildlife managers who are grappling with a public increasingly interested in what has been, until recent decades, a fairly closed professional group going about their business of stewardship without much interference. In fact, there were so few non-professionals (those not official managers or environmentalists) on the speakers' platform, one wondered what might happen if Native elders and other storytellers, poets, and spiritual leaders were invited to join in the dialogue.

Finding myself again surrounded by wildlife managers, many of my father's colleagues, I decided to take off my press badge and just listen—kind of like a proverbial wolf supporter in sheep or woman's clothing.

One member of the Game Board sipped his beer thoughtfully and when asked what he was mulling over, he shook his head in dismay. "You know," he said, "the way that Wolf Fund gal talks, you'd think she believed wolves had souls or something!"

The Eskimos certainly believed in the souls of animals—and they still hunted them to survive. The difference was that instead of assuming attitudes of management or control over animals, the Native shamans respectfully asked the inua or animal spirit to sacrifice its life to feed the village. In return, the villagers, whether they were Pacific Coast whalers or wolf, caribou, and moose hunters gathered in seasonal ceremonies to praise and acknowledge the survival debt we humans owed our animals. There was a relationship between humans and animals, predator and prey, a kinship born of equality.

In the light of this old tradition, the Wolf Summit could be seen as a diluted but important gathering of tribes where clans came together to debate, celebrate, and meditate on the wolf. Though stripped of much of its sacredness, the gathering still called us to confront this predator, who is our equal. That equality and the remnants we still carry of mutual respect explain why aerial hunting, with its disconnected sharpshooters beading down on a prey as if there were no history, no relationship between our species, has provoked a public howl as great as that heard over the Alaska *Exxon Valdez* oil spill.

The next morning as we again trudged through snowbanks to attend the second day of the Wolf Summit, I was approached by a demurely dressed woman who took me aside and said in a whisper, "I'm just hoping that you're sympathetic to the wolf," she began. "I saw your dolphin earrings and thought you might be. I can't go on record with this because I'd lose my job in wildlife management, but you should really research the link between orcas and wolves, top predators. Start from the bottom of the food chain and go up. You see, the herring are depleted—which makes the sea lions starve and disappear. This means the sea lion predators, the orcas, are coming into shallow waters that are not their territory to prey upon gray whales. Everything's out of balance from the bottom up in the predator-prey relationship. We humans have overfished, overhunted, and overkilled. Now we're trying to fix it by taking out the other top predators, such as the wolves. But we don't need the caribou as much as the wolves do; we humans have other food options, don't we? But without caribou, wolves will die from hunger. What do you think might happen if the hunters voluntarily stop taking caribou, so that the wolves might live alongside us as equal predators? What if we stopped ourselves instead of killing the wolf? Could we restore some balance here in the next ten years or so. I wouldn't mind if it took more time, at least I would not be part of destroying the equal balance between human and wolf."

The last night of the Wolf Summit, under a fading New Year's moon the *Farmer's Almanac* calls "Wolf Moon," I sat with some allies I'd made while at the Wolf Summit. We'd found a Wild West bar, complete with trophies. It was warm and as we drank, we found ourselves swapping wolf stories. One story I'll always remember. Someone recounted his grandfather's trapper tale. Seems this trapper found a fierce wolf, his paw clamped shut in the metal teeth of his trap lines. "He just looked at me," the grandfather had said. "Instead of lunging out, that wolf just kept staring at me and wagging his tail. He wagged his tail like that, until I shot him."

His story reminded me of another told me by Linda Hogan, the Chickasaw author. Seems one of her neighbors there in the Colorado mountains was out walking with her young son, when she suddenly felt a terrible pain in her foot. She looked down to find the metal teeth of a trap snapped shut tight around her ankle. Howling in pain, she asked her son to run for help. But the boy had watched a TV show and seen how traps are sprung; after some struggle he was able to open the trap and free her. They searched the trail and found quite a number of other waiting traps. Together, they sprung every last one of them.

"But when they reported the traps to the authorities," Linda said, "they were told they might well be sued for springing those traps; they were legal." Linda concluded, "Lots of terrible things are legal. Any Indian person can tell you that."

She went on to describe the trial of Standing Bear in Missouri in the late 1880s. The Ponca Tribe had been removed from their Oklahoma homeland to Missouri, where they were facing extinction from illness and grief. "The purpose of the trial was to determine if Indians were human beings," Hogan explained. "the judge finally decided we were, but it didn't make any difference. The Poncas still weren't permitted to go back to their sacred land. And remember this, Indians and wildlife are listed under the same agency—Department of the Interior."

Sitting in that Fairbanks bar surrounded by friends and fur-clad hunters, I was reminded of another frontier, another century ago when we didn't have environmental wars; we had the Way the West Was Won. Barely over one hundred years ago there were mountains of buffalo bones piled high across the plains, there were bounty hunters who were sent to capture and kill so-called hostile Indians, there were thousands of ex–Civil War soldiers engaged in Indian wars that decimated a whole nation of Native Americans and scattered them until many faced extinction on tiny reservations where disease and despair set in like slow poison.

As I sat in that Alaskan bar, beneath the familiar eyes of elk and deer, my childhood animal guardians, I realized for the first time that these moose and caribou trophies were like scalps—and that I had been born and raised beneath the eyes and skins of the conquered, the controlled.

* * *

This past winter, during a full moon the Cheyenne Indians call "the Moon When the Wolves Run Together," my father sent me twenty-five pounds of Alaskan caribou meat. It arrived by Federal Express in time for Christmas—my father's gift, just as he had always given his kids wild game even after we left home. In college at the University of California during the sixties, I'd put the moosemeat into the freezer of our communal house. I told my hippie roommates it was hamburger; they never knew we were really eating moosesghetti, sweet 'n' sour moosemeat balls, and moose burgers. When the frozen caribou arrived on my doorstep last winter, I almost couldn't lift the huge, heavy package. As I lugged it to the freezer, my heart felt as heavy as that caribou—because this was the winter of aerial wolf control.

As it turned out, the much-ballyhooed Wolf Summit had simply been a cynical shill to distract attention from the Game Board's true intentions—to increase wolf control by allowing aerial land-and-shoot policies. The snares, already purchased before the Wolf Summit and Governor Hickel's temporary halt on aerial shooting, were simply handed out to trappers contracted by the state as soon as the Game Board announced its decision in favor of wolf control. The Board waited until June 1993 to make official its staunch support of wolf control, June being past the major tourism booking season. Tourists were already locked into summer Alaska tours. It was too late for another boycott. The Board announced that aerial hunting would be allowed in most of the state, with the caveat that the hunters must land their planes, then walk a hundred yards before shooting—a rule that even Alaska's own wildlife agents called unenforceable. A *New York Times* article last spring described the impossible task facing the two federal Fish and Wildlife Service enforcement officers responsible for patrolling and prosecuting a "range of international conspiracies, civil violations and felonies that are virtually unheard of anywhere outside of Alaska." These agents wearily report that they catch "no more than 2 percent of the violators."

In describing one of the few wolf hunters actually brought to justice, the *Times* article shows how brutal aerial hunting actually is. Dr. Jack Frost, an Anchorage surgeon, pleaded guilty in 1991 to hunting wolves from his airplane. "Dr. Frost envisioned himself as a 'mechanical hawk,' according to radio transmissions from his plane that were picked up on the ground, who would chase his prey to exhaustion, then land the plane and kill the wolves."

The federal agents were able to discover Dr. Frost's violations and present him with evidence that lead to his 1991 guilty plea. They showed Dr. Frost transcripts in which a witness in a plane flown by Dr. Frost quoted the doctor as saying: "He wasn't completely dead. . . . We'll go back later. The damn thing jumped up and bit my wing." The federal agent found wolf teeth marks on Dr. Frost's airplane wing. "They had chased the hell out of those animals," the agent said.

There were some independent efforts to monitor the wolf control program once it went into effect last winter. Gordon Haber is a wildlife biologist who has long studied wolves, especially in Denali National Park. During the wolf kill season of 93–94, Haber sued in federal court along with the Alaska Wildlife Alliance and the Alaska Center for the Environment to obtain the frequencies of radio collars worn by twenty wolf packs. Haber's aim was to conduct a census of wolf populations to compare with the state's estimates of wolf numbers. He did receive the radio collar frequencies and found that the Alaska Department of Fish and Game had overestimated the wolf populations by 40 percent. Those radio collar frequencies had long been a flash point in this wolf controversy. Alaska's director of wildlife had originally ordered the wolf packs collared for supposedly scientific reasons. But this was the same man who once had proposed hunting wolves from aircraft equipped with machine guns. It was not too much of a leap to wonder if these wolf packs wearing radio collars would simply make better targets once the wolf control programs were in place. No media were allowed to film or document the actual kills of Alaska's wolf control program. In fact, few of the official photos released ever appeared in the media. But at a Humane Society workshop I attended, we saw a slide show of those official photos. One in particular haunts me still: It is an animal autopsy lab with a fully skinned wolf trussed and hung by his paws. Behind the corpse on a steel shelf is a half-carton of Budweiser. Aside from the obvious good-old-boy beer as an unwitting statement, why did this official photo show a skinned wolf, not simply a dead wolf?

Lt. Mike Reed, a law enforcement officer from Lakewood, Washington, who is a wildlife advocate, answered this question at a Bellevue Humane Society workshop on Alaska's wolves. "It's most likely that the Alaska Department of Fish and Game realized that if they skinned those wolves, the photo would be too gruesome to be on television news or in print. This strategy keeps the media away from fully documenting the wolf kill."

Other slides were so gruesome I had to consciously force myself to sit and see the slaughter. But I reminded myself that the world had not witnessed this official killing and so I must keep my eyes open. In one slide showing snare trappings, I saw wolves lying with their tongues stiffly stuck, the wire snare still tight around their bloodied necks. "These snares will sometimes take days to kill a wolf," Lt. Reed explained. "If a trapper comes upon a wolf still slowly strangling, he is supposed to humanely dispatch the animal with a single shot to the head. But because the University of Alaska has a scientific interest in studying wolf skulls—I have no problem with that—but this has encouraged trappers to aim at the wolf's heart. That's hard to hit; so you often have a wolf with a gut wound that is also strangling—a very slow, and inhumane way to die." Is this hunting or is this something else—something cynical and self-serving and so cruel that it makes one wonder if this species shouldn't call itself *Homo hostilis?*

In last winter's wolf control program the official numbers are disheartening: aside from the thousand plus wolves usually killed, there was an additional kill in Game Management Unit 20A of ninety-eight government-destroyed wolves and another estimated fifty privately trapped wolves in the same unit. Besides wolves, the following animals were accidentally destroyed in snares set by the state: twelve moose, two caribou, six coyotes, thirteen foxes, one wolverine, and two golden eagles.

In a state whose residents strongly oppose wolf control, whose own tourism council chides the Game Board for focusing on hunting to the exclusion of "our natural beauty"; in a country and international community that pleads for wolf preservation, and with a federal government even now proposing legislation to prohibit trappers and hunters from killing free-ranging wolves on the same day in which the person is airborne—how does Alaska continue to sponsor wolf control? The answer is simple—Alaska has a powerful governor who is famous for cronyism and an attitude of control over nature. His most famous environmental comment: "We can't let nature run wild." Add to Governor Hickel a Game Board made up of trappers, hunters, and one woman trapper who delights to pose in fur bikinis—and you have the making of a very unbalanced use of power. This power cannot endure, but it is sustained by a tradition of angry "Alaska for Alaskans" hard-core constituents who have called the shots since this state was a frontier. It is particularly ironic that these Old West traditions hold sway over the nation's largest state, 82 percent of which is federal land and, as such, belongs to all Americans.

"This Game Board is the most hardened group I have ever encountered," contends Dr. Paul Joslin of Wolf Haven International. "Their attitude is simply, we're gonna do what we wanna do."

And that's exactly what they're doing. Not only did the Alaska Game Board put into policy their aerial wolf control plans, this past spring, those policies were made state law. The governor signed into law State Bill 77, a special legislation that requires the state wildlife officials to kill wolves if it will result in achieving higher levels of human harvest of big game. The Board of Game also passed a regulation allowing snowmobile users to simply turn off engines before shooting at animals. But even this kind of calculated wildlife management favoring hunting over any other natural use of wilderness cannot endure if public opinion stays strongly opposed to wolf control. Governor Hickel is up for reelection in November 1994 and so may be more responsive to public protest. Alaska's governor and Game Board, along with those 8 percent of Alaskans who favor an increased wolf take, are not evil people who live to hunt down helpless creatures; they are frontier people in the trapping tradition of Alaska's past. As trappers, they themselves are trapped by a way of thinking about wildlife that underscores why, in Alaska, there is a Fish and Game Department, not Fish and Wildlife, as in much of the lower forty-eight.

One unofficial picture of the recent wolf control killings stays in my mind. It is, oddly enough, not the grisly sight of a skinned wolf nor the strangled wolf. It is the photo of a perfect snow field with six black creatures splayfooted against one another—one wolf pack, an entire family dead. In frenzied, ever-tightening circles around this fallen pack are snowmobile tracks. The tracks seem crazed, out of control. Imagine the wolves loping across frozen tundra for hours on end in their graceful 5 m.p.h. gait; then the whine and roar of the snowmobile engines as several speed behind the wolves, who run for their lives, reaching their fastest dead-heat gallop at 35 m.p.h. The snowmobiles circle, revving motors and rpms capable of 100 m.p.h. This is not the skillful chase of a wolf against caribou, the speed and agility of each animal almost equal so that the kill comes down to strategy and stamina. This is overkill, this is hunter-gatherers run amuck, refusing to grow and change with their diminishing environment. This is a species not learning survival of the fittest, but slaughter of what frightens or competes with us.

I know the hunters of Alaska believe they are becoming an endangered species themselves, but what is really endangered is the balance between predator and prey, that ancient alliance like a slow-motion dance of hunger and hope. And something else—humility. The wolf does not always eat, does not always bring down the prey. The wolf does not hunt its prey to extinction, and wolves rarely prey upon one another. Is it possible that perhaps we humans have something to learn about being predators from our brother and sister, the wolf?

* * *

Alaska, our last frontier, has become a battleground for the wild wolf. If we cannot persuade Alaskans to leave off their obsolete war against the wolf and move into a new century that values wildlife for itself, as well as for how it can serve our human needs—then American wolf hunters will continue to trap and strangle and land and shoot and surround with snowmobiles the wild wolf packs of Alaska. One wishes there were a way to signal to these fellow creatures to migrate out of that last frontier and down to Minnesota, where the wolves are thriving amidst livestock ranchers, more people per square mile, and even hunters looking for deer. One wishes we could send out a call from Washington's mighty Cascade Mountains to rally the Alaska wolves to join the few wolf packs now straggling back into our state.

I also take heart at the decision last summer to reintroduce the wild wolf to Yellowstone National Park. It is curious that on one hand we are inviting the wolf back from extinction in Wyoming, while at the same time we continue to slaughter wolves in Alaska. Such extreme positions on the wolf remind us that we are struggling between last century's American myth of the Old West and the twenty-first century's more enlightened attitude toward wildlife. For example, volunteer research groups in the Cascade Mountains taking field trips into the wilderness and howling their heads off by way of counting the returning wolves. One of the supposed symbols of the lone wolf, his howl, is really a call to community. The lone wolf is a myth based on our misconception that wolves are all individual, heroic adventurers not bound or responsible to any canine community. But scientific studies have proved that the wolf is, in fact, a most pack-centered creature, perhaps more instinctively sociable than our species. The wolf is anything but lonely as he or she—it's also proven that sometimes it is an alpha female that leads the pack—raises a shaggy head to howl; and yet our myths have imprisoned this creature into a symbol of isolation and separation.

I suggest that it is we who are lonely, not the wolves—we who have hunted the wild wolf to near-extinction so that it is a very rare few of us who have ever even heard the call of the wolf in the wild.

The Native Americans use the word "medicine" to describe whatever magic, herb, or potion heals sickness. Often that disease is an inner sickness called soul loss. As defined by Philip Drucker in *Cultures of the North Pacific Coast*, "soul loss was a mysterious malady to which North Pacific Coast Indians were subject." When a soul abandoned its body, the wandering "did not cause immediate death, but rather lassitude and wasting away, which was fatal if the errant soul were not recovered in time."

The tribe's shaman, often wearing animal skin so that he appears to be working from within that animal and its particular power, was responsible for crossing over to the other side and summoning that soul back to its ailing body. The wolf, for many Native American tribes, was the most spiritual creature, capable of moving between the worlds and especially the underworld. It is here so many sick and lost souls wander, even while their bodies still survive on Earth. The shaman would shape-change into the wolf and ask that wolf's spirit to help him track that wandering soul. Imagine the howl, half human, half wolf, as it called the lost soul back to health.

To have wolf medicine is to apprentice oneself to the power to balance, heal, and survive the underworld and return to tell the story, to call our spirits back. How will we call ourselves back if we no longer have the real spirit and body of the wolf to guide us? How will we heal this human soul loss that separates us from other species, as well as from our own animal soul?

In his book *Healing States*, Alberto Villoldo writes about his research with the Incan healers in Peru, "The medicine men and women in North and South America believe that all healing involves an experience of the spiritual, where the ill person rediscovers his connection to nature and to the divine." Rediscovering this ancient connection with the animals is exactly what may happen when women begin to make their voice heard in wildlife circles. Recently the success of Clarissa Pinkola Estes' *Women Who Run With the Wolves* surprised many people. The archetype of the wild wolf was claimed by women for themselves. This claiming is a good first step; it is a symbolic identification with what is most wild and must not ever be tamed or conquered or controlled within us as human beings. Women dreaming and connecting and claiming the archetypal wolf is wonderful. But as Yeats wrote, "In dreams begin responsibility." We must reach out past our own psyches and connect with the literal animals around us. After all, archetypes do not run wild through the woods. Without the real wolf in our world, our human dreams are still disconnected.

I wonder what might happen if, at the next wildlife managers' conference on wolf control, there were more women represented as biologists, as administrators, and simply as spectators. Several other nature writer women friends of mine have made a pact that we will begin to attend these private wildlife conferences, which are, after all, supposedly in the public interest. There where male managers play poker with species, perhaps women might offer another perspective.

Any wildlife manager will tell you that there are three questions that must be asked of any government wildlife program: 1. Is it biologically sound? 2. Are there the financial, personnel, and equipment resources available? 3. Is it acceptable to the public? The Wolf Summit amply showed that biologists have conflicting research on whether wolf control is a sound practice over time for the whole ecosystem. The statistics in on the financial cost of the 93–94 wolf season are startling: Alaska paid around $2000 per wolf killed; this includes expensive air time, personnel, and equipment. And as for the public acceptance of wolf control—92 percent of Alaskans did not want it expanded. Add to this the fierce protests from the lower forty-eight, the demonstrations in over fifty cities—all this spells out a very bad program by the definition of even wildlife managers.

Will wolf control continue next year? There is before the House HR Bill 1391, which proposes to prohibit aerial hunting unless authorized by Congress. This legislation, if passed, would take the wolf control away from state officials, who are managing their wildlife with such short sightedness, and open the discussion up to the entire country, who, after all, hold 80 percent of Alaska in the public trust. HR Bill 1391 is stymied at this moment in Congressional subcommittees, but if there were enough outcry, it could be passed before Alaska's extreme next winter and the wolf control sets in.

Recently when my father spent a day with me en route to a meeting of state Fish and Wildlife agencies in Anchorage, Alaska, I asked him if he would finally tell me just what he personally thought about Alaska's land-and-shoot wolf control program.

He was thoughtful a long time, then said, "You know, I belong to the Boone and Crockett Club. It was started by Teddy Roosevelt and is one of the country's oldest conservation organizations. They have a fair chase ethic and have been known for expelling or disciplining members who violate that ethic. It clearly states that fair-chase hunters must not use snowmobiles or shoot from vehicles or motorized boats. They must not locate animals from air and land and shoot. A hunter also cannot use artificial lights at night to spot animals. Hunters are expected to use only their skills and wait to know an animal; then they plan their hunt. We must take a clear shot and minimize suffering. We are also obligated to use all the meat and other parts of the animal." He looked at me intently, his eyes seemed very old. "Now that's hunting. What is going on in Alaska should not be called a hunt—it's wolf control."

"Like pest control," I said flatly. "Rats in a dump."

"No, honey," my father said gravely, "the wolf is a hunter."

He went on to say that he did believe in some form of wolf control. "We could wait years for the caribou population to rebound, because nature balances things out over time; it's never static, it's cyclical."

"But most hunters don't want to wait years," I said softly. "That's why we have wildlife managers. They're managing most for the hunters."

My father's eyes lit up, elated. We were off again on another debate—a chase, a hunt. "Haven't I already told you that hunters are Alaska's dependable cash crop?" he grinned. "They extend the tourist season and enrich the economy far more than cruise ships or eco-tourists or oil." He stopped and eyed me. "Hey, how did you like that caribou I sent you? Wasn't it a feast?"

In the face of his delight, his gift, I couldn't tell him the whole truth. "A Cuban friend of mine made Cuban caribou meat loaf," I told my father. "And I gave a few caribou steaks to a homeless man in our neighborhood who was so happy to have it."

What I didn't tell my father is that since the wolf control, I haven't been able to eat any more of the Christmas caribou. I am confused; I can almost feel its still life there in hard, red-hewn hunks. Perhaps, I tell myself, I'll start eating game again when they stop killing the wolves in Alaska.

What I told my father was a story, "Who Speaks for Wolf," I thought he might appreciate, one that I'd run across in my research on wolves. It was told by an Oneida Indian, Paula Underwood (Turtle Woman Singing), who heard this thousand-year-old tribal story from her father. Now I told it to my own father, who in his own way had kept some of his Native traditions. When he heard the story of the tribe who had forgotten to take their Wolf Brother's counsel into consideration in all their decisions about land and food, my father was intrigued.

A fine storyteller himself, my father asked, "So what happened to the wolves and the tribe? How did they figure it all out?" He eyed me with those half-lidded eyes, the dark blue Swede eyes with no epicanthic fold on the lids, his Indian trait. There are times my father does look like an old chief.

I told him that the Oneida story ended with the tribe deciding to move themselves, voluntarily, so that they could give back a homeland to their wolf brothers and sisters. "We could do that, too," I suggested, watching my father's face very carefully. I was aware at that moment that he was old, at the end of his long career in wildlife management. I was his daughter, perhaps his future. A sadness flowed over me as I thought of all the years we'd argued, all the times we'd agreed to disagree. I felt strangely close to him, awaiting his answer.

"Yes, honey . . ." he said slowly, "we could to that do. We could voluntarily stop hunting until the caribou population comes back . . . but like I said, that could take years, what with winterkill and all the other unknown factors. How do you suggest we manage our resources and hunters while we wait?"

"You know humans don't need caribou meat to survive. We have many other options. But the wolf depends upon caribou."

"And how about this?" my father's eyes glimmered, as if we were playing some deadly serious game and he would surely win. "How about if it were the humans who were dependent upon caribou and the wolves were managing things? Do you think the wolves would stop hunting so that humans might eat?" He shook his head with a grin. "I seriously doubt it, dear."

"We don't know the answer to that question," I said softly. "We're so out of balance, we can't imagine balance . . . or equality with another predator."

Then my father looked at me strangely, as if struck by my words. But I think he was remembering something I know nothing about: his first hunting trips when he was alone in the forest with nothing but a gun; he was tracking elk and looked up suddenly to see a magnificent buck towering over him. He was a kid, small and seemingly helpless against such animal power. And he shot, and he missed, and my father went home very hungry.

Inside my father will always be that small Depression-era farm boy who is hunting for his supper and feels the tight cramp of hunger. I have never gone hungry because my father always fed us, much of the time on game. What my father knows in his belly, I do not; but what I know in my heart, he doesn't: that it is no longer human hunger that drives us to conquer and control and kill our brother predator as if he were our natural prey—it is a story of hate inherited from another century. And like all hate, our drive to destroy our animal peers, such as the wolf, is rooted in fear.

"Listen," I told my father and took his hand. "I can't eat that caribou you sent. I'm so grateful you raised us on game . . . but I just can't eat that caribou . . . not when I know that this indirectly supports Alaska's wolf kill program."

My father considered this. He seemed both hurt and bewildered. "Well, honey, that's your choice. I'll send it to the other kids." Then he was thoughtful a long time. "I don't know about next fall . . ." he began slowly, "Uncle Bob and I haven't made our hunting trip plans." He looked at me and sighed, then shook his head. "I'll let you know . . . I'll let you know if we go up to Alaska again."

"I'll eat elk," I laughed. "I'll eat rabbit and deer and even rattlesnake again. I'd be proud to. I always tell my friends about growing up on game—that you are a true hunter . . . "

"Like the wolf," my father smiled. "Like the wolf."

Steve Wells, of the Alaska Wildlife Alliance, told me that a total of 1,472 wolves were killed in the state during the 1993–94 hunting and trapping season. That figure includes the 98 wolves killed in the state-sponsored control program.

The controversy over Alaska's wolf control program was at its height when I visited Native villages in northwest Alaska on my lecture tour in early 1993. When I asked Inupiat villagers for their opinions on the issue, I found that they were nearly all against the program. One man summed up what seemed to be the prevailing view: "It's just a plan to make it easier for rich white people from Fairbanks and Anchorage to hunt."

After Brenda completed her essay, several significant developments occurred in Alaska. In November of 1994, Dr. Gordon Haber, an independent wolf biologist, used funds donated by three wildlife organizations (Alaska Wildlife Alliance, Friends of Animals, and Wolf Haven) to purchase flight time over the area where the state was conducting its wolf control program. Haber discovered a site where four wolves—an adult and three pups—had been caught in snares. The snares had not been checked for days and one pup had already died. Another pup had nearly chewed off its leg in its struggle to be free. The biologist filmed an Alaska Department of Fish and Game employee killing the surviving wolves. He needed five shots to finish off one animal. The videotape of the incident hit the news media and immediately created an outraged reaction in Alaska and the rest of the world.

Tony Knowles, the newly elected governor of Alaska, said he was "disgusted as well as disturbed" by what he saw in the videotape. Due to public outcry, the wolf control program was temporarily suspended. Knowles ordered a full investigation of the incident and the entire control program. The subsequent report severely criticized ADFG for inhumane treatment of snared wolves and the high number of non-targeted species, such as moose, caribou, and golden eagles, accidentally killed in the snares. On February 3, 1995, Knowles announced the cancellation of Alaska's wolf control program. Although the Governor terminated this particular program, the ADFG will likely present other wolf control plans to the Alaska Board of Game in the future.

The Gift of a Wolf

Recently, Manuel Iron Cloud and I had a conversation about wolves. I had been telling him about a wolf lecture tour I had just completed in Arizona, California, and Colorado. Then Manuel, who has a habit of speaking openly about spiritual matters, asked a question that startled me: "Why are you doing all these things for wolves? Did they give you a vision?" I thought for a minute and said, "Well no, but I once knew a wolf who gave me a gift and I've been trying to find ways of repaying him. The books and lectures I do on wolves are payments on the debt I owe him." After telling Manuel more about that wolf, he considered my story and commented, "I would say that the wolves did give you a vision."

Whenever I think about wolves I invariably visualize one particular wolf who belonged to the East Fork Pack in Denali National Park. I first saw him in 1979. That initial glimpse was at a distance, perhaps half a mile, but it was close enough to recognize that something was seriously wrong with him. As he traveled across the tundra, he held his left front paw off the ground. His motion was limited to an awkward three-legged hop, rather than the graceful, effortless trot of a healthy wolf. At the time, I assumed he was an old wolf, well past his prime and close to death. Obviously, a predator with such a severe disability could not survive long.

I was wrong. The limping wolf lived on for another eight years. Not only did he survive, but he became the alpha male, the dominant breeding male of his pack. Despite his handicap, the other pack members deferred to him. When the whole pack was out on a hunt, the others periodically waited for the limping male to catch up. They gave him their allegiance and never withdrew it.

His paw never healed, but he somehow managed to adapt to his disability. Later in his life, he was briefly captured by Park Service biologists. To them, it appeared that the wolf had been caught in a steel trap when younger. The border of Denali National Park lies just a few miles north of his territory and wolf trapping is legal beyond that point. His left front foot must have stepped into a trap and, as he struggled to free himself, he yanked it free. The price he paid for his freedom was the loss of part of that foot, a maiming that stayed with him until his death.

When he had to chase a caribou, the limping wolf would run on all fours. There was no chance of catching Denali's fleet game on just three legs. When running at top speed, he appeared to function like any normal wolf. Sometimes he caught his targeted prey, sometimes he failed. Either way, when the pursuit was over, he would collapse on the tundra in exhaustion and begin licking his paw, which would be bleeding profusely from its repeated contact with the rough, rocky ground. There were times when I saw him lick that foot for an entire hour. Sometimes he ran on the maimed foot during pack activities that appeared to be play sessions. An observation I entered into my journal back in the spring of 1981 describes such an incident:

A patch of white, about a mile across the tundra, catches my eye. Looking through my binoculars, I see that it is a wolf. Its coloration — bright white fur — matches the markings of the East Fork alpha female. Hoping to watch her hunt, I set up my forty-five-power scope.

As I focus on her, I notice a second wolf stretched out fifty feet away. Looking over the nearby area, I find a total of five wolves. Except for the white female, all the other pack members are light gray in color. Soon they all get up and trot off to the east. I then see that the largest of the gray wolves has a pronounced limp in his front left leg. He holds his paw in the air and rarely puts his full weight on it. This is my old friend, the alpha male. He and the white female are almost certainly the parents of the other wolves.

As the pack travels, the limping male falls behind. At times he rushes forward on three legs and momentarily catches up. When he drops several hundred yards behind, the other pack members halt and patiently wait for him to reach them.

The wolves frequently stop to socialize. The white female, the mother, invariably is the center of attention. The younger wolves repeatedly come up to her and touch noses or roll on the ground under her. She, in turn, gives most of her attention to the limping male. The pack is in high spirits, like a group of kids on its way to play ball in a vacant lot.

The evening moves on and the pack rests. Suddenly all five wolves simultaneously sense or see something. Jumping up, they run off in close formation, shoulder to shoulder, to the west. The excitement causes the old male to ignore the pain in his crippled foot; he runs on all fours for the first time. One of the younger wolves runs faster than the others; it breaks away from the pack and sprints ahead.

The lead wolf is ten lengths ahead of the others when something new appears in the margin of my scope. The pack is chasing a grizzly bear! The bear is just a few lengths ahead of the first wolf, who is now seventy feet ahead of the pack. Surging forward, the lead wolf closes the gap to five feet. Then the grizzly looks back over its shoulder at the pursuing wolf.

As both animals run, they momentarily lock eyes and communicate with each other in a way that no human can decipher. Whatever passes between them, it causes the wolf to end the chase. The bear continues on a short distance, stops, glances back, then calmly begins feeding on grass.

The wolf who led the charge trots back to its companions, and the pack immediately leaps into exuberant play. They wag tails, touch noses, playfully nip each other, run side by side, and roll on the ground. The wolf who played tag with the bear is the focus of the play. From a human perspective, it looks like a joyous congratulatory celebration. For fifteen minutes, the wolves give uninhibited expression to their emotions. Several hundred yards away, the grizzly eats its dinner in quiet dignity.

The extraordinary aspect of this incident is that the limping wolf endured the agony of running on his maimed foot simply for the joy of participating in the playful activities of his fellow pack members. The events of that evening taught me how important companionship and social involvement are to a wolf. For the limping wolf, it was worth the pain.

On another occasion, I watched the limping wolf and his mate, the alpha female of the East Fork Pack, hunting for caribou:

On this day, the alpha pair is traveling across a broad, flat valley when the female suddenly stops, sniffs the air, and catches sight of a herd of caribou bedded on the tundra. She and her mate, the limping wolf, immediately sprint toward them. The caribou see the charging wolves, jump up, and easily outrun them. After chasing the herd a few hundred yards, the wolves give up, rest a bit, then continue on their rounds, looking for another opportunity. They find and test several other bands, but are unable to make any kills. As the limping wolf rests, he frequently licks his injured paw.

An hour later, they find another caribou herd and charge toward it. At first, it seems that these caribou are also going to escape, but then one young calf falls behind. Recognizing the opportunity, the female wolf shifts to top speed and closes in on the calf. Her mate, hindered by his lame paw, struggles to keep up.

The calf's mother has been running beside her offspring but now sees that the wolves have targeted it. She stays with the calf for a few more moments, then resigning herself to the hopelessness of the situation, distances herself from it.

With every stride, the female wolf gains on the calf. A few seconds later, just as it is about to be seized, the calf collapses, and the alpha female immediately kills it. The limping male joins his mate, and they feast on the carcass. This has been an easy kill, but it comes only after many failed attempts. The wolves have run far and worked hard for their meal.

From this observation, I learned how difficult it is for wolves to find a vulnerable target and make a kill. Based on my experiences in Alaska, I think an average, healthy caribou can run about ten m.p.h. faster that the average wolf. To survive as an individual, and to feed its pups, a wolf must search long and hard for an individual caribou with a weakness that limits its running speed.

A later episode involving the limping wolf taught me about the role of dominance and submission in the politics of a wolf pack:

Late one afternoon, the limping wolf and a younger, slightly larger male member of his pack leave their den and trot upstream on the East Fork River, looking for game. The younger wolf is anxious to travel and quickly outdistances the old alpha male. Struggling to keep up, the old wolf limps along and occasionally uses his bad paw. As they walk, I notice that the two wolves have identical markings. The limping wolf has been the breeding male of his pack for many years now. This younger male is almost certainly his son.

I swing my spotting scope back to the den to check on activity. The alpha female, the limping male's mate, is playing with their pups. After the pups plop down for a nap, I turn back to the two adult males as they continue to hunt the upper regions of the river.

A few minutes later, the lead wolf sees something and charges forward, into a clump of willow. With great agility, he zigzags back and forth through the brush, in hot pursuit of some unseen prey. Suddenly he stops, reaches down, and comes up with a plump Arctic ground squirrel in his jaws.

The second wolf appears on the scene and approaches his companion. Since he faces away from me, I can't read his facial expressions, but it looks like he wants to take the squirrel away from his partner and eat it himself.

The first wolf drops the squirrel and instantly transforms himself into the terrifying image of a snarling, dominant wolf, ready to fight to the death to defend his possessions. Even from my distant position, I can see his erect mane and growling face. The other wolf immediately gives in. He tucks his tail under his stomach, lowers his body, and rolls on the ground under the dominant wolf. From that submissive pose, he watches the other wolf consume the squirrel.

As I witness the confrontation, a great wave of sadness overwhelms me. I had just seen the limping wolf's loss of status to a younger and stronger wolf. I had never seen him submit to another wolf before, but he had clearly done so here. He would never again be the alpha male of his pack. Or so I thought.

When the squirrel was eaten, the wolf who had caught it turns and walks away. Like a chastised puppy, the defeated wolf got up and unobtrusively follows him, maintaining a respectful distance between himself and the dominant animal.

It was then that I saw my mistake. The lead wolf, the one who had caught and eaten the squirrel, walks with a severe limp! I had misidentified the two animals. The limping alpha male still had the agility to capture a squirrel as it raced through a thick patch of brush, and he still had the ability to exert his dominance over a younger and larger wolf.

From this experience, I came to understand how an old wolf, one who is past his prime and suffering from a severe handicap, can still dominate other members of his pack. The limping wolf did this through a fearsome, aggressive display and through the force of his personality. Never, in this case or during other observations, did I see him physically attack another pack member. He could control them in other ways, ways that avoided injuries. This incident taught me about the toughness needed by an alpha male as he leads his pack.

The encounter between the limping wolf and an adult wolf who was probably his son reminded me of an earlier observation at the East Fork Pack's den:

> Standing completely still, the wolf stares straight ahead. With a slow, fluid motion, it lowers its body into a crouch, then charges forward at a dead run. The wolf races toward the center of a small meadow where an animal lies on the ground, seemingly asleep. On the far side of the meadow, three other pack members burst into view, sprinting toward the same target.
>
> At the same instant, the four wolves strike their prey. Two grab his head while the others attack the flanks. Their victim jumps up and vigorously shakes his body, hurling the wolves from him. Each wolf hits the ground, scrambles to its feet, and flings itself back into the battle. In a moment, all four wolves reattach themselves to their quarry.
>
> Their beleaguered prey, with great effort, again tries to dislodge his attackers. First one wolf is thrown off, then all four. The wolves pause to see what their prey will do. He stares back at his assailants, then slowly limps off a few dozen yards, lies down, and goes to sleep. Losing interest in the game, the wolves trot over to him, curl up, and doze off.
>
> The four wolves are six-week-old pups and their intended prey was their father, the limping alpha male of the East Fork Pack. The pups used him to practice their stalking and attacking techniques. The adult willingly played the victim but walked off when the game grew too painful. He did nothing to retaliate against the pups for biting him.

Through this incident, I learned of the gentleness of adult wolves toward pups. The alpha male had enough aggressive power to face down a younger and stronger wolf, but he also possessed enough parental tenderness to let a gang of pups attack him.

Although he was capable of great gentleness, the East Fork alpha male was the toughest animal I've ever known. The final act of his life showed that toughness:

> One summer day, while on a solo hunt, the limping wolf finds a young bull moose. The bull outweighs him by four hundred pounds, but the wolf decides to take the big animal on by himself, challenging the moose to a fight to the death. Over the next thirty-six hours, he attacks the moose at least fourteen separate times. The moose fights back, stomping and kicking his attacker. The wolf's bad paw is hit during the counterattack and bleeds profusely.

Each attack weakens the moose. Near the end of the drawn-out battle, he wades out into a swift river channel. Jumping into the water, the wolf swims to his opponent. As they fight, the moose holds the alpha under water and nearly drowns him. The wolf squirms out from under the hooves, slips away to rest, then comes back for one last round. By this point, the wounds on the bull have taken their toll. Weak from loss of blood, the moose can't fight back any longer, and the wolf finishes him off. After the moose dies, other East Fork pack members arrive and feed alongside their leader.

The limping wolf pays the ultimate price for his hard-fought victory. His injuries slow him down considerably in the weeks ahead. Within a month he disappears, and I never see him again. The beta male, a wolf who is also a skilled hunter, takes over the alpha position. This male, like nearly all the other East Fork wolves, almost certainly was fathered by the limping wolf.

The wolf, during the eight years that I knew him, fought the good fight. And his death was a good one, a fitting death for an alpha male. He lived and died a fighter.

When NPS biologists later inspected the carcass of the bull moose, they discovered that he was in poor health. Somehow, the wolf had sensed this and sought to take advantage of it. This incident, and others like it, taught me about the natural process of predation and the vital, necessary role it plays in an ecosystem.

Another writer once compared wolves to art critics. His analogy caused me to realize that, as critics try to weed out inferior art, wolves seek to evaluate the strengths and weaknesses of their prey. Nature uses wolves to cull the inferior members of a wildlife species so that the species will become stronger, faster, healthier, and fitter. The limping wolf and his pack allowed me to witness this natural process of coevolution as wolves and their prey continually tested each other and counteradapted to each others' strengths and abilities. I gradually came to understand that the limping wolf had given me a gift. His gift was to teach me what it means to be a wolf. He showed me the full spectrum of the life of an alpha wolf by allowing me to watch as he hunted, played with his pups, disciplined a fellow pack member, and pursued a grizzly bear just for the fun of it. Each incident had a point, a lesson to learn, a truth to absorb. He was my teacher and mentor. He showed me the soul of a wolf.

To me, he became the ultimate example of the warrior spirit of the wolf. He never quit; he relentlessly pursued his quest for personal survival and survival of his pack. No adversity, even a lifelong problem with his maimed paw, could deter him. He continued on, despite the pain.

In many ways, he reminded me of the great outlaw wolves of the Old West. The Custer Wolf, Rags the Digger, and Lobo, King of the Currumpaw, like the limping East Fork wolf, never gave up in their arena of battle. They mounted personal guerrilla campaigns against the forces that had decimated their race. They served as champions of their kind and carried out an effective resistance until the moment of their death.

This warrior spirit was the reason the Wolf Nation survived all that our race did to it. They never quit or gave up. They died in huge numbers, they lost 99 percent of their original range in the lower forty-eight states, but they survived to fight another day. Now they are back in many of their former homelands. Soon they will be back in other territories. From the perspective of the late twentieth century, we can look back at the war against the wolf and say that the wolves are now winning the war.

Since the death of the limping wolf, other wolves have carried on his tradition and taught me truths about their race. The limping wolf's son and his fellow East Fork pack members allowed me to observe them as they carried on after their leader's death. In all, during my fifteen years in Alaska, I accumulated nearly five hundred sightings of the limping wolf, his mate, his offspring, and other pack members.

Later, the wolf packs of Glacier National Park allowed me to watch them as they continued their recolonization of Montana. They taught me how well wolf recovery can work, even with nearby herds of livestock. The Glacier wolves hunted deer and other wild prey and completely ignored the local cattle.

While working on *A Society of Wolves*, I spent portions of two years studying a captive pack of wolves in Montana. I came to know Queenie, the alpha female, so well that she let me watch as she nursed, cared for, and played with her pups. She even allowed me to crawl down into her den and experience the underground life of newborn wolf pups. Queenie gave me a vivid demonstration of the emotional bonds that tie a mother wolf to her pups.

All these things are gifts from wolves, gifts that brought me further along in understanding their race.

In researching and tracking down selections for *War Against the Wolf*, I was stuck by the theme common to Native American stories of wolves. Wolf characters are nearly always presented as elders, teachers, mentors, and benefactors. The Blackfeet stories "The Legend of the Friendly Medicine Wolf" and "When Men and Animals Were Friendly," the Dena'ina narrative from Alaska, "Wolf Story," and many others, show wolves as kindred beings who willingly give gifts to humans. These gifts teach people how to relate to the natural and spiritual worlds and frequently save the lives of starving human beings. In return, all the wolves ask is respect and understanding, a small payback for their extraordinary gifts.

Also common to Native wolf stories are human characters who are willing to give the wolves the respect they desire. In response, the wolves give more of themselves to those individuals open to their gifts. Perhaps this is what Chief Dan George was thinking of, the willingness of wolves to respond to humans, when he gave this advice:

> *If you talk to the animals they will talk with you*
> *and you will know each other.*
> *If you do not talk to them you will not know them,*
> *and what you do not know you will fear.*
> *What one fears one destroys.*

Manuel Iron Cloud's grandmother taught him the same lesson about wolves. In telling the story of her encounter with the wolf to young Manuel, she finished with these words, "So when you see a Wolf don't be afraid of him, instead talk to him, he might have something to say to you." Mutual respect between two kindred species can be considered a mutual gift.

During my most recent wolf lecture tour, I did several programs in partnership with Kent Weber of Mission: Wolf, a Colorado non-profit operation that cares for unwanted captive-born wolves. I presented my slide show on wild wolves and then introduced Kent, who explained the purpose of his organization. The climax of each event was the appearance of one of Kent's tame wolves. As the audience responded to the charismatic appeal of the wolf, Kent explained why wolves belong in the wild, not in cages in people's back yards.

After one of our joint appearances, Kent told me a startling story about the gift of a wolf. He often brings wolves to elementary schools and sometimes speaks to groups of kids as large as five hundred. In some cases, he allows a tame wolf to run free in the auditorium. The wolf circles the entire room several times, running at top speed. As the wolf runs, the school children go crazy with excitement.

Kent began to notice that when a wolf was allowed to run free in such situations, it would almost always pick a child to greet and make friends with. It usually was just one kid out of the several hundred in the auditorium. Curious as to why the wolves were picking out certain children, Kent began to ask teachers if there was anything special about the ones the wolves chose.

The teachers were astonished at the behavior of the wolves. They told Kent that the boys or girls selected by the wolves were always the worst outcasts in school, the kids everyone else picked on. The wolves had decided to make friends with those outcasts.

I've been around wolves for eighteen years, and have learned many things about them, but I'm not certain why Kent's wolves behaved that way with those kids. If I had to guess, I would say that they may have sensed that those children were in distress. Wild and captive wolves love to take care of pups, their own or orphaned ones. Wolves instinctively want to care for helpless, defenseless young pups. Perhaps to the captive-raised wolves, those needy, distressed kids were the equivalent of abandoned, orphaned pups, and they wanted to care for them.

Whatever the reasons for the wolves' behavior, I can imagine no greater gift from a wolf to a person. Imagine what it must be like for a young child to be a total outcast in his or her school, to be picked on by all the other kids. Then imagine what it would be like to be sitting in a huge auditorium, surrounded by hundreds of people who don't like you, when a wolf is set free and races around the room, finally stopping beside you. At first, the wolf's approach would likely be interpreted as just one more unfair attack, but then the wolf clearly shows that he is friendly and greets you and licks your face and hands. Such an experience, such a gift, would change a child's life forever. Whatever unfair or negative things might later happen in their lives, they will never forget that once a wolf picked them, out of all the other kids in the entire school, to make friends.

Perhaps, like wolf characters in Native American stories, these wolves were attuned to the needs of people. In the old stories, the needs usually involved food; here it was emotional support. Perhaps the wolves were trying to teach humans a lesson. To the outcast kids and to the rest of the student body the lesson was the same: reach out to people in distress and offer them your friendship.

I feel I owe the East Fork limping male, and the other wolves who have given me gifts, a tremendous debt. They freely gave of their lives to help me understand their race. I have vowed to repay the wolves by passing on their gift to others of my race. With my wolf books and lectures, I try to teach other people about wolves and why they deserve our respect. I explain the horrendous things our country has done to the Wolf Nation and try to show why we should restore them to their former ranges. The best way I can repay the wolves for their gift is to help bring them back to places like Yellowstone National Park, Idaho, Colorado, Arizona, New

Mexico, Texas, New York, and northern New England. If I can help wolves regain those old territories, I'll be able to say that I've repaid the debt I owe them.

In the Oneida story, "Who Speaks for Wolf," as told by Paula Underwood, a Native man, known as Wolf's Brother, tries to repay his debt to wolves by getting his people to move their camp away from the home range of a community of wolves. Through a calm and reasoned approach, acting as a spokesman for his wolf brothers, he succeeds in resolving the conflict that had arisen between the Oneida Nation and the Wolf Nation. I don't claim the honorary title of Wolf Brother. I haven't done enough to deserve it, but I do aspire to serve, like the Native man in the story, as a spokesperson for the wolf. It is part of my debt to the wolves for the gifts they have given me.

A Final Note

Legal challenges delayed but failed to stop the Yellowstone and Idaho wolf reintroduction projects. At 8:45 AM on Thursday, January 12, 1995, the first batch of Canadian wolves arrived in Yellowstone. As reported by the Associated Press, "The once-vilified wolf was given a hero's welcome" by children, park rangers, Washington officials, wolf supporters, and a large contingency of reporters.

On January 14, 1995, the first of fifteen wolves were released into central Idaho. In a ceremony held just prior to the release, elders of the local Lemhi Shoshoni Tribe prayed that the wolf would once again make its home in the territory of the Shoshoni people. Dan Ariwite, a tribal spokesman, summed up the feelings of his people, saying, "He is welcome here."

During the morning of March 24, 1995, after ten weeks in an acclimation pen, the first of three packs of Yellowstone wolves stepped out into Lamar Valley. The following afternoon, NPS biologists observed that pack playing in the snow a quarter-mile from their release site. By March 29, all three packs (fourteen wolves) were out of their pens. The historic moment has finally arrived: Wild wolves are once again living in Yellowstone.

Wolf Spirits

During the final week of production on this book, I discussed the current status of wolf recovery with Joseph Marshall, the Sicangu Lakota author of "The Wolf: A Native American Symbol." We talked about the successful wolf recolonization of Montana; the reintroduction of wolves into Idaho and Yellowstone; the likely return of the wolf to Arizona, New Mexico, and Colorado; and the possibility that the Nez Perce and Wind River Indian reservations might soon initiate their own wolf reintroductions.

As we both voiced our optimism about the reestablishment of the wolf in its traditional homeland, Joseph recalled a prophecy he first heard in 1952, just after learning the terrible story of what had been done to the wolves:

> As a seven year old, I knew that there were no wolves left in my world, and I knew why. One day my grandfather, Isaac Bear Looks Behind, tried to calm my anger and confusion. He told me that the spirits of all the dead wolves had traveled to some far-off mountains. There they would wait until the time was right for them to return and walk again on the earth.

After telling me this, Joseph explained that these Wolf Spirits are waiting until it is safe to be reborn as new wolves. Bounty hunters, wolfers, ranchers, and government predator control agents killed the physical bodies of those wolves, but their spirits lived on, patiently waiting in the mountains until the time was right for them to return.

Joseph and I then compared other references and personal experiences to this concept of Wolf Spirits dwelling in the mountains. When James Willard Schultz lived with the Blackfeet Nation in Montana, he heard a highly respected medicine man named Morning Eagle describe the current location of the Chief Wolf, the Wolf Spirit who is the super-natural keeper or guardian of the Wolf Nation:

> In these late days, the old gods—Chief Wolf, Chief Bear and others—no longer come and talk with us in person; we know that they still roam the earth, that they live in some far part of it which the white men have not yet found and desecrated, and we have assurance that they still visit us in the spirit, unseen and unheard except as they appear to us in our dreams. Yes. And we know that they still heed our prayers and intercede for us with the sun, ruler of all, for her mercy and aid.

Joseph told me that not long after hearing his grandfather's prophecy, a Wolf Spirit came to him in a dream. Perhaps it was the Chief Wolf spoken of by Morning Eagle. The Wolf talked with young Joseph and assigned him a mission that gave direction to the rest of his life. The Wolf Spirit returned numerous times to Joseph's dreams and spoke with him on many matters. Joseph tells the story of that Wolf Spirit in his book, *On Behalf of the Wolf and the First Peoples*.

Some Native people say that animal spirits live in the mountains that encircle the Medicine Wheel in Wyoming, a sacred ancient ceremonial site used jointly by many tribes. The Medicine Wheel sits at ten thousand feet in the Big Horn Mountains, one hundred miles east of Yellowstone, in the heart of the traditional homeland of the wolf. The location certainly fits Morning Eagle's description of a "far part" of the earth that has not yet been desecrated.

Bill TallBull, a highly respected tribal elder from Montana, tells of a vision he had at the Medicine Wheel. When he was on his way to the site, he saw a wolf step out from a rock wall. The wolf looked at Bill, then disappeared down the mountain. The white people in his party didn't see the animal, and when Bill checked the snow-covered ground where the wolf had walked, he couldn't find any tracks.

In telling this story to Jim Boggs, an ethnographer at Montana State University, Bill spoke of how the spirits of animals moved to the mountains around the Medicine Wheel site. Then he added:

> And they'll be dormant until such time that the conditions are right. And then they'll come back out.

As we talked of these things, Joseph and I concluded that Isaac Bear Looks Behind's prophecy of the early 1950s is now being fulfilled. As expressed by Joseph, "The time is right for them to come back home." Jack Gladstone, the Blackfeet singer/songwriter, expressed exactly the same thought to me: "The time is ripe right now for the Wolf Spirit to reemerge into the twentieth century." Our country's war against the wolf is now drawing to a close. We have learned, thanks in part to the example set by Native Americans, that we can coexist and share this continent with fellow species.

Perhaps we should seek to speak to the Wolf Spirit who dwells in our dreams and give it this message:

> Wolf Spirit—the time is right
> for you to be reborn
> and once again walk the earth.

Aerial view of an ancient Medicine Wheel at Big Horn Mountains, Wyoming. (U.S. Department of Agriculture Forest Service)

Albright, Horace M. 1931. The National Park Service's Policy on Predatory Mammals. *Journal of Mammalogy* 12(2):185–86. Reprinted by permission of the American Society of Mammalogists.

American Society of Mammalogists. 1931. Report of the Committee on Problems of Predatory Mammal Control. *Journal of Mammalogy* 12(3):340–44. Reprinted by permission of the American Society of Mammalogists.

Bowden, Charles. 1992. Lonesome Lobo. *Wildlife Conservation* January–February, 1992. Reprinted by permission of the author.

DeBlieu, Jan. 1992. A Song for the Smokies. *American Way* April 15, 1992, 66–72 and 103–06. Reprinted by permission of the author.

Ellanna, Linda J. and Andrew Balluta. 1992. *Nuvendaltin-Quht'ana: The People of Nondalton.* Washington: Smithsonian Institution Press. Reprinted by permission of the authors.

Emerson, Everett, Editor. 1976. *Letters From New England: The Massachusetts Bay Colony 1629–1638.* Amherst: The University of Massachusetts Press. (*Source for the modernized version of "Edmund Browne: Letter to Sir Simonds D'Ewes."*)

Fouquet, L. C. 1925. Buffalo Days. In *Kansas State Historical Collections 1923–1925* (Volume XVI). Topeka: Kansas State Printing Plant. Reprinted by permission of the Kansas Historical Society.

Haley, J. Evetts. [1929] 1953. *The XIT Ranch of Texas and the Early Days of the Llano Estacado.* Reprint. Norman: University of Oklahoma Press. Reprinted with permission of the University of Oklahoma Press.

Hogan, Linda. 1993. The Fallen. In *The Book of Medicines.* Minneapolis, Mn.: Coffee House Press. Reprinted by permission of the author.

Howell, A. Brazier. 1930. At the Cross-Roads. *Journal of Mammalogy* 11(3):377089. Reprinted by permission of the American Society of Mammalogists.

Laramie County Protective Association. 1890. Wolf Fund letter. Teschemacher and DeBillier Collection #340, American Heritage Center, Laramie, Wyoming. Reprinted by permission of the American Heritage Center.

Leopold, Aldo. 1920. The Game Situation in the Southwest. *Bulletin of the American Game Protective Association* April, 1920. Reprinted with permission of Nina Leopold Bradley.

Leopold, Aldo. 1947. Foreword. In J. Baird Callicott, Editor. 1987. *A Companion to A Sand County Almanac: And Sketches Here and There.* Madison: The University of Wisconsin Press. Reprinted with permission of Nina Leopold Bradley.

Leopold, Aldo. [1949] 1977. Thinking Like a Mountain. *In A Sand County Almanac: And Sketches Here and There* (Special Commemorative Edition). New York: Oxford University Press, Inc. Reprinted with permission of Oxford University Press.

Marshall, Joseph M. 1992. The Wolf: A Native American Symbol. *The Wolf Fund Newsletter* Winter/Spring 1992. Reprinted by permission of the author.

McIntyre, Rick. 1993. *A Society of Wolves: National Parks and the Battle Over the Wolf.* Stillwater, Mn.: Voyageur Press. Selections reprinted by permission of the author.

Mooar, J. Wright. 1927. Letter to J. Evetts Haley, November 25, 1927. Collection of the Panhandle-Plains Historical Museum, Canyon, Texas. Reprinted by permission of the Panhandle-Plains Historical Museum.

Olson, Sigurd F. 1938. A Study in Predatory Relationship with Particular Reference to the Wolf. *The Scientific Monthly* 46:323–36 Reprinted by permission of the American Association for the Advancement of Science.

Seton, Ernest Thompson. 1937. Wosca and Her Valiant Cub or The White Mother Wolf. In *Great Historic Animals: Mainly About Wolves.* New York: Charles Scribner's Sons. Reprinted by permission of Dee Seton Barber.

Seton, Ernest Thompson. 1940. *Trail of an Artist-Naturalist.* New York: C. Scribner's Sons. Reprinted by permission of Dee Seton Barber.

Townshend, R. B. [1923] 1968. *A Tenderfoot in Colorado.* Reprint. Norman: University of Oklahoma Press. Reprinted by permission of the University of Oklahoma Press.

Tubbs, Nancy jo. 1994. Cry Wolf—Tracking Down an Alleged Wolf Attack on a Human. *International Wolf* Summer 1994. Reprinted by permission of the author.

Underwood, Paula. 1983. *Who Speaks for Wolf.* Austin: Tribe of Two Press. Reprinted by permission of the author.

Young, Stanley P. 1946. *The Wolf in North American History.* Caldwell, Id.: Caxton Printers. Reprinted by permission of Caxton Printers.

Young, Stanley P., and Edward A. Goldman. [1944] 1964. *The Wolves of North America.* Reprint. Mineola, N.Y.: Dover Publications. Reprinted by permission of Dover Publications.

The following material is copyrighted by the respective authors and used by their permission:

Baldes, Richard. 1995. The Wolf as a Fellow Hunter.

Bangs, Ed. 1995. Wolf Hysteria: Reintroducing Wolves to the West.

Boyd, Diane. 1995. The Return of the Wolf to Glacier.

Fischer, Hank. 1995. Supply-Side Environmentalism and Wolf Recovery in the West.

Fritts, Steven. 1995. The Story of Wolf 5105.

Gipson, Philip. 1995. Wolves and Wolf Literature: A Credibility Gap.

Gladstone, Jack. 1987. Wolf.

Gladstone, Jack. 1995. A Blackfeet Song of Brotherhood.

Iron Cloud, Manuel. 1995. Sungmanitu Tanka Oyate: Wolf Nation.

LoBello, Rick. 1995. Aqui No Hay Mas Lobos.

McIntyre, Rick. 1995. Witnesses to an Ecological Murder. Hunting Their Lost Tribe. The Gift of a Wolf. Wolf Spirits.

Peterson, Brenda. 1994. Wolf Medicine.

Underwood, Paula. 1992. Wolf Song for Wolf Haven.

Adams, Andy. 1906. *Cattle Brands: A Collection of Western Camp-Fire Stories.* Boston: Houghton, Mifflin and Company.

Albright, Horace M. 1931. The National Park Service's Policy on Predatory Mammals. *Journal of Mammalogy* 12(2):185–86.

American Society of Mammalogists. 1931. Report of the Committee on Problems of Predatory Mammal Control. *Journal of Mammalogy* 12(3):340–44.

Anonymous. 1834. *Visit to Texas: Being the Journal of a Traveller.* New York: Goodrich & Wiley.

Anonymous. 1886. Montana Wolves and Panthers. *Forest and Stream* July 22, 1886.

Anonymous. 1935. Hunter Who Slew Famed Killer Wolves Retires. *Rocky Mountain News* April 14, 1935.

Anonymous. 1948. World Champion Wolfer Lives Quietly on Ranch Near Delta. *Delta (Co.) County Independent* January 8, 1948.

Arnold, Samuel Greene. 1874. *History of the State of Rhode Island and Providence Plantations.* New York: D. Appleton & Company.

Audubon, John James. 1835. *Ornithological Biography* (Volume III). Edinburgh.

Bailey, Vernon. 1907. *Wolves in Relation to Stock, Game, and the National Forest Reserves.* Washington: U. S. Department of Agriculture.

Bailey, Vernon. 1908. *Destruction of Wolves and Coyotes: Results Obtained During 1907.* Washington: U. S. Department of Agriculture.

Bailey, Vernon. 1930. *Animal Life of Yellowstone National Park.* Springfield, Il.: Charles C. Thomas Publisher.

Banta, Captain William. [1893] 1933. *Twenty-Seven Years on the Texas Frontier.* Reprint. Council Hill, Ok.: L. G. Park.

Bass, Rick. 1992. *The Ninemile Wolves.* Livingstone, Mt.: Clark City Press.

Batty, Joseph H. 1884. *How to Hunt and Trap.* New York: Orange Judd Company.

Bliss, Charles. 1922. *Annual Report, New Mexico District, Fiscal Year 1922.* U.S. Bureau of Biological Survey.

Bowden, Charles. 1992. Lonesome Lobo. *Wildlife Conservation* January–February, 1992.

Bowman, Elbert F. 1938. *Wolves: Being Reminiscent of My Life on an Eastern Montana Ranch.* Unpublished manuscript in the collection of Montana Historical Society, Helena, Montana.

Browne, Edmund. 1638. Letter to Sir Simonds D'Ewes. British Museum, Manuscript Harley 388, folio 19. *(See also, Everett Emerson)*

Brown, David E., Editor. 1983. *The Wolf in the Southwest: The Making of an Endangered Species.* Tucson: University of Arizona Press.

Cahalane, Victor. 1939. The Evolution of Predator Control Policy in the National Parks. *Journal of Wildlife Management* 3(3):229–37.

Caine, S. A., *et al.* 1972. *Predator Control—1971: Report of the Council on Environmental Quality and the Department of the Interior by the Advisory Committee on*

Predator Control. Washington: U.S. Government Printing Office.

Caras, Roger. 1966. *The Custer Wolf: Biography of an American Renegade*. Boston: Little, Brown.

Carhart, Arthur, 1939. World Champion Wolfer. *Outdoor Life* September, 1939.

Carhart, Arthur H., and Stanley P. Young. 1928. Rags the Digger. *The Red Book Magazine* January, 1928.

Carhart, Arthur H., and Stanley P. Young. 1929. *The Last Stand of the Pack*. New York: J. H. Sears and Company.

Colorado, State of. 1984. *Colorado Revised Statutes* (Volume 14). Denver: Bradford Publishing Co.

Cook, John R. 1907. *The Border and the Buffalo*. Topeka, Ks.: Crane & Company.

Corbin, Ben. 1900. *Corbin's Advice or The Wolf Hunter's Guide*. Bismarck, N.D.: The Tribune Co.

Curnow, Edward. 1969. *The History of the Eradication of the Wolf in Montana*. Masters thesis, University of Montana.

Day, Albert, and Almer Nelson. 1928. *Wild Life Conservation and Control in Wyoming Under the Leadership of the United States Biological Survey*. Laramie: The University of Wyoming.

DeBlieu, Jan. 1991. *Meant to be Wild: The Struggle to Save Endangered Species through Captive Breeding*. Golden, Co.: Fulcrum Press.

DeBlieu, Jan. 1992. A Song for the Smokies. *American Way* April 15, 1992, 66–72 and 103–06.

Director, National Park Service. 1917–23. *Annual Reports*. Washington: U.S. Government Printing Office.

Dunlap, Thomas. 1988. *Saving America's Wildlife: Ecology and the American Mind: 1850–1990*. Princeton, N.J.: Princeton University Press.

Ellanna, Linda J., and Andrew Balluta. 1992. *Nuvendaltin-Quht'ana: The People of Nondalton*. Washington: Smithsonian Institution Press.

Emerson, Everett, Editor. 1976. *Letters From New England: The Massachusetts Bay Colony 1629–1638*. Amherst: The University of Massachusetts Press. *(Source for the modernized version of "Edmund Browne: Letter to Sir Simonds D'Ewes.")*

Fouquet, L. C. 1925. Buffalo Days. In *Kansas State Historical Collections 1923–1925* (Volume XVI). Topeka: Kansas State Printing Plant.

Freeman, Frederick. 1860. *The History of Cape Cod: The Annals of Barnstable County*. Boston: Geo. C. Rand & Avery.

Grinnell, George Bird. 1897. Wolves and Wolf Nature. In George Bird Grinnell and Theodore Roosevelt, Editors. 1897. *Trail and Camp-Fire*. New York: Harper & Brothers, Publishers.

Grinnell, George Bird. 1911. *The Wolf Hunters*. New York: Charles Scribner's Sons.

Haley, J. Evetts. [1929] 1953. *The XIT Ranch of Texas and the Early Days of the Llano Estacado*. Reprint. Norman: University of Oklahoma Press.

Hastings, Lansford W. [1845] 1932. *The Emigrants' Guide to Oregon and California*. Reprint. Princeton, N.J.: Princeton University Press.

Hening, William Waller, Editor. 1823. *The Statutes at Large; Being a Collection of*

All the Laws of Virginia. New York: R. & W. & G. Bartow.

Hogan, Linda. 1993. The Fallen. In *The Book of Medicines*. Minneapolis, Mn.: Coffee House Press.

Howell, A. Brazier. 1930. At the Cross-Roads. *Journal of Mammalogy* 11(3):377–89.

Huidekoper, Wallis. 1916. *The Wolf Question and What the Government Is Doing to Help*. Denver: American National Live Stock Association.

Humphreys, Col. David. 1818. *An Essay on the Life of the Honorable Major General Israel Putnam*. Boston: Samuel Avery.

Hutchinson, Thomas. 1764. *The History of the Colony of Massachusetts-Bay*. Boston: Thomas and John Fleet. *(Source for "Anonymous: Letter from a Colonist.")*

Iowa, State of. 1857. *Journal of the Senate, of the Sixth General Assembly of the State of Iowa*. Iowa City: P. Moriarty, State Printer. *(Source for "Jarius Neal: Proposed Amendment to Iowa's Wolf Bounty Law.")*

Josselyn, John. [1672] 1972. *New-England's Rarities Discovered*. Reprint. Boston: Massachusetts Historical Society.

Kennedy, James J. Understanding Professional Career Evolution—An Example of Aldo Leopold. *Wildlife Society Bulletin* 12:215–26.

Kellert, Stephen. . Public Perceptions of Predators, Particularly the Wolf and Coyote. *Biological Conservation* 31(2):167–89.

Laney, L. H. 1946. *Annual Report, Predatory Animal Control, New Mexico District, Fiscal Year 1946*. U.S. Fish and Wildlife Service.

Laney, L. H. 1950. *March Quarter Narrative (1950), Predatory Animal Control, New Mexico District*. U.S. Fish and Wildlife Service.

Laney, L. H. 1958. *Annual Report, Predatory Animal Control, New Mexico District, Fiscal Year 1958*. U.S. Fish and Wildlife Service.

Laramie County Protective Association. 1890. Wolf Fund Letter. Unpublished letter in Teschemacher and DeBillier Collection #340, American Heritage Center, Laramie, Wyoming.

Leopold, Aldo. 1915. The Varmint Question. *Pine Cone* December, 1915.

Leopold, Aldo. 1920. The Game Situation in the Southwest. *Bulletin of the American Game Protective Association* April, 1920.

Leopold, Aldo, 1944. Review of *The Wolves of North America* by Stanley Young and Arthur Carhart. *Journal of Forestry* 42(12):928–29.

Leopold, Aldo. 1947. Foreword. In J. Baird Callicott, Editor. 1987. *A Companion to A Sand County Almanac: And Sketches Here and There*. Madison: The University of Wisconsin Press.

Leopold, Aldo. [1949] 1977. Thinking Like a Mountain. In *A Sand County Almanac: And Sketches Here and There* (Special Commemorative Edition). New York: Oxford University Press, Inc.

Ligon, J. Stokley. 1916. *Annual Report, Predatory Animal Control, New Mexico–Arizona District, Fiscal Year 1916*. U.S. Bureau of Biological Survey.

Ligon, J. Stokley. 1917. *Annual Report, Predatory Animal Control, New Mexico–Arizona District, Fiscal Year 1917*. U.S. Bureau of Biological Survey.

Ligon, J. Stokley. 1919. *Annual Report, Predatory Animal Control, New Mexico Dis-

trict, Fiscal Year 1919. U.S. Bureau of Biological Survey.

Ligon, J. Stokley. 1920. *Annual Report, Predatory Animal Control, New Mexico District, Fiscal Year 1920.* U.S. Bureau of Biological Survey.

Lopez, Barry Holstun. 1978. *Of Wolves and Men.* New York: Charles Scribner's Sons.

Marshall, Joseph M. 1992. The Wolf: A Native American Symbol. *The Wolf Fund Newsletter* Winter/Spring 1992.

Marshall, Joseph M. 1995. *On Behalf of the Wolf and the First Peoples.* Santa Fe, N.M.: Red Crane Books.

McClintock, Walter. 1910. *The Old North Trail.* London: Macmillan and Co. *(Source for "Brings-down-the-Sun: The Legend of the Friendly Medicine Wolf.")*

McClure, S. W. 1914. The Wolf at the Stockman's Door. *The Country Gentleman* November 14, 1914.

McIntyre, Rick. 1993. *A Society of Wolves: National Parks and the Battle Over the Wolf.* Stillwater, Mn.: Voyageur Press.

Mech, L. David. [1970] 1981. *The Wolf: The Making of an Endangered Species.* Reprint. Minneapolis: University of Minnesota Press.

Merritt, Dixon. 1921. *World's Greatest Animal Criminal Dead.* Washington: U.S. Department of Agriculture.

Montana, State of. 1905. *Laws, Resolutions and Memorials of the State of Montana Passed at the Ninth Regular Session of the Legislative Assembly.* Helena, Mt.: State Publishing Company.

Mooar, J. Wright. November 25, 1927. Letter to J. Evetts Haley. Collection of the Panhandle-Plains Historical Museum, Canyon, Texas.

Murie, Adolph. 1944. *The Wolves of Mount McKinley.* Washington: U.S. Government Printing Office.

Murray, John A. 1993. *Out Among the Wolves.* Portland, Or.: Graphic Arts Press.

National Park Service. no date. *Condensed Chronology of Service Predator Control Policy.* On file in the Yellowstone National Park Library.

National Park Service. 1919–32. *Minutes of National Park Conferences.* Washington: National Park Service.

National Park Service. 1936. National Park Policy for the Vertebrates. *National Park Supplement to Planning and Civic Comment* October–December 1936.

Neal, Jarius. 1857. Proposed Amendment to Iowa's Wolf Bounty Law. *Journal of the Senate, of the Sixth General Assembly of the State of Iowa.* Iowa City: P. Moriarty, State Printer.

O'Callaghan, E. B., Editor. 1868. *Laws and Ordinances of New Netherland, 1638–1674.* Albany: Weed, Parsons, and Company.

Olson, Sigurd F. 1938. A Study in Predatory Relationship with Particular Reference to the Wolf. *The Scientific Monthly* 46:323–36.

Peirce, Milton P. 1890. The Great Hinckley Hunt. *American Field* January 4, 1890.

Pennsylvania, State of. 1896. *The Statutes at Large of Pennsylvania from 1682 to 1801* (Volume II: 1700–1712). Harrisburg: State Printer of Pennsylvania.

Piper, Stanley. 1922. In *The Rocky Mountain News* December 21, 1922.

Pulsifer, David, Editor. 1861. *Records of the Colony of New Plymouth in New England*

(Laws: 1623–1682). Boston: William White Press.

Roosevelt, Theodore. 1902. Wolves and Wolf-Hounds. In *Hunting the Grisly and Other Sketches*. New York: G. P. Putnam's Sons.

Schultz, James Willard. 1901. The Eagle Creek Wolfers. *Forest and Stream* January 5, 12, and 19, 1901.

Schultz, James Willard. 1974. *Why Gone These Times: Blackfeet Tales by James Willard Schultz*. Norman: University of Oklahoma Press.

Seton, Ernest Thompson. 1898. Lobo: King of the Currumpaw. In *Wild Animals I Have Known*. New York: Charles Scribner's Sons.

Seton, Ernest Thompson. 1909. *Life-Histories of Northern Animals*. New York: Charles Scribner's Sons.

Seton, Ernest Thompson. 1937. Wosca and Her Valiant Cub or The White Mother Wolf. In *Great Historic Animals: Mainly About Wolves*. New York: Charles Scribner's Sons.

Seton, Ernest Thompson. 1940. *Trail of an Artist-Naturalist*. New York: C. Scribner's Sons.

Shoemaker, Henry W. 1914. *Wolf Days in Pennsylvania*. Altoona, Pa.: The Tribune Press.

Shurtleff, Nathaniel B., Editor. 1853. *Records of the Governor and Company of the Massachusetts Bay in New England*. Boston: William White Press.

Shurtleff, Nathaniel B., Editor. 1855. *Records of the Colony of New Plymouth in New England* (Court Orders: Volume I 1633–1640). Boston: William White Press.

Skinner, Milton P. 1927. The Predatory and Fur-Bearing Animals of the Yellowstone National Park. *Roosevelt Wildlife Bulletin* 4(2):163–282.

Stuart, Granville. 1925. *Forty Years on the Frontier*. Glendale, Ca.: The Arthur H. Clark Company.

Superintendent, Yellowstone National Park. 1880–1920. *Annual Reports*. On file in the Yellowstone National Park Library.

Superintendent, Yellowstone National Park. 1918–28. *Monthly Reports*. On file in the Yellowstone National Park Library.

Taylor, Joseph Henry. 1891. *Twenty Years on the Trap Line*. Bismarck, N.D.: Published by the Author.

Thoreau, Henry David. [1906] 1962. *The Journals of Henry David Thoreau*. Reprint. New York: Dover Publications.

Townshend, R. B. [1923] 1968. *A Tenderfoot in Colorado*. Reprint. Norman: University of Oklahoma Press.

Tubbs, Nancy Jo. 1994. Cry Wolf—Tracking Down an Alleged Wolf Attack on a Human. *International Wolf* Summer 1994.

Underwood, Paula. 1983. *Who Speaks for Wolf*. Austin: Tribe of Two Press.

U.S. Army. 1907. *Rules, Regulations and Instructions for the Information and Guidance of Officers and Enlisted Men of the U.S. Army, and of the Scouts Doing Duty in the Yellowstone National Park*. Washington: U.S. Government Printing Office.

U.S. Biological Survey. 1924. *Report of the Chief of the Biological Survey*. Washington: U.S. Government Printing Office.

U.S. Biological Survey. 1926. *Report of the Chief of the Biological Survey.* Washington: U.S. Government Printing Office.

U.S. Fish and Wildlife Service. 1992. *Transcript of Proceedings: Public Hearing on Wolf Environmental Impact Statement.* Helena, Mt.: Hendrickson Court Reporting.

U.S. Fish and Wildlife Service. 1994. *The Reintroduction of Gray Wolves to Yellowstone National Park and Central Idaho: Final Environmental Impact Statement.* Helena, Mt.: U.S. Fish and Wildlife Service.

U.S. Senate. 1915. Debate on Funding Predator Control Program. *Congressional Record* February 25, 1914, 4572–83.

Vest, Jay Hansford C. 1988. The Medicine Wolf Returns: Traditional Blackfeet Concepts of *Canis lupus. Western Wildlands* 14(2):28–33.

Victor, Mrs. Frances Fuller. 1870. *The River of the West.* Hartford, Ct.: R. W. Bliss.

Weaver, John. 1978. *The Wolves of Yellowstone.* NPS Natural Resources Report #14. Washington: U.S. Government Printing Office.

Webb, James Josiah. 1931. *Adventures in the Santa Fé Trade: 1844–1847,* edited by Ralph P. Bieber. Glendale, Ca.: The Arthur H. Clark Company.

Webb, W. E., 1872. *Buffalo Land: A Manual for Sportsmen and Hand-book for Emigrants Seeking Homes.* Chicago: E. Hannaford & Company.

Wilder, Doris. 1922. U.S. Agents Stalk 'Desperadoes' of Animal World thru Deserts and Over Mountain Ranges of the West. *The Rocky Mountain News* December 31, 1922.

Williams, H. P. 1961. The Custer Wolf—Greatest Killer. *Denver Post.* September 24, 1961.

Wood, William. [1634] 1977. *New England's Prospect.* Reprint. Amherst: University of Massachusetts Press.

Wyoming, Territory of. 1876. *Compiled Laws of Wyoming 1869–1876.* Cheyenne, Wy.: Leader Steam Book and Job Print.

Wyoming, Territory of. 1879. *Session Laws of Wyoming, 1879.* Cheyenne, Wy.: Leader Steam Book and Job Print.

Wyoming, Territory of. 1884. *Session Laws of Wyoming, 1884.* Cheyenne, Wy.: Leader Steam Book and Job Print.

Wyoming, Territory of. 1890. *Session Laws of Wyoming, 1890.* Cheyenne, Wy.: Leader Steam Book and Job Print.

Wyoming, State of. 1913. *Session Laws of Wyoming, 1913.* Sheridan, Wy.: Mills Printing Co.

Young, Stanley P. 1930. November 24 letter to Arthur Carhart. Stanley Young Collection, Western History Department, Denver Public Library.

Young, Stanley P. 1946. *The Wolf in North American History.* Caldwell, Id.: Caxton Printers.

Young, Stanley P., and Edward A. Goldman. [1944] 1964. *The Wolves of North America.* Reprint. Mineola, N.Y.: Dover Publications.

Young, Stanley P. 1970. *The Last of the Loners.* New York: Macmillan.

Acknowledgments

I would like to thank the following libraries, historic societies, and other collections, facilities and organizations for their assistance in tracking down historic documents used in *War Against the Wolf* (names in parentheses indicate staff members who were especially helpful):

Amon Carter Museum, Ft. Worth, Tx. (Rick Stewart)
American Heritage Center, Laramie, Wy.
Arizona Historical Society, Tucson
The Center for Research Libraries, Chicago, Il. (Catherine Nich)
Colorado State University
DeGolyer Library, Southern Methodist University (David Farmer and Cammie Vitale)
Denver Public Library, Western History Dept. (Barbara Walton, Lisa Backman, and Kathey Swan)
Ernest Thompson Seton Memorial Library and Museum (Stephen Zimmer)
The Free Library of Philadelphia
Harvard University Archives (Danielle Green)
The Historical Society of Pennsylvania
Jefferson National Expansion Memorial Archives, St. Louis, Mo.
Kalispell (Mt.) Public Library
Kansas State Historical Society (Susan Forbes)
National Park Service, Harpers Ferry Center (David Nathanson)
National Park Service, Rocky Mountain Regional Office
Northwestern University
Montana Historical Society
Ohio Historical Society (Vernon Will)
Oregon Historical Society (Steven Hallberg)
Palm Desert (Ca.) Public Library
Panhandle-Plains Historical Society, Canyon, Tx. (Betty Bustos)
Plimoth Plantation, Plymouth, Ma. (James Baker)
Scituate (Ma.) Town Archives (Dorothy Clapp Langley)
Smithsonian Institution Archives (Bruce Kirby)
State Historical Society of Iowa (Susan H. Rogers)
Sol Ross State University, Alpine, Tx.
South Dakota State Historical Society (Marvene Riis)
St. Louis Mercantile Library (Charles E. Brown)
Teton County Historical Society, Jackson, Wy. (Rita Verley)
University of Alaska
University of California, Berkeley
University of California, Riverside

University of Massachusetts
University of Montana
University of Nevada, Las Vegas
University of New Mexico
University of Texas, Austin
University of Wisconsin, Aldo Leopold Collection (Bernard Schermetzler)
University of Wyoming
Wyoming State Archives (Cindy Brown and Ann Nelson)
Yellowstone National Park Library and Archives (Elsa Kortge, Beverly Whitman,
    Lee Whittlesey, and Barbara Zafft)

I would also like to thank Dee Seton Barber, Jenny Baum, Kena Bell, Ted Birkedal, Norm Bishop, Jim Boggs, Elaine Boni, Nina Leopold Bradley, Dara Carpenter, Andrea Gunderson, Ellen Hardy, Linda Howard, Paul Joslin, Bob Landis, John Malloy, Garth McCarty, Alan McIntyre, Gus Sanchez, Sandi Schenck, Morris Snider, Carol Sperling, Tom Tankersley, Steph Tatel, Carol Tenney, Vic Van Ballenberghe, Dennis Vasquez, and Steve Wells.

Finally, I would like to thank the following people at Voyageur Press: Bob DuBois and Tom Lebovsky (for having faith in the concept of the book), Helene Anderson (for helping to organize the project), Kathy Mallien and Andrea Rud (for their work on the layout), Todd Berger (for the drudgery he endured in proofreading my transcription of the historical documents), and freelance editor Jane McHughen (for doing such a great job on giving me advice on the final organization and fine-tuning of the material). This book was greatly improved by the efforts of the above people.

Non-Profit Organizations Involved With Wolf Issues

Adirondack Wolf Project
Box 1300
Lake Placid, New York 12946

Alaska Wildlife Alliance
Box 202022
Anchorage, Alaska 99520

Defenders of Wildlife
1244 19th Street NW
Washington, DC 20036

International Wolf Center
1396 Highway 169
Ely, Minnesota 55731

Maine Wolf Coalition
RFD #6, Box 533
Augusta, Maine 04330

Mexican Wolf Coalition of New Mexico
207 San Pedro NE
Albuquerque, New Mexico 87108

Mexican Wolf Coalition of Texas
Box 1526
Spring, Texas 77383

Mission: Wolf
Box 211
Silver Cliff, Colorado 81249

National Wildlife Federation
1400 Sixteenth Street NW
Washington, DC 20036

Preserve Arizona's Wolves
1413 East Dobbins Road
Phoenix, Arizona 85040

The Red Wolf Fund
Tacoma Zoological Society
5400 North Pearl Street
Tacoma, Washington 98407

RESTORE: The North Woods
Box 440
Concord, Massachusetts 01742

Sinapu
Box 3243
Boulder, Colorado 80307

Wolf Education and Research Center
Box 3832
Ketchum, Idaho 83340

Wolf Education Fund
Zion Natural History Association
Springdale, Utah 84767

Wolf Haven
3111 Offut Lake Road
Tenino, Washington 98589

Wolf Park
Rural Route 1
Battle Ground, Indiana 47920

Wolf Society of Great Britain
Prospect House
Charlton, Kilmersdon
Bath BA3 5TN

Index

Rick McIntyre has served as a seasonal park ranger for twenty years at Yellowstone, Denali, Glacier, Big Bend, Sequoia, and Kings Canyon national parks, Death Valley and Joshua Tree national monuments, and Padre Island National Seashore. He has also worked for the U.S. Forest Service on the White Mountain and Tonto national forests and at California's Anza-Borrego Desert State Park.

During his eighteen summers in Alaska and Montana, Rick accumulated nearly six hundred observations of wild wolves. He has also closely studied mating season and pup rearing behavior in captive wolf packs.

Rick's previous books include *Denali National Park: An Island in Time* (Albion Publishing Group, 1986), *Grizzly Cub: Five Years in the Life of a Bear* (Alaska Northwest Books, 1990), and *A Society of Wolves: National Parks and the Battle Over the Wolf* (Voyageur Press, 1993). Rick's wildlife photos have appeared in over 150 books and most of the major American and European nature magazines, including *Audubon, National Geographic*, and *National Wildlife*.

During the past few years, Rick has traveled extensively, giving lectures on wolves, grizzly bears, and ravens throughout the lower forty-eight states, in Native villages in Alaska, and in Ireland and England.